INSPIRED BY TRUE EVENTS AND I

MW00782819

SMELL THE
GUNPOWDER

THE LAND OF THE
MORNING CALM

WILLIAM R. GRASER
FOREWORD BY LTC WAYNE L. PARSONS, US ARMY (RET)

Smell The Gunpowder
The Land of the Morning Calm
All Rights Reserved.
Copyright © 2023 William R. Graser
v8.0 r1.3

The opinions expressed in this manuscript are solely the opinions of the author and do not represent the opinions or thoughts of the publisher. The author has represented and warranted full ownership and/or legal right to publish all the materials in this book.

This book may not be reproduced, transmitted, or stored in whole or in part by any means, including graphic, electronic, or mechanical without the express written consent of the publisher except in the case of brief quotations embodied in critical articles and reviews.

Ramasun Thunder Publishing

Paperback ISBN: 978-0-578-26472-1
Hardback ISBN: 978-0-578-26473-8

Library of Congress Control Number: 2022906662

Cover Photo © 2023 William R. Graser. All rights reserved - used with permission.

PRINTED IN THE UNITED STATES OF AMERICA

Dedication of

Smell the Gunpowder:
The Land of the Morning Calm

Is Simple:

… to Those Who Served

"All that is necessary for the triumph of evil is for good men to do nothing."

> — Edmund Burke (1729–1797), British statesman, parliamentary orator, and political thinker, played a prominent part in all major political issues for about thirty years after 1765 and remained an important figure in the history of political theory.

"History never looks like history when you are living through it."

> — John W. Gardner (1912–2002), Secretary of Health, Education, and Welfare, President Lyndon B. Johnson's Administration

"*Smell the Gunpowder: The Land of the Morning Calm* is the most comprehensive history of our involvement in Korea that I believe is out there."

> — Private First-Class Gerald P. Page, 93, 1952-1954, A Company, 3rd Battalion, 14th Infantry Regiment, 25th Infantry Division

CONTENTS

Part Three: 2nd Korean Conflict

Part Four: Preparations for War

Part Five: Korea in the 21st Century

Part Six: Appendices

Part Seven: References

FOREWORD

My name is Wayne L. Parsons. I served in the US Marine Corps with a tour in Vietnam (69-70). After completing college, I served as a US Army military police officer with tours of duty overseas in Germany, Israel, Desert Storm, and Operation Enduring Freedom (Afghanistan). I retired as a Lieutenant Colonel.

I met the author William R. Graser (Bill) in 2010. He was actively writing *Veterans' Reflections: History Preserved*, his first book. He wanted to capture the stories of service and sacrifice of the veterans who served from World War II to Afghanistan living in our retirement community. We also started working together organizing Veterans Day and Memorial Day ceremonies honoring 60 veterans.

Bill is dedicated to recognizing veterans wherever he goes. I have gained a friend and learned a great deal about military history through his knowledge and commitment to telling stories that are not only true but put the reader in the middle of the action. The author inspired me to write my story for inclusion in *Veterans' Reflections* from the time I enlisted in the US Marines to my various assignments throughout the world. The Pacific Book Review and The US Review of Books highly recommends *Veterans' Reflections*.

Smell the Gunpowder: The Land of the Morning Calm is inspired by true events and tells the Cold War story of the Republic of Korea and the Democratic Republic of Korea and the 2018 Singapore and 2019 Hanoi summits between the United States and North Korea.

Bill's newest project is professionally written and extremely informative. My personal interactions with him, from organizing veterans' programs to accompanying him on several discussions and book signings, put me in a unique position to write this foreword for *Smell the Gunpowder* and to tell you about him. My experiences both in war and peace provide a perspective that lends itself to this foreword.

William R. Graser was a Sergeant First Class was recruited by the US Army Security Agency in 1965, and upon completion of basic training completed specialty training at the US Army Security Agency Training Center and School, Fort Devens, MA. During the Cold War era, his assignments included South Korea, Vietnam, Thailand, West Germany, occupied West Berlin and US Army Security Agency's headquarters at Arlington Hall Station in Virginia. He was awarded the Legion of Merit Medal for his exceptionally meritorious conduct in the performance of outstanding services and achievements while serving with the US Army Field Station Berlin.

The author's background contributes directly to his ability to tell the story about the Republic of Korea. He served during 1966/67 north of the Imjin River near the Korean Demilitarized Zone southern boundary line and was present the night of November 2, 1966, when North Korean commandos ambushed a United Nations command patrol, killing six American soldiers and one South Korean. One American was severely wounded and was the sole survivor. The author's emphasis is on post-World War II, First Korean Conflict 1950–1953, 2nd Korean Conflict 1966–1969, the forgotten chapter in US military history, and Korea in the 21st century.

Most people have never heard of the 2nd Korean Conflict, which includes the capture of the USS *Pueblo* (GER-2) and the shoot down of a US Navy EC-121M warning star surveillance aircraft, code name *Deep Sea 129*.

During the latter part of the 1960s, 2462 North Korean agents were captured, and more than 440 incidents/clashes took place both in the demilitarized zone and interior South Korea. The 2nd Korean Conflict was a victory for the United States and South Korea, but the Vietnam Conflict overshadowed the outcome of the conflict. North Korea has been continually violating the armistice signed in 1953 which ended hostilities with a ceasefire. During its 77-year existence, North Korea has been ruled by three generations of the same family, all brutal dictators.

The author concludes that during 1994, Bill Clinton's administration faced the same concern about a nuclear North Korea as Presidents Barack Obama, Donald J. Trump, and Joseph R. Biden, Jr. A nuclear North Korea presents serious threats to the world.

Today the world is facing many challenges and North Korea is at the top of the list. *Smell the Gunpowder: The Land of the Morning Calm* is timely, given the current situation on the Korean peninsula. The author, William R. Graser, views his latest project as a history lesson seen through historical content and firsthand accounts of veterans who served in Korea since World War II.

His method weaves the veterans' own stories into a historical overview of Korea. The soldiers' accounts go well beyond the war's scorecard and reveal the actual fears and experiences of the participants.

This is an excellent book and highly informative for anyone. I learned more about modern American history reading this book than I did taking American history classes. The history lessons on the wars themselves, what led up to them, and all the key events are there in a concise, but unbiased way. Most important are the gut-wrenching, heart-touching, first-person accounts. Those are why you cannot pull yourself away.

In conclusion, my military background recognizes the importance of *Smell the Gunpowder: The Land of the Morning Calm*, and therefore I chose to write this foreword.

Lieutenant Colonel Wayne L. Parsons, United States Army (Ret)

United States Korean Service Medals since 1950

1950s Korean Conflict

The Korean Service Medal was awarded to service members who participated in operations in the Korean war zone between June 27, 1950, and July 27, 1954.

1960s Korean Conflict

The Armed Forces Expeditionary Service Medal (AFEM) was awarded to service members who participated in operations between October 1, 1966, and June 30, 1974. The AFEM is a military medal, which was first created in 1961 by Executive Order 10977, December 4, 1961 of President John F. Kennedy.

Korean Defense Service Medal Post June 27, 1954

The Department of Defense approved the Korean Defense Service Medal in February 2004 to be given as recognition for military service in the Republic of Korea and the surrounding waters after July 28, 1954 and ending on such a future date as determined by the Secretary of Defense.

Republic of Korea War Service Medal is Categorized as a Foreign Decoration

The Republic of Korea (ROK) War Service Medal is a decoration presented by South Korea to recognize members of a military who served with South Korea during the Korean War from June 25, 1950 - July 27, 1953. Personnel must have served 30 consecutive days or 60 non-consecutive days to be eligible for the award. To receive the ROK Medal the veteran must apply to their respective service branch.

ACKNOWLEDGMENTS

No book is ever the product of one person's efforts, and this one is certainly no exception. It would not have become a reality without the help and suggestions of supportive friends and especially the veterans who provided their stories. It is an immense pleasure to acknowledge the assistance I received.

I am thankful for the support of my wife, Florence, who tolerated the period of writing and rewriting. She, more than any other person, made it possible to complete this project.

I am thankful to Lieutenant Colonel Wayne L. Parsons, US Army (Ret), and his wife, Lora Parsons, whose reviews led to revisions. Throughout the writing process, Wayne and Lora provided continued support, for which I am profoundly grateful.

My special thanks to Wayne for writing the foreword and for his insight, along with the ability to write a clear and concise explanation of the content.

My special thanks to Lora, for the hours spent working on this project. Her diligence and self-motivation are appreciated. Thank you once again for all your effort.

I am thankful to Charles H. McDaniel, Jr., of Indianapolis, Indiana for permitting me to tell the story of his father, Master Sergeant Charles H. McDaniel, Sr., who was killed in action during the Battle of Unsan and Chongchon River area in North Korea during the opening months of the first Korean Conflict. His father went missing in November 1950, and it would be 71 years before his identification tag (dog tag) was returned.

I extend my sincere appreciation to Billy Kobin, reporter for the *IndyStar*, Indianapolis, Indiana for connecting me with Charles H. McDaniel, Jr., son of

Master Sergeant Charles H. McDaniel, Sr. Without his assistance, this important piece of history would have been missed.

I am thankful to Ted Barker, Korean War Project, and Major Vandon E. Jenerette, US Army (Ret), (koreanwar.org) for providing critical background information about the 1960s Korean Conflict.

PREFACE

Smell the Gunpowder: The Land of the Morning Calm is the product of a five-year effort beginning in 2017. It is a collection of Korean Conflict veterans' own personal stories and firsthand accounts blended with historical content to include the Republic of Korea (South Korea) and the Democratic People's Republic of Korea (North Korea) perspective. It provides a snapshot of American military history in Korea from the end of World War II through the Cold War to include two Korean Conflicts (1950–1953) and (1966–1969). *Smell the Gunpowder* continues with the Singapore Summit 2018 (Singapore), the Hanoi Summit 2019 (Socialist Republic of Vietnam), and North Korea's hostile threat of nuclear conflict, along with the economic and social impact of the coronavirus pandemic.

First and always, within the limits of his knowledge and ability, the author has neglected no effort nor passed over any details that seemed likely to further his purpose of writing a true history of Korea.

The author is not entirely a stranger to Korea; he arrived there in April 1966, for a thirteen-month tour of duty. He was assigned to Company B (Forward) 508th US Army Security Agency Group Camp Alamo, the "US Army Northernmost Outpost," located near the village of Sabanggeori, north of the Imjin River, within view of the southern boundary line known as the South Tape of the Military Demarcation Line (MDL) in the Chorwon district.

Korea was beautiful and dangerous. The green hills and patchwork-patterned rice paddies have an enchanting beauty when seen from a distance. The weather was a combination of scorching heat or pelting rain in the summer, and numbing cold of a Siberian-type winter, with the realization that Korean infiltrators could be waiting over the next rise of the ground.

How easy it would have been to author a story of the conflicts based on records alone. The author chose to interview veterans who served not only in combat, but in the relative peace between the 1950s and 1960s armed conflicts. The author asked each veteran interviewed to provide a copy of his DD214 form — that is, certificate of release or discharge from active duty. The DD214 is an official document that verifies the service branch, service dates, rank, awards, and decorations. Using this document, the author was able to personalize the stories provided by the former military men.

Their firsthand accounts capture war, love, and peace. Once a First Korean Conflict combat veteran called the author at home three weeks after his story was completed. He said, "When reading my own story, those days in Korea rushed back like it was yesterday." The author listened as the veteran wrestled with his emotions. Months later, he told the author how he appreciated his story being recorded for future generations, especially his grandchildren.

Smell the Gunpowder: The Land of the Morning Calm concludes on a cautiously optimistic note that peace on the Korean peninsula may be in reach. The United States had imposed various economic sanctions against North Korea over its nuclear weapons program.

Former Presidents Barack Obama and Donald J. Trump took different approaches to secure a deal with North Korea in which Chairman Kim Jong-un would relinquish his nuclear weapons. Obama took a hands-off approach and Trump chose to meet face-to-face.

The Singapore Summit 2018 provided the stage for a sitting United States (US) president to meet face-to-face with the North Korean leader. On June 12, 2018, President Trump and North Korean leader Chairman Kim Jong-un shook hands to kick off the historic summit. In a joint statement by President Trump and Chairman Kim Jong-un, President Trump committed to provide security guarantees to North Korea, and Chairman Kim Jong-un reaffirmed his firm and unwavering commitment to complete denuclearization of the Korean peninsula. President Trump and Chairman Kim hoped to develop lasting relations between the two countries and end the long history of hostility. On June 13, 2018, President Trump declared that North Korea is "no longer a nuclear threat" to the United States and regional allies. The true test of success is whether the follow-up negotiations can close the gap between the US and North Korea on the definition of denuclearization and lay out specific, verifiable steps that Pyongyang will take to reduce the threat posed by its nuclear weapons.

On February 27 and 28, President Trump and Chairman Kim met for a second time in the Socialist Republic of Vietnam at the Hanoi Summit. North Korean leader Kim Jong-un restated his commitment to denuclearization and President Trump reaffirmed his belief that North Korea has tremendous economic potential. The goal of the summit was to determine what variable steps Chairman Kim would take toward eliminating North Korea's nuclear arsenal and what the US might offer in exchange. The summit failed for an amazingly simple reason: North Korea would not agree to eliminate its nuclear arsenal unless the US immediately lifted all economic and financial sanctions. The US remained firm to the position that North Korea should remove its nuclear threat first before sanctions could be addressed. President Trump walked away from the table but kept the door open to continue negotiations. Following the summit, both sides announced the resumption of "working level" nuclear talks. Behind the scenes, discussions continued until working-level nuclear talks held in Stockholm, Sweden, in October 2019, broke down without an agreement.

In January 2020, the Coronavirus Pandemic (COVID-19) resulted in North Korea closing its border with China, its primary trading partner. This action caused economic and social hardships to worsen. COVID-19 dominated 2020, and North Korea took extensive measures to protect itself, to include the establishment of quarantine facilities, and strict travel restrictions. Concurrently, North Korea continued to build its nuclear capabilities. With the dawn of the new year, 2021, concerns about North Korea's intentions remained as high as they have been since the end of the two conflicts. The United States, the Republic of Korea, and the Democratic People's Republic of Korea continued to have a "shared" vision for the future of the Korean peninsula. That vision is to maintain peace and stability on a nuclear-free peninsula.

When Joseph R. Biden, Jr., was inaugurated as President of the United States on January 20, 2021, his administration ushered in a fresh look at US policy with North Korea. One year has passed and as 2022 begins, the concerns about North Korea remain the same. History has shown it would be a big mistake to underestimate North Korea as many initially did.

Just days after the US-North Korea summit held in Hanoi ended in a stalemate, workers became active at the Sohae Satellite Launching Station, a partially disassembled missile test facility located in northwest North Korea. In January 2022, North Korea conducted seven missile tests, including two short-range ballistic missiles from separate trains. The test was to evaluate the response time and alert posture of its new railway-borne missile regiment. On January 29 a Hwasong-12 mid-range ballistic missile was tested with an estimated range of 2796 miles with ability to carry a nuclear warhead and which could reach the US territory of Guam. It was last tested in 2017.

In May 2022, Presidents Joe Biden and Yoon Yeol met in Seoul to discuss expanding the scope and scale of combined military exercises and training. Large scale exercises were canceled by President Trump who tried to encourage N Korea to end its nuclear missile programs.

On May 25, 2022, N Korea increased tensions when it fired three missiles including its largest ballistic missile (ICBM), with an estimated range of about 9320 miles, enough to reach the United States.

On August 21, 2022, S Korea and the US resumed field exercises and military drills. It was nearly five years since the last large scale military exercise. The joint exercise known as Ulchi Freedom Shield was conducted over a two-week period. The drills included live fire from US and S Korean howitzers and tanks at the Rodrequez Live Fire Complex, 20 miles from the DMZ, and real-life scenarios including protecting facilities such as seaports, airports, and nuclear power plants.

N Korea once again criticized the joint drills as a rehearsal for invasion.

On September 22, 2022, N Korea announced it was ruling out denuclearization with a new law adopting a more aggressive nuclear position.

The author hopes the personal stories and historical content in *Smell the Gunpowder: The Land of the Morning Calm* promotes an understanding and appreciation for our veterans and the political developments that affect US foreign policy.

INTRODUCTION

The United States and Korea established diplomatic relations under the 1882 Treaty of Peace, Amity, Commerce, and Navigation; the first US diplomatic envoy arrived in Korea in 1883. United States-Korea relations continued until 1905 when Japan assumed direction over Korean foreign affairs at the end of the Russo-Japanese War. The Japanese period of rule over the whole of Korea began in 1910. At the end of World War II, after 35 years of colonial rule, Japan was defeated and left Korea divided and occupied by two superpowers, the United States (US), and the Union of Soviet Socialists Republics (USSR). The Soviet Union would take control of Korea north of the 38th Parallel, and the United States, the southern territory.

The history of North Korea (N Korea) began with the partition of Korea and its first leader Kim Il-sung. He created the country's policy of "self-reliance," which cut off N Korea economically and diplomatically from the rest of the world. The formation of South Korea (S Korea) was through United Nations-sponsored elections that led to the creation of the Republic of Korea (ROK) on August 15, 1948, under the leadership of President Syngman Rhee.

The Democratic People's Republic of Korea (DPRK-N Korea) formed its own government, and its capital became Pyongyang. The Republic of Korea (ROK-S Korea) made Seoul its capital city.

The Cold War came to dominate United States (US) foreign policy. N Korea's main allies were the Soviet Union, which supplied it with arms, fighter pilots, and anti-aircraft artillery crews; and China, officially the People's Republic of China (PRC), which later sent thousands of troops and fighter pilots. S Korea, with aid from the US, began to fortify its defenses south of the 38th Parallel.

Then on June 25, 1950, the N Koreans crossed the 38th Parallel and surged into S Korea in what the United Nations (UN) termed an unprovoked act of aggression. The following day, President Harry S. Truman approved the use of

American forces below the 38th Parallel. The UN Security Council approved a resolution to assist in repelling N Korean aggression. The First Korean Conflict would continue for more than three years.

The N Korean point of view is that the start of the conflict was initiated by the US and conducted by S Korea with an armed invasion forcing N Korea to launch a counterattack. The N Korean *Home Ministry of the Republic* on June 23, 1950, stated that the army units of S Korea went into a large-scale artillery bombardment over the area north of the 38th Parallel. The bombardment was the preliminary firing signaling the start of an all-out armed aggression of the US imperialists.

On July 27, 1953, all fighting stopped; the conflict ended. The armistice agreement, while it stopped hostilities, was not a permanent peace treaty, but a ceasefire between United Nations Command, N Korea People's Army, and China. The S Koreans abided by the armistice agreement but refused to sign it because it was not a peace treaty; it was a ceasefire arrangement.

The First Korean Conflict (1950s Korean Conflict or First Korean War 1950-1953) devastated S Korea, killing and injuring millions of people and scarring those who survived. The US bombing destroyed N Korea's industry, agriculture, transportation, and communications systems.

In the decade that followed, N Korea received abundant financial and technical aid from the USSR and China to rebuild, and rapid industrialization occurred in the 1950s and early 1960s. In addition, the German Democratic Republic (East Germany), Poland, Czechoslovakia (the Czech Republic in 1992), Hungary, Romania, Bulgaria, and Albania contributed to N Korea's reconstruction. Each of the Eastern European Communist countries agreed to undertake rehabilitation projects. In 1962, reconstruction completed, the East Europeans went home. During the early years following the armistice, S Korea was entirely dependent on the US for food and consumer goods. From 1953 to 1962, US aid financed an average of 70 percent of imports. The US also provided significant aid to S Korea under the auspices of the UN Korea Reconstruction Agency (UNKRA).

UNKRA focused on aiding war refugees and the homeless. South Korea rose from the days of conflict to developing a strong economy.

Beginning three months after the ceasefire ended the conflict, N Korea steadily increased tensions along the 38th Parallel. During the years 1953–1965, there were more than 360 clashes between the Koreas. These clashes occurred on land within the Demilitarized Zone (DMZ), the Yellow Sea, and various locations along the S Korean eastern coastline (the Sea of Japan [East Sea]).

In the autumn of 1966, events were in motion that would assess the willpower of the US and S Korea. As the US involvement in the Vietnam conflict escalated, the tempo of incidents and violations of the armistice also increased. By mid-October 1966, N Korea infiltrators attacked two S Korean patrols south of the DMZ, killing 17 soldiers. S Korea promptly retaliated, sending an attack team north of the DMZ, which killed three dozen N Korean soldiers. US soldiers stationed in and near the DMZ were on a heightened sense of alert as N Korean began probing the DMZ. The 2nd Korean Conflict (1960s Korean Conflict or 2nd Korean War 1966-1969) began November 2, 1966, when N Korean commandos ambushed an eight-man UN command patrol composed of soldiers of the US 2nd Infantry Division south of the DMZ. The ambush was one of the deadliest engagements and the first major action involving Americans. The ambush resulted in the death of six Americans and one S Korean soldier, along with one American seriously wounded. During the 12 months beginning in November 1966, more than two dozen Americans were killed and scores more were wounded in combat. Violence followed a seasonal pattern, dropping in winter months and peaking in springtime. During 1967, N Korea infiltrated S Korea more than 440 times. In late 1967, it was clear that the N Koreans were attempting to develop a full-scale insurgency in S Korea. The N Koreans hoped to create a guerilla uprising in the South like the Viet Cong insurgency in South Vietnam. In 1967, there were 143 firefights and 280 actions against N Korean positions.

In 1968, the frequency of infiltration increased to 500, resulting in more than 236 firefights. US and S Korean troops fired upon N Korean positions 223 times. S Korea conducted commando raids into N Korea, destroying military targets and ambushing N Korean troops. The number of casualties is unknown. N Koreans were putting one crisis on top of another.

It was during this time the N Koreans expanded their operations and on January 23, 1968, captured the USS *Pueblo* (GER-2), a "spy" ship operating off the N Korean coast, resulting in a second major incident. The crew of 83, including two civilian oceanographers, was taken as prisoners of war and held in N Korea until December 23, 1968. (One US sailor was killed in action.)

The ship, disguised as an environmental research vessel, was captured at the height of the Cold War. The capture also provided the N Koreans, Russia, and China with specialized top secret signal intelligence equipment and highly classified documents.

The *Pueblo* officially remains a commissioned vessel of the US Navy and subjected to exhibition at the Victorious War Museum, moored along the Taedong River in Pyongyang. It is the only ship of the US Navy currently held "captive" and is used as a war museum.

115th Congress 2nd Session House Resolution 894 sought the return of the *Pueblo* to the US Navy. On May 15, 2019, in the House of Representatives, Mr. Scott Tipton of Colorado submitted the following resolution which was referred to the Committee on Foreign Affairs.

Resolved, That the House of Representatives—

(1) desires the return of the USS *Pueblo* to the United States Navy.

(2) would welcome the return of the USS *Pueblo* as a sign of good faith from the North Korean people to the American people; and

(3) directs the Clerk of the House of Representatives to transmit copies of this resolution to the President, the Secretary of Defense, and the Secretary of State.

On February 25, 2021, more than half a century after the *Pueblo* incident, a United States Federal Court in Washington, DC ordered N Korea to pay compensation totaling $2.3 billion to the crew and surviving families of the ill-fated "spy" ship for psychological and physical damages inflicted by Pyongyang's interrogators. Of the total damages $22 million to $48 million awarded to each of the forty-nine surviving crew members. N Korea is unlikely to pay the bill, but in the future, it could be used as a bargaining tool in future negotiations. In 2017, N Korea was declared a sponsor of terrorism by former President Donald J.

Trump, which allowed it to be ordered to pay. This continues to be an "urgent priority" for President Joseph Biden, Jr., administration.

On April 15, 1969, the third major incident happened when the N Koreans shot down a US Navy EC-121M, Warning Star call sign *Deep Sea 129* surveillance aircraft, over the Sea of Japan (East Sea) killing all 31 crew members. The year, 2019, marked the 50th anniversary since N Korean fighter planes shot down *Deep Sea 129*. The US Navy Information Operations Command Hawaii held a remembrance ceremony, May 2, 2019, in honor of the crew.

The commemoration included a wreath-laying ceremony and the firing of three volleys to honor the dead, along with remarks from Commander Joseph Overstreet, the son of Lieutenant Commander James Overstreet, who was the pilot and officer-in-charge of *Deep Sea 129*.

The *Pueblo* and the *Deep Sea 129* incidents almost started an all-out war on the Korean peninsula.

As 1969 ended, provocative incidents by the N Koreans decreased as quickly as they had started three years earlier. In mid-October 1969, a team of N Korean soldiers patrolling the DMZ ambushed four unarmed Americans driving a jeep displaying a white flag on the left bumber. Each soldier was executed. The white flag was a recongnized sign of the ceasefire and provided freedom of movment for vehicles and personnel within the DMZ. This ambush signaled the last American deaths in the final days of the conflict.

Whatever the reasons for winding down the conflict, it is officially considered to have ended on December 3, 1969, the day N Korea released three captured US Army aviators whose observation helicopter had been shot down four months earlier after having strayed into N Korean airspace.[1][2]

The 1960s Korean Conflict resulted in American casualties: 92 killed in action, and 111 wounded suffered in 42 firefights directly between US and N Korean forces of the 440 firefights during the 37 months. S Korean forces suffered 229 killed and 553 wounded; N Korean losses 427 killed and twelve soldiers

---

1   The Korean War That Almost Was (historynet.com)
2   https://www.armyupress.army.mil/ (*Shadows of War Violence Along the Korean Demilitarized Zone* by Captain Michael Anderson, US Army, November-December 2019.)

along with 2462 agents captured and 33 defected to S Korea; an unknown number were wounded. Through the 1970s, 1980s and 1990s, the N Koreans continued their covert attempts to destabilize the S Korean government. N Korean infiltrators continued to probe the DMZ, and communist spy rings were continually discovered in the South. From 1954 to 1992, it was reported that N Korea infiltrated 3693 armed agents into S Korea.

In December 1991, as the world watched in amazement, the Soviet Union/Russia disintegrated into fifteen separate countries, thus ending the Cold War. The breakup of the USSR transformed the entire world political situation, leading to a complete reformulation of political, economic, and military alliances all over the globe. N Korea no longer received military aid.

The US nearly went to war with N Korea in June 1994 to stop its nuclear weapons program. The N Korea missile program was developed with help from the USSR in the 1970s. President Bill Clinton's administration considered a cruise missile strike on an N Korea nuclear complex site that could provide fissile material capable of sustaining a nuclear fission chain reaction. In nuclear weapons, the fission energy is released all at once to produce an explosion. In the end, high-level diplomatic intercession of former President Jimmy Carter diffused the immediate crisis and allowed Washington and Pyongyang to resolve their nuclear stalemate peacefully.

Kim Jong-un emerged onto the world stage as a virtual unknown in 2011, a young man thrust into power as the head of North Korea – a nuclear-armed state – after the unexpected death of his father, Kim Jong-il. In the decade since, he has ruthlessly purged alleged political opponents and extended his country's nuclear capabilities.

Presently, by 2022, N Korea is almost able to threaten the US mainland directly with nuclear strikes; the possibility of conflict looms as it did in 1994.

South Korea has risen from the days of armed conflict to develop a strong economy. Over the past several decades, S Korea has achieved a remarkably high level of economic growth and is now the 6th-largest goods trading partner with the US. The largest industries are electronics, telecommunications, automobile production, ship building, and steel production. Agriculture also plays a role in the country's economy.

The June 2018 summit in Singapore between US President Donald J. Trump and N Korean leader Chairman Kim Jong-un resulted in only assurances to denuclearize, with no timeline to achieve it. President Trump committed to provide security guarantees to N Korea. In January 2019 Kim extended an invitation to meet again with President Trump.

A second summit was held in Hanoi, in the Socialist Republic of Vietnam, February 27 and 28. Chairman Kim restated his commitment to denuclearization and insisted that all sanctions be lifted before addressing nuclear concerns. President Trump committed again to provide security guarantees. Kim resisted what Trump presented as the means to grant sanction relief. Specifically, N Korea would trade all its nuclear weapons, materials, and facilities for an end to the American-led sanctions.

President Trump and Chairman Kim departed the summit early because no agreement was reached regarding rolling back N Korea's nuclear program; consequently, sanctions remained. With the failure of the summit to provide a substantial outcome, N Korea continues to have a nuclear arsenal. The US reaffirmed pressure will continue against N Korea until denuclearization takes place. President Trump, while attending the G20 Summit in Osaka, Japan on June 28 and 29, 2019, made a trip to Korea, landing at Osan Air Force Base near Seoul. He met again with the N Korean leader at the Korean demilitarized zone (DMZ). Except for a handshake and a symbolic gesture, President Trump setting foot in N Korea, nothing of substance was announced regarding a commitment by N Korea to cease its nuclear weapon programs. (The primary agenda addressed at the G20 Summit meeting was focused on issues related to the global economy, trade and investment, innovation, environment and energy, employment, development, and health.) In typical N Korean fashion, Chairman Kim showed displeasure at the lack of progress with the US and conducted four short-range ballistic missile tests during July and August 2019. History has shown it would be a big mistake to underestimate N Korea, as many did. The N Koreans have for decades been in the game to get, not give.

The linkage of the tests marks another escalation in rhetoric; Kim threatened to withdraw from dialogue unless N Korea gets concessions and insisted that all sanctions be lifted before the end of 2019. The Trump administration chose not to overreact to the tests, which could jeopardize any chance of diplomatic progress.

In 2021, President Joseph R. Biden Jr.'s administration took a fresh look at US policy between the US and N Korea. Reaffirmed sanctions will not be eased until denuclearization is complete. In May 2021, Biden's administration concluded its N Korean policy review and offered the public a glimpse of its rough outline. Like its predecessors', the full content of the administration's policy review remains classified.

While the US and N Korea might agree on little else, their shared acceptance of this language dates to 1993, and more recently, "complete denuclearization of the Korean Peninsula" is the phrase that appears in the June 2018 joint statement from the Singapore summit—the sole US—North Korea document that bears Kim Jong-un's signature. On August 29, 2021, The UN International Atomic Energy Agency reported North Korea appeared to have resumed operation of its plutonium-producing reactor at Yongbyon in a move to expand its nuclear-weapons arsenal adding a new challenge to President Biden's foreign policy agenda. The agency described the development as "deeply troubling" and a clear violation of United Nations Security Council resolutions.

In September 2021, N Korea successfully test-fired a new model of long-range missile in the latest sign N Korea is trying to bolster its nuclear capability. The missile flew for more than two hours covering 930 miles over land and sea off the east coast of the Korean peninsula. As September ended, N Korea test-fired a ballistic missile and a newly developed anti-aircraft missile. The ballistic test was the first since President Biden took office. The US State Department viewed these missile launches as another violation of multiple UN Security Council resolutions and posed a threat to its neighbors and the international community. N Korea accused the UN Security Council of applying double standards over military activities among UN member states amid criticism over recent missile tests. Reference to S Korea's test firing a new submarine-launched ballistic missile from a submerged submarine.

In October 2021, N Korea justified its country's weapons development as necessary in the face of the continued US and S Korea hostile policies. N Korea's threats are intended to deflect from the coronavirus pandemic restrictions, economic failure, and international sanctions because of its nuclear programs. N Korea faced one of the worst crises in its 77-year history.

President Biden's special envoy, Sung Kim, Special Representative for N Korea, conveyed that he is ready to meet N Korean counterparts "anywhere and at any time" over stalled nuclear talks.

To support the larger story about Korea, selected information from this introduction is repeated in subsequent chapters.

Smell the Gunpowder: The Land of the Morning Calm provides a historical perspective from the post-World War II years 1945-2022, a 77-year span of time. This nickname, "the land of the Morning Calm," was coined by Percival Lowell in his book *"Chaohsien (Choson) The Land of the Morning Calm,"* published in 1885. He stated, "If you have ever awakened to a view of Korea's cloud-enshrouded mountains, walked through the green grasses or tasted the waters of a fresh mountain stream, you will know why they call it 'the land of the morning calm.'

The current population of the Korean Peninsula (October 2021) is Republic of Korea 51.3 million and the Democratic People's Republic of Korea 26 million, for a combined population of 77.3 million. South Korea's economy following the 1950s and 1960s Korean Conflicts was based on farming and fishing. Today, The Land of the Morning Calm, through its "tiger economy" growth, has made S Korea the 11th-largest economy in the world through its raw materials and industrial production base. Products such as electronics, textiles, ships, automobiles, and steel are some of its most important exports.

The economy of N Korea is a centrally planned economy. Following the collapse of the Soviet Union in 1991, a principal source of external support, N Korea announced a three-year transitional economic policy, placing primary emphasis on agriculture, light industry, and foreign trade. In 2013 and 2014, the State Economic Development Administration announced several smaller special economic zones covering export handling, material processing, high technology, gaming, and tourism, resulting in a limited degree of success. During 2021, N Korea experienced extreme food shortages and a poor economic performance. The Coronavirus Pandemic (COVID-19) resulted in border lockdowns, and limited imports from China added to the already desperate situation. After 10 years in office, Kim Jong-un was struggling to overcome what appears to be the toughest period of his rule. In December 2021, South Korea, United States, and North Korea agreed, in principle, to mark a formal end to the 1950s Korean Conflict, which spanned 1950-1953.

Speaking at a joint press conference in mid-December 2021 with Australian Prime Minister Scott Morrison after bilateral summit talks in Australia, former South Korean President Moon said he believes that an end-of-war declaration will assist in reviving talks between North and South Korea, as well as between North Korea and the United States. As of January 2022, N Korea continues its policy of "juche" adherence to self-reliance.

How has North Korea's Kim Jong-un held on to power so long?

Thank you for reading the introduction, and I hope you will enjoy this story. I trust you will find the information tables along with firsthand accounts interesting and gain a greater understanding of veterans' sacrifices.

Table 1. Official Country Name, Short Names,
Abbreviations, and Organizations

United States of America	United Nations/United Nations Command
U.S. or US	U.N., UN, and UNC
Republic of Korea	**Democratic People's Republic of Korea**
ROK	DPRK
South Korea	North Korea
S Korea, S Korean and SK	N Korea, N Korean and NK
Republic of Korea Armed Forces founded August 15, 1948. Headquarters, Ministry of National Defense, Yongsan, Seoul. Republic of Korea Army (ROKA) Republic of Korea Navy (ROKN) Republic of Korea Air Force (ROKAF)	Korean People's Army (KPA) founded February 8, 1948. Headquarters, North Korean Armed Forces, Pyongyang. The KPA is divided into five branches: Ground Force, Navy, Air Force, Special Operations Force, and Rocket Force. Example: North Korean People's Army Air Force (KPAAF)
People's Republic of China	**Union of Soviet Socialist Republics**
China or PRC	U.S.S.R. or USSR
Chinese People's Liberation Army (CPLA)	Soviet Union or Russia
Chinese People's Volunteer Force (CPVF)	Russian
Chinese People's Liberation Army Air Force (PLAAF) Chinese Communist forces (CCF) Chinese Communist Party (CCP) By the third week of November 1950, thirty CCF divisions [300,000 troops] crossed their border into N Korea. The N Korean XVII Army Group committed eighteen divisions opposing the 8th US Army, and twelve Chinese divisions of IX Army Group attacked the US X corps. From November 1950 forward, the CCF carried the Communists' effort until the Armistice. Reconnaissance units were organic in the Chinese forces from the Army Group through the regiment.	Russian Involvement: Between 1950/53 72,000 Russian troops (among them 5,000 pilots) served along the Yalu River in Northeast China, and Northwest N Korea. On November 1, 1950, Russia entered the conflict. Sixty-Fourth Fighter Aviation Corps, Order of Battle, June 1952. Based at Antung Airfield Complex Northeast China. Aircraft Strength 246 MiG-15/MiG15bis. Peak strength of 25,000 men reached in 1952. Casualties: 299 killed and 335 MiGs lost. Unified Air Army Chinese & N Korean Pilots Aircraft Strength 275 MiG-15/MiG-15bis. The Chinese lost 224 MiGs. N Korean claims were viewed as inaccurate regarding UN losses.

US Far East Air Force lost 2,714 aircraft of several types including 109 B-29 Heavy Bombers, and seventy-eight F-86 Sabres. The US Navy and US Marine Corps focused on close air support compared to the US Air Force's focus on interdiction and strategic bombardment. The Chinese acknowledged losing 224 MiGs, 3 La-11s post-World War II Soviet long-range piston-engine fighter, and 4 Tu-2S, World War II Soviet high-speed twin-engine bomber, but also claimed to have shot down 211 F-86s, 72 F-84s turbojet fighter-bomber, and forty-seven other aircraft. The small N Korean People's Air Force of 132 lost 110 aircraft of different types during the Air Battle of South Korea, June 25 to July 20, 1950. North Korea claims were widely inaccurate, asserting that they shot down 5,729 UN aircraft and damaged another 6,484! [3]

Table 2. Military Organization Order of Battle Structure

United States of America Ground Forces Order of Battle	Democratic People's Republic Republic Republic of Korea Ground Forces Order of Battle
Eighth US Army Korea (EUSAK) - 8th Army An army is the highest command level in each theater of operations and typically has about 100,000 to 300,000 men. It is an element of a joint command; the Army's component is commanded by a general (4-Star). Includes support brigades and support commands. Composed of two or more Corps.	General Headquarters North Korean Army Kim Il-sung Commander-in-Chief General Nam Il Chief of Staff Planned and directed the fighting from Pyongyang during the initial stages of the conflict.

---

3   MigAlley(Y'Blood).qxd (defense,gov) media.defense.gov., page 44, second paragraph.

Corps	Korean People's Army and Border Constabulary Force
US Army Corps commanded by a lieutenant general and includes two to five divisions, support brigades and subordinate commands. The corps has about 20,000 to 100,000 men.	Supreme Commander of the Korean People's Army Choe Yong-gon ordered the attack on S Korea on June 25, 1950, with a combined force of 135,000 men.
The US Marine Corps - Marine Expeditionary Force similar in size, organization, and commanded by a lieutenant general.	Army I and II Corps Headquarters in June 1950, had about 5,000 men; they commanded NK Divisions on the eastern sector, in the Seoul area. II Corps commanded the First, 3rd, 4th, 6th Infantry Divisions, and Thirtieth Mechanized Division in the initial attack. III, IV, V, and VII Corps commanded a mix of infantry divisions, infantry brigades and mechanized artillery brigades. Corps VI and VIII, composition Unknown. Each Infantry Corps fields a Reconnaissance Battalion.
The US Air Force – Numbered Air Force organizations or a Major Command commanded by a lieutenant general.	
Lieutenant Generals are picked and appointed by the President of the United States.	
Division	**Division**
The division is commanded by a major general and has about 6,000 to 25,000 men including two to five brigades, an artillery brigade, an engineer brigade, and a logistic brigade. The First Cavalry Division (1CD) was organized as an Infantry Division.	The infantry division basic tactical formation has about 10,000 to 11,000 men including three regiments, one artillery regiment, and one reconnaissance company. The only armored division in name only being the size of a brigade had about 6,000 men and estimated 120 T 34 medium tanks with an 85 millimeter (mm) anti-aircraft/anti-tank gun.
First Marine Division (1stMARDIV) has an authorized strength of about 23,000 men and is commanded by a major general. In early 1950, the division had 5,000 men, the strength of a reinforced regimental combat team. By mid-June it expanded to 75,000 regulars.	NK Twelfth Division at Inge, east central N Korea estimated 30 T 34 / 85 tanks before it crossed the 38th Parallel.
Brigade	**Brigade/Regiment**
A brigade is commanded by a colonel and has about 4,000 to 4,700 men, depending on whether it is armored or infantry. Command of 2-6 regiments. Cavalry brigades are referred to as regiments.	Brigade Strength 2,600 to 5,000 men.
	Five Brigades Uneven in Size and Armament.
	Three Independent Reconnaissance Brigades; Deployed anywhere on the battlefield. Conducts additional intelligence-gathering signals and tactics.
Marine Corps units at this level are also called regiments. (The term "Marine Expeditionary Brigade" refers to a task force, which is larger.)	Fields Ten Reconnaissance Battalions. Brigade Strength 3,600 to 4,200 men. Regiment Fields a Reconnaissance Platoon.

Regiment	Regiment
A regiment is commanded by a colonel and has about 1,000 to 3,000 men and commands two-plus battalions.	Regiment Estimated Strength 2,290 men. One Infantry, One Mortar, One Howitzer Artillery, Three Motorized Anti-Aircraft-Artillery Regiments. Motorcycle Regiment 2,000 men. Independent Infantry Regiment 3,000 men.
Battalion/Cavalry Squadron	**Battalion**
A battalion commanded by a lieutenant colonel and usually includes two to six combat companies and one support company. It has about 300 to 1,000 men. A Cavalry battalion is called a Squadron.	Infantry Battalion Strength 622 men 76 MM Mortar Battalion Strength 292 men 122 MM Mortar Battalion Strength 292 men Reconnaissance Battalion Strength 500 men Includes: Radio Direction Finding (RDF) to Determine Location and Operational Procedures of the Enemy.
Company/Troop/Battery	**Company**
Company/Troop/Battery: A company commanded by a captain and includes two to five subordinate platoons (usually three or four). It has about 80 to 250 men. Cavalry companies are called troops; artillery companies are called batteries.	Infantry Company Strength 125 men Mortar Company Strength 81 men Artillery Company Strength 78 men Reconnaissance Company Strength 120 men Motorcycle Reconnaissance Company Strength Varies Signal Company Strength 74 men Engineer Company Strength 75 men

The N Korean ground forces and the Border Constabulary-June 1950 estimated 135,000 men. Estimated total included 77,838 men in seven infantry assault divisions: 6000 in the tank brigade, 3000 in an independent infantry regiment, 2000 in a motorcycle regiment, 23,000 in three reserve divisions, 18,162 in the Border Constabulary, and 5000 in Army and First (I) and 2nd (II) Corps Headquarters. The S Korean ground forces at the 38th Parallel were composed of four divisions and one infantry regiment. Its divisions were unprepared and ill-equipped. S Korea had no tanks.

Table 3. Tactical Name, Short Names, Abbreviations, and Military Organization

8th US Army (EUSAK)		
501st Communication Reconnaissance Group (CRGp) Administrative and Operational Control of all in-country assets. Organization Strength July 1952 – July 1953. 113 Officers 1 Warrant Officer 1,565 Enlisted. Group Strength 1,679 men plus 119 Department of the Army Civilians		
Communication Reconnaissance Company 351st (Security) CRCo. Direct communication security support (COMSEC) to the 8th US Army. (Commonly referred to as 8th Army). COMSEC Support to the 9th (IX) and 10th (X) Corps. Company strength 221 men	Communication Reconnaissance Company 352nd CRCo. Direct Tactical Intelligence Support to 8th US Army 1st (I) Corps, and the Korean Military Advisory Group (KMAG). (Commonly referred to as 8th Army). Company Strength 261 men. June 1953, strength declined to 125 men	
1st (I) Corps Communication Reconnaissance Battalion 303rd CRBn. Battalion Strength Varied ——— Communication Reconnaissance Company 326th CRCo. Company Strength 180 men ———	9th (IX) Corps Communication Reconnaissance Battalion 304th CRBn. Battalion Strength Varied ——— Communication Reconnaissance Company 329th CRCo. Company Strength 201 men and 6 Chinese Nationals ———	10th (X) Corps Communication Reconnaissance Battalion 301st CRBn. Battalion Strength Varied ——— Communication Reconnaissance Company 330th CRCo. Company Strength 35 men June 1952, and by June 1953, Company Strength 120 men ———

Official Name
501st Army Security Agency (ASA) Group

In mid-September 1950, a small ASA element arrived in S Korea, assigned to support combat operations.

The 60th Signal Service Company, Fort Lewis, Washington, was the best prepared ASA tactical unit and was dispatched to the Far East Command S Korea. It did not arrive, however, until early October, a little more than three months after the conflict commenced.

On October 20, 1950, ASA activated the 501st Communication Reconnaissance Group (CRGp) to supervise operations of subordinate battalions and companies in support of the 8th US Army.

In December 1950, the 301st Communication Reconnaissance Battalion (Comm Recon Bn) arrived, and in Mid-1952, the remaining two battalions and three companies (Comm Recon Co) were in-country. By the end of the conflict, CRGp was supervising the operations of three attached battalions, and five companies.

The Army Security Agency's (ASA's or the Agency's) Mission: Communications Intelligence (COMINT), Communications Security (COMSEC), Radio Direction Finding (RDF) and support to the Armed Forces Security Agency (AFSA) through fixed station operations, support to Army Field Forces through tactical unit operations.

At the close of the conflict, ASA units were recognized for their service and awarded the Meritorious Unit Citation and the Republic of Korea Presidential Unit Citation for "exceptionally meritorious service."

On July 1, 1956, the 501st Army Security Agency Group inactivated, and its personnel and mission transferred to the 508th US Army Security Agency Group as part of the worldwide reorganization occurring within the Army Security Agency to provide greater flexibility in support to tactical units. The ASA would go on to provide critical intelligence information during the 1960s Korean Conflict. There were three major incidents that almost led to another all-out conflict. In the early morning of November 2, 1966, the first incident happened when N Korean commandos ambushed an UN patrol south of the DMZ. Six US soldiers and one S Korean soldier were killed in action, while the 7th American soldier was severely wounded. On January 23, 1968, the USS *Pueblo* (GER-2) a seaborne signal intelligence collection vessel, was attacked by N Korean patrol boats and MiGs resulting in the death of one US sailor and capture of the *Pueblo*. The crew was held for 11 months and released on

December 23, 1968. On April 15, 1969, an airborne signal intelligence collection reconnaissance aircraft, an unarmed US Navy EC-121M, was shot down by a single N Korean MiG killing all 31 crew members.

The ASA was unique; it was within but not part of the overall military establishment. As a separate entity within the US Army, the agency was completely self-sufficient. In addition to conducting its own operational missions, it administered its own personnel system, ran its own school, arranged for its own supplies, and conducted its own research and development.

Military Intelligence (army.mil). [4] [5]

Table 4. Casualties 1950s Korean Conflict

Korean Conflict 1950 – 1953			
American Casualties		**South Korean Casualties**	
Killed in action Died of Wounds Total		Killed in action	
23,613 2,460 26,073		137,899	
Wounded in Action (Not Mortal)		Wounded in Action (Not Mortal)	
103,284		450,782	
Prisoner of War Defected		Prisoner of War Defected	
4,714 21		8,343 333	
North Korean Casualties		**Chinese Casualties**	
Killed in Action		Killed in Action	
215,000 (406,000+ US est.)		184,084 (400,000+ US est.)	
Wounded in Action		Wounded in Action	
303,000		486,000 US est.	
Prisoner of War/Defected		Prisoner of War/Defected	
120,000; 947 ~ 1998 [6]		7,110; 14,190	
Soviet Union (Russia) [7]		Intentionally Left Blank	
Killed in Action		Intentionally Left Blank	
299 (355 planes lost)		Intentionally Left Blank	

4   Military Intelligence (army.mil)
5   https://history.army.mil.
6   Status of N Korean defectors entering S Korea 1953-1998.
7   Krivošeev, Grigorij F. (1997). *Soviet Casualties and Combat Losses in the Twentieth Century.*

Unidentified – DAPP lists 111 Cold War losses in the vicinity of the Korean Peninsula.

Korean Conflict 1950-1953, First Korean Conflict, Korean War 1950-1953, and 1950s Korean Conflict interchangeable descriptions. During the 1950s Korean Conflict and the reconstruction period following the signing of the Armistice Agreement, 22 nations contributed either combat forces or medical assistance to support S Korea under the United Nations Flag. Their contributions made it possible for the ROK to remain a free and sovereign nation.

Table 5. Casualties 1960s Korean Conflict

Korean Conflict Casualties 1966 – 1969				
American Casualties		**South Korean Casualties**		
Killed in Action		Killed in Action		
102* includes		299		
Wounded in Action		Wounded in Action		
111**		553		
Captured***		Intentionally Left Blank		
North Korean Casualties				
Killed in Action	Wounded in Action		Captured	
427	Actual Total Unknown		12 Soldiers	
Intentionally Left Blank	Intentionally Left Blank		33 Defected to South Korea	
North Korean Agents Captured				
1966	**1967**	**1968**	**1969**	**Total**
205	787	1,245	225	2,462

Table 6. 1960s Korean Conflict DMZ Incidents: A Statistical Summary

DMZ Incidents of Violence Frequency			
1966	1967	1968	1969
Firefight			
22	143	236	39
Korean People's Army Harassing Fire			
3	5	19	4
Korean People's Army Mining Roads, Rivers, and Trails			
56	118	19	4
US-S Korea Fire on Suspected Korean People's Army Positions			
12	280	223	24
Korean People's Army Infiltration Land/Sea			
Detection by Chance****	440	500	14

Table 5.

Significant US-KPA Firefights November 1966 – December 1969. There were 42 incidents fought directly between US and N Korean forces. During this period S Korea conducted 200 raids or incursions into N Korea. In 1967, sabotage missions by S Korean forces attacked 50 N Korean facilities.

* On January 23, 1968, N Koreans killed one sailor and captured the USS *Pueblo*.
  On April 15, 1969, N Korean MiG-15 shot down a US Navy EC-121M Surveillance Aircraft off the N Korean coast operating in international waters outside the N Korean territorial 12-mile limit, killing 31 crewmen.

** On March 16, 1969, a medivac helicopter carrying soldiers wounded in a clash with N Korean troops crashed along the DMZ approximately three miles southwest of Panmunjom.

*** On January 23, 1968, 82 USS *Pueblo* crewmen were captured and held for 11 months.
  The crew and remains of the one sailor killed in action were released December 23, 1968.

On August 17, 1969, 3 US Army helicopter crewmen were captured in the DMZ.

The helicopter was shot down and the crew was released on December 3, 1969.

Their return signified the end of the 1960s Korean Conflict. [8]

Table 6.

> ******** Detection by chance simply is a coincidence without any prior knowledge of an infiltration plan.

Korean People's Army reconnaissance infiltration units, sometimes referred to as line-crossers, were made up of two officers, and three 10-man squads. A third of the unit was issued civilian clothes and performed in a semi-agent capacity in S Korea, others wore US and S Korean uniforms. Line-crossers infiltrated by land/sea to identify and mark artillery positions, command posts and the location of US and S Korean forces. Infiltration units hid anti-personnel wooden box mines, sabotaged military infrastructures and ambushed American and S Korean military personnel. Details refer to Appendix T: Enemy Tactics, Techniques and Doctrine - Infiltration and Guerrilla Activities.

No one reason explains the US-ROK victory in the 1960s Korean Conflict. Still, one can fairly argue that it derived from three causes: the flawed execution of the DPRK campaign plan, the UNC's ability to decern the northern threat and choose sound countermeasures, and eventually comprehensive ROK reaction to the danger of an insurgency. Source: Major Daniel P. Bolger, US Army (Ret). *Scenes from an Unfinished War: Low-Intensity Conflict in 1966-1969*. Combat Studies Institute, US Army Command and General Staff College Fort Leavenworth.

A monument was dedicated on June 12, 2012, in honor of the American and Korean Augmentees to the US Army service members who were killed in active combat in Korea during the 1960s Conflict. The monument is located at the US Army Garrison 8th Army Camp Humphreys near Anjeong-ri and Pyeongtaek S Korea.

---

8   Bolger, Daniel (1991). Scenes from an Unfinished War: Low intensity conflict in Korea 1966-69. Diane Publishing Company. ISBN: 978-0-7881-1208-9. This work incorporates text from this source, which is in the public domain.

Table 7. Chapter 3. Korean Conflict North Korean Perspective

Korean Conflict 1950-1953 Echoes of the Korean War & US Imperialists Started the Korean War	
Echoes of the Korean War	*US Imperialists Started the Korean War*
National government publication by Propaganda & Agitation Department Foreign Languages Publishing House, 1996. No specific author and no ISBN. Contributor: Oegungmun Ch'ulp'o. Printed in the Democratic People's Republic of Korea, Pyongyang, North Korea.	National government publication by the Propaganda & Agitation Department Publisher Foreign Languages Press, 1993 Contributors: Candidate Academician Ho Jong-ho, Doctors Kang Sok Hui and Pak Thae Ho. Printed in the Democratic People's Republic of Korea, Pyongyang, North Korea.
Distribution No. 604173: Shifoying Dongli 105, Building 5, Unit 10, Room 302, Beijing, Chaoyang District 0024, China.	Intentionally Left Bank
Appendix R Booklet Cover Image and Title Description	Appendix S Book Cover Image and Title Description
Printed copy only available from third-party sellers. 1) Hippo-books 2) Discover-Books 3) Breaktimebooks and eBay Canada. ISBN: There is no international standard book numeric commercial book identifier. The booklet is not available in mainstream bookstores, or online.	South Korean puppet army men going on an armed attack against the northern half of Korea on instruction of the US imperialists. Printed copy available from Amazon, and 3rd-party sellers. 1) Hippo-books 2) Discover-Books 3) Breaktimebooks and eBay Canada. Not available in mainstream stores. Unique Amazon Standard Identification Number: ASIN: 0000CP2AZ.
Smell the Gunpowder: The Land of the Morning Calm includes selected written material directly from the booklet/book and is identified in an *Italicized* font.	
Echoes of the Korean War provides a concrete description of the course and outcome of military actions on the Korean Peninsula in 1950-1953 as viewed by N Korea.	
The US Imperialists Started the Korean War is a sweeping indictment of American aggression, arguing that the US provoked the Korean War in the 1950s as part of a much broader strategy of post-WWII global domination. The conflict pitted communist N Korea, backed by the Soviet Union and later China, against S Korea, backed by the United States.	

Table 8. Chapter 11 – Strategic Air Command and
the US Air Force Far East Command

B-29 Superfortress American Four-Engine Propeller-driven Heavy Bomber Boeing Airplane Company	
B-29s flew on all but 21 days of the 37-month war. In 21,000 sorties Far East Command dropped 167,000 tons of bombs and claimed 16 MiGs and seventeen other fighters shot down. Figures on total B-29 losses vary widely depending on the source. Based on the Korean Conflict Aircraft Loss Database, published by the Department of Defense, a total of 109 B-29s were lost to operational causes and enemy action.	
Top Speed	365 miles-per-hour
Cruising Speed	220 miles-per-hour (mph)
Range	3250 miles
Ceiling	31,850 feet
Power	Four 2200-horsepower Wright Duplex Cyclone Engines
Accommodation	10-man crew
Armament	12-.50-caliber remote-control machine-gun turrets, 1 20milimeter (mm) cannon, 20,000-pound bomb load.
3,970 B-29s Built 1943 - 1946	Only 22 complete airframes are currently restored in the US. Only two of these are airworthy and able to fly. (12/24/2021)
The B-29 featured the first ever fully pressurized nose and cockpit in a bomber; an aft area for the crew was also pressurized. Since the bomb bays were not pressurized, a pressurized tunnel was devised to connect the fore and aft crew areas.	

Table 9. Chapter 14 – 1950s Korean Conflict Ground, Sea, and Air Combat

Korean Conflict 1950-1953	
Red Wings over the Yalu, China, the Soviet Union, and the Air War in Korea, by Xiaoming Zhang Publisher Texas A&M University Press, College Station (2002) *Air Combat over the Eastern Front & Korea, a Soviet Fighter Pilot Remembers,* by Sergei Kramarenko Publisher Pen & Sword Books Ltd, 47 Church Street, Barnsley, South Yorkshire S70 2AS (2008)	
Amazon ISBN: 1-58544-201-1 (Cloth cover) ISBN: 1-58544-340-9 (Soft cover)	Translators Vladimir Krupnik and John Armstrong English Text Christopher Summerville
Selected written material from these sources is identified in an *Italicized* font.	
Casualties Analysis System and Statistical Snapshot dcas.dmdc.osd.mil. January 4, 2022	
As of January 4, 2022, total US hostile deaths of 33,739 in-theater includes missing in action declared dead and captured declared dead. Total casualties were 36,574, representing all military branches.	
To view the complete statistical snapshot, refer to Chapter 14.	

Table 10. Chapter 15 – Prisoners of War Exchange
- Armistice Signed Fighting Ends

Armistice Agreement for the Restoration of the South Korean State (1953)
US National Archives & Records Administration 700 Pennsylvania Avenue NW, Washington, DC 20408
Korean War, Korean Conflict, and 1950s Korean Conflict interchangeable.
To view the complete text, refer to Chapter 15.

Table 11. Chapter 1 – Land of the Morning Calm

Chapter 21– Political Gamble of the 21st Century

Coronavirus Pandemic Cases/Deaths/Population Coronavirus COVID-19 Statistics January 3, 2020 - June 12, 2022			
Country	Total Cases	Total Deaths	Population
South Korea	18,225,460	24,321	51,344,120
North Korea	4,432,800	72	25,997,845
United States	87,305,419	1,035,828	334,765,837
Mainland China	2,054,342	15,819	1,450,084,182
To view the complete text, refer to chapter content. Chapter 1, Land of the Morning Calm Chapter 21, Economic Hardship and Coronavirus Pandemic Impact on North Korea			

COVID Live - Coronavirus Statistics - Worldometer (worldometers.info)

Sources: Cases, and deaths John Hopkins COVID-19 Map Coronavirus Resource Center.

Population Data United Nations Population Division World Health Organization.

On May 10, 2022, North Korea reported its first COVID-19 outbreak and ordered a lockdown. An Omicron variant was detected in the capital, Pyongyang. North Korea sent aircraft to China to pick up medical supplies after it confirmed the outbreak. On August 11, 2022, N Korea declared victory over COVID-19 and ordered the lifting of maximum anti-epidemic measures. N Korea reported 74 deaths, but the World Health Organization cast doubt for the reported cases and deaths.

Table 12. Appendices D, J, K, L, and M – Documents Declassified and Approved for Release.

Mandatory Declassification NSA, Fort George G. Meade, MD. National Archives at College Park, MD.	
DOCID Document Identifier	REF ID Reference Identification
NSA National Security Agency	FOIA Freedom of Information Act
CIA Central Intelligence Agency	DIA Defense Intelligence Agency
E.O. The President's Executive Order	MOR Memo of Record
NCA National Security Council	OSD Office Secretary of Defense
GPO Government Printing Office	MDR Mandatory Declassification Review

ISCAP Interagency Security Classification Appeals Panel

To access the complete document, enter the DOCID into the computer search engine.

Appendix D – DOCID 3997429 The Capture of the USS *Pueblo* and Its Effect on SIGINT Operations. Approved for release by NSA on September 14, 2012. FOIA Case # 40722

Appendix J – DOCID 523682 American Cryptology during the Cold War, 1945-1989

Chapter 10 SIGINT in Crisis 1967-1969

Book II: Centralization Wins, 1960-1972, 1995 (nas.gov)

Declassified under authority of the Interagency Security Appeals Panel. E.O. 13526, Section 5.3 (b) (3) ISCAP No. 2008-021. Document 1 Date July 26, 2013. FOIA Case # 40722.

The USS *Pueblo*, specific pages 439-449

The Shootdown of the US Navy EC-121, specific pages 462-467

Link: American Cryptology during the Cold War, 1945-1989. Book II: Centralization Wins, 1960-1972, 1995 (nsa.gov)

Appendix K – DOCID 3997434 Cryptologic/Cryptographic Damage Assessment USS *Pueblo* (GER-2) Approved for Release by NSA on September 14, 2012.

USS Pueblo Record Group: 526 National Archives ID: 56032. FOIA # 40722

Appendix L – DOCID 4047116 The National Security Agency and the EC-121 Shootdown

Approved for Release by NSA, CIA, DIA on April 23, 2013. MOR # 60085. FOIA # 40722

Appendix M – DOCID 3997686 [H.A.S.C. No. 91-12] Inquiry into the USS Pueblo and EC-121 Plane Incidents by the United States Congress July 28, 1969. Use the link to access content: Inquiry_into_the_USS_Pueblo.pdf (nsa.gov). Approved for Release by the NSA on September 14, 2012. FOIA Case # 40722

5 FAM 480.3 DECLASSIFY NATIONAL SECURITY INFORMATION E.O. 13526.

The President's Executive Order establishes a uniform system for classifying, marking, safeguarding, and declassifying national security information. The full text of E.O. 13526, which supersedes all previous Executive Orders on the subject, is on the Government Printing Office website. All classified records that are more than 25 years old and considered to have permanent value are subject to automatic declassification.

Declassification Marking: All classified records, regardless of media format, must be marked in such a manner as to leave no doubt about the declassified record and identify the declassification authority. The classification marking must be marked through by Xs or a line and include the date of declassification.

Source Documents: *Smell the Gunpowder: The Land of the Morning Calm*

PART ONE
ANCIENT KOREAN KINGDOM
Kingdom of Goguryeo

CHAPTER 1

THE LAND OF THE MORNING CALM

The name *Korea* is derived from the ancient Kingdom of Goguryeo, also spelled as *Koryŏ*. This kingdom was first mentioned in Chinese records in the early 7th century before Christ (BC). [9] The poetic interpretation of the word *Korea* — "Land of High Mountains and Sparkling Streams" — derives from the word Koryo, the name of the ancient kingdom on the peninsula. Mountains and streams are indeed the dominant characteristics of Korean terrain. People have been living on the Korean peninsula since prehistoric times, slowly developing their own distinct culture and civilization. The first settlement of the Han River area, where present-day Seoul is located, began around 4000 BC, and Pyongyang was founded in 1122 BC. The Korean peninsula was settled by Tungstic-speaking peoples who migrated in waves from Northeast China and North-Central-and-northeastern Siberia. They settled along the coasts and moved up the river valleys. These peoples formed the dominant ethnic foundation of the Korean people and developed the Korean language.

The Ming Dynasty of China (1368 – 1644), the Celestial Empire of the East, gave Korea the title of "Chaohsien" (Korean: Chosŏn), meaning morning freshness. The title was most suited to South Korea (S Korea) because of its spellbinding natural beauty of picturesque high mountains and clear waters and its splendid tranquility, particularly in the morning, which later further confirmed the title of S Korea as the "land of the morning calm." The Chaohsien state was founded along the Taedong River. Prior to the development of this early state, nomadic

---

9   Placing the "AD" abbreviation before the year number. However, BC is placed after the year number (for example: AD 2018, but 68 BC). BC does stand for "before Christ." AD is from the Latin phrase anno domini, which means "in the year of our Lord."

tribes migrated throughout the peninsula and Northeast China with little regard for contemporary boundaries between China and Korea. The Yalu and Tumen Rivers were easily crossed with rafts or during winter when the rivers froze. The Chao Hsien state rose to power over time, as tribes gathered for common defenses. Before its unification in AD 668 in the Christian Era, Korea became divided by warring tribes, with the Northern tribes tending to be more developed than their southern neighbors because of their proximity to the more advanced societies in China. Competing tribes unified into a single dominion on the Korean Peninsula. Successive regimes maintained Korean political and cultural independence for more than a thousand years; the last of these ruling kingdoms would be the Joseon Dynasty, founded by Taejo of Joseon, born Yi Seong-gye. After ascending to the throne, he changed his name to Yi Dan. He reigned from 1392 to 1398 and was the main figure in the overthrow of the Goryeo Dynasty. The Joseon Dynasty lasted for more than five hundred years and is also known as Chosun, Choson, and Chosŏn. Traditional culture and social structure during this period of independent rule were deeply influenced by Chinese civilization. In general, and throughout their history, Koreans have led productive lives while enjoying the attractiveness and serenity of their peninsular homeland, which they still refer to as "The Land of the Morning Calm."

Beginning in 1871, Japan began to exert more influence, forcing Korea out of China's traditional sphere of influence. On October 8, 1895, at the age of forty-three, Empress of Mveongseing Korean, wife of emperor Gojong, was assassinated by Japanese agents. In 1897, the Joseon Dynasty proclaimed the Empire of Korea.

The Korean Empire was an independent unified Korean state proclaimed by emperor Gojong of the Joseon Dynasty. During this period, Korea had success in modernizing the military, economy, real property laws, education system, and various industries. Russia, Japan, France, and the United States all invested in the country and sought to influence it politically. The empire stood until Japan's annexation and occupation in August 1910.

The United States and Korea's Joseon Dynasty

The US and Korea's Joseon Dynasty established diplomatic relations under the 1882 Treaty of Peace, Amity, Commerce, and Navigation, and the first US diplomatic envoy arrived in Korea in 1883. US-Korea relations continued until 1905, when Japan assumed direction over Korean foreign affairs at the end of the Russo-Japanese War. The Russo-Japanese War was a military conflict fought between the Russian Empire (1721–1917) and the Empire of Japan from 1904 to 1905. In 1904, the Japanese attacked the Russian fleet at Port Arthur, Northeast China, before the formal declaration of war was received in Moscow, surprising the Russian navy, and earning an early victory. Over the course of the next year, the two forces clashed in Korea and the Sea of Japan (East Sea), with the Japanese scoring significant, but costly, victories. By 1905, the combination of losses and the economic cost of financing the war led both countries to seek an end to the war. The Japanese asked US President Theodore Roosevelt to negotiate a peace agreement, and representatives of the two nations met in Portsmouth, New Hampshire. The negotiations took place August 6th to the 30th, at the Portsmouth Naval Shipyard in Kittery, Maine. The chief aims of the Japanese negotiator included first control in Korea and Northeast China. The Russians wanted to maintain Sakhalin Island and refused to pay war costs indemnity to the Japanese. The final agreement was signed on September 5, 1905, and it affirmed the Japanese presence in Northeast China and Korea and ceded the southern half of the island of Sakhalin to Japan. The Treaty of Portsmouth formally ended the Russo-Japanese War. The Hotel Wentworth in New Castle, New Hampshire hosted the members of the delegations and signers of the treaty.

The years of colonization by imperial Japan (1910–1945) humiliated Korea, depriving it of freedom and creating a skewed economy. In 1905, Japan declared a virtual protectorate over Korea and in 1910 formally annexed the country. The Japanese period of rule over the whole of Korea began on August 29, 1910, when His Majesty the Emperor of Korea made complete and permanent cession to His Majesty the Emperor of Japan. Japan's declaration of annexation ended the 518-year rule of the Joseon (Choson-Chaohsien) Dynasty and began the most horrific period of Korean history. The first year of Japanese control was characterized by its consolidation of power, implementation of colonial rule, and complete repression of any form of resistance. The Japanese instituted vast social and economic changes, building modern industries and railroads; but their rule was harsh and exploitative.

Sporadic Korean attempts to overthrow the Japanese were unsuccessful, and after 1919, a provisional Korean government, under Syngman Rhee, was established at Shanghai, China. In the 1930s, Japan invested heavily in industry in the North, making it the next most advanced industrial region in East Asia. At the end of World War II, after 35 years of colonial rule (1910−1945), the Japanese were now defeated, leaving Korea divided and occupied.

Much more damaging to the ancient culture and society was the division in 1945 into North Korea and South Korea. Syngman Rhee returned to S Korea from exile. The defeat of Japan led only to the replacement of one colonial power with two military superpowers and thrust the Korean peninsula into the front lines of the Cold War.

The defeat of the Japanese by the US, and the 11th-hour declaration of war on Japan by Russia, placed Korea squarely in the middle of an escalating conflict between two post-war world powers, to the dismay of Koreans by most measures. The combination of disparate superpower objectives in Korea, and the diverse groups striving for power in a liberated Korea, created the conditions that led to the Korean nation being divided.

On August 11, 1945, General Order No. 1, [10] the protocol for the surrender and occupation of Japan, was completed in Washington, DC. The 38th Parallel, which runs across the Korean peninsula, had been just one line on a map of the globe. On the night of August 10-11, 1945, members of the State-War-Navy Coordinating Committee [11] (assistant secretaries from each department) and the Joint Staff planners (military staff officers) met in adjoining rooms in the Pentagon to draft the documents that would spell out the steps Japan must take to complete the surrender. Key among those documents was General Order No. 1. By the morning of August 11, the territorial provisions of the general order were completed. General Order No. 1 approved by the President of the United States, Harry S. Truman, and issued to the Japanese government on August 17, 1945, by the Supreme Commander for the Allied Powers, General Douglas MacArthur. General Order No. 1 became known to the world when it was announced at the Japanese surrender ceremony on September 2, 1945, aboard the battleship USS *Missouri* (BB-63) in Tokyo Bay. The order instructed

---

10   Appendix B, Department of State, Office of the Historian, Revision of General No. 1.

       The document spelled out the steps to be taken by Japan to complete the surrender.
11   State-War-Navy Coordinating Committee (SWNCC) planned for the occupation of Europe and Japan along with its occupied areas aimed at anticipating and addressing the issues that might confront US forces tasked with occupying and running former enemy states. *On Active Service in Peace and War* by Henry L. Stimson and McGeorge Bundy, Publisher: Hippocrene Books, June 1, 1971.
       https://www.amazon.com/Active-Service-Peace-War/dp/0374976279

Smell The Gunpowder

the Japanese Imperial General Headquarters to direct its military and naval commanders in the field to surrender their forces and weapons to specifically designated representatives of the Allied Powers (the United States, Great Britain, Soviet Union, and the Republic of China).

The order set in motion military operations that would have profound political implications, because whoever took the surrender of enemy forces in each area would gain immediate control of that territory by virtue of having the only armed forces on the ground.

The Soviet Union had just—somewhat belatedly—declared war on August 8, 1945, against the Japanese Empire, and already started to move troops into the Japanese protectorate of Korea. The Soviet Union committed more than 1 million soldiers into Japanese-occupied Manchuria. The Russians wasted no time and on August 12, 1945, had their troops in northern Korea. American combat units, deployed throughout the Pacific, did not enter Korea until early September 1945. The Russians would take the surrender of Japanese forces in Northeast China (Manchuria) and Korea north of the 38th Parallel, and the US, the southern territory. The two superpowers agreed on the 38th Parallel as the temporary line of demarcation between their forces. The US envisioned a trusteeship lasting five years and managed by the United Nations, with Russia agreeing in principle. At that time, the US did not foresee the 38th Parallel becoming the border between divided countries.

The US and Russia agreed to restore a Korean government to lead a free and independent Korean people. However, the superpowers fundamentally disagreed on the nature of that government. Thus, the political and cultural landscape of modern Korea was born.

President Truman had already learned not to trust Russia, referencing its attempt to force the US, French, and British from occupied Berlin, Germany. Truman wanted a border that kept the USSR from occupying all of Korea, a "demarcation line," between the northern part of the Korean peninsula and the southern part, where the US planned to station troops. Dividing Korea about equally at the 38th Parallel, the US would control Seoul, the capital, and the major ports of Inchon (near Seoul) and Pusan at the southern tip of the peninsula. The division at the 38th Parallel was proposed to the USSR as the demarcation line, and they had no objections.

The agreement led to the creation of the Democratic People's Republic of Korea (DPRK-N Korea) "Strong and Prosperous Nation," and the Republic of Korea (ROK-S Korea) "The Land of the Morning Calm."

While the end of World War II brought peace and prosperity to most Americans, it also created a heightened state of tension between Russia and the US. Fearing that Russia intended to "export" communism to other nations, America centered its foreign policy on the "containment" of communism, both at home and abroad. Although formulation of the Truman Doctrine, the Marshall Plan, and the Berlin Airlift suggested the US had a particular concern with the spread of communism in Europe, America's policy of containment extended to Asia as well. Indeed, Asia would prove to be the site of the first major conflict waged in the name of containment. The establishment of the US military government in Inchon on September 8, 1945, signaled the beginning of S Korean history. On September 9, 1945, the Japanese flag was lowered in Seoul and the United States flag raised. In November 1945, the US military government in Korea was established. Army Lieutenant General (LTG) John R. Hodge named the first Commander, US Army Forces in Korea (USAFK), and thereby became essentially S Korea's chief executive. A December conference in Moscow led to a Russo–American commission to work out the postwar problems of Korean independence. Concurrently, a pro-Russia, ideologically communist government was established in the North, officially succeeding the Provisional People's Committee for N Korea, colloquially known as Soviet Korea, a quasi-government composed of five provinces in 1946. The government was modeled after the USSR-Russia system of government. It co-existed alongside the Russian Civil Administration.

On February 8, 1946, a provisional government formed under Kim Il-sung, who had spent the last years of World War II training Russian troops in Northeast China. Meeting for the first time in March 1946, the commission was short-lived.

Its failure, due to lack of Russian cooperation, paved the way for politico-military factions within the country that set up two separate Koreas. The Russians and Americans failed to reach agreement on a unified government, and in 1948, two separate governments were established, each claiming to be the legitimate government of all Korea. The history of N Korea began with the partition of Korea and its first leader Kim Il-sung. Kim did not appear in N Korea until late September 1945 and was 34 years old when he came to power. Kim was the founding father of socialist Korea and ruled North Korea from 1948 until his death on July 8, 1994. Following the death of his father, Kim Jong-il ruled from 1994 until his death on December 17, 2011. Kim Jong-un, 40, grandson of Kim Il-sung, came to power in 2011 following the death of his father, Kim Jong-il.

"Juche" Policy of Self-Reliance

Kim Il-sung created the country's policy of "juche," translated as self-reliance, which cut off N Korea economically and diplomatically from the rest of the world, even in times of great need, such as famines. Kim announced his juche policy in 1972, and this national ethos places an emphasis on self-reliance, independence, resourcefulness, a display of one's strength, self-defense, and the responsibility to internally solve problems without outside assistance. Songun, begun by Kim Jong-il in the mid-1990s, was a continuation of his father's juche policy, with added emphasis on military capability at the expense of civilians and N Korean fundamentals. Despite the juche policy, N Korea relies on imports to make up for shortages in raw materials, finished products, and technology that are not available in the country. During the Cold War, N Korea relied heavily on support from Russia and China, especially for its economy and military.

N Korea seemed to be on a war footing in early 1949. Tens of thousands of Koreans who were veterans of the Chinese Communist forces that had defeated Chiang Kai-shek's National Army in China during the Chinese civil war (1945–1949) filtered back into Korea. Five Divisions formed in N Korea around these veterans, and each was well-equipped with robust combat support.

By the end of 1949 N Korea was a full-fledged communist state and established a political system that was partly styled on the 1991 failed socialist system. On December 25, 1991, the Soviet hammer-and-sickle flag was lowered outside the Kremlin for the final time.

United States Korean Military Advisory Group

Preoccupied with Russian intentions in Western Europe, the US placed little strategic importance to Korea in the late 1940s. The US Army withdrew its combat forces from S Korea in June 1949. In July 1949, the United States Military

Advisory Group (KMAG) East Asia to the Republic of Korea (S Korea) formed and authorized 472 soldiers to assist the S Korean military.

Americans assigned to the KMAG East Asia were armed only with their individual weapons. The KMAG's mission was to organize, administer, equip, and train the Korean Security Forces, which consisted of the Korean Army, the Korean Coast Guard, and the Korean National Police. To accomplish this mission, the advisory group assigned a US officer to each key position in the Korean national defense establishment, from the Minister of National Defense down to the battalion level. The organization is called the "counterpart" system. US and S Korean colleagues had desks in the same offices, inspected troops together, attended social functions together, and otherwise shared intimately all daily tasks and problems. The efforts of the advisers provided a cornerstone of the present S Korean Armed Forces. As the Cold War developed, the peninsula became a pawn in a larger, international ideological struggle. After three years, the US turned the problem over to the United Nations (UN), which mandated elections to decide on a unified government in Korea. UN-sponsored elections led to the formation of S Korea on August 15, 1948, under President Syngman Rhee, with its capital in Seoul. S Korea's first constitution was established on July 17, 1948, following the general election of May 10, 1948. North Korea declined to participate in the UN elections and formed its own government, Kim Il-sung as its leader and its capital in Pyongyang.

Treaty of Friendship, Cooperation and Mutual Assistance

In 1961, leaders of China and N Korea made the far-sighted strategic decision to sign the China-N Korea Treaty of Friendship, Cooperation, and Mutual Assistance, a treaty which laid important political and legal foundations for consolidating friendship and promoting bilateral friendly cooperation for the long run. In July 2021, the 60th anniversary of the signing of the treaty, Chinese President Xi Jinping and N Korean Leader Kim Jong-un reaffirmed its provisions. The treaty also calls for each country to come to the aid of the other if attacked. China adamantly supports N Korea in developing its economy, which it views as reasonable, and improving its people's wellbeing. N Korea's only ally and major benefactor is China, with bilateral trade involving over half of N Korean exports and eighty-five percent of its imports. North Korea also serves as a buffer between China and the economically capitalistic and democratic S Korea. The historical ties between China and N Korea continue to bind the two countries together, and China's fear of a unified and economically powerful Korean Peninsula under a democratic-style government drives Chinese actions to preclude such an event. N Korea and China are separated by two rivers, the Yalu and Tumen, and the border is 880 miles long. Of note, the border with Russia measures only ten miles.

Until January 2020, the border with China was the gateway for most of N Korea's trade with the outside world. N Korea shut its border as the coronavirus (COVID-19) pandemic spread around the world, and trade with China dropped nearly 90 percent. Dismal trade figures for 2021 attest to the toll the North's border closures took on its food supply, medicine, and fuel shortages. Factories closed because of a lack of parts. N Korea's strict COVID-19 policies undermined N Korean leader Kim Jong-un's goal of ending hunger and improving the daily lives of its people.

CHAPTER 2

EARLY WARNINGS OF THE CONFLICT TO COME

As the Cold War came to dominate United States foreign policy, America extended security commitments to two nations in Northeast Asia: South Korea and Japan. The Department of State under Secretary Dean Acheson implemented a series of agreements to build a permanent American presence in the region and support these two nations, creating alliances that have lasted to this day.

After Japan's unconditional surrender to the Allied Powers in August 1945, the US military occupied the defeated nation and began a series of far-reaching reforms designed to build a peaceful and democratic Japan by reducing the power of the military and breaking up the largest Japanese business conglomerates. On September 8, 1945, Army Lieutenant General (Lt. Gen.) John R. Hodge arrived in Inchon to accept the Japanese surrender south of the 38th Parallel. However, growing concern over communist power in East Asia, particularly the success of the Chinese Communist Party (CCP) against Chiang Kai-shek's Nationalist forces, led the United States to halt reforms in 1947 and 1948 to focus on the economic recovery and political rehabilitation of Japan.

In this "reverse course," General Douglas MacArthur, as Allied commander of the Japanese occupation in 1945–1951, focused on strengthening, not punishing, what would become a key Cold War ally.

The USSR supported Kim Il-sung in N Korea; the US backed Syngman Rhee in S Korea. On September 9, 1945, N Korea Communists established the Democratic People's Republic of Korea.

The US did not consider S Korea of vital interest until 1950, when the N Korean forces began a military buildup along the 38th Parallel. N Korea fortified the 38th Parallel, and soon border incidents began breaking out. Neither side recognized the parallel as a legitimate boundary; S Korea wanted to unify Korea, by force if necessary. N Korea's main allies were Russia, which supplied it with arms, fighter pilots, and anti-aircraft artillery crews; and China, which later sent thousands of troops and fighter pilots. In turn, S Korea, with aid from the US, began to fortify its defenses south of the 38th Parallel. In the summer of 1949, S Korea provoked the fighting along the 38th Parallel, according to declassified US CIA documents [12] –fighting that sometimes took hundreds of lives. In 1949, the US Congress approved a $150 million dollar aid bill to S Korea. Since Syngman Rhee had so often talked about invading N Korea, US leaders believed that if they had provided, for example, heavy artillery, he might have used it to invade N Korea. S Korea had also denied modern aircraft, tanks, and other military hardware, by the same reasoning. For this reason, S Korea provided only rifles, bazookas, and light artillery.

This attitude was a prime reason the US limited fuel supplies and ammunition while providing enough resources to sustain a defensive posture for two-weeks. This fear would last for decades to come and feed the N Korean assertion that joint military exercises between S Korea and the US were a prelude to invasion.

Military exercises, no matter the size or form, are viewed as a rehearsal for conflict. N Korea has threatened unspecified countermeasures that would cause a "security crisis" for the US and S Korea.

On August 10, 2021, joint exercise between US and S Korea continued for nine days, mostly consisting of defensive computer-simulated command post training with minimal personnel but no live field training. N Korea viewed this military training as an act of aggression and has for decades reacted angrily.

---

12   https://www.cia.gov/library/center-for-the-study-of-intelligence/csi-publications/index-of-Declassified articles.

Armed Forces Security Agency and Army Security Agency Operations

On May 20, 1949, all cryptologic activities were centralized under a national organization called the US Armed Forces Security Agency (AFSA).

The intelligence community in June 1950 was in turmoil. Extensive reorganization, personnel reductions, equipment inadequacies, and disjointed training created a state of general unreadiness. The shortcomings of various intelligence organizations and disciplines led to poor tactical and operational outcomes on 1950s Korean Conflict battlefields and go far to explain the failure of intelligence to predict the N Korean attack of S Korea and the intervention of the Chinese in the conflict. There were early warnings of the conflict to come, but no alarm was raised. The AFSA intercepted communications intelligence hints of more than usual interest in the Korean peninsula by China and Russian, but neither was sufficient to provide specific warnings of an attack. In the spring of 1950, a Russian intelligence network located in their port city of Vladivostok, home base to the Russian Pacific Fleet, increased its targeting of communications in S Korea. Russian targeting of S Korea was quite low until early February, then rose dramatically after February 21. This coverage continued at an extremely elevated level until May 15, when it ceased altogether.

The US intercept facilities in the Pacific region focused on higher-priority signal intelligence (SIGINT) collection requirements, such as Chinese activities. With no specific guidance on collecting against N Korea from the Far East Command, AFSA concentrated on obvious items of importance, primarily China and Russia. When N Korea crossed the 38th Parallel, there was only one analyst at AFSA working on N Korean intercepts, and he did not have a Korean typewriter, a Korean dictionary, or Korean language books. The AFSA began an expanded effort against China that included increased intercept and crypto analysis studies. The N Korean attack reflected the intelligence community's lack of tactical readiness. On November 2, 1952, AFSA, by order of President Truman was redesignated as the National Security Agency (NSA).

The Army Security Agency (ASA), the Army's cryptologic organization, was created on September 15, 1945, and was under the operational control of the War Department and later the Director of the NSA, mostly focused upon signal communication intelligence.

In mid-April 1950, the ASA undertook a limited "search and development" study of N Korean communications traffic. It revealed large shipments of bandages and medicines went from Russia to N Korea and Northeast China (Manchuria), beginning in early spring. These actions made sense only in hindsight, after the attack on S Korea occurred. At the start of the conflict, two fixed ASA stations and three mobile units were performing fixed-station missions in the Pacific.

A signal collection unit from ASA Pacific deployed to S Korea on September 18, 1950, and on October 9, the 60th Signal Service Company finally arrived in Korea. The ASA was revitalized for the conflict by assuming a new role to provide support to tactical operations.

Initially, because of problems with mountainous terrain, no steady or reliable information was available from the direction-finding operations to identify, triangulate, and analyze N Korean and Chinese radio communications. Not until 1952 could traffic analysis detect from military communications when communist Chinese units entered and left Korea. In addition, the ASA planned to support with a communications reconnaissance group at the 8th Army-level the 501st Communication Reconnaissance Group (CR Group), and a reconnaissance battalion for each of the three US Army corps, the 1st (I Corps), 9th, (IX Corps) and 10th (X Corps), in the theater. In July 1951, the CR Group became operational, having been ordered by the National Security Agency (NSA) to Korea from Camp Pickett, Virginia. The ASA also encountered problems finding Chinese linguists to translate voice communications. The severe shortages of trained military linguists were "acute and persistent" and continually plagued intelligence units in Korea. Recognizing a severe shortage of linguists, ASA scrambled to provide training in Chinese Mandarin dialect. Recruitment began among the large Chinese population in the US but provided few candidates because most American-born Chinese spoke a southern dialect rather than the Mandarin used by People's Liberation Army (PLA) radio operators. To fill the need, several Chinese Nationalists from Taiwan were hired as civilians to work with ASA, although some special training was needed to acquaint them with differences in military vocabulary between the nationalist and communists. Meanwhile, the US Army deployed its only two Korean linguists to provide translation of signal intelligence (SIGINT) for UN forces in Korea. The results of this lack of adequate intelligence support were strategic surprises both when the N Koreans attacked S Korea and when the Chinese intervened in Korea in massive, overwhelming numbers. These strategic surprises led to the near tactical defeats of Task Force Smith at Osan and elements of the 8th Army in northwest N Korea and X Corps at the Chosin reservoir.[13] The official description and the tactical name and organization described in the introduction, Table 3.

In April 1950, N Korea's leader, Kim Il-sung, traveled to Moscow for a meeting with Joseph Stalin. They discussed Kim's plan to invade S Korea. Stalin advised Kim to discuss the invasion plan with Chinese leader Chairman Mao Zedong, who was also in Moscow. Mao agreed to support the invasion of S Korea, and Stalin approved the invasion with the understanding that no Russian forces would be committed.

Russian advisors prepared the invasion plan; Stalin, however, reiterated that he would not permit Russian soldiers to accompany the N Koreans once its forces crossed into S Korea. A report forwarded routinely dated June 20, 1950, to Washington from KMAG East Asia reflected a strong possibility of action toward the end of June. It reported significant troop movements and concentrations along the 38th Parallel, forward stockpiling of supplies, border evacuation of all civilians, suspension of civilian freight service, and transportation of military supplies only. But this information was poorly evaluated in the field and at higher echelons. Then the communist N Koreans crossed the 38th Parallel and surged into S Korea in what the UN termed an unprovoked act of aggression. This action seemed at first just another incident in a five-year standoff marked by mutual threats and hostility. Each side had postured, threatened reunification by force, and engaged in border fights. In noticeably short order, the UN and the US realized this was not a border fight but an invasion.

The 1950s Korean Conflict, (interchangeable reference to the Korean War, and a police action) the first hot war, was America's first experience with the concept of "limited war." President Truman referred to the US response to the invasion as a "police action" under the aegis of the UN. Truman did not seek a formal declaration of war from the US Congress. The unexpected involvement by China soon turned the "police action" into an armed conflict.

The United States' aim initially was not the complete and total defeat of the enemy, but a "limited" goal of protecting S Korea. The N Koreans refer to the

---

13 Sources: 1. T.R. Fehrenbach, This Kind of War: A Study in Unpreparedness. 2. Culp, Robert A.II, "North Korean invasion and Chinese intervention in Korea: failures of intelligence" (2004). https://digitalcommons.lsu.edu/gradschool_theses/309. Free and open access by the Graduate School at LSU Digital Commons. Information, please contact gradetd@lsu.edu. Louisiana State University.

conflict as the "Fatherland Liberation War" and the S Koreans use the term "6-25 War" (June 25, 1950). The N Korean point of view is that the start of the conflict was initiated by the US and conducted by S Korea with an armed invasion, and N Korea launched a counterattack. The S Korean position was simple; it responded to the armed invasion of its territory.

Landscape Setting and Climate Patterns

The Korean peninsula is 683 miles long, but at its shortest width near the Demilitarized Zone (DMZ), it is only 120 miles from coast to coast and is mountainous and frequently cut by waterways of all sizes flowing down from the mountains into the sea. At nearly the same latitude as the US state of Utah, the combined territories of North and South Korea are about the same size as the United Kingdom or the US state of Minnesota. The entire landmass of the Korean peninsula measures 84,565 square miles. The DMZ division allocated more territory to the North than to the South, fifty-five percent and forty-five percent, respectively. S Korea is very hilly and mountainous in the East, where the Taebaek Mountains dominate the landscape. The mountain range is steep and rugged, with narrow, winding gorge-like valleys. Summit heights are 2000 to 5000 feet. The rugged land slopes west into undulating, flatter coastal plains, where most people live. The western and southern coastlines of the country are covered by thousands of islands and narrow channels. Its longest distance is 309 miles. The southernmost point of the peninsula is only 120 miles from southern Kyushu, one of Japan's four main islands. S Korea covers 37,541 square miles and in 1950 was inhabited by 20 million people. Based on UN data as of June 12, 2022, the current population is 51 million.

N Korea is a series of large and medium-size mountain ranges and large hills, separated by deep, narrow valleys. Along the Yellow Sea, (West) coast are wide coastal plains, while along the Sea of Japan (East Sea) coastline (N Korea's lowest point at 0 feet), narrow plains rise into the mountains. Like S Korea, dozens of small islands dot the western coastline. Its longest distance is 374 miles. According to the UN Statistics Division, N Korea covers 46,541 square miles and in 1950 was inhabited by 10.5 million people. The current population is nearly 26 million as of June 12, 2022, based on the latest data.

Long summers and cold winters dominate Korea's climate. In the summer, the monsoon rains hit. It rains heavily, and then after 15 minutes, it stops, and becomes sunny and hot … 100, 110 degrees. Cross-country travel is limited by the heavy rainfall and extremely wet lowland areas. The rugged terrain and wetness of the lowlands along with large rivers and irrigated fields presented obstacles, making fighting in Korea tough. The high humidity in the summer months required special precautions and protective measures for food not in airtight containers, and technical equipment, radios, and electronics. Dust, mud, and snow at times limited US Air Force operations. The winter months are especially brutal, with high wind and freezing temperatures sometimes reaching -35 °F degrees. Frostbite was the worst malady brought on by the freezing weather. Soldiers also suffered from frozen rations, icy terrain, jammed weapons, and shortage of cold-weather gear.

The mean temperature in combat areas was always below freezing during the winter months. Soldiers recall this period in Korea as the coldest times of their lives. The weather conditions were the most severe ever experienced by American forces since the World War II Aleutian Island Campaign, US Territory of Alaska, during the winter of 1942-1943. The most favorable season for general operations was October through March.

PART TWO
1ST KOREAN CONFLICT

CHAPTER 3

KOREAN CONFLICT: NORTH KOREAN PERSPECTIVE

"Strong and Prosperous Nation"

Early in the morning of June 25, 1950, a large-scale aggression started against N Korea, according to a report released by the Ministry of the Interior of N Korea. The S Korean puppet army, under the direct command of the US, launched an armed invasion all along the 38th Parallel on a preconceived war plan, intruding one-to-two-and-half miles deep in the directions of Haeju, Kumchon, and Chorwon.

North Korea Propaganda and Agitation Department

The N Korean perspective of the events of June 1950 is presented in *italicized font* from *Echoes of the Korean War (EOTKW)Booklet* and *The US Imperialists Started the Korean War*. The publishing house is under the control of the Propaganda and Agitation Department of the Workers' Party of Korea located in Pyongyang, N Korea. These writings were published in 1996 and 1993. *EOTKW* written by war historians, political scientists and based on study of documents in the USSR-Russia and N Korea-DPRK archives, critical analysis of military-political and military-historical literature published after 1945 in the USSR, N Korea, S Korea, Japan, the United States (US), the People's Republic of China (PRC), and other countries. The present head of the department is Kim Yo-jong, powerful sister of N Korean leader Kim Jong-un. Selected information is in *italicized font* and includes excerpts from *Red Wings over the Yalu* by Xiaoming Zhang. It has been 72 years since the outbreak of the 1950s

Korean Conflict. However, people still argue the controversial questions of why the conflict was ignited and by whom.

Echoes of the Korean War & *US Imperialists Started the Korean War* national government publications described in the introduction—specifically, Table 7.

S Korea is turned into a Military Bridgehead

Wars do not break out of their own accord. They mature gradually, and war itself is a continuation of policy by military means. The march to war on the Korean peninsula began in the autumn of 1945.

Containment of Communism; the United States designated S Korea as the forward base in the Far East for its military-strategic and political importance. In August 1947, Syngman Rhee said, "It is posed as an urgent task to form in the first place a 100,000 strong army."

The United States handed over to S Korea 105-and 57mm guns (mm-millimeter), warships, and many Japanese weapons received as the result of disarmament of the Japanese army. Formation of a regular S Korean Army was proclaimed on September 1, 1948.

On June 19, at a meeting of the National Assembly of S Korea, Advisor to the State Department John F. Dulles said to Syngman Rhee (president of S Korea) that the 38th parallel had left a deep impression on him and if Rhee was ready to attack communist N Korea, the US would give aid to him through the United Nations.

However, he advised Rhee to fabricate the story that S Korea had been invaded first and to make up an action programme on that basis. This programme was translated into practice.

According to the report of the Home Ministry of the Republic, from 2200 hours (10:00 p.m.) on June 23 the puppet army units at the 38th parallel which had been in a "state of emergency" went into a large-scale artillery bombardment over the area north (Ongjin region) of the 38th parallel. By the 24th they had fired more than 700 of 105-mm howitzer and 81-mm mortar shells. This bombardment was the preliminary firing signaling the start of an all-out armed aggression of the US imperialists and the prelude to their "great drama" and "positive action."

The government of the republic resolutely demanded that the US imperialists and Syngman Rhee clique (sharing a common purpose) stop their adventurous act of war at once, warning that if they did not stop the aggression, it would take a decisive step to pressure the enemy and they would then bear full responsibility for all the consequences arising from their hazardous act of war.

At dawn of June 25 the S Korean troops launched intensive offensives along the whole length of the 38th parallel.

President Kim Il-sung lost no time to call a political committee meeting of the Party Central Committee and an emergency session of the cabinet and took resolute steps for administering an annihilating blow at the enemy. He ordered the Republic's Security Forces and People's Army to go over to a counter offensive immediately. Thus started the Korean people's just Fatherland Liberation War to repulse the US invasion and defend the freedom and independence of the fatherland. The start of a counteroffensive by the Korean People's Army was a crushing blow to the aggressors.

The news of the start of the Korean War (conflict) was a quite unforeseen event for the majority of USSR (Russian) people, in particular specialists in Far Eastern affairs.

Russian newspapers carried articles about China and N Korea, grave warnings from Beijing concerning "US aggressive actions" and messages about "new provocations" of the S Korean troops, dispatched by Pyongyang. Although the world smelled gunpowder, it was not until June 25 that anyone knew the date and place of large-scaled military action on the Korean peninsula."

Conclusion: "The US imperialists, who had occupied S Korea in place of the Japanese imperialists following the 2nd World War, forced reactionary fascist colonial rule upon it from the first day of their occupation, perpetrated ceaseless military provocations against the northern half of Korea in the foolish hope of invading the whole of Korea and Asia, and at last on June 25, 1950, unleashed a war of aggression against the Korean people."

"At the first moment of war, the US rulers stated that the Korean Conflict (War) was quite an unforeseen event and tried to describe the situation as if they had been "invaded by surprise."

The US rigged up and expanded the S Korean puppet army with a view to keeping the balance of forces at a "ratio of ten to one" over the N Korean army and trained it the American way. It (the US) also seized its prerogative of supreme command over the puppet army. From 1945 to 1949, the US offered S Korea military aid worth over 1 billion dollars. While stepping up the combat readiness of the puppet army, it deployed its reinforced forces in the areas along the 38th parallel. It also built or repaired military roads and conducted the work of building positions on a large scale.

At the same time, the US imperialists egged the puppet army on to launch armed provocations against N Korea in the areas along the 38th parallel. Their (puppet) armed provocations from 1947 to June 1950, numbered over 5,000. Such provocations were not simple "armed conflicts" but "test wars" committed repeatedly with a focus on the directions of main attack according to military action plans for "northward expedition."

The US scheme to unleash a war in Korea did not kick off unexpectedly on June 25, 1950, which is usually called the day of the outbreak of the First Korean Conflict (Korean War). It started in 1947, right after the 2nd World War.

After rounding off war preparations, the US imperialists buckled down to action. President Harry S. Truman sent Secretary of Defense Louis L. Johnson, Chairman of the US Joint Chiefs of Staff Omar N. Bradley, and Advisor to the State Department John F. Dulles to Seoul and Tokyo on the pretext of discussing a "peace treaty" with Japan to ultimately make sure of the preparations for war against N Korea and take relevant measures. Dulles arrived in Seoul in mid-June 1950 and made a final examination of the war preparations of the puppet army in a trench along the 38th parallel.

Giving instructions to ignite a war to President Syngman Rhee, he said he came here with Truman's order to inspect the preparations for a "northward march" with his eyes and kick it off in case everything is OK, adding that there is no need for further delay.

According to it, in January 1950, when the Secretary of Defense of the United States, (Kenneth C.) Royall, and the chief of public relations of (General) MacArthur's command, (William J.) Sebald, visited Seoul, the latter assured Syngman Rhee: "If the expedition against the North is launched, American naval and air force unit's stationed Japan will be sent immediately to support S

Korea. As far as naval and air forces are concerned, you have nothing to worry about."

"According to the testimony (September 26, 1950, Documentary Evidence for the Provoking of a Korean Civil War by the US Imperialists, Pyongyang) of Kim Hyo Sok, in June 1950 (John F.) Dulles who visited Seoul assured Syngman Rhee and Sin Sing Mo (Acting Prime Minister S. Korea):

"If the ROK army can hold out for two weeks, everything will go smoothly, for during this period the USA, by accusing N Korea of attacking S Korea, will compel the United Nations to act. And in the name of the United Nations, land, naval and air forces will be mobilized."

On June 25, 1950, the S Korean puppet army, in combat readiness under the direct command of the American Military Advisory Group (AMAG), launched a sudden armed invasion of the DPRK all along the 38th parallel. But the US imperialists suffered an ignominious defeat in the war by the Korean people who turned out in the heroic struggle to firmly defend the destiny of their country and nation.

Marxists Internet Archive: At dawn on Sunday, June 25, Syngman Rhee launched a sudden attack which took the N Koreans by surprise. His forces crossed the 38th parallel at several places and captured Haeju, some miles to the north on the road to Pyongyang. The N Koreans staged a counteroffensive and then drove on across the parallel and staged a full-scale invasion of S Korea.

There is overwhelming evidence that Syngman Rhee and his American supporters started the civil war on June 25, 1950, and it was to prevent this evidence being produced and sifted that the United States Government insisted that a Security Council resolution condemning the North Koreans should be adopted the same day.

Korean history since 1945 is one of partition and at the same time one of interrupted struggle against it. The 1950-53 war (conflict) delayed the reunification of the Korean peninsula and made it more difficult. The war clearly indicated that resorting to force is not the way to reunify the country.

Despite an atmosphere of mutual distrust and hostility after the Korean War (conflict), there were and are attempts to realize contact and cooperation between the north and the south. The Korean nation can solve the reunification question by its own strength.

The North Korean People's Army (NKPA) spearhead consisted of experienced Korean veterans of the Chinese Civil War and World War II. These Koreans were serving in the People's Liberation Army (PLA), embedded with Chinese communist forces, and returned to serve in the NKPA.

The attack aimed at reuniting the country under communist rule. After initial resistance, the Republic of Korea Army (ROKA) gave way before the larger, stronger Korean People's Army (KPA), and a chaotic and disorderly retreat quickly developed.

The Lie that Led to War

Author Sir John Pratt in 1951 wrote the pamphlet *"Rearmament and East Asia"* explaining briefly how the 1950s Korean Conflict (interchangeable with War) broke out. It was not an international war but a civil war, with which the United Nations would not normally be concerned. For a year, both North and South Koreans had been expecting civil war to break out, and each side was confident of victory. Border skirmishes were common; 10,000 North and South Korean soldiers were killed in battle before the conflict began. The United States Government decided, however, to treat it as an international war and to secure the condemnation of the North Koreans before any evidence could be presented and before the Soviet delegate could resume his place on the UN Security Council.

There is evidence that Syngman Rhee and his American supporters started the civil war on June 25, 1950. The United States (US) insisted that a UN Security Council resolution condemning the North Koreans should be adopted the same day. The conflict had its origin in the hysterical fear that the mere word Communism produced in America.

Disclaimer: The pamphlet *Rearmament and the Far East* was issued by the Britain-China Friendship Association, 17 Bishops Bridge Road, London W2. The association noted it did not necessarily agree with its content.

Report of the Democratic People's Republic of Korea

Ministry of Internal Affairs

To Cde. Andrei Andreyevich Gromyko

I am sending a report of the Ministry of Internal Affairs transmitted by radio on 25 June 1950.

Report of the DPRK Ministry of Internal Affairs.

Early on the morning of 25 June 1950, troops of the so-called 'army of national defense' of the puppet government of South Korea began a surprise attack on the territory of North Korea along the entire 38th parallel.

Having begun a surprise attack, the enemy invaded the territory of North Korea to a depth of one or two kilometers north of the 38th Parallel in the area west of [Haeju] and in the areas of [Geumseung] and [Cholwon].

The DPRK Ministry of Internal Affairs has issued an order to security detachments to repel the attacks of the enemy, which has invaded the territory of North Korea. Now, the security forces of the Republic are stubbornly resisting the enemy. Security detachments of the Republic have repulsed attacks of the enemy, which has invaded the territory of North Korea around [Yang yang].

The government of the DPRK has charged the Ministry of Internal Affairs of the Republic with warning the authorities of the puppet government of South Korea that if they do not immediately halt their reckless military operations in the areas north of the 38th Parallel, decisive steps will be taken to subdue the enemy and that they will bear full responsibility for all the serious consequences of these reckless military.

Chichkova wrote and sent the letter, which was received by Kirsanova on behalf of Gromyko.

Comrade (Cde) Andrei Andreyevich Gromyko was a Soviet Belarusian communist politician and diplomat during the Cold War.

Reception of US Ambassador Alan G. Kirk by Gromyko

From the Journal of Andrei Andreyevich Gromyko, "Reception of US Ambassador Kirk, June 29, 1950." Gromyko delivers a statement on the start of the Korean War to US Ambassador to the Soviet Union Kirk.

[Handwritten]: to Cde. G. S. Sazhin/Saksin to Cde.? N. I. Molyakov?

FROM THE JOURNAL
OF A. A. GROMYKO 30 June 1950

N° 210/AG

RECEPTION OF US AMBASSADOR KIRK

29 June 1950

Today, I invited US Ambassador Kirk and delivered a statement of the Soviet Government to him in response to the statement of the US Government of 27 June.

Having familiarized himself with the text of the statement, Kirk asked whether this was also a reply to the point in which the US Government asked the Soviet Government to influence the North Korean authorities.

I replied to Kirk that the statement given to him was the response of the Soviet Government to the statement of the US Government of 27 June, including the point mentioned by the Ambassador.

At Kirk's request the text of our reply was (verbally) translated into English for him.

The conversation lasted 10 minutes.

Present at the reception were Cde. V. N. Pastoyev, Assistant to the Chief of the Protocol Department, and N. I. Molyakov, First Secretary of the US Department.

DEPUTY USSR MINISTER
OF FOREIGN AFFAIRS

/ A. Gromyko/

Authenticated by [illegible signature]

> [Handwritten]: Ref N 854/SShA 30 June 1950
> Delivered to US Ambassador Kirk
> by Cde. A. A. Gromyko
> during a conversation on 29 June 1950

In connection with the statement of the Government of the United States of America which you sent on 27 June, the Soviet Government has charged me with stating the following.

1. According to reliable information of the Soviet Government, the events, which are occurring in Korea, were provoked by an attack on border areas of North Korea by forces of the South Korean authorities. Therefore, the responsibility for these events rests on the South Korean authorities and on those who are behind them.

2. As is well known, the Soviet Government withdrew its troops from Korea before the United States did and thereby affirmed its traditional principle of non-interference in the internal affairs of other countries. Now, the Soviet Government stands by the principle of the impermissibility of the interference of foreign powers in the internal affairs of Korea.

3. It is not correct that the Soviet Government refused to participate in the Security Council meetings. Much as the Soviet Government would have liked, it was impossible to take part in the Security Council meetings since a permanent member of the Security Council, China, has not been admitted to the Council by virtue of the position of the US Government, which has made it impossible for the Security Council to make legally valid decisions.

Statement of the Government of the United States of America reads in part:

June 27, 1950

STATEMENT BY THE PRESIDENT

In Korea the Government forces, which were armed to prevent border raids and to preserve internal security, were attacked by invading forces from North Korea. The Security Council of the United Nations called upon the invading troops to cease hostilities and to withdraw to the 38th parallel.

This they have not done, but on the contrary have pressed the attack. The Security Council called upon all members of the United Nations to render every assistance to the United Nations in the execution of this resolution.

In these circumstances I have ordered United States air and sea forces to give the Korean Government troops cover and support. The attack upon Korea makes it plain beyond all doubt that communism has passed beyond the use of subversion to conquer independent nations and will now use armed invasion and war. It has defied the orders of the Security Council of the United Nations issued to preserve international peace and security.

President Harry S. Truman

Communist International Archive – Reception of US Ambassador Alan G. Kirk

In 2015, the Russian Federation made freely available the scanned papers of the Communist International Archive digitized in the 1990s. The Woodrow Wilson International Center, Washington, DC, International History and Public Policy Program Archive Reception of Ambassador Kirk, Document ID 114910. (Admiral Alan G. Kirk US Navy, (Ret) subsequently embarked on a diplomatic career.)

Today, the Victorious Fatherland Liberation Museum (Korean War Museum) in Pyongyang explains the 1950s Korea Conflict from the N Korean perspective. In N Korea, children are taught in school that the US started the conflict and N Korea won.

CHAPTER 4

FIRST KOREAN CONFLICT 1950 – 1953

Because of the International Date Line, when it is Sunday in Korea, it is Saturday in New York City and Washington, DC.

The North Korean Communists ignited the 1950s Korean Conflict. In early 1947, the United States (US) had drawn the line in Korea, and its purpose was to pursue the basic containment policy of US President Harry S. Truman to prevent the spread of communism. In 1948, the N Korean government began the stockpiling of equipment, including tanks, artillery, aircraft, large-caliber ammunition, vehicles, major items of engineer material petroleum products, medical supplies, and uniform material. N Korea utilized nearby Dongbei Pingyuan depots (Northeast China) for the storage of war supplies. The Korean People's Army (KPA) had 60,000 troops by the end of 1948, including three infantry divisions—the 1st, 2nd, and 3rd. In late 1948, it also created a tank battalion and expanded to a division shortly after the outbreak of the conflict. N Korea under the leadership of Kim Il-sung seemed to be on a war footing in early 1949. Tens of thousands of Korean soldiers who fought in the Chinese civil war (1946–1949) filtered back into Korea. All through 1949, tough, crack troops with Chinese, not Soviet, experience returned to be integrated with the KPA. The N Korean Army doubled, with an estimated 40,000 conscripts and over 20,000 returnees from three Korean divisions embedded with the Chinese People's Liberation Army (CPLA), and fielded another three infantry divisions—the 4th, 5th, and 6th. In January 1950, the training of the N Korean military was in high gear. Growth accelerated in the first half of 1950, when the KPA brought four more divisions online—the 7th, 10th mechanized, 13th, and 15th. Of these organizations, the 5th, 6th and 7th divisions were very potent since they were composed entirely of combat veterans of the CPLA. The KPA produced ten divisions in just over 28 months. N Korea fortified the 38th Parallel by constructing large underground pillboxes for the housing of weapons and ammunition, and soon border incidents began breaking out. Neither side recognized the parallel as a legitimate boundary. S Korea, under the leadership of President Syngman Rhee, (1948–1960), wanted to unify Korea, by force if necessary. Rhee often referred to a "northern expedition" or "dash north" to "recover the lost territory," and in the summer of 1949 his army provoked the fighting along the 38th Parallel that sometimes took hundreds of lives.

This attitude was the prime reason the US refused to supply tanks, anti-aircraft artillery, and airplanes. There was evidence that American officials feared that President Rhee would embark upon military adventures of his own into N Korea if it had "offensive-type" equipment. In 1949, the US Congress provided a $150 million dollar aid bill to S Korea and sent only rifles, bazookas, and light artillery. Their infantry divisions contained only 15 105-millimeter (mm) howitzers apiece and their ammunition supply was limited to prevent S Korea from initiating military action.

In April 1950, Premier Joseph Stalin of the Union of Soviet Socialist Republics gave President Kim Il-sung [14] leader of N Korea, permission to attack the South under the condition that Chairman Mao Zedong, leader of the Chinese Communist Party (CCP) of China, would agree to send reinforcements if needed. Stalin made it clear Russian forces would not openly engage in combat, to avoid a direct war with the United States. Upon passage of a resolution to assist North Korea by the Russian government, Stalin announced: "We can give Korea more arms." The Russians began sending arms, ammunition, fuel, and medications to N Korea. In April and May 1950, large shipments of arms flowed from Russia, and these shipments served to equip both the army and air force, giving them considerable heavy artillery, trucks, tanks, automatic weapons, and additional aircraft. During this period, N Korea's preparations for conflict had become readily recognizable. Intelligence collectors reported the North's implementation of a draft, its growing order of battle, and the movement of N Korean forces southward, taking positions on the line of departure. Before the outbreak of the conflict, the US and S Korea believed the N Korean Army possessed over 150 modern tanks. During June,

---

[14] N Koreans believed Kim Il-sung was an "almighty god" who "created the world" in seven days as a divine spirit millions of years ago, and came to Earth as a human in 1912, as a Messianic figure. President Kim Il-sung died July 8, 1994.

Smell The Gunpowder

intelligence reports from US and S Korean intelligence, including the Central Intelligence Agency (CIA), provided clear descriptions of N Korea preparations for the conflict. However, the intelligence community had received repeated rumors of a N Korean invasion, and talk of invasion was almost routine during 1949–1950. These premature warnings undermined trust in such reporting and desensitized analysts. The possibility of an actual attack was not taken seriously.

Although the world smelled gunpowder in early 1950, it was not until June 25 that the gunpowder ignited.

The official descriptions of the countries involved, their official titles, battle structures, their tactical names, and casualties are described in the introduction – specifically, Tables 1-4.

The Soviet Union also provided technical assistance and aircraft for reconnaissance and fighter bombers to support ground forces. All the planes were of old types. No jet plane was supplied to N Korea. The Soviet assault plane, Il-10, was the most powerful, but it could be used successfully only against S Korean infantry.

The operational formation of the N Korean army in mid-June 1950 showed that Pyongyang did not intend to take offensive action.

On the morning of June 25, 1950, a large-scale battle started all along the 38th parallel of Korea. Units of the Korean People's Army frustrated the attack launched by the S Korean troops on the main front areas and their appalling blows on the enemy in the direction of Seoul. (N Koreans advanced southward, breaking through the S Korean defense line.)

The Ilyushin Il-10 Shturmovik was a Soviet ground attack aircraft developed at the end of World War II. It was a single-engine two-seat monoplane, with a metal-covered frame. It was highly armored. The N Korean People's Air Force (NKPAF) received about 50 Il-10s, all from World War II production. The Fifty-Seven Assault Aviation Regiment flew the Il-10s during the early phase of the 1950s Korean Conflict.

The Il-10 was initially used with success against the weak anti-aircraft-artillery defense of S Korean forces, but then they suffered heavy losses in encounters against the US Air Force (USAF) fighters.

The wet season had begun, and heavy rain fell along much of the 38th Parallel, the 160-mile boundary between N and S Korea. In the Ongjin region, an isolated area on Korea's West-Central coast, the crackle of small-arms fire and the boom of artillery interrupted the pattern of the raindrops. Who started the firing in the predawn hours of June 25, 1950, on a dreary morning remains in doubt. The Ongjin region has long been the setting for border skirmishes between N and S Korean forces, and often the South initiated the combat action. [15]

> The Ministry of the Internal Affairs of the DPRK announced the first official report that early morning of June 25, 1950, the S Korean side had launched a surprise attack on the N Korean regions, and to cope with it the government of the Republic had resolutely demanded that the south side stop its war action at once, warning that if it refuses the demand, it will then bear full responsibility for all future consequences. A second report of the Ministry of Internal Affairs said that the security forces and units of the People's Army of the DPRK went over to counteroffensive from defense.

The evidence for this day in June is ambiguous and contradictory. [16] What followed the outbreak in Ongjin, however, is less uncertain. The Koreas were already waging a civil conflict when N Korea attacked and opened the conventional phase of the conflict.

The N Korean operational approach, developed with the assistance of Russian planners, was a swift style offensive of an initial breakthrough, a deep exploitation, and a rapid consolidation and conclusion. The N Koreans organized its 10 divisions, along with one independent infantry regiment, a motorcycle reconnaissance regiment, border constabulary, and one armor brigade into two corps. First (I) Corps was the main effort and comprised the 2nd, 5th, and 7th Infantry Divisions, three border brigades, one infantry regiment, three reconnaissance companies supported by the 105th Armor Brigade. (After the capture of Seoul, the Armor Brigade's operational status changed to a division at the end of June before it crossed the Han River to continue the attack southward.) Second (II) Corps was a supporting effort and comprised the 1st, 3rd, 4th, 6th, Infantry Divisions, four reconnaissance companies and the 13th Mechanized Division.

---

15   https://www.cia.gov/library/readingroom and https://cia.gov/about-cia-policies/index.htlm.
16   S Koreans initiated most of the border clashes with N Korean forces at the thirty-eight parallel beginning in the summer of 1948, and reaching a high level of intensity and violence in 1949, a year later.
      https://www.arechives.gov/publications/proloruw/2002/summer/korean-myths-2.html#nt17.

I Corps (DPRK) was to cross the 38th Parallel through the cities of Chongchon and Inge 75 miles east of Seoul to Hong Chen and Yeongcheon converging on Seoul. II Corps (DPRK) was to cross the 38th Parallel near the Hwasheon Dam and support I Corps operations with two divisions by attacking Seoul from the east. The II Corps also conducted a supporting amphibious landing along the east coast of the peninsula with one division. It was a sound operational approach.

North Korea Rolled Across South Korea

During the period June 15-24, the N Korean Command moved all regular army divisions to the close vicinity of the 38th Parallel and deployed them along their respective planned lines of departure for the attack on S Korea. Altogether, 80,000 men with their equipment joined those already along the border. They succeeded in taking their positions for the assault without alerting the S Korean defenders. Under cover of darkness, units began moving to the forward edge of the battle area (FEBA). Officers told their men they were on maneuvers, but most realized this was more, and prepared for conflict. Destined to endure the impending attack were four S Korean divisions and one infantry regiment in their thinly held defensive border positions. An attack was unexpected, and a substantial number of officers and men, as well as American advisors, were in Seoul and other towns on weekend passes.

In early June, the 105th Armored Regiment became a brigade with a strength of 6000 men and 120 superb T 34/85 medium tanks. The brigade had three mechanized regiments—the 107th, 109th, and 203rd, each with 40 tanks. Its equipment – tanks, weapons, and vehicles – were Russian made.

Shortly before daybreak on Sunday, June 25, 1950, at approximately 0440 hours (4:40 a.m.) Korean (local) Standard Time amid squalls of rain, and a 45-minute artillery barrage, N Korean infantry advanced into S Korea in six columns with an estimated 135,000 [17] men comprising ten infantry divisions; (five of the infantry divisions and the armored brigade had well-trained combat personnel), an armored brigade, and three border brigades.

---

17   US Department of Defense, Privacy Policy: The defense.gov website is provided by the Office Of the Assistant Secretary of Defense for Public Affairs. Information presented may be copied and distributed, unless otherwise specified. Use of an appropriate credit by line/photo/image is requested. https://www.defense.gov/Resources/Privacy.
https://www.uskf.mil/About/United/Nations-Command.

The T 34 had a large 85-millimeter (mm) anti-aircraft/anti-tank gun and was the best medium tank in the world in 1945 and could outmatch its best American counterparts in 1950. No US armor (particularly the Light Tank M24 Chaffee) or anti-tank rockets (such as the M9 2.36-inch Bazooka) could penetrate its heavy-sloped armor.

The sequence of attacks seemed to progress from west to east, with the earliest attack striking the western Ongjin Peninsula. In an arc of 40 miles stretching from Kaesong on the west to Chorwon on the east, the N Koreans concreted more than half of their infantry and artillery along with half of their tanks for a converging attack on Seoul. The main attack was to follow the Uijeongbu Corridor, an ancient invasion route leading straight south to Seoul. N Korean troops also struck by sea, landing south of Kangnung on S Korea's east coast.

The NKPA's spearhead consisted of experienced Korean veterans who fought in the Chinese Civil War, [18] and with the Russians against the Japanese during World War II. The N Korean army was well-disciplined, well-trained, and well-equipped.

N Korea had Russian-built, single-engine Yakovlev Yak-9 (YAK), fighter/bombers that initially gave it control of the skies. The battle for air supremacy ensued on the first day of the war. NKPAF, with no anticipation of intervention from the UN, exerted superior air prowess over S Korea and dominated the skies. By late morning, nine YAK fighter/bombers attacked S Korean and US Air Force (USAF) aircraft, including a USAF C-54 Skymaster cargo/transport aircraft, and facilities at Suwon airfield and Kimpo Air Base (AB), just south of Seoul.

On June 27, N Korean aircraft met US fighter aircraft flying F-82 Mustangs from the Fifth Air Force's 35th and Eightieth Fighter Squadrons escorting transports engaged and destroyed seven N Korean propeller-driven fighters in what would become the first air battle of the 1950s Korean Conflict — the Battle of Suwon Airfield. The F-82 Twin Engine Mustang, the last American piston engine fighter, flew against N Korea's Lavochkin La-7, a piston-engine Russian fighter, and Ilyushin Il-10, a twin-seat single-engine ground attack

---

18 Chinese Civil War, was a military struggle for the control of China waged between the Nationalists (Kuomintang) under Chiang Kai-shek and the Communists under Mao Zedong.
The two-decade struggle reached its conclusion in 1949. Mao Zedong led the Chinese Communists to victory and proclaimed the formation of the People's Republic of China. Chinese Communists Party (CCP).

Smell The Gunpowder

Russian aircraft. The 5th Air Force embarked on a mission to establish air superiority over S Korea.

Meanwhile, the quick capture of the Ongjin Peninsula, located at the westernmost end of the 38th Parallel, protected the west flank of the main thrust on Seoul. Prior to the Battle of Ongjin, the two opposing forces already had three clashes near these mountains in 1949. The attack on June 25 was led by one division and a border brigade with fifty tanks and 8,000 to 10,000 troops. An additional effort involved a column with forty tanks driving from Kaesong to Seoul. By June 26, the N Koreans were in complete control of the Ongjin Peninsula. The east flank was covered by a strong attack on Chongchon, pinning down the S Koreans. N Korean forces captured Chongchon, Pichon, Tongduchon, and continued its offensive southward toward the S Korean capital.

On the evening of June 27, three mechanized infantry regiments, and tanks, advanced to the suburbs of Seoul, and fierce street fighting took place. By midnight June 27, Seoul's defenses nearly collapsed, and, in panic, created a rapid evacuation. In the early morning of June 28, the N Koreans captured Seoul, forcing the S Korean government to move to Taejon, 100 miles south of Seoul. The N Korean forces hoisted their flag over the capital building. The N Korean objective was to reunite the country (peninsula) under communist rule. After the capture of Seoul, the N Korean forces regrouped, brought additional units south, and continued the attack.

However, lacking detailed plans for operations south of the Han River, N Korean forces had been slow to proceed. S Korean troops took advantage of the lull and blew up a key bridge over the Han River before critical supplies and military units had escaped across it.

With no warning given, two tons of TNT were detonated by S Korean engineers, destroying the bridge, killing 1000 civilian refugees of the estimated 4000 on the bridge.

The S Korean Army had adequate supplies to sustain defensive operations for five days. The US decision not to provide tanks, 155mm (millimeter) and 105mm howitzers, anti-aircraft-artillery, in hindsight, was a serious mistake. On June 30, a 1000-man advance battalion from the 24th Infantry Division, including specialists and noncommissioned officers transferred from the First Cavalry Division (1CD) arrived with additional forces on the way. The S Korean forces were unprepared for the attack by infantry, armor, and air. Although they numbered 95,000 men at the start of the conflict and had the benefit of 1000 US troops and 500 American military advisers, their members trained only to the company level. Although four of S Korea's nine divisions, a total of twelve regiments, guarded the border, no more than one-third of the force, four regiments, was in position on the day of the attack. Even if they had been at full strength, it was doubtful the S Koreans could have done much more than delay the enemy onslaught. The S Koreans possessed US Army motor vehicles and 105mm howitzers, but ammunition for all their weapons was in short supply and they lacked anti-aircraft-artillery, heavy mortars, recoilless rifles, and anti-tank weapons capable of stopping the T 34/85 Russian-built tanks.

They had no tanks of their own because the US had decided not to supply them, and US advisers had judged the land, roadways, and maintenance capabilities of S Korea poorly suited to the efficient use of armor. They were surprised, and, by contrast, were frightened, confused, and retreated. (The S Korean howitzer ammunition, 105mm high-explosive [HE] rounds had no effect on the tanks. They did not have armor-piercing high-explosive [HE] anti-tank [HEAT] rounds.) The S Koreans, outranged, outgunned, and with little ammunition, pleaded for more 105mm shells. In a magnificent effort, 119 tons of munitions were immediately shifted from Ikego Ammunition Depot near Tokyo to Tachikawa Air Base and then airlifted to Suwon—where the N Koreans promptly overran them. The S Koreans were no match for N Koreans at all, and the disposition by the S Koreans of their logistic potential was extraordinarily poor. They had put their supplies and equipment close to the 38th Parallel. They had not developed any positions in depth. Everything between the 38th Parallel and Seoul was their area of depot. When they lost that immediate line, they lost their supplies. They were not able to destroy the supplies. N Korea attacked *en masse*; so that at one initial stroke the N Korean army had a new supply base in the area between the 38th Parallel and Seoul, which enabled them to press south with the full strength of their base being immediately behind them. They no longer had to rely on the long distance from the Yalu River to get their supplies.

The first word of the attack reached the Pentagon about 2000 hundred hours (8:00 p.m.) Eastern (local) Standard Time Saturday night, and at about the same time, the United Nations Commission in Korea managed to get UN Secretary

Trygve Lie, from the first Secretary-General of the UN 1946–1952, on the telephone at his home on Long Island, New York.

President Harry Truman learned of the attack from his home in Independence, Missouri, early Sunday morning and immediately returned to Washington. (The date becomes one day later as one travels across it in a westerly direction, and one day earlier as one travels across it in an easterly direction.)

In the evening of June 26, President Truman received General Douglas MacArthur's report that the S Korean forces could not hold Seoul, that the forces were in danger of collapse, and the evacuation of American nationals was underway.

United Nations Security Council Resolutions 83 and 84

The United Nations Security Council Resolution 83, adopted June 27, 1950, determined that the attack on S Korea by forces from N Korea constituted a breach of peace.

The Council called for the immediate cessation of hostilities and for the authorities in N Korea to withdraw their armed forces to the 38th Parallel. N Korea ignored the UN resolution. The Council then recommended that members of the UN furnish such assistance to S Korea as might be necessary to repel the attack and to restore international peace and security. The US responded by pushing a resolution through the United Nations Security Council (UNSC) calling for military assistance to S Korea. The UNSC voted to invoke military action by the UN for the first time in the organization's history. The Soviet Union refused to attend the Security Council meetings and did not participate. The UN resolution passed to "render every assistance to the UN in the execution of the resolution" providing aid to S Korea. This was the first conflict in which the UN played a role. The resolution succeeded because the Soviet Union, N Korea's supporter, was absent and unable to veto or reject the measure.

On July 7, 1950, UN Secretary-General Lie convened an emergency meeting of the UNSC at 1400 hours (2:00 p.m.) Sunday afternoon and Resolution 84 was adopted. UNSC Resolution 84 authorized the US to establish and lead a unified command composed of military forces from UN member states and authorized that command to operate under the UN flag. With this resolution in hand, President Truman rapidly dispatched US land, air, and sea forces to S Korea to engage in what he termed a "police action." Truman sanctioned the use of American air and naval forces below the 38th Parallel. At that point, the US intervened militarily to support S Korea. Truman then extended American air and naval actions to N Korea and authorized the use of US Army troops to protect Pusan. The UNSC approved a resolution, introduced by the US, asking member nations to assist in repelling N Korea's aggression, and other UN members sent troops or supporting forces.

The UN empowered the American government to select a commander, and the Joint Chiefs of Staff unanimously recommended General Douglas MacArthur. MacArthur, at the age of seventy, became Commander-in-Chief of the United Nations Command (UNCOM or UNC). General MacArthur ordered the entire 24th Infantry Division (ID) to Korea. On July 1, a small forward element arrived. On July 18, the 1CD was ordered to Korea.

Under the flag of the UN, 16 countries sent military forces to S Korea's defense; but most forces came from the US. Other countries contributed equipment, supplies, and other support. In all, 53 UN-member nations promised troops to assist S Korea. The nations of the British Commonwealth were mostly ready to fight when war broke out. Great Britain, Australia, New Zealand, and Canada were first to send air, sea, and ground forces. Eventually, UN allies sent over 19,000 troops to S Korea, all assigned to the 8th Army.

The United Kingdom and Australia also participated in the conflict with elements of their Navy and Air Force. During August, troops from Turkey, the Philippines, and the 27th British Commonwealth Brigade from Hong Kong were welcomed.

If US forces had not entered the conflict, the N Koreans would have won easily in just days.

Unofficially, Japan provided hundreds of laborers in critical Korean industries and in the peninsula's harbors, operating dredges, and minesweepers. [19]

---

19   http://www.dtic.mil/dtic/tr/fulltext/u2/a157032.pdf.

In keeping with the UNSC [20] Truman announced that he had authorized the US Air Force (USAF) to conduct missions on specific targets in N Korea wherever militarily necessary and had ordered a naval blockade of the entire N Korean coast. President Truman directed the US 7th Fleet, Task Force 77, based at Subic Bay in the Philippines, to head north into troubled waters off N Korea. At the outset of the conflict, the N Koreans had sent a merchant ship loaded with 600 combat troops on a nighttime mission to capture the critical S Korean port of Pusan. A vigilant US-built patrol vessel of the S Korea Navy spotted the ship and sank it.

On July 2, 1950, the anti-aircraft cruiser USS *Juneau* (CLAA-119), assigned to Naval Forces, East Asia, engaged in the only surface battle of the conflict, along with the British cruiser *Jamaica* and British frigate *Black Swan* destroying five of the attacking N Korean torpedo boats in the waters off the east coast of S Korea near the port of Jumanji.

On July 3, carrier aircraft went into action. Warplanes from the aircraft carrier USS *Valley Forge* (CV-45) and the British carrier *Triumph* attacked the capital of N Korea, Pyongyang, and Chunghwa military airfield twenty-six miles northwest of the capital. The attack-plane squadrons bombed fuel-storage tanks, runways, nearby bridges, and rail yards. The Navy's new jet fighter, the F9F Panther aerial victory, shot down two N Korean Yak-9s (multipurpose fighter aircraft). The *Valley Forge* was the only operational US carrier in the western Pacific when the conflict began. The clashes on the ground during the first six months demanded flexibility of force. Carrier aircraft flew deep support missions, attacked supply lines, roamed over enemy territory for targets of opportunity, bombed bridges; interdicted highways and railroads, attacked refineries and railroad yards, attacked hydroelectric plants, and escorted land-based bombers on special missions. Helicopters assumed an increasingly significant role as they rescued downed aircrew, evacuated wounded, flew short-range supply missions to Marines and soldiers ashore, spotted shore bombardment gunfire for ships, and scoured coastal areas for mines.

Only recently established, the S Korean Navy compensated for its small size by fighting with determination throughout July and August. S Korean naval forces doubled down the effort to destroy communist junks, motorized sailboats, and

---

20   Appendix C: United Nations Security Council request for support to the Republic of Korea.

sampans trying to deliver reinforcements and supplies to the N Korean ground forces besieging Pusan. Fighting side by side with the US Navy were naval forces from eight other members of the US coalition. The Royal Navy contingent included the carriers *Glory*, *Theseus*, *Triumph*, and ten cruisers and destroyers. Australian, New Zealand, Canadian, Colombian, French, Dutch, and Thai naval forces also sent vessels into combat in the defense of S Korea.

In early October, airstrikes from the USS *Leyte* (CV-32) were directed against the Linjiang Yalu River Bridge, the Changbai-Hyesan International Bridge, and the Tumen Bridge, all of which connected China with N Korea. These bridges were used to move troops and supplies. These were the first carrier-based air strikes against Chinese and N Korean targets during the conflict. The *Leyte* spent 92 days at sea from October 9, 1950, through January 16, 1951, and launched aircraft against N Korea completing 3933 sorties.

Combat power projected from the sea by Task Force 77 had another source — the battleships, cruisers, and rocket vessels. The World War II-built US battleships *Iowa* (BB-61), *New Jersey* (BB-62), *Missouri* (BB-63), and *Wisconsin* (BB-64) attacked along the Korean coast, shelling railways, roads, supply caches, and troop concentrations.

The battleship USS *New Jersey* (BB-62), part of Task Force 77, an aircraft carrier battle group of the US 7th Fleet, served two tours of duty off the east coast of N Korea from 1951 to 1953, shelling coastal areas with its nine 16-inch guns. On March 20, 1951, the *New Jersey* was slightly damaged after being hit by a shore battery at Wonsan, N Korea. US and British naval units were also active on the west coast, where major carrier-borne air strikes occurred.

Five US Navy ships were sunk and 95 damaged in action during the conflict. Losses and damage contributed to striking mines and damage inflicted by N Korean coastal artillery. The first ship sunk in action was the USS *Magpie* (AMS-25). It was performing minesweeping duty off the east coast of N Korea when it struck a floating mine and sank.

Magpie was struck from the Navy list October 20, 1950. Twenty-one sailors, including the commanding officer, were never found. The USS *Merganser* (AMS-26) picked up 12 survivors and transported them to Pusan. The first

Smell The Gunpowder

of 95 damaged in action was the destroyer USS *Collett* (DD-730). The *Collett* sailed up a difficult Inchon channel to Wolmi-do Island on September 13, 1950 and participated in the pre-invasion bombardment of the island. The *Collett* on September 14-15 returned, accompanied by five US destroyers to provide gunfire support for the Inchon landings. In the intense ship-shore duel, the *Collett* received seven hits and sustained considerable damage, along with five wounded. On August 27, 1952, minesweeper USS *Sarsi* (AT-111) was patrolling the edge of the windswept waters in the dark off the N Korean coast between Wonsan and Hungnam. It also struck a drifting mine cut loose by a storm. It exploded against her hull. The *Sarsi* sank in twenty minutes, the last of five ships sunk. Four men were killed.

The remainder, including four wounded, spent the night in, or clinging to, life rafts, life preservers, and the ship's whale boat. Rescue ship USS *Boyd* (DD-544), and minesweepers USS *Zeal*(AM-131) and USS *Competent* (AMS-316) arrived in the morning; and carried survivors to friendly territory for medical treatment. On August 27, 1952, the *Competent* suffered superficial damage and loss of minesweeping gear after a shrapnel near miss from a N Korean shore battery. No casualties. The last ship to be damaged was the cruiser USS *Saint Paul* (CA-73) on July 11, 1953. It suffered damage after a direct hit from a shore battery at Wonsan, N Korea. No one was killed or wounded, and only a 3-inch anti-aircraft mount was damaged. On July 27, 1953, at 2159 hours (9:59 p.m.), *Saint Paul* conducted the last gun strike and had the distinction of firing the last round shot at sea in the conflict.

Details and insight can be found online at the Navy History and Heritage Command, a complete list of ships sunk and damaged during the 1950s Korean Conflict.

During the three years of conflict, Navy and Marine aircraft flew 276,000 sorties and dropped 177,000 tons of bombs. They reached within 7,000 sorties of World War II totals in all theaters and surpassed the bomb tonnage by 74,000 tons. The Navy was essential to the US and UN effort in the first major conflict of the Cold War.

As of January 4, 2022, the Defense Casualties Analysis System reported 503 hostile deaths, 1576 wounded in action, and 154 non-hostile deaths (officers and enlisted personnel succumbed to injury or disease). Total combined deaths in-theater were 657.

The official casualty summary described in the introduction, Table 9, and Chapter 14 Ground, Sea and Air Combat - US Military Casualties – 1950s Korean Conflict Snapshot. [21]

On July 27, 1950, the US Air Force (USAF) 3rd Bombardment Group (BG) 11th Air Force flew reconnaissance sorties and protected allied shipping in Korean waters. The next day, the group flew 20 Douglas B-26 Invaders a twin-engine light bomber and attacked Munson railroad yards near the 38th Parallel and rail and road traffic between Seoul and the N Korean border. A day later, 18 B-26s attacked Heiko airfield near Pyongyang claiming up to 25 enemy aircraft destroyed on the ground. In August 1951, the 3rd BG moved to Korea to continue combat missions.

US Combat Forces Caught Off Guard

The US military was caught off guard and the invasion exposed a hollow army. In June 1950, the 8th Army had only four infantry divisions. But two months earlier, it had two corps, they had been eliminated to meet end strength and budget limits. Actual combat forces located in East Asia were four under-strength infantry divisions — all were in Japan on occupation duty. Only the 25th Infantry Division (ID) in south central Honshu was near full strength, with 13,000 soldiers assigned. The under-strength combat divisions were the First Cavalry Division (1CD) organized as infantry in central Honshu with just over 11,000 soldiers; the 7th Infantry Division (ID) in northern Honshu and Hokkaido; and the 24th Infantry Division (ID) in Kyushu — each had fewer than 11,000 soldiers.

Also in the Pacific were the Fifth Regimental Combat Team (RCT) in the Hawaiian Islands and the 29th Infantry Regiment (IR), along with an Anti-Aircraft-Artillery Group in Okinawa. All lacked reconnaissance, military police, replacement companies, and medical detachments. The tank battalion in the divisions had the Light Tank M 24 Chaffee in the opening weeks of the Korean Conflict. It was the principal tank available to UN forces rather than the Medium Tank M 46 Patton.

---

21   The Cold War's First Conflict | Naval History Magazine - June 2010 Volume 24, Number 3.

Although the M 24 was no match for the N Korean T 34/85 tank, the M 24's compact size, mobility, and maneuverability, combined with its hefty armament, made it an asset. The M 46 "Patton", with its 90mm gun, began arriving at the end of July 1950. Finally, the 8th Army lacked anti-tank ammunition and adequate anti-tank weapons. [22]

In February 1952, the M 48 "Main Battle Tank" arrived.

By the end of July 1950, the US committed the Army, Navy, and Air Force in the first major conflict since World War II. The US and S Korea provided more than 90 percent of the military power.

The N Korean forces continued southward unopposed for five days, and General MacArthur was convinced that US troops must fight a delaying action to allow time to deploy additional troops. General MacArthur sent a TOP SECRET message to the Joint Chiefs of Staff on June 30, 1950, requesting authorization to immediately move a US regimental combat team to S Korea for the reinforcement of the S Koreans and to organize two US divisions from troops in Japan for an early counteroffensive. President Truman read MacArthur's request and approved the request to send one regimental combat team to Korea but delayed approving division-sized forces until the UN decided on a course of action.

---

22   https://. ausa.org/articles/korean-war-echoes-today%E2%80%99s-challenges.

CHAPTER 5

US ARMY FIRST OPERATION

For the US Army, the conflict in Korea began with the 24th IDs' attempt to delay the N Koreans advancing along the Seoul-Pusan (Busan) Highway. The gains the 24th ID achieved in delaying the N Koreans were not decisive. The subsequent successful defense of the Pusan Perimeter occurred despite, not because of, the 24th ID's delaying operation. On June 30, 1950, General MacArthur ordered the 24th ID under the command of Army Major General (MG) William F. Dean Sr., from Japan to Pusan. The 24th ID was stationed at Camp Wood near Kumamoto on the southern island of Kyushu, 1945-1950, the southernmost of Japan's four major islands during the occupation of Japan. In retrospect, the 24th ID was an unfortunate choice. Of the four divisions in Japan, it had both the lowest aggregate strength (12,197 men on June 30) and the lowest combat effectiveness rating (65 percent on May 30). Like the other divisions in the Far East Command, troops were not ready, lacking training and equipped for sustained combat, nor even conditioned for rigorous physical activity. The 24th ID was chosen solely based on its location. Stationed in southern Japan, it was the nearest division to S Korea. The division was undermanned, requiring thousands of men to meet authorized strength. Needed men transferred to the 24th ID from other units, raising its strength to 15,965 men by the time of its departure. When the 24th ID deployed, it experienced a series of defeats from July 5–20 while trying to delay the invading N Koreans.

Army Lieutenant General (LTG) Walter H. Walker, Commander of the 8th Army, received battle orders formally committing forces to the 1950s Korean Conflict. On July 1, LTG Walker issued orders for the division–stationed in Kyushu, Japan–to airlift its headquarters and one Infantry Regiment to Pusan

(Busan). Walker conveyed preliminary verbal instructions to MG Dean that he was to send a small delaying task force to "contact the enemy." The rest of the division would follow by sea, entering S Korea through the port of Pusan. Given the shortage of transport aircraft, and the fact the order came from General MacArthur's headquarters, the force was reduced to fit into six USAF C-54 Skymaster cargo/transport aircraft. The task force had a regimental combat mission, without its assets: two rifle companies instead of sixteen, two 4.2 mortars instead of two 75mm recoilless rifles, zero tanks instead of fourteen, and one artillery battery of six 105mm howitzers instead of one battalion of 155mm howitzers.

(Task Force Smith and the 24th Infantry Division in Korea July 1950, *Task Force Smith, the Lesson Never Learned,* was required reading at the School of Advanced Military Studies United States Army Command and General Staff College Fort Leavenworth, Kansas, approved for Public Release; Distribution is Unlimited.)

On the morning of July 1, 1950, the small delaying force with 406 soldiers from the 21st Infantry Regiment (IR), boarded transports at Itazuke Air Force Base, and flew to S Korea.

Upon arrival, the men climbed into trucks and transported 17 miles from the airstrip to the railroad station in Pusan. The troops then climbed aboard trains in Pusan and moved north, arriving at Taejon July 2.

The delaying force was the under-strength 1st Battalion, 21st IR, commanded by 34-year-old Army Lieutenant Colonel (LTC) Charles B. Smith, who built a task force around the two rifle companies, dubbed Task Force Smith (TF Smith). Smith was a seasoned combat veteran. A 1939 graduate of the US Military Academy at West Point, Smith was stationed at Oahu, Hawaii when the Japanese attacked Pearl Harbor in December 1941, and he fought in the Pacific throughout World War II. Smith's men were 20 years old or younger, and only a fraction of the officers and soldiers had seen combat.

While in Japan preparing for departure, the force commander met with MG Dean and was told to head for Taejon and stop the N Koreans as far north of Pusan as possible. That night, TF Smith traveled by train north to Pyeongtaek and Ansong. On July 3, the task force took defensive positions to guard the

Ansong River bridges in the Pyeongtaek-Ansong area. The next morning, Army Brigadier General John H. Church, Commander, General Headquarters Advance Command, greeted Smith and pointing to a place on the map explained the mission to delay the N Korean advance. The location pointed out was 34 miles below Seoul, on the main highway and railroad line connecting the capital with the southeastern port of Pusan. The location was the tiny agricultural village of Osan. (In late July 1950, Church, a member of MacArthur's staff, was promoted and assumed command of the 24th ID on July 20, 1950, because MG Dean was listed as missing in action.)

While his men went to their rest area, Smith and his principal officers got into Jeeps and set out over the 80 miles of bad, bumpy roads to the village of Osan. All along the way they saw thousands of S Korean soldiers and refugees cluttering the roads and moving south. Three miles north of Osan, Smith found an excellent infantry position which commanded both the highway and the railroad. The highest point rose about three hundred feet above the low ground which stretched northward toward Suwon. Its purpose was accomplished; the group returned to the Taejon airstrip well after dark. In the morning of July 4, 1950, Army Lieutenant Colonel (LTC) Miller O. Perry, commanding the 52nd Field Artillery Battalion, arrived in Pyeongtaek with part of his battalion along with six 105-millimeter (mm) howitzers and his support troops. Perry brought 1200 rounds of ammunition, including six high-explosive anti-tank rounds. An artillery battery is roughly equivalent to a company of infantrymen. The artillery traveled by sea aboard a Landing, Ship, Tank (LST) from Japan on July 2 to Pusan, disembarking late that night. From there, they moved north by rail. It was a matter of good fortune to the UN forces that Pusan had dock facilities able to manage sizable amounts of cargo. Its four piers could berth 24 or more deep-water ships, and its beaches provided space for unloading of fourteen LST's at the same time. Colonels Smith and Perry, and a small force, went forward in the late afternoon of July 4 to make a final reconnaissance of the Osan position. At this time, Perry selected the positions for his artillery.

On the road, Smith and Perry noted the S Korean engineers preparing demolitions on all bridges. The engineers were encouraged not to destroy the bridges, since they were going to be needed as means to withdraw, if necessary.

At one bridge, after talk failed to influence the S Korean engineers, Smith had the boxes of dynamite thrown into the river. Smith had to commandeer Korean trucks and miscellaneous vehicles to move his men. Driving was difficult, given there were no two-lane roads. Existing roads were narrow, poorly drained, and surfaced only with gravel or broken rocks. The primary road traffic was by oxcart.

The 34th IR, also part of the 24th ID, followed immediately behind 21st IR and was to defend the Pyeongtaek line with one infantry battalion at Pyeongtaek and one 11 miles east, at Ansong. If the delaying force, 21st IR, was unable to hold at Osan, it was to fall back to Pyeongtaek-Ansong and reinforce the 34th IR.

Just after midnight on July 5, the combined infantry and artillery moved north out of Pyeongtaek in dozens of the commandeered trucks and vehicles. In blackout conditions, with fleeing S Koreans troops and civilians clogging the road, it took more than two hours arriving at their position at Chikni-Ryong, just south of Suwon, and three miles north of Osan about 0300 hours (3:00 a.m.). Upon arrival, in the pouring rain, it prepared to set up a roadblock on the main road to Pusan, south of the S Korean capital of Seoul. Each soldier carried 120 rounds of .30-caliber rifle ammunition and enough C-rations for two days. At the same time, the N Korean 4th Infantry Division, on the night of July 4-5, had taken Suwon. TF Smith and three N Korean infantry regiments and one N Korean Armored Regiment were just eight miles apart and ignorant of each other. The enemy forces facing TF Smith were well trained and ready. It was raining and unseasonably cold during the dark early-morning hours of July 5 when the 34th IR reached Pyeongtaek-Ansong. They took defensive positions to guard the Ansong River bridges in the Pyeongtaek-Ansong area. The command post (CP) was in Pyeongtaek, 15 miles southeast of Osan. The village of Pyeongtaek, 40 miles south of the capital city of Seoul, was on the main road and railroad line between the capital city and Taejon, Taegu, and Pusan to the south. In cold, rainy weather, they dug foxholes, forming a mile-wide defensive line that flanked the road. Meanwhile, men used Jeeps to tow all but one of the howitzers up a steep hillside 2,000 yards to the rear of the infantry. The standard artillery gunnery procedures followed, specifically outlined in the US Army Field Manual, January 1950. Smith had chosen an advantageous position and placed his weapons to best advantage. The sky showed no sign of clearing, eliminating any possibility of air support. Volunteers from the artillery Headquarters and Service batteries made up four .50-caliber machine guns and four 2.36-inch bazooka teams and joined the infantry in their positions. When first light came, the infantry test fired their weapons, and the artillerymen registered their guns relative to expected target positions. TF Smith prepared for a fight, not a police action, delay, or demonstration. The infantry parked most of the trucks and Jeeps along the road south of their positions, and artillerymen left their trucks concealed in yards and sheds and behind Korean houses along the road just north of Osan. Smith and his men did not have to wait long for the enemy. At around 0730 hours (7:30 a.m.), observers spotted 33 medium T 34/85 tanks rolling toward them.

First Engagement: Battle of Osan Began and Ended July 5, 1950

Shortly after 0800 hours (8:00 a.m.) on July 5, the Battle of Osan began; it was the first engagement between US and N Korean forces. A force of 406 infantry soldiers, supported by 134 men of the artillery battery, were ordered to fight as a rearguard to delay advancing N Korean forces.

Nearly 5,000 N Korean troops of the 4th Infantry Division (ID) along with the 105th Armored Division (AD) participated in the battle. Today, the 105th AD remains a military unit of the North Korean People's Army and is N Korean leader Kim Jong-un's most powerful weapon in any future war.

The division was equipped with T 34/85 tanks, armored vehicles, and its mission to rapidly exploit any breakthrough in the lines and drive deep into the heart of S Korea.

Simultaneously both sides cut loose with their entire firepower. At a range of 4000 yards, the American artillery fired on the forces of N Korea. The 52nd Field Artillery Battalion became the first American artillery unit to fire on the N Korean forces, leveling its 105mm howitzers at advancing enemy tanks. The standard high explosive (HE) 105mm rounds merely bounced off the tanks. The artillery fire adjusted, and shells began landing among the tanks. The T 34s soon opened fire with their turret-mounted 85mm gun and 7.62mm machine guns. The tanks kept coming, undeterred by the exploding artillery shells. The forward 105mm howitzer, and a 2.36-inch bazooka fired from the infantry position, damaged two tanks and they pulled to the side of the road, clearing the way for those following. One of the two tanks caught fire and burned. There were 32 tanks remaining in the column, and the last passed through the infantry position by 0900 hours (9:00 a.m.), about an hour after the battle began. TF Smith was not able to use anti-tank mines—one of the most effective methods of defense against tanks—as there were none available in S Korea at the time. The tanks did not stop to engage the infantry; they merely fired on them as they came through. The artillery had stopped two tanks in front of the battery position, while three others, though damaged, had managed to get out of range moving toward Osan. The last of the tanks passed the artillery positions at 1015 hours (10:15 a.m.) heading south. Outnumbered and without armor, effective anti-tank weapons or air support, TF Smith held their ground until they expended their ammunition. With no reserve or reinforcements or even the promise or hope of such support, Smith decided that if any of his command was to get out, the time to move was at hand. He planned to withdraw at about 1430 hours (2:30 p.m.), six and a half hours after the battle began, by leapfrogging units toward Osan.

Each jump of the withdrawal was covered by fire protection from the next unit ahead. Before the withdrawal began, enemy forces were on both flanks and moving toward his rear, nearly overwhelming the task force. The remnants of the task force made their way clear and retreated in disorder through rice paddies, leaving behind all crew-served weapons—recoilless rifles, mortars, and machine guns, along with the dead and wounded litter cases. TF Smith suffered its heaviest casualties in the withdrawal. Some of the enemy machine-gun fire was at close quarters. As the advancing N Koreans came upon the injured Americans, they shot them where they lay or bound and executed them.

Smith had no communications with Perry's artillery, so he struck off west through the rice paddies to find Perry and tell him the infantry was leaving. While crossing the rice paddies, Smith met Perry's wire party stringing communication lines and together; they hurried to Perry's artillery battery.

Smith had assumed that the enemy tanks had destroyed all the artillery pieces and had made casualties out of most soldiers. His surprise was complete when he found that all the guns at this battery position were operable and that only Perry and another man were both wounded. Enemy infantry had not yet appeared at the artillery position. Smith told Perry to withdraw, and upon receiving the order, the artillerymen immediately removed the sights and breech locks from the guns and carried them and the aiming circles used as the primary means of orienting the cannon battery to a target, to their vehicles.

Smith, Perry, and the artillerymen walked back to the outskirts of Osan where they found the artillery trucks as they left them, being only slightly damaged by tank and machine-gun fire. Loaded, the column headed eastward toward Ansong, and soon came upon groups of men from Smith's battalion. The infantry parked trucks and Jeeps along the road found destroyed by the N Koreans. The trucks stopped and waited while groups of soldiers came up and climbed on them. About one hundred infantry soldiers joined the artillery group, and then the vehicles continued unmolested.

Perry and Smith planned to take a road at the south edge of Osan to Ansong if the enemy tanks had gone down the main road toward Pyeongtaek. Smith and Perry in the lead vehicle came suddenly upon three enemy tanks halted just ahead of them, turned around quickly, and, without firing a shot, drove back to the north edge of Osan. There they turned into a small dirt road that led eastward. The vehicles continued uncontested, arriving at Ansong after dark. The next morning, Smith led his men to Chonan. Upon arrival, there were 185 men. Subsequently, 65 men arrived, increasing the total to 250 officers and men—half of the original force. TF Smith slowed the N Korean advance by seven hours, buying valuable time for organizing an effective defense around Pusan. Perry lost five officers and 26 men of the artillery force. Survivors straggled into American lines at Pyeongtaek, Chonan, Taejon, and other points during the following days. Dramatically outgunned and outnumbered more than ten-to-one, TF Smith confronted two regiments of enemy infantry and three dozen tanks and killed or wounded about 127 N Korean soldiers and destroyed or immobilized four tanks. Task Force Smith had fought one of the most disappointing yet one of the most necessary forms of warfare, the delaying action, and succeeded.

Smith had 406 soldiers and suffered 198 casualties; 60 killed in action, 56 wounded in action or missing in action, and around 52 captured.

The artillery force suffered 77 casualties; 21 killed in action, 25 wounded in action, and around 31 captured. None of the five officers and ten soldiers of the artillery forward observer group with the infantry survived. This casualty count accounted for 50 percent of the task force.

Later, General MacArthur credited LTC Smith, and his men with buying the necessary time for the other UN units rushing to the war-torn peninsula to build a defensive line at the Naktong River west of Pusan. This action would not be the last American force precipitately thrown into combat with tragic results in the early days of the 1950s Korean Conflict. [23] In mid-September, Smith's 1st Battalion of the 24th ID 21st IR helped lead the breakout from the Pusan perimeter — coinciding with the US amphibious landing at Inchon.

TF Smith's 21st IR and 34th IR fought additional delaying actions against the advance of the N Korean 3rd and 4th Divisions along the corridor that ran south of Osan toward Taejon. These battles unfortunately differed little from the TF Smith battle; they were outnumbered, outflanked, and withdrew under pressure, without support.

The delaying actions fought by TF Smith and the 34th IR enabled the rest of the 24th ID to land in Pusan and establish and hold the "Pusan Perimeter" along the Naktong River.

The 24th ID left from five ports on Japan's Kyushu's coast, and the combat troops of the division were in Korea by July 5, little aware of the hell through which troops of TF Smith were going that day. The 24th ID's mission was to take the initial "shock" of N Korean advances, delaying larger N Korean units to stalling follow-up forces to arrive. The division's delaying actions allowed the 7th ID, 25th ID, 1CD, organized as an infantry division, and other 8th Army supporting units to move into position.

In early November 1950 LTC Smith was awarded the Distinguished Service Cross for heroism.

Smith retired in 1965 a Brigadier General. He died on May 23, 2004, at the age of 88, in Scottsdale, Arizona.

---

23   Rush to Disaster: Task Force Smith (historynet.com).

Smell The Gunpowder

CHAPTER 6

US ARMY 2ND OPERATION

At 0001 hours (00:01 a.m.) on July 4, 1950, General MacArthur notified MG Dean that United States Army Forces in Korea (USAFIK) activated under his command. Dean established his headquarters at Taejon. Dean, on July 8, sent to General MacArthur an urgent request for speedy delivery of 105mm howitzer high-explosive anti-tank shells for direct fire against tanks. Dean also stated that those of his troops who had used the 2.36-inch rocket launcher against enemy tanks had lost confidence in the weapon, and he urged immediate air shipment from the US of the 3.5-inch rocket launcher.

LTG Walker, upon instructions from General MacArthur, assumed command on July 13 of the 8th Army, headquartered in Taegu, and took command of USAFIK, relieving Dean. Walker's advance party opened its command post on July 9 at Taegu. In World War I Walker had commanded a machine gun company and won a battlefield promotion, awarded two Silver Stars for gallantry in action. In World War II, he was promoted to major general and commanded the 3rd Armored Division. On July 7, 1944, he was awarded a third Silver Star for gallantry in action. He at once established tactical objectives to delay the enemy advance, secure the current defensive line, and build up units and materiel for future offensive operations. Just four days later, he received word from MacArthur that he was to assume command of all the Republic of Korea ground forces, in accordance with S Korea's President Syngman Rhee's expressed desire. On July 24, the first United Nations Command (UNC) was organized. During the day, its flag hung in the 8th Army headquarters in Taegu.

Once N Koreans ran into American soldiers, US commanders thought the N Koreans would turn around and run. Walker, on the contrary, was under no illusions about the capabilities of the 8th Army. He had the unenviable task of conducting a delaying action with the 8th Army until sufficient reinforcements could be available to launch a counteroffensive into the N Korean Army's rear area.

2nd Engagement: Battle of Pyeongtaek, Began July 6 and Ended July 8, 1950

The Battle of Pyeongtaek began on July 6 in western S Korea. Uncommitted elements of the 24th ID 34th IR, which had a strength of 1981 men, under the command of Colonel (COL) Jay B. Loveless, began arriving in the afternoon of July 2 at Pusan by ship. The next afternoon two LSTs arrived with equipment. Just after daylight on July 4 the 1st Battalion 34th IR started north by rail. When Colonel Loveless met Dean at Taejon (Daejeon), it was clear that the Pyeongtaek-Ansong line must be held for as long as possible.

If enemy troops succeeded in penetrating south of Pyeongtaek, delaying and blocking the N Korean advance would be difficult in the western part of Korea.

In accordance with General Dean's orders, Loveless placed the 1st Battalion north of Pyeongtaek and sent the 3rd Battalion to Ansong, 12 miles east of Pyeongtaek, and set up regimental CP at Songhwan-ni, six miles south of Pyeongtaek on the main highway.

Dean was expecting the 1st Battalion to hold its position without artillery, tank, or anti-tank weapons against a vastly superior enemy force. A reconnaissance unit consisting of bazooka teams was sent north to Sojong-ni, five miles south of Osan, and exchanged fire with enemy tanks. The group returned to Pyeongtaek and reported the presence of N Korean tanks south of Osan. The fate of TF Smith was still unknown. That evening, Dean and his aide drove to Pyeongtaek. There was still no word from Smith and his men, but the presence of enemy tanks south of Osan raised all sorts of conjectures in Dean's mind. After midnight, he started back to Taejon. Survivors of the Osan fight arrived at Pyeongtaek shortly after Dean had left, and then LTC Perry arrived from Ansong and made his report about what had happened to TF Smith. About the same time Smith, with remnants of his task force (86 men), passed through

Colonel Loveless's regimental CP Songhwan-ni on the way to Chonan, leaving four gravely wounded men. The decision was to keep the 1st Battalion in its blocking position but to destroy the highway bridge just north of town now that enemy tanks were sighted.

At 0300 hours (3:00 a.m.) July 6, the bridge was blown up. As dawn broke the morning of July 6 in the fog and rain and water in foxholes, the men huddled in small groups as they broke open C-rations cans for an early breakfast. Then suddenly the outline of tanks was seen, and beyond the first tanks, soldiers were seen and a line of more tanks and trucks came into view. It took only a minute or two to realize that the force moving up to the blown bridge was N Koreans. The lead tank stopped at the edge of the blown bridge as other tanks moved up behind it. The infantry came up and without halting crossed the stream on both sides of the blown bridge and engaged the American forces. That same morning, news came that the enemy had overrun TF Smith. The regimental CP Songhwan-ni had no communication with its 1st Battalion at Pyeongtaek. The distances between Ansong, Pyeongtaek, and Songhwan-ni were so great the command radios could not connect with each other on the radio-net. Land lines were laid from the regimental CP to the 1st Battalion, but it was impossible to keep them intact. Retreating S Korean soldiers and civilians cut out sections of telephone wire to improvise harnesses to carry packs and possessions. The decision to withdraw the 1st Battalion was made and by mid-morning was withdrawing down the road to Chonan. By afternoon, advance elements of the 1st Battalion 34th IR began arriving. The withdrawal became disorganized, and discarded equipment and clothing littered the Pyeongtaek-Chonan road. The 1st Battalion joined elements of the 21st IR in a defensive position two miles south of the town. The 3rd Battalion 34th IR arrived at Chonan from Ansong the afternoon of July 6 and during that night. Concurrently, the 34th Regimental Combat Team (RCT), including the 63rd Field Artillery Battalion, arrived and set-up defenses. By 1700 hours (5:00 p.m.) the 3rd Battalion 21st IR was in a defensive position along the railroad tracks west of Chonan. A night battle developed at Chonan and lasted through July 7 resulting in the 34th IR being pushed out of their defensive positions by overwhelming force. The N Korean 4th ID supported by elements of the 105th AD captured Pyeongtaek.

The 21st had arrived in Pusan from Japan and sent north to fight a delaying action at Chonan, supporting the 34th IR. On July 8 the 34th RCT engaged a powerful N Korean force reinforced by scores of T 34/85 tanks, and the fight ended in another N Korean victory.

On July 12, US forces withdrew south toward Kong-Ju and Kum River near Chochiwon. Dean emphasized the importance of holding the town of Chochiwon. If lost, Dean stressed, it meant that the S Korean Army would have lost its Main Supply Route (MSR). Meanwhile, TF Smith, re-equipping at Taejon, had received 205 replacements and on July 10 rejoined the 21st IR at Chochiwon. Smith arrived before dawn July 11, reuniting the 1st Battalion with other elements of the regiment. LTC Smith had his battalion together for the first time. At 0730 hours (7:30 a.m.), the 1st Battalion was in position along the highway two miles north of Chochiwon. Smith was ready to engage the N Koreans in the next battle. In a series of battles between Cheonan and Chochiwon, the understrength two-battalion 21st IR delayed the N Koreans for three days. As July progressed, disasters struck Dean's command. The 24th ID pushed south at and around the villages of Cheonan and Chochiwon in Western S Korea and Pyeongtaek, Handog, and central S Korea at Yechon. The US forces retreated south to Cheonan, 51 miles south of Seoul. The N Korean forces advanced toward Pusan, following a string of victories mostly unopposed.

N Korea's ally China had not yet decided to intervene in the conflict. "Chinese leaders were impressed by the rapid progress N Korean troops made during the first days of the conflict.

After the 8th Army entered the conflict in early July, Chinese leaders were still confident that the Americans were unable to reverse the course of the war and would only delay S Korea's defeat." (Red Wings Over the Yalu)

The US imperialists were driven out of Seoul on the third day after their provocation of war due to President Kim Il-sung's outstanding military strategy and wise leadership.

In the wake of it, "Smith's special attack" unit was smashed to bits at the Osan line, and Suwon, the enemy's "second stronghold," gave way like a landslide at the hand of the mighty Korean People's Army (KPA) that advanced like angry waves.

The US troops who were driven back to the bridgehead of Pusan were trembling with horror of "death, sorrow, and despair," comparing their lot to the "calves in a public slaughterhouse."

Smell The Gunpowder

These and other battles through July 21 did delay the N Koreans and allowed time for the 1CD and the 25th ID to deploy from Japan. Between July 10 and 18, MacArthur moved these divisions to Korea.

The 1CD, under the command of Army Major General (MG) Hobart Gay, alerted to move from Japan to Korea on July 1 and told to prepare for an amphibious landing at Inchon.

During July 12-14, the division moved from its garrisons in central Honshu and loaded onto ships in the Japanese port city of Yokoyama. With N Korean successes south of the Han River near Seoul, the Inchon landing was canceled.

The destination changed, and on July 18 the 1CD with its three regiments (5th, 7th, and 8th) landed on the east coast of Korea at Pohang-dong, a fishing village 80 miles northeast of Pusan.

The N Koreans were 25 miles away when elements of the 1CD came ashore to successfully carry out the first amphibious landing of the conflict. Lead elements of the division's first regiment, the 8th Cavalry Regiment, were ashore by 0610 hours (6:10 a.m.). By July 22, all regiments were deployed in battle positions—a remarkable achievement in the face of Typhoon Helene that pounded the coastline. The 1CD promptly reinforced and provided direct support to the faltering 24th ID and assumed responsibility for blocking the enemy along the main Taejon-Taegu (Daejeon-Daegu) corridor. On July 22, the 5th and 8th Cavalry Regiments (5CR and 8CR) relieved the 24th ID 21st IR from its positions in the rugged and hilly countryside, and northwest of Yongdong. At that point, the 1CD assumed responsibility for blocking the N Koreans along the main Taejon-Taegu corridor to Pusan. The last elements of the 24th ID passed through the 1CD lines at Yongdong, temporarily the 8th Army reserve. On July 23, the 8CR was hit by a heavy artillery and mortar barrage and the N Koreans advanced toward their positions. As the space between the battalions became increasingly threatened, the 1st Battalion, 5CR moved into the gap to absorb the increasing pressure on the 8CR. The next day, the troopers suffered their first severe combat losses. Only 26 men from the relief units managed to escape and return to friendly territory. Since the 1CD could not defend Yongdong indefinitely, the division conducted a delaying action on the way back to the Naktong River. Walker was disappointed over the inability of the 1CD to check the advance of the enemy. He questioned MG Gay about the withdrawals and ordered there be no more. The 1CD's actions from this point were able to delay the N Korean advance for several days, giving the UN forces valuable time to set up the Pusan Perimeter. During its first 10 days of action the 1CD suffered 497 casualties–78 killed in action, 419 wounded in action, and more than nine hundred missing.

The 25th ID under the command of Army Major General (MG) William B. Kean prepared for moving to Pusan. It was the second US unit to be committed to the conflict. The 25th ID moved from Japan to Korea arriving during July 5-18, with its three regiments. Upon landing at Pusan, the division was positioned one hundred miles north of Pusan and given the mission of blocking and delaying advancing N Korean forces down the Naktong River. On July 8, MG Kean, accompanied by an advance party of his staff, flew from Osaka, Japan to Pusan. Kean and a small party then flew to Taejon for a conference with the commander of all US Forces in Korea, MG Dean, and plans for the deployment of the division were discussed. LTG Walker, upon his arrival on July 13 assumed command of USAFIK and ordered the 25th ID to bolster S Korean defenses of the central mountain corridors. The first to arrive was the 27th IR followed by the 24th IR, an all-African American regiment under the command of Colonel Horton V. White, and the only regiment within the 8th Army having three battalions, and lastly, the 35th IR at Pusan. The Division's initial objective was the relief of the 24th ID 19th IR. As the 24th IR prepared for deployment, three all-African American units, the 159th Field Artillery Battalion, the 77th Engineer Combat Company, and the 512th Military Police Company, were assigned to accompany it. With their addition, the 24th Infantry became a regimental combat team. When the 24th ID arrived July 12 and 13, S Korea seemed on the verge of collapse.

The 24th IR was initially positioned 100 miles north of Pusan in the central mountains in support of the S Koreans (ROK) and given the mission of blocking and delaying advancing N Korean forces down the Naktong River valley. Kean, with his 25th ID, had to guard two main approaches to Sangju.

On the first main road, Colonel (COL) Henry G. Fisher's 2nd Battalion 35th IR held a block position northwest of Hamchang supported by a platoon of tanks. COL Fisher's 1st Battalion was sent to reinforce the 27th IR defending the Pound-Hanggan (Poun) road to check the N Korean advance toward the

Smell The Gunpowder

main Seoul-Pusan highway. On July 23 the 27th IR under the command of Colonel (COL) John H. Michaelis was north of Huanggang and able to delay the N Koreans for almost a week. The N Koreans eventually were able to overwhelm the US forces, pushing the 27th and the 1st Battalion 35th IR further south. (John H. Michaelis became an Army four-star general and served Commander United Nations Command/United States Forces Korea/ 8th United States Army 1969−1972.)

On the second road, led into Sangju from the west, the 24th IR under the command of COL White assembled two, later three, of its battalions and assumed a hill position on the south side of a stream that flowed past Sangju to the Naktong River. The 24th IR entered combat under a cloud of racism against the N Korean Army on July 18 and experienced the same dismal performance common among many US Army units in the first few months of the conflict as they all fought for survival against the numerically superior N Koreans. Nonetheless, they were branded as poor soldiers because of their race. By July 31 as the 24th IR engaged in heavy fighting, desertions reached pandemic proportions. Conditions on the battlefield made it impossible for the 8th Army to order the 24th IR disbanded. The reason the 8th Army was unable to organize a new regiment was that the 24th IR continued to serve as an active regiment. Despite problems, individual soldiers in the 24th continued to show great courage. The 24th IR fought throughout the entire Korean peninsula, from the defense of the Pusan Perimeter to its breakout and the pursuit of communist forces well into N Korea.

On July 22, the N Koreans attacked the 2nd Battalion 35th IR, then pushed out of its position. The 27th IR was tasked with contacting the enemy, and on the morning of July 23 the 1st Battalion 27th IR moved northward toward Poun. Its original mission was to relieve the decimated S Korean troops retreating down the Poun road. Unable to obtain from the retreating S Korean troops information on the size of the N Korean force following them, or how close the N Koreans were, a patrol from the 1st Battalion proceeded northward to locate the enemy. Near Poun, the patrol sighted an enemy column approaching. A firefight began and the N Koreans, believing it had encountered a major position, held back until dawn. When the enemy turned back, the patrol withdrew and returned to the 1st Battalion lines. The battalion prepared for an attack, which came at 0630 hours (6:30 a.m.) on July 24, shortly after daybreak, and in heavy fog that enabled the N Koreans to approach the battalion positions. The fight lasted throughout the day, with the high ground changing hands three times. Late in the evening after dark, the battalion disengaged and withdrew. The N Koreans were unaware the battalion had left; the next morning, as they prepared to attack, they realized the US forces had departed. In late July both the 25th ID and the 1CD withdrew steadily in the face of aggressive N Korean attacks. The N Koreans, overwhelming US forces repeatedly, were able to push the 8th Army south.

As the 8th Army neared a natural defensive position along the Naktong River, the N Koreans accelerated their efforts to cut off the withdrawal to stop the 8th Army from reaching Pusan. The 24th and 25th IDs, aided by the S Korean 17th Infantry Regiment, finally managed to slow the progress of the N Korean 4th and 6th Divisions at what would become the southernmost sector of the Pusan Perimeter.

On August 1, the 8th Army issued an operational directive to all UN ground forces in Korea for their planned withdrawal east of the Naktong River. UN units would then establish main defensive positions behind what would become the Pusan perimeter. On August 3, the 24th ID, along with the 1CD, except for the 1st Battalion 8CR, began withdrawing across the river to the east side. The 8CR (the rear guard) had been blocking the Sangju Road southwest of the Waegwan bridges. The main line railroad bridges and the highway bridge across the Naktong at Waegwan were to be blown up as soon as all units of the 1CD had crossed. Both bridges were blown up after the rear guard crossed. By nightfall, UN, US, and S Korean units had averted the immediate threat of a N Korean drive all the way to Pusan. With the destruction of the Waegwan bridges, the 8th Army by the morning was in defensive positions on the east bank awaiting enemy crossings. The Naktong River Line, as it came to be known, was the vital position where the 8th Army intended to make its stand. The Battle of the Pusan perimeter would culminate in the eventual defeat of the N Korean Army.

Disaster at the Kum River

In a series of actions at the Kum River the N Korean 3rd and 4th Infantry Divisions again outflanked the defenders. Taejon, located a hundred miles south of Seoul, served as an important road and communications center. The Kum River makes a semicircle to the north around Taejon that constitutes a protective moat. Dean placed his 24th ID in a horseshoe-shaped arc in front of Taejon—the 34th IR on the left, the 19th IR on the right, and the 21st IR in reserve. By positioning elements of the 34th IR at Kongju, located about 20 miles northwest of Taejon, Dean hoped to prevent the N Koreans from an early crossing of the Kum River and an immediate drive to Taejon. On July 13, the day before the action began, the division intelligence officer estimated that two N Korean divisions with fifty tanks were closing on his position. Defensive positions were set-up along the south bank of the Kum River extending along the river to a point above Taejon, eighty miles south of Seoul. The 24th ID had less than 4000 men and was in poor condition for what was certain to be the hardest test yet. Action against the Kum River Line began first on the left (west), in the sector of the 34th IR. On the first day of the attack the N Koreans had widely breached the Kum River Line. Not only was the line breached, but the 19th IR's left flank was exposed. After dark on July 16 the 34th IR, on orders from Dean, fell back approximately 20 miles to a new defensive position west of Taejon. The N Koreans inflicted substantial casualties on the defensive positions on the south side of the Kum River. Not all the men along the river line withdrew with their units. Men scattered into the hills and moved off singly or in small groups south and east toward Taejon. All night long and into the next day stragglers and those who escaped through the hills filtered into Taejon.

In the afternoon of July 17, the 34th IR took over the entire defensive line north and west of Taejon. The 19th IR was being re-equipped, leaving the 34th IR to defend the entire line. Dean viewed the fight as another in a series of delaying actions to slow the N Korean advance.

On July 18, Dean made the decision to evacuate Taejon the next day. The plan changed with the arrival of Walker before noon on July 18. Walker's decision was to hold Taejon until July 20, delaying evacuation to allow time for deploying other American units from Japan. The 24th ID and the S Korean Army units were to hold positions and execute maximum delay of the N Koreans.

The conference between Walker and Dean changed the plan to withdraw from Taejon. In the afternoon, Dean went to the 24th ID CP and he took steps to bolster the defense of Taejon for an extra day. On July 19, two NK divisions plunged into the city's outskirts. Dean had moved the division's CP to Yongdong but stayed behind in Taejon at the 34th IR CP. During the early hours of July 20 N Korean infantry, supported by tanks, shattered and overran the 34th IR and the attached 2nd Battalion, 19th IR. The battle became confused as enemy infantry and tanks infiltrated into Taejon, cutting off American troops. Small battles broke out all over the town as isolated American units fought desperately to escape the enemy trap. The events of July 20 made it clear to Dean that Taejon could no longer be held, and his regiments had been decimated in earlier fighting.

The men at Taejon enjoyed one positive development. They had just received a weapon that was effective against the T 34/85 tank: the new 3.5-inch rocket launcher. The five-foot hand-carried launcher fired a two-foot-long, eight-and-a-half-pound rocket with a shaped charge designed to burn through any tank then known. Dean personally led tank-killer teams armed with the newly arrived 3.5-inch rocket launchers to destroy the attacking N Korean T 34/85 tanks. Seven kills were scored for the first seven rounds fired. Those who last saw Dean in combat remember his heroism and his victory cry: "I just got me a tank." He attacked and destroyed an enemy tank armed with only a hand grenade and handgun. After assaulting a tank with grenades, he had crawled to within 10 yards of its blazing guns and destroyed it with a launcher. On July 20, 10 enemy tanks were destroyed: eight of them with the 3.5-inch rocket launcher. The 24th ID was ultimately defeated on July 20 in the Battle of Taejon; the town Dean hoped to defend. He ordered his men to withdraw to the south, but he refused to depart with the leading elements. He remained behind to organize his retreating units and provide directions to stragglers. [24] The 3rd and 4th N Korean Divisions had established bridgeheads over the Kum River and encircled the town. The N Koreans, in five days, had executed two phenomenally successful maneuvers against American positions, one at the Kum River and the other at Taejon. Each time, they combined strong frontal attacks with movements around the left flank to establish roadblocks and obstruct the escape routes. The fight ended in another N Korean victory following unsuccessful attempts by US forces to inflict damage or delays on advancing N Korean units. The N Korean forces continued to advance toward Pusan, following a string of victories.

The 24th ID suffered heavy losses in the battle. The 24th was composed of untested and green troops. Lacking adequate numbers of heavy weapons, the soldiers of the 24th could do little. When the men who escaped from Taejon had rejoined their units, a count showed 1150 casualties out of 3933 of the forces

---

24   1956_brief_history_24th_division_Korea_OPT_SM.pdf (24thida.com).

engaged. Representing 30 percent of those who participated, soldiers were missing in action, including Dean, the division commander.

Major General William F. Dean, Sr.: Captured by North Korean Forces

During the confused retreat, MG Dean became separated from his soldiers and was severely injured. He hid alone in the woods and spent the next 36 days wandering around the countryside. Dean ate whatever meager food he came across, including handouts from friendly S Koreans. Dean also traveled at night to reach safety, but this was the period when the N Koreans were advancing southward rapidly. On August 25, after a hand-to-hand struggle, Dean could no longer resist and was captured by N Korean soldiers.

His capture took place near Chinan, 35 miles south of Taejon. As a prisoner of war (POW), Dean was transported to Seoul on the back of a truck and paraded through the streets. As the highest-ranking US prisoner of the war, he underwent endless interrogation, often lasting for days without end. On the day of capture, Dean was betrayed by two S Koreans who turned him into the N Koreans. After the conflict, S Korean police arrested the two men who turned Dean in to the N Koreans. Both had received 30,000 won (the equivalent of five dollars) at the time from the N Koreans. One sentenced to death, the other to life in prison. In 1951, while listed as missing in action, the US Congress voted to award Major General Dean the Medal of Honor for his actions during the defense of Taejon.

On July 23, 1950, the 24th ID received a new commander, Army Major General (MG) John H. Church, a former member of General MacArthur's staff. A veteran of both world wars and recipient of the Distinguished Service Cross, for his extraordinary heroism in action at Cantigny, France, May 28-31, 1918.

MG Church was serving in General Douglas MacArthur's headquarters in Tokyo. Church's new command was given a two-day period to rest, but then Walker decided that he needed the 24th ID to guard the southwest line (the Naktong Bulge) of the Pusan Perimeter. On August 4 Church issued to the 24th ID an order typical of those issued to American troops at this time. He directed that every man in the division know the order.

It said: "Defensive and alternate positions must be prepared, routes reconnoitered, intensive patrolling of the river at night, communications perfected, and everyone knows his job. There will be no withdrawal, nor will there be any if everyone contributes his share to the preparation, and, if attacked, has the will to fight it out here. Every soldier will under all circumstances retain his weapon, ammunition, and his entrenching tool. Without these he ceases to be a soldier capable of defending himself. Many of our losses have been occasioned by failure to dig a foxhole when the time permitted." Church remained in command of the 24th ID until January 25, 1951. He retired in June 1952 and died on November 4, 1953. (Frail and suffering from arthritis, his health meant that he was not often in the field.) Church was replaced by Army Brigadier General (BG) Bryan. Before the Pusan Perimeter, all through July and into the first days of August, there was seldom a continuous line beyond a battalion or a regimental position.

Both flanks were wide open, and enemy troops moving in the hills could easily penetrate and turn a defensive position. It did not take long before American soldiers realized the isolated nature of their positions; often they would not stay to fight a losing battle.

Few in July 1950 saw any good reason for dying for Korea; with no inspiring incentive to fight, self-preservation became the dominating factor.

Reinforcements Arrive

The 24th ID would soon share the defense of S Korea with the rebuilt S Korean Army. On July 24, the S Korean Army reorganized itself into five divisions. The claim that enemy forces outnumbered UN troops at least four to one had no basis in fact. The N Korean forces had outnumbered those of the UN after the near collapse of the S Korean Army at the end of June and until about July 20, but never by more than two to one.

By July 22, the UN forces in Korea equaled those of the N Koreans. American ground combat units as of August 4 totaled more than 47,000 men. The principal S Korean combat strength at this time was in five infantry divisions filled to a strength of 45,000 men. Thus, on August 4 the UN combat forces outnumbered the enemy at the front 92,000 to 70,000, and in the closing days of the month the

UN gained a numerical superiority, which constantly increased until near the end of the year. The 2nd Infantry Division (ID) under the command of Army Major General (MG) Laurence B. Keise was quickly alerted for movement from Fort Lewis, Washington, to the Far East Command.

The division arrived in Korea via Pusan on July 23. During July, the Korean augmentation to the United States Army [25] (KATUSA) program was established when Korean President Syngman Rhee provided Korean soldiers to augment US Army units. Their unique knowledge of the geography of Korea, and the ability to distinguish S Korean soldiers from enemy troops (N Korean) directly benefited US forces. KATUSA had an elevated level of English fluency. After training, the KATUSAs were assigned to the 2nd, 7th, 24th, and 25th Divisions.

During the conflict, a total of 43,660 KATUSA soldiers fought for S Korea with US forces. Of these soldiers, 11,365 went missing or were killed in action. After the ceasefire agreement the US decided to keep the KATUSA system. (The mission in 2022 of the KATUSA Program is to augment the US Army in Korea with S Korean soldiers to increase the S Korean/US combined defense capability on the Korean peninsula.)

Due to the urgency of the situation, Chief of Naval Operations Admiral Forrest P. Sherman, the youngest officer to hold the post and at the urging of Commandant of the Marine Corps General Clifton B. Cates convinced the Joint Chiefs of Staff to offer MacArthur a Marine regimental combat team accompanied by a Marine air group for immediate deployment to the Pusan perimeter.

MacArthur enthusiastically accepted the offer. (Admiral Sherman, age 54, died unexpectedly on July 22, 1951, in Naples, Italy.) There were no Marine units in the Far East at the outset of the conflict.

On July 7, the First Provisional Marine Brigade, organized as an ad hoc unit, accompanied by a Marine air group, under the command of Marine Brigadier General (BGen) Edward A. Craig, activated at Marine Corps Base Camp Pendleton, California, and just five days after its activation, the Brigade, with a

---

25   It was at this time that the 2nd Infantry Division received a crucial new support element, S Korean soldiers embedded into the division. The Korean Augmentation to the United States Army KATUSA program is still an important part of the US military and the defense of S Korea today. These valiant new 2nd Infantry Division troops helped turn the tide of the conflict (war) for American forces.

strength of over 6,500, sailed from San Diego, California enroute to Pusan. The core of the ground element was the Fifth Marine Regiment/ "Fifth Marines."

On August 2, 1950, the Brigade arrived in Korea. The marines went ashore at Pusan and proceeded immediately to Masan in the 8th Army reserve. On August 6 the Marine brigade became attached to the 25th ID. The brigade was commanded by Lieutenant Colonel (LtCol) Raymond L. Murray. Officers and about 65 percent of the noncommissioned officers of the brigade were World War II combat veterans. The Brigade had African Americans assigned during the fighting on the Pusan Perimeter, marking the first time African Americans integrated as individuals in significant numbers in combat. These Marines earned respect and commendation for fighting alongside whites.

Because of the 1950s Korean Conflict, African American Marines grew to 17,000. The high competence of African Americans fighting in Korea and the general absence of racial tension during their integration destroyed long-accepted beliefs against integration. Immediately after the conflict, the Marines participated in the defense of the Korean Demilitarized Zone from July 1953 until February 1955. The regiment returned to Camp Pendleton in March 1955.

CHAPTER 7

US ARMY AND US MARINE CORPS: 3RD OPERATION

3rd Engagement: Battle of the Pusan Perimeter

Began August 4 and Ended September 18, 1950

After the battle debacles during July and early August, along with more than 100 miles of retreating, the 8th Army morale was low. LTG Walker stabilized the lines on August 4 around a defensible area along the meandering Naktong River, S Korea's longest river that came to be known as the "Pusan Perimeter." The defensive perimeter formed an arc about the seaport of Pusan, in a rectangular area that stretched about 100 miles north to south and 50 miles from east to west.

During a conference in Taegu, Walker met with General MacArthur and determined that there could no longer be any retreat. Shortly after the meeting, Walker issued an order to the defenders of the Pusan Perimeter not to withdraw under any circumstance. The command was timely, for an all-out N Korean offensive was launched against the perimeter in five different spots. The Naktong River, west of Pusan, and, after turning east, close to Naktong-ni, about 50 miles to the coast above Pohang Dong. The city of Taegu is near the middle from north to south, but only about 10 miles from the western and threatened side of the Perimeter. From the southwest to the northeast, the UN line is held by the 25th, 24th, and 1CD Divisions, and then by the ROK 1st , 6th, 8th, Capital, and 3rd Divisions. Walker moved his forces quickly and astutely to blunt repeated N Korean attacks. This was part of the last line of defense for the S Korean, American and other UN forces who had temporarily retreated to the southeastern tip of the Korean peninsula. Initial orders were to engage the N Korean Army as far north as possible and defeat it. The prevailing order that applied to all American troops was that each soldier knew his job.

The First American Counterattack - Task Force Kean

General Walker's primary objective in August was to retain a foothold in Korea.

The first American counteroffensive was approved by the 8th Army to relieve enemy pressure against the perimeter in the Taegu area. On August 6, the 8th Army issued the operational directive for the attack, naming Task Force Kean (TF Kean) as the attack force, giving the hour of attack at 0630 hours (6:30 a.m.) the next day. The task force was named for 25th ID commander Army MG William B. Kean. Kean had about 20,000 men under his command at the beginning of the attack. TF Kean was composed of the 25th ID, Fifth Regimental Combat Team (RCT), and the First Provisional Marine Brigade along with First Marine Air Group 33 (MAG 33) attached. The division now had three infantry battalions in each of its regiments, although they were all under-strength. The plan called for TF Kean to strike west and secure the line of the Nam River, a tributary of the Nakdong River.

While TF Kean attacked west, the 24th IR, under the command of COL White, was to clean out the enemy from the rear area of unknown size from the rough ground surrounding Sobuksan. It was presumed by White that the enemy would be a small group.

On August 6, the day preceding TF Kean's attack, N Koreans ambushed a company of the 24th IR west of Haman and scattered another company. On August 7, the 24th IR units panicked and abandoned their positions and equipment. Sobuksan remained in enemy hands. As a result, Colonel (COL) Arthur S. Champney replaced Colonel White in command of the 24th IR.

The 24th IR and S Korean troops were unable to clear the mountainous region. The old, abandoned coal mines of the Tundok region on Sobuksan were crawling with enemy troops. Kean pushed his unit commanders hard, and the pace was fast, the sun bright and hot. Casualties from heat exhaustion sometimes exceeded those from enemy action. Throughout TF Kean's attack, well-organized enemy forces controlled the Sobuksan area and from there struck at its rear and cut its lines of communications.

The principal enemy units pressing toward Masan and Pusan in the southern sector were identified as the N Korean 6th Infantry Division and the 83rd Motorcycle Regiment. Composed entirely of Chinese civil war veterans. The N Korean 6th Infantry Division took heavy losses in the fighting, but so did TF Kean.

On August 7, the Marines participated in their first battle with the N Koreans, the First Battle of Naktong River. The Marines and US Army forces conducted local offensives, defended hills, and fought extremely violent and close engagements with tenacious and well-disciplined N Korean troops. Although it lost hundreds of men, the joint Army and Marine forces inflicted heavy casualties on the enemy. The Marine Air Group 33's (MAG 33) two fighter squadrons, flying from carriers, and its night fighter squadron, operating from Japan's Kyushu Island, steadily bombed, strafed, and rocketed N Korean positions. The first offensive action of the air group came on August 3 when an eight-plane strike against the N Korean 6th Infantry Division in the vicinity of Jinju. MAG 33 deployed the first helicopters ever deployed by the US in combat. The helicopter was used to deliver water and other critically needed supplies to Marines on the ground. They were often used to carry wounded Marines. On August 14 after a week of fighting, TF Kean was back approximately in the positions from which it had started its attack. The 35th IR held the northern part of the line west of Masan, the 24th IR the center, and the 5th RCT the southern part. The 1st Marine Brigade moved to another part of the 8th Army line. Mid-afternoon August 16 in a radio message to Kean, the 8th Army dissolved TF Kean. The task force had not accomplished what the 8th Army had believed to be easily possible—the winning and holding of the Chinju-pass line. From this time on, except for the 24th IR, the division troops fought well and displayed a battleworthiness that paid off handsomely and sometimes spectacularly in the oncoming perimeter battles. Walker's use of US Army troops and Marines as a fire brigade to contain any N Korean breakthrough proved to be a sound strategy and forestalled a forced withdrawal from the Korean peninsula.

The N Koreans now focused on crossing the Naktong River and no one doubted that they planned to cross the river without delay. Time was now against them. Every passing week brought closer the prospect of more American reinforcement—troops, tanks, artillery, and planes. The first enemy crossings of the Naktong came on August 5 in three separate places. Two were north of Waegwan and the third was thirty miles south of Waegwan in the 24th ID sector. Over the next week, battles raged, and Walker had become impatient at the lack of progress in driving the enemy back across the Naktong. On August 13 MG Church, 24th ID, told Walker the entire 4th N Korean ID was in the 24th ID sector. Walker's response was "attack" and maintain contact. US and S Korean forces increased pressure on the N Koreans. The stubborn forces of the N Korean 4th ID held their position through attacks and counterattacks. (On January 25, 1951, Church was replaced with Army Brigadier General (BG) Blackshear M. Bryan.)

The 1CD successfully defended Waegwan. However, elements of the 2nd Battalion, Fifth CR were surrounded by N Korean troops crossing the Naktong River near Hill 303. On August 17, retreating N Korean regulars of the 206th Mechanized Infantry Regiment, 105th AD who had gained temporary control of the area, committed a notorious mass execution upon 41 American prisoners of war (POWs). The massacre happened during one of the smaller engagements of the Battle of Pusan Perimeter. Of these, four survived, who later provided details of the massacre.

The massacre provoked a response from both sides in the conflict. US commanders broadcast radio messages and dropped leaflets demanding the senior N Korean commanders be responsible for the atrocity. The N Korean commanders, concerned about the way their soldiers were treating prisoners of war, laid out stricter guidelines for managing enemy captives. Every year since 1953, a wreath-laying ceremony to honor the fallen on Hill 303 has been held near Camp Carroll in Waegwan, S Korea.

The weather was overcast, preventing the use of close air support, but the N Korean resistance, including those at Waegwan, began to crumble as the weather cleared—which allowed the use of air assets. Walker's forces gained the initiative on the northern, northwestern, and western fronts with successive assaults against the crumbling N Korean Army. While the S Korean Army led the attack up the eastern seaboard, the 1CD and others attacked the main highway leading northwest toward Taejon and recaptured the city.

N Korean leader Premier Kim Il-sung had set August 15 as the day of final victory and the liberation of all Korea; however, it became clear that this would not happen by the evening of August 18 when the N Korean 4th ID suffered a high number of casualties and was stopped. The entire 2nd ID, under the command of Major General (MG) Laurence B. Keise, was committed on August 24 to assist the 24th

ID, which was then struggling to restore the front line following the crossing of the Naktong River by the N Korean 4th ID with 7000 men. The combined forces of the 24th and 2nd IDs led to the destruction of the N Korean 4th ID and was the greatest setback suffered thus far by the N Korean Army. The N Korean 4th ID never recovered until after the Chinese entered the conflict and it was reconstituted.

General Walker reported to the Far East Command in Japan that at this time the 24th ID was short of personnel and equipment, in accordance with its table of organization and equipment (TOE), to complete its wartime mission.

On August 25, after 55 days of combat, Walker relieved the 24th ID from combat along the Naktong River Line. The stand-down allowed time to rest and to re-equip the division. Every man who served with the 24th Infantry Division from July 2 to September 15, 1950, was awarded the Bronze Star Medal for Meritorious Service. The division received the US Distinguished Unit Citation for the same period, in recognition of the individual and collective heroism displayed by all ranks. Additional honor was bestowed upon the 24th by the Republic of Korea, by Doctor Syngman Rhee, when it received the Korean Presidential Unit Citation.

In late August from south to northeast, the N Korean units positioned opposite the UN units were the 83rd Motorized Regiment of the 105th AD and then the 6th, 4th, 3rd, 2nd, 15th, 1st, 13th, 8th, 12th, and 5th Divisions and the 766th Independent Infantry Regiment. On August 28, the 8th Army intelligence officer warned that a general attack "may be expected at any time along the 2nd and 25th IDs front," aimed at severing the Taegu-Pusan railroad and highway and capturing Masan. On the night of August 31/September 1, the N Korean First Corps launched an aggressive attack, crossing the Naktong River at five points along the 2nd ID's front. In the first hours of September, N Koreans crossed the lower Naktong at points of departure in a well-planned attack.

The N Koreans struck the perimeter in a desperate human wave attack, and in the 16-day battle that followed, the 24th ID returned to the line and its clerks, bandsmen, technical and supply personnel joined in the fight to defend against the attackers. On August 31, the 25th ID held the front of 30 miles, beginning in the north at the Namji-ri bridge over the Naktong River and extending westward on the hills south of the river to the Nam River. In the left center of the division line, the 2nd Battalion, 24th IR, held the crest of the second ridge west of Haman, a little more than a mile from the town. COL Champneys's 24th ID CP was at Haman. Shortly before midnight the N Koreans struck the north side of the pass on the Chungam-ni Haman Road. The N Koreans passed through the line quickly and overran the 2nd Battalion CP; Haman was then open to direct attack, resulting in a high number of casualties. The 2nd Battalion was no longer an effective fighting force. When the enemy attack broke through the 2nd Battalion, Champney ordered the 1st Battalion, about three miles south of Haman on the Chindong-ni road, to counterattack and restore the line. Upon contact with the enemy, the 1st Battalion broke and retreated to the rear. Thus, shortly after daylight the scattered and disorganized men of the 1st and 2nd Battalions had fled to the high ground two miles east of Haman. When General Kean learned of the breakthrough, he immediately asked for and received approval from the 8th Army to send Colonel (COL) Check's 1st Battalion 27th IR toward Haman, and to be attached to the 24th ID upon arrival at Champneys's CP. COL Check arrived at the CP two miles east of Haman at 1000 hours (10:00 a.m.). The scene was chaotic. Vehicles of all descriptions, loaded with soldiers, were moving down the road to the rear. Soldiers on foot were on the road. Champney tried repeatedly but in vain to get these men to stop. COL Check observed that none of the retreating troops from the 1st and 2nd Battalions could not be stopped from fleeing.

Check reported the situation to Kean and then sent a platoon of tanks with a platoon of infantry to find out what had happened. On September 6, a sniper severely wounded Champney and he was evacuated at once. Colonel (COL) Corley, commanding officer of the 3rd Battalion, succeeded to the command of the regiment.

On July 18, 1950, the 24th IR entered combat under a cloud of racism and was branded as poor soldiers because of their race. The African American soldiers experienced the same dismal performance common among many US Army units in the first few months of the conflict. Rumors circulated that 8th Army command was considering disbanding the regiment. In 1987, the Secretary of the Army, John O. Marsh, Jr., (1981-1989), directed that the US Army Center of Military History study and analyze the history of the 24th IR during the 1950s Korean Conflict to determine the quality of its performance. On April 29, 1996, the result of the study resulted in the African American US Army 24th IR having its honor restored in an official US Army report made public. Chapter 8, Segregation – Integration of the 24th Infantry Regiment provides an historical overview, African American contributions, and military service honors.

On September 10, the 8th Army ordered the First Provisional Marine Brigade along with the First Marine Aircraft Group 33 released from the 25th ID control, reverting to the 8th Army reserve. The next day the Marines departed Pusan, arriving in Kobe, Japan and on September 11 rendezvous with the First Marine Division (1st MARDIV) at sea. The 7th ID departed the same day from Yokohama and joined the Inchon invasion force. In mid-September, the 8th Army and the S Korean Army were still engaged with N Korean forces at all points of the Pusan Perimeter. After two weeks of the heaviest fighting of the conflict, the all-out N Korean assault on the Pusan Perimeter had forcibly turned back. By September 17, the 2nd, 24th and 25th IDs, along with the 1CD, beat the N Koreans back across the river again. On September 19, the enemy cordon around the Pusan Perimeter was destroyed, and the 8th Army pushed out of the Pusan Perimeter and advanced north. Former TF Smith's 1st Battalion 21st IR 24th ID helped lead the breakout. The N Korean soldiers in the south had disintegrated as an effective military force; while a small number escaped to the north and others became guerrillas in the south, most were casualties. The Battle of Pusan Perimeter was a large-scale battle lasting from August 4 to September 18, 1950. It was one of the major engagements of the 1950s Korean Conflict. An Army of 140,000 UN troops, having been pushed to the brink of defeat, rallied to make a final stand against the N Korean army, 98,000 men strong. The breakout from the Pusan Perimeter cost the 8th Army 4,443 casualties—790 killed in action and 3653 wounded in action. But 10th (X) Corps and 8th Army soldiers had captured 23,000 enemy personnel and killed thousands more.

The 24th Infantry Division was the first to respond at the outbreak of the conflict, and for the first 18 months the division was heavily engaged on the front lines. N Korean and Chinese forces, suffering over ten-thousand casualties.

In January 1952, the division withdrew from the front lines to the reserve force in Japan. During the conflict, 10 soldiers of the division were awarded the Medal of Honor. The division returned to Korea in July 1953 to restore order in prisoner of war camps, and for patrol duty at the end of major combat operations. It arrived two weeks before the end of the conflict. It remained on front-line duty after the armistice until October 1957, patrolling the 38th Parallel and being prepared if combat resumed. (Fire and Ice Varhola 2000, p 97) [26]

---

26   *Fire and Ice: The Korean War, 1950-1953 (Conflict)* by Michael J. Varhola (2000). Publisher: Capo Press, Iowa. *Fire and Ice* Varhola 2000.

CHAPTER 8

SEGREGATION — INTEGRATION OF THE 24TH INFANTRY REGIMENT

While some African Americans had seen combat in World War II, they did so in segregated units. By 1950, the military had made huge strides to integrate its units. Integration of the combat units and service units in Korea was not completed until May 1952.

The 1950s Korean Conflict was the last American conflict involving segregated units. Among the 25th Infantry Division's three infantry regiments was one of the US Army's last segregated units. The unit was the 24th Infantry Regiment (IR) first constituted by Act of Congress on July 28, 1866, with African American (Negro) enlisted soldiers. In 1951, the 7th US Army's 94th Engineer Battalion in France remained composed of African American enlistees and mostly White officers. In Europe, a heavy influx of White replacements with transportation specialties allowed the European Command to complete integration with the deactivation. It took six years to desegregate America's armed forces. On November 27, 1954, the deactivation of the 94th Engineer Battalion, the Army's last African American unit, completed the process. Segregation officially ended in the active armed forces with the announcement by the Secretary of Defense Charles E. Wilson that the last all-African American unit had been abolished in accordance with Executive Order 9981, signed President Harry S. Truman on July 26, 1948, mandating the racial integration of America's long-segregated armed forces. Original order filed, stamped imprint "July 17, 10:39 AM 48" at the US National Archives and made available for public inspection. Despite the issuing of the order, there was initially considerable resistance. Many experienced racism through other institutionalized and personal acts of discrimination, but in time, integration became the norm. Truman's order set in motion a wave of reforms for equality for African Americans. In the six years after the order, a quarter of a million African Americans had been intermingled with Whites in the nation's military units.

From the end of World War II, the 24th IR occupied Okinawa, Japan, and on February 1, 1947, reorganized and was assigned permanently to the 25th Infantry (ID), which was then serving in the occupation of Japan with Headquarters in Osaka on the main island of Honshu. Despite the desegregation of the US armed forces in 1948, the regiment remained African American with White officers. In late June 1950, soon after N Korea invaded S Korea, the division moved from Japan to Korea, arriving during July 5-18, 1950. Upon landing at Pusan, the 25th ID was initially positioned 100 miles north of Pusan and given the mission of blocking and delaying advancing N Korean forces down the Naktong River valley. The 24th IR entered combat against the N Korean Army on July 18. The 24th IR experienced the same dismal performance common among many US Army units in the first few months of the conflict as they all fought for survival against the numerically superior N Koreans. Again, and again US forces were not only outnumbered, but they were outgunned, and outflanked by the initiative-taking N Korean People's Army.

The defense battles on the Mason front during August and early September brought to a head a problem that had bothered the division commander MG William B. Kean ever since the 25th ID entered the conflict; in a larger sense, it was a problem that had concerned the 8th Army as well. Two of the division's regiments, the 27th and 35th, had performed well in Korea. Not so for the 24th IR, the division's third regiment. Ever since its entrance into combat in the Sangju area, the all-African American regiment had given deficient performance, although there were exceptions.

During the last 10 days of August, elements of the 24th IR defended positions along Sobuksan Mountain near Haman, from advancing N Korean troops. Two of the mountain's peaks--Phil-bong a towering peak of 1135 feet, and the Hill 655, at 2148 feet—were sites of continued back-and-forth fighting, and the area came to be known as "Battle Mountain." The front lines on "Battle Mountain " fluctuated repeatedly during this period, as US soldiers pushed forward against enemy forces and then drove back. The unstable nature of the regiment demonstrated in the fighting during August solidified the evaluation by Kean. Then on the night of August 31-September 1, the N Koreans launched an aggressive attack crossing the Naktong River, and 1st and 2nd Battalions evaporated in the face of the enemy. Four nights later, on September 5, this performance repeated, and an undetermined number abandoned their positions ignoring commands from officers to stay in place. The regiment had clearly become a weak link in the 25th ID line. The situation was so severe that those who stayed in their positions were often awarded Bronze Star Medals with Valor Devices because there were so far outnumbered in the fighting.

Battle Mountain changed hands so often during August and early September that there is no agreement on the exact number of times. On September 9, MG Kean recommended to LTG Walker the immediate removal of the 24th IR from combat, and that the troops of the regiment transfer as replacements on a percentage basis to other US Army units in S Korea. However, Walker did not act on MG Kean's recommendation, since unrelated considerations seemed to make such action impossible at the time. These considerations included heavy fighting at the Pusan perimeter and disturbing reports indicating that Chinese troops were concentrating along the Yalu River on the N Korean border. The 24th IR continued to serve for another year. The regiment moved north on November 19, 1950, into the front lines, which by then were deep into N Korea near Anju and the Chongchon River Valley. Taking the offensive, the division quickly ran into stiff resistance and pushed into the defensive posture as massive Chinese forces attacked and penetrated the 8th Army line to the right of the 25th ID and opened the division's right flank held by the 24th IR. Taking heavy casualties on November 26 as the Chinese hit the right flank of the 2nd Battalion, 24th IR, soldiers left their positions. With Chinese troops moving to their rear, the 24th IR, along with the rest of the 25th ID, began a series of delaying actions back down the peninsula, reaching Kaesong on December 8 and then south of the Imjin River in S Korea by December 14.

Continuing Chinese pressure forced the 8th Army, including the 25th ID, to withdraw further south of the 38th Parallel to the 37th Parallel near Osan, arriving on January 3, 1951. A new offensive was launched in late January, and by the end of February, Inchon and Kimpo Air Base were recaptured.

On March 6, after several successful assaults moving across difficult terrain against an entrenched enemy, the 24th IR, along with the division, advanced across the Han River, south of Seoul, pushing the Chinese/N Korean forces north back across the 38th Parallel.

After the death of General Walker on December 23, 1950, Army Lieutenant General (LTG) Matthew B. Ridgeway was assigned as Walker's replacement in command of the 8th Army. LTG Walker relieved MG Kean as part of an overall "shakeup" of the Army's frontline generals. In 1951, MG Kean was assigned to command 3rd (III) Corps at Camp Roberts, California. MG Kean had recommended that the 24th IR be disbanded, and its soldiers assigned as "fillers" in white units. LTG Ridgeway embraced Kean's assessment of the 24th IR and took action to dissolve the regiment.

To replace the regiment, LTG Ridgway decided on the 14th Infantry Regiment, which had been recently assigned, minus men and equipment, to the Far East Command. The 14th Infantry Regiment (IR) was filled with troops and equipment from the 24th IR, and replacements training in Japan and assigned to the former 24th IR's zone of responsibility in the 25th ID's line.

The story of the 24th Infantry Regiment in Korea is a difficult one, both for the veterans of the unit and for the Army. In the early weeks of the 1950s Korean Conflict, most American military units experienced problems as the US Army attempted to transform under-strength, ill-equipped, and inadequately trained forces into an effective combat team while at the same time holding back the fierce attacks of an aggressive and well-prepared opponent. In addition to the problems other regiments faced in Korea, the 24th IR also had to overcome the effects of racial prejudice. Soldiers of the regiment, despite steadfast courage on the part of its soldiers, paid the price on the battlefield for the attitudes and misguided policies of the Army and their nation.

US Army Center of Military History Executive Directive "Honor Restored"

In 1987, the Secretary of the Army, John O. Marsh, Jr., (1981-1989), directed that the US Army Center of Military History study and analyze the history of the 24th Infantry Regiment during the 1950s Korean Conflict to determine the quality of its performance.

The 25th Infantry Division, along with the 24th Infantry Regiment (one of the Buffalo Soldier regiments 1866-1951) and its associated engineers and artillery units left Japan, arriving in Korea in early 1950. Almost immediately, rumors began to circulate among White and African Americans that the regiment would never go into combat because of the supposed deficient performance of all-African American units in earlier wars.

As the project proceeded, it became clear that what happened to the 24th IR was, in part, the result of injustices that had affected African Americans from the very beginning of the American Republic. The 24th's conduct was always blamed on race. They were written off because of their color, and no unit suffered as much as the 24th.

The 24th IR was one of several outnumbered American units overwhelmed in June 1950 by the surprise N Korean invasion of S Korea. It took part in the frantic, confused, and disorderly retreat to the small Pusan perimeter, where the conflict was nearly lost.

Fueled by passages in the US Army's official history of the 1950s Korean Conflict, published in 1961, and others works on the conflict, the controversy over the 24th IR performance continued for decades after the actual fighting. The results of the study clearly suggest that what happened to the 24th IR in Korea was a product of injustices that afflicted African Americans prior to the formal integration of the Army.

Until recently, historians have tended to interpret the regiment's performance without recognizing those prejudices and the corrosive effects they had on cohesion within the unit. The whole story is much different. If it reflects lapses of command and deficiencies in leadership, training, and equipment—it also contains displays of honor, commitment, selflessness, and heroism that are in keeping with the best traditions of the US Army.

Indeed, that the 24th IR achieved what it did at Yechon, in the early weeks in Korea, the Han and Hant'an River crossings South of Seoul, and elsewhere—can only underscore the courage and determination of those among its members who chose to preserve and to do their duty in the face of adversity. Medals of Honor were awarded to two African Americans serving in the 24th IR and others recognized for their great courage and capable performance of duty, awarding them the Bronze Star Medal for Valor in combat.

On April 29, 1996, the African American US Army 24th Infantry Regiment had its honor restored in an official US Army report made public.

On August 6, 1950, Sergeant William Thompson of Brooklyn, New York, during the Battle of Masan, S Korea singlehandedly stymied an enemy attack while his platoon withdrew to reorganize. He died from wounds two weeks later and was awarded the Medal of Honor. Thompson was part of M (Mike) Company, 3rd Battalion, 24th IR heavy weapons (machine gun) support company for the battalion. On June 21, 1951, General of the Army Omar Bradley presented Thompson's mother with the Medal of Honor, posthumously recognizing Thompson's actions.

In the summer of 1951, the second time in the conflict, an African American soldier from the 24th IR received the Medal of Honor. Sergeant Cornelius H. Charlton, a squad leader in May 1951 was under consideration for a battlefield commission. Before that could happen, however, the C (Charlie) Company 24th IR was tasked with leading the charge up heavily defended terrain near the village of Chipo-ri, S Korea.

He decided to take over command of his platoon after its platoon officer was shot and killed. He led the platoon on successive assaults against heavily entrenched enemy positions. Despite a gaping wound in his chest, Charlton encouraged his men in dislodging the enemy from their positions. Within minutes, an enemy mortar position on the reverse slope of the hill began dropping mortar shells down upon them. Sergeant Charlton charged the enemy position alone and succeeded in destroying the bunker and relieving his men, but at the cost of his own life.

On March 12, 1952, Secretary of the Army Frank Pace presented Charlton's parents with the Medal of Honor, posthumously recognizing Charlton's actions.

Stories such as these about African Americans received little press attention at the time and were never taken into consideration by those in the Army who wanted to see the end of the 24th IR. On October 1, 1951, the 24th IR was relieved from front line duty. Despite "acts of heroism and capable performance of duty" by individuals, the 24th IR performed poorly. LTG Ridgeway inactivated the 24th IR in accordance with Executive Order 9981 to end segregation in the military.

The US Army cited President Truman's executive order as the official reason for the end of the 24th IR. Source: Center of Military History, US Army 1996, Washington, DC. [27] These actions marked the end of the 82-year history of the regiment.

The regiment was re-instituted in 1995 and assigned to the First Brigade, 25th Infantry Division in Fort Lewis, Washington. The regiment served in the Iraq War from 2004 to 2005 and was decorated for its service. In 2006, during a reorganization of the Army, the regiment was re-flagged; however, the 1st Battalion was not included, and so it alone retains the regimental designation and carries on its legacy. It is now part of the First Brigade Combat Team (Stryker), 25th Infantry Division at Fort Wainwright, Fairbanks, Alaska.

The 24th IR was not the only all-African American unit to serve in Korea.

During early August 1950, the 9th Infantry Regiment's African American 3rd Battalion and the 503rd Field Artillery Battalion arrived in Korea with other 2nd Infantry Division elements. Initially, the African American artillery battery, tank company, and an engineer company were withheld from frontline action and assigned to guard an airfield near Pohang. In early September, heavy combat losses among the 9th Infantry's two white battalions led to the assignment of 200 African American soldiers as individual replacements, a practice heartily endorsed by the regimental commander, Colonel (COL) Charles C. Sloane Jr. During mid-September, having been introduced gradually to combat action near Pohang and elsewhere, the 3rd Battalion rejoined in time to strengthen the 9th Infantry Regiment in attempting to break out from the Pusan Perimeter.

The 3rd Infantry Division, complete with the African American 3rd Battalion 15th Infantry Regiment, disembarked at Wonsan in northeast Korea in mid-November 1950, joining X Corps. After familiarizing itself well with its defensive role during the evacuation of Hagaru and Hungnam, code-named *Operation Christmas Cargo "Miracle of Christmas"* in N Korea, the Corps level 58th Artillery Battalion excelled at providing artillery fire support and did so again in early February 1951, and on May 19 and 20 at Pungnam.

---

27   https://history.army.mil/books/korea/24th.htm and details and insight visit online website:
      https://blackpast.org/aah/24th-infantry-regiment-korea-1950-1951.

The performance of African American artillery and armor battalions in Korea was consistently superior. The 3rd Infantry Division included the Puerto Rican 65th Infantry, the African American 64th Tank Battalion, and the Corps-level African American 58th and 999th Field Artillery Battalions.

As the conflict progressed, attitudes began to slowly change. In the last two years of the 1950s Korean Conflict and throughout the services, African Americans held command positions, and were posted to elite units such as combat aviation and served in a variety of technical specialties.

Yearly during the month of February, US armed forces pay tribute to historic contributions made by African Americans. Throughout the history of the United States, racism and segregation were motivating factors for not properly recognizing worthy people for the merits they deserved. To this day, the US Congress has enacted laws expanding impartial reviews for medals for valor, giving proper credit that were previously overlooked.

There are more than 3527 service members who have earned the nation's highest military decoration, including a total of 92 African American veterans. There are a total of 66 living recipients, including African Americans, according to the American Legion and the Congressional Medal of Honor Society, United States of America. Sources: *American Legion Magazine* December 2021 and Website: cmohs.org.

On July 9, 2020, Army General Mark A. Milley, Chairman of the Joint Chiefs of Staff, condemned systemic racism, saying, "There is no place in our armed forces for manifestations or symbols of racism, bias or discrimination." Milley also said: "The US military is a cohesive team consisting of people of different races and genders and religious and sexual orientations working to accomplish their mission in peace and war, all over the globe. Equality and opportunity are matters of military readiness, not just political correctness." US Department of Defense news stories. [28]

African American Military Service Honors/Historical Moments

The history of American Americans serving in the US Army is a long and proud one. In 1776, Congress passed legislation that allowed African Americans to enlist

---

28   No Place for Racism, Discrimination in US Military, Milley Says.
     https://www.defense.gov/news/news-stories/article/article/2269438/

in the Armed Services. In response to this Congressional Act, approximately 7000 African Americans enlisted and defended the colonies in the American Revolutionary War.

The first African American service member who earned the Medal of Honor was Landsman Joachim Pease for his conduct while loader of the No. 2 Gun on the USS *Kearsarge* as she battled the CSS *Alabama* off Cherbourg, France on June 19, 1864. Inscription engraved on the back of his medal reads: "Personal Valor/ Joachim Pease/(Colored Seaman)/U.S.S *Kearsarge*/Destruction of the *Alabama*/ June 19, 1964.

Pease was one one of eight African American sailors awarded the Medal of Honor from among about 18,000 African Americans who served the Union during the Civil War. (Navy image: poster of Joachim Pease US Naval History and Heritage Command) President Abraham Lincoln signed the bill creating the Medal of Honor in December 1861.

US Army Sergeant William H. Carney, a man born a slave in 1840, in Norfolk, VA, according to the Department of Defense. In March 1863, Carney joined the Union Army and was assigned to Company C, 54th Massachusetts Colored Infantry Regiment, the first official African American unit for the Union. He earned the Medal of Honor for his actions on July 18, 1864, during the battle at Fort Wagner on Morris Island, SC. Carney received the Medal of Honor on May 23, 1900. [29] [30] [31]

In the late 1800s, six regiments organized consisting of African Americans and these soldiers became known as the "Buffalo Soldiers." They got their nickname from Native American tribes who sometimes fought against them: These troops were tough, like buffalo, with dark curly hair.

Thirty-nine were awarded the highly prestigious Medal of Honor.

Sergeant William Henry Johnson performed heroically in the first African American unit of the US Army to engage in combat in World War I. On watch in the Argonne Forest on May 14, 1918, he fought off a German raid in

---

29   Meet Sgt. William Carney: The second African American Medal of Honor recipient.
30   www.cmohs.org/recipients/william-h-carney (Photo).
31   William Harvey Carney | US Civil War | US Army | Medal of Honor Recipient (cmohs.org)

hand-to-hand combat, killing multiple German soldiers and rescuing a fellow soldier while experiencing 21 wounds. In 1918, the French awarded Sergeant Johnson with a Croix de Guerre with a star and bronze palm. He was the first US soldier in World War I to receive that award. It took Johnson 97 years to receive the Medal of Honor for his tenacity and grit in defending his fellow soldiers from German troops.

Now, 103 years after Johnson's regiment served in World War I for 191 days, the longest of any unit, the storied 369th Infantry Regiment became known as the Harlem Hellfighters.

On June 2, 2015, he received the Medal of Honor by President Barack Obama in a posthumous ceremony at the White House. Johnson's medal was received on his behalf by Command Sergeant Major Louis Wilson of the New York National Guard. Obama said, "The least we can do is to say, 'We know who you are, we know what you did for us. We are forever grateful.'"

The Tuskegee experiment made it obvious to many leaders, including President Truman, that segregation by race in the military, in addition to being morally wrong, was simply inefficient and should be ended. The US Air Force was the first service to erase the color line, thanks largely to the pioneering efforts and courageous legacy of the African Americans who showed their worth in combat in World War II.

In the 1950s Korean Conflict, the US Marine Corps' First Provisional Marine Brigade had African Americans assigned during the fighting on the Pusan Perimeter, marking the first time African Americans integrated as individuals in significant numbers in combat. These Marines earned respect and commendation for fighting alongside their fellow Marines.

Ensign (Ens.) Jesse L. Brown was the first African American to complete US Navy flight training and the first African American naval aviator killed in combat. He flew with Fighter Squadron 32 (VF-32) from the USS *Leyte* (CV-32). On December 4, 1950, flying a close support mission in an F4U-4 Corsair over Hagaru-ri, N Korea anti-aircraft fire struck his aircraft. Ens. Brown made an emergency landing on a snow-covered mountain west of the Chosin Reservoir. Attempts to rescue him were unsuccessful, and his remains were not recovered.

Smell The Gunpowder

Ens. Brown posthumously received the Distinguished Flying Cross for his twenty missions over N Korea, he also earned the Air Medal and the Purple Heart for his actions. He was also honored with a ship bearing his name: USS *Jesse L. Brown* (DE-1089), a KNOX Class-Frigate. Korean War Movie 'Devotion' an Epic Story of Friendship and Courage. 'Devotion' a movie drama released in September 2022, is about the real-life friendship between Navy aviators Jesse Brown and Tom Hunter. Tom passed up Harvard to fly for his country. Jesse became the navy's first African American carrier pilot.

On August 10, 2021, the Senate passed legislation to award the Congressional Gold Medal to the Harlem Hellfighters regiment, the third Congressional Gold Medal to go to an African American unit, after the Tuskegee Airmen in 2007 and the Montford Point, North Carolina Marines in 2011.

"It's unfortunate that it's taken so long for this country to recognize their bravery because so many of our soldiers of color were not recognized for their service," Sen. Chuck Schumer, D-NY, said in a press release following the vote.

The Harlem Hellfighters are an example of bravery and courage under fire. Even though this regiment consigned to racial segregation, they still loved America, and fought hard for America, and died for America. The Hellfighters, enlistees from Harlem, initially formed as the 15th New York National Guard Regiment in 1916. The Hellfighters prepared for US involvement in what would become known as the Great War. Renamed the 369th Infantry Regiment for its trip to Europe, the regiment of 2000 arrived in Brest, France, on January 1, 1918, and was assigned to supply, where they unloaded ships and provided organizational support in the region. By April 15, 1918, well before the American Expeditionary Forces engaged in their first major battle, the Hellfighters were on the front lines, fighting in skirmishes and enduring the onslaught of German forces. They returned home to a heroes' welcome with a victory parade on Fifth Avenue in New York City in February 1919. On August 26, 2021, President Joe Biden signed the legislation awarding the Congressional Gold Medal to the Harlem Hellfighters.

Overall, if American history shows anything, it reveals that racially segregated combat units have succeeded in battle. Segregated regiments performed well during the American Civil War and up to the middle of the twentieth century in the United States. The African American regiments of the 93rd Infantry Division in World War I fought to high acclaim, as did segregated platoons thrown into the line after the German offensive during the December 1944 to early January 1945 known as the Battle of the Bulge in World War II.

Today the US Armed Forces value diversity in its ranks and benefit from having both men and women service members," says Sergeant First Class William R. Graser, (Ret), and Author.

CHAPTER 9

BATTLE OF INCHON: CODE-NAMED OPERATION CHROMITE

During the first week of July 1950, with the first Korean Conflict little more than a week old, General Douglas MacArthur told his staff to begin considering plans for an amphibious operation to strike the enemy center of communications in Seoul, and to study a location to accomplish this task.

At a Far East Command (FEC) headquarters meeting on July 4 attended by Army, Navy, and Air Force representatives, MacArthur discussed the idea of an amphibious landing in the enemy rear. The early amphibious operation received the code name *BlueHearts* and proposed the 1st Cavalry Division (organized as an infantry division) (1CD) be prepared for that purpose. On July 6, he ordered Army Major General (MG) Hobart R. Gay, commander of the 1CD, to plan the division's amphibious landing at Inchon. The operation called for driving the N Koreans back across the 38th Parallel, and the proposed date for it was July 22, but the operation was shelved by July 10 because of the inability of the US and S Korean forces in Korea to halt the southward drive of the enemy. The 1CD was sent to reinforce the 24th ID inside the Pusan Perimeter. Meanwhile, the planning went ahead in the Far East Command despite the cancellation of *BlueHearts*. On July 23, General MacArthur devised a secret plan to attack behind N Korean lines at the port city of Inchon. This risky strategy was not supported by leaders of the other military branches or his own colleagues. They knew too little about the dangerous tides, even though the US had occupied Korea south of the 38th Parallel for four years. With a tidal range over 30 feet, accurate intelligence of Inchon and its water approaches was vital, along with seawalls and fortifications. They were right; they did know too little, which forced

MacArthur to devise a clandestine operation to gather essential information from within occupied Inchon.

Inchon Reconnaissance Code-Named Operations *X-Ray* and *Trudy Jackson*

On September 1, *Operation X-Ray*, a small reconnaissance team to check the conditions in Inchon harbor, landed on Yonghung-Do, an island at the mouth of the ship channel only 14 miles from Inchon (Incheon) proper. From there, the team would relay intelligence back to UNC. Commander (then Lieutenant) Eugene F. Clark, US Navy, a geographic specialist on MacArthur's intelligence staff, led the team — which included two S Korean operatives along with their squad.

Clark observed the tides at Inchon for two weeks, noted N Korean artillery positions and fortifications on the island of Wolmi-do, at Inchon, and on nearby islands.

A separate reconnaissance mission, code-named *Trudy Jackson*, dispatched Lieutenant Youn Joung of the S Korean Navy and S Korean Army Colonel Ke In-Ju (Counterintelligence) and their squad, infiltrated Inchon, Kimpo air base, and Seoul to collect further intelligence on the area. The members of the unit disguised themselves as a N Korean inspection team and infiltrated the N Korean army command center in Inchon.

Their prime objective was to determine the placement of N Korean defenses (such as mines and artillery) and the tactical characteristics of the Inchon harbor, notorious for swift currents and major tidal surges, among the highest on earth, and secure a lighthouse on Palmido Island crucial to the landing's success. The lighthouse provided navigational guidance to the landing force. Inchon lay 25 miles west of the capital on a jagged stretch of coast. (The Palmi Lighthouse, the first lighthouse built in 1903 in Korea, still exists on Palmido Island and has been inactive since 2003.) Only once during the month of September — on the 15th — was water deep enough to accommodate the 29-foot draft of American landing ship tanks (LST) and even then, for only brief intervals shortly after sunrise and sunset.

The S Korean operatives reported enemy forces in the Inchon-Seoul area consisting of a major headquarters, a troop replacement center, anti-aircraft-artillery defenses,

Smell The Gunpowder

and air crews along with ground personnel for 19 aircraft, coastal defenses, and a marine/army garrison force with approximately 6500 N Korean marines and artillery soldiers. Clark reported to UNC, General MacArthur, that the Japanese-prepared tide tables, originally done during the Japanese rule 1910-1945, were accurate, that the mud flats fronting Inchon would support no weight, and that the harbor's area walls were higher than estimated. Clark's team and the S Korean reconnaissance squad were still in the inner harbor when the invasion fleet entered it.

On September 8, MacArthur announced September 15 as the Inchon landing date.

US commanders did not anticipate any air opposition, for, as far as intelligence knew, the N Koreans had only 19 planes. However, by April 1950, Russia had provided 63 World War II Il-10 and UII-10s one-engine two-seat monoplanes, its basic ground attack aircraft, to the N Korean Air Force's estimated 178 aircraft. [32] With the landing at Inchon scheduled for September 15, the Marines 1st Provisional Brigade and 1st Marine Aircraft Wing (MAW) had departed the Pusan line and joined the 1st Marine Division, at sea.

At 0050 hours (00:50 p.m.) on September 15, Lieutenant Clark and his S Korean squad would activate the lighthouse on the island of Palmido. Later that morning, the ships carrying the amphibious force followed the destroyers toward Inchon and entered the Flying Fish Channel, and the US Marines of the invasion force got ready to make the first landings on Wolmi-do Island. Lieutenant Clark along with a S Korean squad watched from the hills south of Inchon, plotting locations where N Korean machine guns were firing at the ships. This information was relayed to UNC via Japan. The US Navy awarded Lieutenant Clark the Silver Star Medal for "conspicuous gallantry and intrepidity" in obtaining "vital intelligence information."

Clark received the Legion of Merit Medal by the US Army. Commander Clark retired from the US Navy in 1966 and died June 26, 1998. *Battle Report, The War in Korea*, relates the Clark mission in detail; US Naval Institute (USNI) [33]

---

32   Historical Dictionary of the Korean War, p 151 by Matray, edited by James I. (1991).
       Publisher: Greenwood Press, New York, Special Book Sources: ISBN: 0-3132-5924-0.

33   https://www.navalhistory.org/2010/09/01/it-clark-and-the-inchon-landing.

Stories about S Korean troops are few, and it is important to note that they, too, fought to preserve their country. Just before the landings at Inchon, a small, inexperienced S Korean battalion of student soldiers was tasked with a diversionary action at Jangsari Beach to distract N Korean troops. With little ammunition, low food supplies, and second-hand weapons, 772 soldiers landed under fire and fought a battle that took place over two days (September 14-15, 1950), at Jangsari in Yeongdeok, North Gyeongsang Province, S Korea.

The Battle of Jangsari was released on Blu-ray, DVD and digital on January 20, 2020. The movie's real stars are Kim Myung-min (from the "Detective K" movies) and Choi Min-ho (K-pop boy band SHINee) along with American actors Megan Fox (*Transformers*) and George C. Eads III (*CSI,*) and television series *MacGyver*).

Battle of Inchon: Code-Named Operation *Chromite*

Began September 15 and Ended September 19, 1950

On September 10, five days before the landing, 43 US Navy warplanes took off from the escort aircraft carriers USS *Sicily* (CVE-118) and USS *Badoeng Strait* (CVE-116). Their target was the island of Wolmi-do (Green Beach), their payload of 50 tons of napalm. The planes dropped 93 napalm canisters to "burn out" its eastern slope to clear the way for American troops. On September 11, the invasion force left Kobe, Japan and on September 13, the largest naval force assembled since the invasion of Okinawa at the end of World War II near the Korean port city of Inchon. US Vice Admiral Arthur D. Struble commanded the flotilla of ships that landed and supported the amphibious force during the battle. His flagship was the heavy cruiser USS *Rochester* (CA-124). The Joint Task Force 7 (JTF 7) consisted of 261 vessels, including four aircraft carriers and two escort carriers, along with cruisers, destroyers, frigates, and at least 120 landing craft. JTF 7 included vessels from six nations: the United States, the United Kingdom, New Zealand, Canada, France, and S Korea, alongside hired civilians and transport ships from Japan. Among Admiral Struble's ships were the Gunfire Support Group, consisting of *Rochester*, the heavy cruiser USS *Toledo* (CA-133), the British light cruisers HMS *Jamaica* and HMS *Kenya*, and the six US destroyers USS *Collett* (DD-730), USS *Mansfield* (DD-728), USS *De Haven* (DD-727), USS *Swenson* (DD-729), USS *Gurke* (DD-783) and USS *Henderson*. (DD-785). Royal Canadian Navy destroyers HMCS *Cayuga*, HSCS *Athabaskan* and

HMCS *Sioux* also participated in the invasion task force. In total, 70,000 men participated in the operation. Overhead aircraft from the US Navy, US Marine Corps, and the British Royal Navy would support the assault.

The first of 95 US ships damaged in action during the 1950s Korean Conflict was the destroyer USS *Collett* (DD-730). She sailed up a difficult channel to Inchon on September 13 to begin the pre-invasion bombardment, along with US and British cruisers positioned at sea. The *Collett*, along with destroyers *Mansfield*, *De Haven*, *Swenson*, *Gurke*, and *Henderson* arrived on station prepared to begin the bombardment.

In the early afternoon, cruisers from seven to ten miles offshore out of range of the N Korean artillery batteries began the bombardment of Wolmi-do Island, targeting N Korean fortifications and gun emplacements. Between them, the cruisers and six American destroyers fired almost 1000 shells onto the fortifications.

In the ship to shore exchange, N Korea's coastal artillery returned fire, hitting *Collet* seven times, and sustained considerable damage along with five wounded.

The *Gurke* hit three times, causing minor damage by N Korean coastal guns and no casualties, and the *Swenson* twice with two casualties, one killed and one wounded. The destroyers withdrew in the early afternoon. The *Mansfield, De Haven,* and *Henderson* were not hit by N Korean artillery.

During the night of September 13-14, Struble, an expert in amphibious warfare, decided on another day of bombardment, and the US destroyers moved back up the channel off Wolmi-do on September 14. The destroyers and the cruisers bombarded the island again, and planes from the carrier task force bombed and strafed it.

Operation *Chromite*, which began on September 15, 1950 under the command of Army Major General (MG) Edward Almond, was an amphibious invasion at Inchon on the West Coast (Yellow Sea) of S Korea.

On September 15, the destroyers once again returned with the invasion force to provide gunfire support. The destroyers proceeded, under cover of air strikes close to Wolmi-do, to begin the bombardment. In an hour and fifteen minutes, the cruisers and destroyers fired 1732 5-inch shells into Wolmi-do and Inchon. Once the landings were made, the destroyers withdrew and there was no return fire; the Wolmi-do batteries were silent. The *Sicily* and the *Badoeng Strait*, in company with the 1st Marine Aircraft Wing 33, launched air strikes on communist troop concentrations and furnished close air support for the First Marine Provisional Brigade. The *Sicily* and *Badoeng Strait* launched more than 344 ground-support sorties during the amphibious landings and subsequent operations at Inchon and Kimpo airfield between September 14 and 22. Sicily would serve three deployments to Korean waters, and the *Badoeng Strait* served three tours off Korea.

The major units were the First Marine Division (1st MARDIV), the 7th Infantry Division (ID), the 92nd and 86th Field Artillery Battalions (both with 155mm howitzers), and the 5th Anti-Aircraft Artillery Battalion, the 56th Amphibious Tank and Tractor Battalion, the 19th Engineer Combat Group, and the 2nd Engineer Special Brigade. The 1st MARDIV on invasion day had a strength of 25,040 men — 19,494 Marines and Navy personnel along with 2760 Army troops and 2786 Korean marines. Later, after the 7th Marine Regiment/ "7th Marines" arrived, the Marine strength increased to about 4000 men.

The UNC reserve consisted of the 3rd Infantry Division (ID) and the 187th Airborne RCT (composed of troops from the 11th Airborne Division). The S Korean 7th Infantry Regiment (IR) was in the process of moving from the 8th Army to join 10th (X) Corps with a battlefield formation composed of more than two divisions.

Chromite's objectives were simple: Land and secure the initial beachhead on the morning tide, land again in the evening with army troops and then, with the Marines, wage the battle to defeat the surprised N Koreans, cross the Han River, take Kimpo Airfield and then Seoul. MacArthur's planners had identified three landing sites designated as Green Beach, Red Beach, and Blue Beach.

Just after 0600 hours (6:00 a.m.), about one hour before high tide, Marines from the 3rd Battalion, 5th Marine Regiment (3/5MR) boarded their landing craft and 30 minutes later waded toward Wolmi-do Island, with the objective of securing Green Beach. N Korean resistance consisted of six or so sporadic shots; then the defense ceased.

Having captured Green Beach, the 3/5MR was forced to wait until the evening tide before advancing to take Red Beach, which was west of Inchon, and the First Marine Regiment/ "First Marines" (1MR) could advance toward Blue Beach, which was Inchon's port.

As the Marines rested, positions were attacked by air strikes and naval bombardment. The Marines secured their objectives just before midnight; D-day was over. The Marines suffered 21 killed in action and 174 wounded in action. The next day, US Navy landing ships (LST) unloaded tanks, trucks, supplies, and equipment on Red Beach.

N Korean forces were not expecting an assault as far from the Pusan Perimeter as Inchon. By September 18 Inchon was secure, enabling the 7th ID and S Korean forces to land. The Inchon landing put the X Corps in the enemy's rear. The Battle of Inchon initiated the second phase of the conflict and ended September 19. The battle ended a string of victories by the invading N Korean Peoples' Army. The 8th Army and UN forces led by the 2nd Infantry Division (ID), and the S Korean 1st (I) Corps launched a general attack all along its front to hold the enemy's main combat strength and prevent movements of its units from the Pusan area to reinforce Inchon. Suddenly, the troops of the NKPA were between two fronts, with General MacArthur's troops to the north and Walker's forces to the south. The effect of the Inchon landing and the battle around Seoul on enemy action at the Pusan Perimeter from September 1950 onward was clearly apparent. The N Korean High Command began to withdraw its main forces committed to the south and started them northward.

By September 23, 1950, the enemy cordon around the Pusan Perimeter was no more. MacArthur's Inchon landing reversed the course of the Conflict. UN Forces around Pusan at the time numbered 160,000 men, of whom more than 76,000 were in the 8th Army and about 75,000 in the S Korean Army. The 8th Army pressed the attack from Pusan, retaking Taejon, and pushed the N Korean forces north, linking up on September 26 with the 7th ID just north of Osan, approximately 21 miles south of Seoul. In preparation for the pursuit of the N Korean forces, the 8th Army moved its headquarters on September 23 from Pusan back to Taegu. Of the approximately 100,000 N Korean soldiers surrounding the Pusan Perimeter, only 25,000 to 30,000 disorganized N Korean soldiers reached N Korea after the UN breakthrough.

General Walker's 8th Army fought its way over 185 miles through winding mountain roads to Osan, the location of the first engagement against N Korea troops by TF Smith. The N Korean Army and its ability to fight were destroyed as the 8th Army pushed north.

The S Korean capital was defended by 7000 of N Korea's best-trained soldiers, and they did their best to delay the Marines with counterattacks using T 34/85 tanks and planes, but the damage inflicted on the Marines failed to stop the advance. The Seoul area is one of the few lowland tracts in mountainous Korea. The attack on Seoul occurred from three sides: west, south, and southeast.

When the Marines moved into Seoul on September 22, heavy fighting followed as they fought their way from house to house chasing the N Koreans from their entrenched positions. The city was reduced to ruins, and on September 25 victory was declared despite the fact that gunfire could still be heard.

On September 27 the 2nd Battalion, 1st Marines (2/1MR), drove into the center of the city, capturing the French Embassy. In the afternoon, the Russian Embassy was occupied, and their Red Flag was pulled down and the American flag was raised. Marines then secured the American consulate and raised the American flag.

The UN recapture of Seoul by the X Corps, 1st MARDIV under the command of Marine Major General (MajGen) Oliver P. Smith and 7th ID under the command of Army Major General (MG) David G. Barr partially severed NKPA's supply lines in S Korea. Most UN ground forces involved were US Marines and were the driving force behind the operation, overcoming the strong misgivings of more cautious generals adverse to a risky assault over extremely unfavorable terrain. With MacArthur's forces at Seoul, the US and S Korean forces would drive the N Koreans back to the 38th Parallel—and later beyond it. The impressive gains by the S Korean units did not go unnoticed and prompted Walker to remark on September 25: "Too little has been said in praise of the S Korean Army which has performed so magnificently in helping turn this conflict from the defensive to the offensive." *New York Times*, Tuesday, September 26, 1950. MacArthur began to plan for a ceremony to re-establish President Syngman Rhee, his cabinet, senior members of the legislature, and the UN Commission domiciled in Seoul. The combat situation in Seoul did not permit final plans for the ceremony until September 27/28. On September 29 at the National Assembly Hall in the Government House, General MacArthur came into the chamber accompanied by President Rhee and delivered his short address and said in part, "On behalf of the United Nations I am happy to restore you, Mr. President, the seat of your government that from it you may better fulfill your constitutional responsibilities." Rhee was the first President of S Korea, July 24, 1948-April 26, 1960. As the month of September ended, Operation *Chromite* reached a complete successful conclusion. This victory marked a turning point in the conflict. The Inchon invasion was undoubtedly the right choice of action at that juncture in the fighting; there were multiple options for how, when, and where to end the conflict. Although minor skirmishes continued into October, decisive results were achieved in the brief space of 15 days after the landing. The victory cost approximately 3500 UN casualties. N Korean losses were estimated at 14,000 killed in action and 7000 captured. From the beginning of the conflict to September 15, American battle casualties totaled 19,165 men. Of this number, 4280 men were killed in action, 12,377 were wounded in action, 401 reported missing, and 2107 reported missing in action. [34]

Shortly after the capture of Seoul, the 24th ID was assembled at Chonan-Pyeongtaek on the south side of the Han River, and from there they were transported by truck north to Munson, about 25 miles above Seoul. Although not committed to action, the division on its way captured and interned thousands of defeated N Korean troops.

N Korean forces were withdrawing northward in the direction of the Uijeongbu corridor, located close to the 38th Parallel, just 90 days after they had victoriously entered Seoul in their bid for the conquest of S Korea. Morale in the N Korean Army was at a low point. No more than 30 percent of the original troops of the divisions remained. The extent of the collapse of the N Korean Army was a death blow to the enemy's hopes for continuing the conflict with N Korean forces alone.

As the fighting wore on in the fall of 1950, US policy changed. Had the US simply sought to contain the N Korean thrust into S Korea, it would have restored the 38th Parallel when it crushed the N Korean army. As of September 30, UN ground combat forces number exceeded 198,000 of which 113,500 were

---

34   *South to Naktong, North to the Yalu, Breaking the Cordon* p 547.

US ground forces. By October, the N Koreans had fled back across the 38th Parallel. On October 4 and 5, Chinese leaders decided to assist North Korea.

The success of Operation *Chromite*, MacArthur's grand amphibious invasion at Inchon, resulted in his rejection of sound advice from anyone beyond his most trusted advisors. MacArthur headed on a path that would lead to his army's defeat two months later in N Korea. [35]

---

35   Battle of Inchon: Operation Chromite streaming on Amazon.com.

Smell The Gunpowder

CHAPTER 10

THE PLAN FOR COMPLETE VICTORY: LOOKING BEYOND THE 38TH PARALLEL

The question of whether UN forces should cross the 38th Parallel became a most difficult one as soon as the Pusan Perimeter broke out and the Inchon landing succeeded. As a result of long and detailed consideration at elevated levels on the future course of action, the UN General Assembly on October 7 approved crossing the dividing line and pursuing the N Koreans to destroy their armies completely and unify the peninsula so UN-supervised elections might take place.

The Joint Chiefs of Staff sent MacArthur a comprehensive directive to govern his future decisions. Included were instructions to unite all of Korea under Syngman Rhee, if possible, and make special efforts to determine whether Chinese or Russian intervention appeared likely.

"After the Inchon landing, Moscow became more actively involved in managing the Korean situation." "The Soviets made significant attempts to rescue Kim (N Korea) and his regime from a catastrophic defeat; however, by the end of the month, the situation in Korea appeared hopeless.

Seoul fell on September 29, and it did not look like US/UN forces would stop at the 38th parallel." (Red Wings over the Yalu)

MacArthur's calculation was to land a huge armed force in Incheon in September 1950 and occupy the whole of Korea in a short time.

That was a great mistake. Although the US imperialists, taking advantage of their absolute numerical superiority, could force their way through the People's Army positions in the Naktong River line and the Inchon-Seoul line and then intrude into the area north of the 38th parallel, they were unable to occupy it completely.

8th Army and X Corps Enter North Korea

UN forces crossed the 38th Parallel, despite warnings from Communist China to remain below it, and pressed north to the Yalu River that served as the border between N Korea and China. The 8th Army expected strong enemy resistance at the 38th Parallel and a stubborn defense at Pyongyang. Walker continued leading the 8th Army in its attack across the 38th Parallel into N Korea. Ready for the attack, the 1CD was deployed in three regimental combat teams just below the 38th Parallel. The 1CD sent patrols across the parallel late on the afternoon of October 7 and others crossed Sunday night, October 8, 1950. Then on Monday, October 9, the 1CD moved up to the Parallel and started fighting its way northward. American, UN, and S Korean forces marched into N Korea.

At the close of October 14, with US troops in the principal enemy positions between the 38th Parallel and the N Korean capital, enemy front lines as such ceased to exist. X Corps began loading the attack force at Inchon aboard Amphibious Group One LSTs. X Corps, including the newly arrived 3rd ID under the command of Army Major General (MG) Robert H. Soule, was set for a "race to the Yalu ``against crumbling N Korean opposition. During the conflict, the division was known as the "Fire Brigade" for its rapid response to the crisis. On October 17, the main body of the attack force with the 1st MARDIV aboard departed Inchon, moved into the Yellow Sea, and headed south to round the tip of Korea. From Inchon it was 830 miles to Wonsan by the shortest sea route. The 1st MARDIV landed on the East Coast of N Korea at Wonsan and Iwon and headed north toward the Chosin (Korean: Changjin) Reservoir with the goal of driving to the Yalu River to complete the UN's control of N Korea. Marine MajGen Oliver P. Smith moved slowly north from Hungnam, a port city along the coast, through Koto-ri to Hagaru-ri and Yudam-ni in the vicinity of the Chosin Reservoir. The 7th ID had remained afloat at Pusan for ten days. Upon receipt of orders the division proceeded on October 27 to Iwon, 150 miles above Wonsan, unloading on November 9 across their beaches.

President Truman arranged a conference with General MacArthur on Wake Island, a small atoll in the central Pacific Ocean on October 15, 1950. There were a few items on the agenda, but the real reason for the conference was to discuss the possibility of China or Russia intervening in Korea. That being the big question, MacArthur assured Truman there was a truly little chance either country would become involved. MacArthur added that the Chinese were able to mass no more than 60,000 men near the Yalu River and they had no air force. They never discussed what to do should China become involved. Chinese Communist Party Chairman Mao Zedong received a plea for direct military aid from Kim Il-sung. Mao Zedong was willing to intervene, but he needed assurances of Russian air power. Stalin promised to extend China's air defenses (staffed by Russians) to a corridor above the Yalu, thus protecting air bases in Dongbei Pingyuan and hydroelectric plants on the river, and he also promised new weapons and armaments factories. After a lengthy debate, Mao ordered the Chinese People's Volunteers Force (CPVF) to cross into Korea. Beginning in early October 1950, troops from the Chinese People's Liberation Army (CPLA), under the cover of darkness, undetected, began to cross the border to assist their N Korean ally. By mid-October, the Chinese had concentrated more than 400,000 troops close to N Korea. The Chinese had secretly moved 200,000 troops, referred to as "volunteers," into Korea on October 19 and readied itself to counterattack US and S Korean forces.

"The US troops are going to cross the 38th Parallel to extend the war. If the US troops really do so, we cannot sit idly by and remain indifferent. We will intervene."

— Chinese Foreign Minister Zhou En-Lai communicating his country's final warning to the US through India's Ambassador to Beijing twelve days prior to the PLA's infiltration into N Korea.

MacArthur claimed there might be around 30,000 Chinese soldiers in N Korea and again believed no more than 60,000 men were near the Yalu River. The Yalu River of northeastern Asia forms the northwestern boundary between N Korea and the Northeast region (also known as Manchuria) of China. MacArthur and his staff were soon to make one of the worst military intelligence blunders in US Army history.

Ignoring reports of contact with Chinese Communist Forces (CCF), and the Armed Forces Security Agency (AFSA) clear and convincing evidence of the massing of Chinese troops north of the Yalu, along with MacArthur's chief of staff LTG Edward Almond, reported he had seen Chinese prisoners of war (POWs) being held by a S Korean unit, MacArthur ordered the 8th Army and X Corps to push on to the Yalu River. MacArthur continued his attempt to destroy the N Korean Army and unify the Korean Peninsula. The assessment of the CCF threat was published by AFSA in reports available to the Joint Chiefs of Staff (JCS), the White House, and to MacArthur.

The 24th ID was part of the northward drive in the western sector. UN forces, primarily American and S Korean troops, advanced swiftly against negligible opposition, and on October 19 took Pyongyang, the N Korean capital, and its seaport. Walker on October 25 established his advance headquarters in N Korean Premier Kim Il-sung's abandoned headquarters building. October 25 had been a frigid day and carried the promise of the bitter N Korean winter that lay ahead. After the capture of Pyongyang, the 24th ID, its soldiers and equipment, were transported by truck north and then attacked north from Sinuiju. Briefly the 24th halted, and then throughout November the division alternately attacked and regrouped. The division held a line defending bridge heads on the Chongchon and Taeyong Rivers north of Anju and Sinuiju. UN forces led by the US destroyed N Korean resistance in less than two weeks. Morale was high as they crossed the Chongchon River, which formed the last major water barrier in the western part of N Korea short of the Chinese border. The 8th Army operation above Chongchon began as a continuation of the pursuit that had started with the breakout from the Pusan Perimeter. The UN forces had disregarded a warning from China's Communist government that it would not allow the destruction of N Korea. China claimed the UN advance threatened its borders and their intervention in November changed the nature of the conflict. Around the same time the Russian government began to send pilots, aviation maintenance teams, and anti-aircraft-artillery defense units to provide cover from aerial attacks on important centers in Northeast China and N Korea. It was not long before the presence of Chinese troops impacted UN forces as pressure by the CCF increased. Concerned about these developments, and despite US air superiority, China's Chairman ordered the Chinese People's

Smell The Gunpowder

Volunteer Army (CPLA) to intervene in Korea. The Chinese were waiting in ambush, and their goal was to destroy MacArthur's forces. By late October, as the leading UN forces crossed the Chongchon River, MacArthur issued an order to his ground commanders in Korea which changed all earlier orders drastically. He now changed all restrictions on the use of UN forces south of the border and instructed all commanders to press forward to the extreme northern limits of Korea, utilizing all their forces. In an unexpected encounter with S Korean troops in the Unsan area on October 25, the CPVA launched its first-phase offensive campaign in Korea. Unsan was one of the few access points into the Yalu and Chosin Reservoir area. The conflict took a grim new turn.

On the last day of October 1950, the 1CD 8th Cavalry Regiment (8th Cavalry/8CR) and B Company, 7th Tank Battalion was positioned at the lead edge of the UNC advance into N Korea near the village of Unsan, only 65 miles from the Chinese border. The mission was to relieve S Korean elements in the area. The CCF had set the stage for an attack that night against the 8th Cavalry Regiment (8CR) and the S Korean 15th Regiment. The 8th Army was to go on the defensive for the first time since September.

This battle represented the last opportunity for MacArthur and his senior intelligence officer, Major General Charles A. Willoughby, to make the assessment that China had entered the Korean Conflict on a decisive scale.

On the evening of the 8CR disaster at Unsan, 8th Army intelligence realized there were enemy forces in the vicinity of Unsan, two Chinese units of regimental size. When dusk fell that evening, enemy forces were on three sides of the 8CR—the north, west, and south. Only the ground to the east, held by the S Korean 15th Regiment, was not in Chinese possession. Within hours, the S Korean regiment on the 8CR's right flank collapsed. The 8CR fell back in disarray into the city of Unsan, fighting a series of battles with the CCF. On November 2, the 25th ID 2nd Battalion, 24th IR participated alongside the 8CR. They pushed back and began heading south. On November 4, the strength of the CCF was re-evaluated, indicating the two Chinese units were division size, and the next day the estimated strength increased to three division-size units. Severe fighting continued November 5–6, and the 8CR was overwhelmed and forced back from positions in and around the town of Unsan by vastly superior Chinese forces. The regiment was severely battered, suffering heavy casualties, including missing in action.

In less than two weeks, the CPVA pushed S Korean and US troops from the Yalu River to the Chongchon River. The 8CR and the S Korean 15th Regiment withdrew to positions above the Yongsan-dong-Yong-byon-Unhung east-west road. This amounted to a general withdrawal of approximately 12 miles. Over the next two weeks, there were replacements of 22 officers and 616 soldiers for the 8CR. By November 21, UN forces reached the Yalu River. The N Korean Army was in full retreat. A quick end to the war was near; UN commanders presumed that the conflict was over. General MacArthur's headquarters informed Walker that the possibility of Chinese intervention was very slight. This optimistic view would change quickly as the situation on the northern front lines rapidly deteriorated. In a series of vicious firefights, the 8th Army success stalled in its tracks and put them on the defensive. On November 21, the 8th Army advised IX Corps, X Corps and the S Korean Army that H-hour for the counterattack was 1000 hours (10:00 a.m.) November 24. Up to the launching of the November 24 attack, the 8th Army and X Corps had suffered a total of 27,827 battle casualties: 21,529 in the 8th Army and 6,298 in X Corps. Of the 8th Army total, 4157 had been killed in action, 391 had died of wounds, and 4834 were missing in action.

With another 230,000 troops available, plus 150,000 heading to the Chosin Reservoir, the Chinese on November 22, 1950, began the 2nd Phase Campaign.

> *The US Imperialists Started the Korean War. The Korean people and the People's Army heroically surmounted the hard trial of the strategic retreat through their devoted struggle and went over to the overall counteroffensive from late October 1950, frustrating the enemy's plan to reach the Amnok River, (also called the Yalu River) by a 'win-the-war-quick operation' and cutting the comb of MacArthur, who had blared: 'The war is just about to end.' The main force of the enemy was utterly crushed at the regions around the Chongchon River and Lake Jangjin by the large-scale encircling operation of the People's Army, and there started the so-called "December general retreat of the UN Forces."*

Battle of Chongchon River Valley

On November 24, 1950, General MacArthur ordered the final offensive, which became known as the "home by Christmas" offensive. Battle of the Chongchon River was a decisive battle, and took place from November 25 to December 2, 1950, along the Chongchon River Valley in the northwestern part of N Korea.

The Chongchon valley is a wide one for Korea, varying in width from three miles to twenty miles. On Friday, November 25, preceded by a heavy and lengthy artillery barrage, Walker's 8th Army had begun its march to the Yalu River. Initially, there was little resistance. The 8th Army advanced close to the Yalu River and stopped its advance on the afternoon of November 25, the Chinese launched a massive frontal attack against the entire UN line from Yongsan-dong to Yongdong-ni. Hoping to repeat success, the Chinese continued with a series of surprise attacks on the night of November 25, effectively destroying the 8th Army's right flank while allowing Chinese forces to move rapidly into UN rear areas. The 2nd ID had been advancing on the right flank of 9th (IX) Corps, which was then pushing to the Yalu River, and was positioned north of Kunu-ri with the 25th ID on its left flank. In a swift attack, the Chinese threatened to encircle the 8th Army, with the 2nd ID exposed on the right and bearing the brunt of the movement. The 25th ID was able to withdraw to Anju, but the 2nd ID was eventually cut off and forced to fight its way through the Chinese to safety at Sunchon. By mid-afternoon November 28, all US forces and S Korean units were in retreat. In the subsequent battles and withdrawals during the period of November 29 to December 2, the 8th Army managed to avoid being cut off and surrounded by Chinese forces, but the Chinese were still able to inflict heavy losses onto the retreating UN forces, which had lost all cohesion.

The withdrawal of the 8th Army units was difficult because of the thousands of fleeing Korean refugees who blocked the roads. In addition, the large numbers of refugees gave excellent cover to Chinese and N Korean infiltrators, who often dressed in Korean clothing, went through US checkpoints, and then turned and opened fire on the startled US forces. The tactics repeated those used by the N Koreans during the initial invasion of the South and were often equally effective. MG Keiser, commander of the 2nd ID, ordered a full-scale retreat from its base at Kunu-ri while being attacked by several Chinese divisions. As the division began its withdrawal under pressure, it found itself literally "running the gauntlet" as its trucks and vehicles became trapped on a congested valley road under fire from Chinese positions on the high ground to the east and west. Soldiers were forced to crouch in the ditches as their vehicles were raked with enemy fire; while hundreds were killed or wounded, others were forced to proceed on foot down the long road to Sunchon, almost 20 miles to the south of Kunu-ri. Chinese roadblocks halted the columns repeatedly as the casualties mounted. Artillery units abandoned their guns. As the road became clogged with abandoned vehicles, men left the column and made their way south as best they could. Unit integrity broke down under the murderous fire.

With heavy losses, the division broke through the Chinese ambush that was waiting on a mountainside along the road just north of Sunchon. Following the battle, during which the division suffered almost 4500 battle casualties, Kaiser was relieved of his command. He was replaced with Army MG Robert B. McClure.

Officially, Kaiser was relieved for medical reasons. Kaiser felt he was made a scapegoat for the reverses suffered by the UN following the Chinese intervention in the conflict. Finally, late on November 30, the last units arrived in Sunchon. The shattered 8th Army established a hasty defensive line from Sunchon to the west to Sinchang-ni in the east, 25 miles south of their initial positions on the Chongchon River line.

The battles along the Chongchon River were a major defeat for the 8th Army and a mortal blow to the hopes of MacArthur and others for the reunification of Korea by force. Although not closely pursued by the Chinese, Walker decided that his Army was not in shape to hold the Sunchon–Sinchang-ni line and ordered a retreat farther south before his forces could be surrounded by fresh Chinese forces.

Battle of the Chosin Reservoir

General Almond's X Corps, including the 1st MARDIV, began to strike for the Yalu. Chinese Communist forces in N Korea had grown to around 300,000 and each soldier carried a personal weapon, 80 rounds of ammunition, three or four "stick" hand grenades [36], and a week's supply of rations, dried fish, rice, and tea. For one US Army unit, the intervention of CCF resulted in absolute disaster. The 31st Regimental Combat Team (RCT), commanded by Colonel (COL) Allan MacLean, better known as Task Force MacLean (later known as Task Force Faith), comprised elements of the Army 7th Infantry Division (7th ID). By late November 1950, two geographically separated American forces, the 8th Army and X Corps, augmented by their S Korean allies, were spread out on

---

36 Stick grenade was a Chinese Type 67 defensive hand grenade. The grenade is a so-called "stick" grenade, aka a "potato masher." Invented by the German Army in World War I, stick grenades contained an explosive charge in one end of the weapon. A pull string runs through the length of the handle and is concealed by a screw-on cap on the other end of the grenade. Pulling on the string ignites the fuse, and the grenade is then thrown at the enemy.

Smell The Gunpowder

the Chongchon River Valley in the west and at the Chosin Reservoir in the east the 1st MARDIV and the 7th ID.

The Chinese attack on November 25-26 caught the US Army forces by surprise and the American positions and units were overrun. The 31st RCT had the mission of relieving the 1st MARDIV East of the Chosin reservoir and attacking to the North toward the Yalu River. The unit's battalions and separate companies were spread out along the road from the port of Hungnam in the south to forward positions east of the reservoir over 90 miles away when it was hit in the evening of November 27 by the surprise attack of the Chinese Eightieth PLA Division. The attack virtually annihilated the 31st RCT of the 7th ID on the east side of the Chosin Reservoir. The RCT consisted of about 3000 soldiers, and over 1000 died on a 10-mile stretch of frozen and snow-covered dirt road on the east side of the reservoir. One thousand were wounded in action or missing. (The Changjin Reservoir was known to the Americans by its Japanese name, Chosin.) Of the 1050 survivors who eventually reached the Marine lines, only 385 were able-bodied. During the withdrawal, COL MacLean was shot several times and taken prisoner; he died four days later. Organizational leadership failures of the X Corps, 7th ID, the 31st RCT and attached battalions all contributed to the almost complete destruction of the RCT.

By the evening of December 1-2, Army Lieutenant Colonel (LTC) Don C. Faith Jr. took command. Faith, a World War II veteran, was killed in action on December 2, 1950, east of Chosin, and was posthumously awarded the Medal of Honor for his courage in five days of bloody fighting near Hagaru-ri. His body was not recovered by US forces at that time. In 2004, a US and DPRK team surveyed the area where Faith was last seen. His remains were located and returned to the US for identification. The experiences of the American soldiers, who fought in rough terrain and died in the frigid cold of the Chosin area, proved to be some of the most harrowing and tragic in the history of the US Army.

The 1st MARDIV commander, Lieutenant General (LtGen) Eric M. Smith had positioned about 7000 Marines to lead the strike for the Yalu. But when CCF troops attacked the UN lines, the 1st MARDIV on the west side was overwhelmed by the Chinese 9th Army Group and made an escape through treacherous terrain and a 40-mile roadblock. Under the worst possible weather conditions, the Marines turned and fought their way south. It turned extremely cold and made fighting exceedingly difficult. The temperature was below zero and the wind howled. Temperature rarely climbed above freezing; even along the western coastal plain, snow driven by biting winds added to the arctic feel. American units had no training and inadequate equipment for the bitter temperatures. Many wore long woolen underwear, two pairs of socks, a wool shirt, and cotton field trousers over a pair of woolen trousers, shoepacs, pile jackets, wind-resistant reversible parkas with hoods, and trigger-finger-mittens of wool insert and outer shell. To keep ears from freezing, wool scarves were tied around their heads underneath helmets. Still, the cold seeped through.

After conferring with MG Almond, Smith decided to withdraw his division to Hungnam. Smith, never doubting the ability of the Marines to fight, was determined to conduct "an orderly and honorable withdrawal" and bring out his equipment, the wounded, and as many of his dead as possible. The long retreat took six weeks. Opposed by the Chinese 9th Army Group (12 divisions in 3 armies) numbered 300,000 soldiers—mostly infantry with mortars and machine guns, the Marines fighting through numerous enemy roadblocks as they made their way south, and forced to endure subzero temperatures, the Marines suffered thousands of battle casualties and cases of frostbite. By December 11, after 13 harrowing days, Smith's force finally arrived at Hungnam, where his division landed in late October and would prepare to be evacuated by sea. In a brilliant feat of military management, Smith had saved his division. Concurrently, the 8th Army retreated to the Imjin River, south of the 38th Parallel. The 8th Army line would be stabilized, running from Pyeongtaek in the west to Wonju in the east. The 1st MARDIV suffered 718 killed in action, 3508 wounded in action, and 7313 "noncombat" casualties due to frostbite. There were 192 missing in action. Between 25,000 and 30,000 Chinese troops were killed, and another 12,500 wounded, along with 30,000 who were frostbitten.

The offensive began on November 24 and ended December 24; UN forces pushed back from the Chinese border to the 38th Parallel. The 1st MARDIV, 24th and 25th IDs, and the S Korean First ID were still relatively intact, but the US 2nd ID, the Turkish Brigade, and three S Korean Infantry Divisions were shattered units that would need extensive rest and refitting to recover combat effectiveness.

Smell The Gunpowder

Intelligence Failure

Accession Number: ADA501969

Title: Intelligence Failure in Korea: Major General Charles A. Willoughby's Role in the United Nations Command's Defeat in November 1950

Defense Technical Information Center
8725 John J. Kingman Road
Fort Belvoir, Virginia 22060-6218

Source: View original document - https://apps.dtic.mil/docs/citations/ADA501969

Descriptive Note: Master's thesis

Corporate Author: Army Command and General Staff College Fort Leavenworth, Kansas

Personal Author(s): Haynes, Justin M

Full Text: https://apps.dtic.mil/dtic/tr/fulltext/u2/a501969.pdf

Report Date: 12 Jun 2009

Pagination or Media Count: 144 pages

Abstract: "In November 1950, the United States Army suffered one of its most devastating defeats ever in the frozen mountains of North Korea at the hands of the Chinese People's Liberation Army.

This defeat fundamentally changed the nature of the Korean Conflict from a near-certain United Nations victory into a fight for its very survival. It was, however, avoidable.

Despite overwhelming evidence that the new Communist Chinese state was poised to enter the conflict, MacArthur and Willoughby ignored the evidence.

Instead, MacArthur continued his attempt to destroy the N Korean Army and unify the Korean Peninsula. This Chinese victory was partially the result of one of the most glaring failures in US military intelligence history.

The officer most responsible for this failure was the Far East Command Assistant Chief of Staff for Intelligence, Army Major General Charles A. Willoughby.

His inaccurate intelligence picture contributed to General MacArthur's flawed understanding of the nature of the Chinese Communist intent.

Willoughby correctly identified the potential threat of a Chinese Communist intervention in Korea in late 1950 yet failed to acknowledge the significance of China's strategic warnings, operational preparations for war, and tactical confirmation of their intentions.

Willoughby's actions also had significant second and third order effects on the Joint Chiefs of Staff, the Central Intelligence Agency (CIA), as well as the President, compounding errors made at the national, strategic level. The grim fate that awaited the Soldiers and Marines of the US 8th Army and Tenth Corps was the result of informational, institutional, and personality factors that distorted Willoughby's judgment and effectiveness."

Subject Categories:

Humanities and History
Military Intelligence
Military Operations, Strategy and Tactics
Distribution Statement: Approved for Public Release; distribution is unlimited.

While Willoughby successfully identified Chinese military preparations, he failed to determine their intentions prior to MacArthur's final offensive on November 24, 1950. On November 24, General MacArthur ordered the *"home by Christmas"* offensive. On the evening of November 25, as UN forces approached the Yalu River, the border between Korea and China, Beijing decided to intervene.

Contrary to MacArthur's expectations, this action put an end to any thoughts for a quick or conclusive UN victory. Chinese Communists forces (CCF) struck along a 300-mile front. The Chinese offensive caught the UN forces off guard, and the CCF intervention reinvigorated the N Korean army. It took several days for MacArthur and his staff to face the fact that his *"home by Christmas"* offensive toward the Yalu was over, and victory was not near. A gap had opened between the 8th Army and X Corps as they moved close to the Chinese border due to a lack of coordination between Walker, MG Almond, and General MacArthur's headquarters in Tokyo.

China's decision to intervene in the conflict was determined by concerns more complicated than safeguarding the Chinese Korean border. Chairman Mao Zedong, commonly known as Chairman Mao, sought "to win a glorious victory" that would restore China's world status as the "Central Kingdom." Mao also wanted to repay a debt to N Korea, which had sent thousands of soldiers to fight in the Chinese civil war. [37] [38] Finally, on November 28, MacArthur reported that he faced 400,000 Chinese People's Liberation Army (CPLA) troops and a completely new war. By the end of the year, CPV and N Korean troops had recovered the lost territory in the north. In January 1951 Seoul would be once more in N Korean hands.

Hungnam Evacuation: Code-Name Operation *Christmas Cargo*

By late November 1950, Communist Chinese forces numbering 250,000 men operating in the mountains of N Korea threatened to cut off and destroy UN units. To prevent that catastrophe, on December 9, General MacArthur ordered evacuation by sea of the X Corps. As the Marines and soldiers, in bitter cold and wind, fought their way out of encirclement at Chosin Reservoir and elsewhere in northeast Korea, several hundred Navy and Marine aircraft, operating from airfields ashore and from the ships of Task Force 77, pummeled enemy ground troops. The ships included cruisers, destroyers, and rocket ships, which put a ring of fire between the troops and the enemy. On December 23, the USS *Missouri* (BB-63) added shells from her 16-inch guns to the gunfire support mission. The already bloodied Chinese army wisely chose not to contest the evacuation.

---

37   Professor Chen Jian, *China's Road to the Korean War: The Making of the Sino-American Confrontation* (1994), New York: Columbia University Press pp 3-5, 20.
38   Taewoo Kim (2012) Limited War, Unlimited Targets, Critical Asian Studies, 44:3, pp 467-492, DOI 10.1080/146715.2012.711080.

The *Sicily* (CVF-118) and *Badoeng Strait* (CVF-116), and the First Marine Air Wing 33 provided air support from the Chosin Reservoir to Hungnam Evacuation. (Navy and Heritage Command – Official US Navy website.) The Hungnam evacuation, code-named Operation *Christmas Cargo*, was also known as the *Miracle of Christmas*. A 173-ship armada assembled at the port and evacuated not only the UN troops, but also their heavy equipment and Korean refugees. The evacuation of X Corps between December 9 and 24, 1950, approximately 105,000 troops, 17,500 vehicles and 350,000 tons of cargo, material, and 100,000 civilians were loaded onto merchant ships and military transports and they were transported to safety in Pusan (today, Busan) and other destinations in S Korea. One ship, the SS *Meredith Victory,* a type of cargo freighter transport built during World War II, evacuated more than 14,000 refugees in a single trip. The *Meredith Victory* was designed to carry only 12 passengers with a 47-person crew. This operation was the culmination of the Battle of Chosin Reservoir, in which the embattled UN troops fought their way out of a Chinese trap. The presence and fate of Army troops east of Chosin, in November and December 1950, are not well known. [39] Many accounts of the Chosin campaign tend to overlook or minimize the Army's role. US Army elements of the 7th ID, many of which had been in fighting as severe as that of the Marines, rejoined their division without a break and assumed a role in the defense of the perimeter. From November 27-December 2, the Army's 31st RCT of the 7th ID was virtually annihilated on the east side of the Chosin Reservoir. The Army accomplished at least part of its mission; it successfully guarded the right flank of the surrounded 1st MARDIV, protecting it from additional Chinese attacks for four days. If not for the presence of the 7th ID, Communist Chinese forces might have captured the key Marine base and airstrip at Hagaru-ri before the Marines concentrated sufficient units to defend it.

The withdrawal of X Corps units by sea was in the following order: 1st MARDIV, S Korean 1st Corps (3rd Infantry Division and Capital Division), US 7th ID, and US 3rd ID. Beginning with the 1st MARDIV loaded on waiting ships from December 9 to 14, the Korean I Corps from December 15 to 17, the 7th ID from December 18 to 21, and last was the 3rd ID, loading from December 21 to 24. The withdrawal of the mangled 7th ID, after the destruction of Task Force Faith at Chosin, was virtually a two-regiment division. The 3rd ID African American 3rd Battalion 15th Infantry Regiment, and 64th Tank Battalion, along with the 58th and 999th Field Artillery battalions, provided supporting firepower in a defensive role during the evacuation of Hagaru and Hungnam. The

---

39   https://www.armyhistory.org/nightmare-at-the-chosin-reservoir/

performance of African American artillery and armor battalions in Korea was consistently superior. During the final stages of the withdrawal, conventional artillery, naval gunfire, and close air support effectively prevented any major enemy forces from endangering the evacuation.

Finally, on December 24, the last three battalions (one from each regiment) of the 3rd ID, which had been covering the removal of its regiments from the perimeter, abandoned their final strongpoints and loaded onto LSTs. Explosive teams destroyed bridges, facilities, vehicles, tanks, and abandoned supplies. The few military supplies left (mostly unserviceable or, in the case of some frozen dynamite, too dangerous to move) were detonated as the convoy sailed from Hungnam for S Korea. The dynamite that was usable was set as booby traps for the Chinese to discover. The acting operations officer for the 3rd ID had the engineers mine all the toilets. The toilets had pull-type chains, so the first person who pulled the chain on a toilet was going to get the shock of his life. The results of these booby traps are not known.

The ships assembled at the port left and steamed south, reaching Pusan on Christmas Eve. In the morning of December 25, the Chinese People's Volunteer Armies (PVA) 27th Corps entered Hungnam. The evacuation from Hungnam was not Dunkirk (reference to Dunkirk France, May 26 and June 4, 1940, and the evacuation of 338,226 Allied soldiers during World War II), but it was still a retreat and a demoralizing defeat after the high hopes of November. The race to the Yalu and the Chosin Reservoir campaign were painful defeats because, to a great extent, X Corps did not follow its own doctrine of foreseeing events and planning for all contingencies. The X Corps jeopardized its own operations and almost presented the 8th Army and the US government with a catastrophic defeat due to its lack of vision. The Far East Command and General MacArthur share in this blame. [40]

From late October until mid-December 1950, Chinese forces killed or captured thousands of American and S Korean soldiers, decimating the 2nd ID. By December 22, 1950, the 8th Army's front had stabilized along the 38th Parallel. Just days before his death, LTG Walker placed the US 1st (I) Corps, the IX Corps, and the S Korean Army's 1st (I) Corps along the 38th Parallel to defend Seoul. The 3rd Battle of Seoul took place from December 31, 1950 to January 7, 1951 around the S Korean capital of Seoul. On December 31, 1950, 500,000 Chinese

40   https://www.armyupress.army.mil/Portals/7/combat-studies-institute/csi-books/stewart.pdf.

troops attacked the 8th Army's line at the Imjin River, and the S Korean Army along the 38th Parallel. Prior to the attack, Chinese infiltration platoons, elite groups, slipped into the UN lines sometimes disguised as S Korean soldiers, and would attack from within. Massive Chinese attacks, accompanied by kettle drums and trumpets, broke through the 8th Army's lines. Chinese troops used both grenade and submachine gun platoons that led the attacks followed by infantry units. The grenade platoons saturated 8th Army positions, attempting to stun and injure as many defenders as possible so that they could be overrun by the next wave of attacking platoons. When they ran out of grenades, they would pick up weapons either from the fallen American or S Korean soldiers or members of the submachine gun platoons.

Waves of infantry would follow, overwhelming the 8th Army by concentrating on the weakest points. The Chinese attacked the line without pausing until it was breached, usually because of casualties or lack of ammunition. On January 1, 1951, the defenses at the 38th Parallel completely collapsed. In the aftermath of the Chinese attacks along the 38th Parallel, the new commander of the 8th Army, LTG Ridgway, worried that the Chinese would exploit the breakthrough to circle the entire 8th Army. To prevent the Chinese forces from overwhelming the defenders, the 8th Army evacuated Seoul on January 3, 1951, falling back 50 miles. Seoul was again in N Korean and in Chinese hands. The S Korean government in Seoul, which was reduced to essential personnel before the battle, also left the city with little difficulties. On the afternoon of January 4, the communists entered Seoul and raised the N Korean flag over the capital building; by January 7, the offensive ended. The Chinese People's Volunteer Armies (PVA) were exhausted after months of non-stop fighting since the start of the Chinese intervention, thereby allowing the UN forces to regain the initiative in S Korea. The Chinese were still moving south, accompanied by a small number of N Koreans.

Most decisions about the conflict were now being made in Beijing. China hoped to repeat N Korea's rapid conquest of the south in the summer and early autumn in 1951. However, on January 25, the UN's first counteroffensive by the 8th Army attacked the Chinese with Operation *Thunderbolt*. *Thunderbolt* was also known in China as the Defensive Battle of the Han River Southern Bank. The attack was heavily supported by artillery and air support, and between February and March 1951, UN troops, including the 24th ID, slowly but stubbornly moved northward again, retaking Seoul for the 4th time and pushing Chinese and N Korean forces north of the Han River.

On March 24, the 1stMARDIV assumed responsibility for approximately 35 miles of the front, which overlooked Panmunjom and included the defense of the Pyongyang–Seoul corridor. By mid-April, the division had advanced north of the 38th Parallel. [41]

Operation *Thunderbolt* was the first offensive under the command of LTG Ridgway, and it started less than three weeks after the Chinese forced UN forces south of Seoul. In March 1951, Major General (MG) Blackshear M. Bryan was part of the first rotation of combat commanders since the start of the conflict, taking charge of the 24th ID. Between April and mid-September, the Chinese launched counterattacks against the 24th and 25th IDs along with the 1stMARDIV, and they were able to hold their ground. The last Chinese ground offensive, the spring counterattack on April 22, was another of the "human wave" attacks supported by hours of steadily pounding artillery. Then the bugle-blowing Chinese struck the American and S Korean positions. US artillery fire against the Chinese was so extensive that in one day, April 23, the 24th ID 52nd Field Artillery fired 15,712 rounds at the attacking forces. The 24th ID Division commander, MG Bryan, knew that the best way to stop the attack was to concentrate all available firepower and then wait until the enemy supply lines were disrupted to support the attack satisfactorily. By April 25, the Chinese had expended everything they had, and their supply lines were stretched and inefficient. However, the vast human resources of the Chinese had hardly been dented, despite the mass slaughter of the first few waves. On May 16, the Chinese attacked again in a last-ditch effort to push the UN forces from the Korean Peninsula. For three days, the attack continued, but the battle line held. The enemy lost three divisions, reducing its force to a few disorganized units. By June, both sides were entrenched along the 38th Parallel where the conflict began. The Russians proposed negotiations for a ceasefire at the UN on June 23, 1951. Representatives of the two sides first met at Kaesong on July 10, behind communist lines. This location was unsatisfactory to the UN side, so the meetings were moved to Panmunjom [42], 34 miles north of Seoul, an obscure village in "no-man's land."

The US aggressors were bewildered by the string of defeats. Caught in such a dilemma, the US rulers racked their brains for a loophole. Finally, in June 1951,

41 *Fire and Ice: The Korean War, 1950-1953* (Conflict) by Varhola, Michael J. (2000). Publisher: Capo Press, Mason City, Iowa.

42 Panmunjom is in the most sensitive area of Korea's demilitarized zone. Panmunjom is a small village, about 34 miles (55 Kilometers) north of Seoul that lies at the de facto border between N and S Korea. The truce that ended hostilities between the two countries was signed here in 1953, but as peace was never agreed to, the two sides are still officially at war (conflict) over 69 years later and a million men stand guard around the demilitarized zone (DMZ).

they found themselves compelled to propose ceasefire negotiations to the side of the Korean People's Army. On July 10, 1951, ceasefire negotiations started at Panmunjom near Kaesong.

Beginning July 11, 1951, the day after the opening of the ceasefire negotiations on August 20, a total of more than 10,000 US military planes including B-29s dropped 4,000 incendiary, and other bombs plus gasoline tanks over Pyongyang on more than 250 occasions. As a result, 4,000 innocent inhabitants were killed and more than 2,500 heavily wounded. Most of the cultural establishments including the Pyongyang Moranbong Theater and priceless historic relics such as Yongmyong Temple and Pubyok Pavilion were destroyed or burned down."

After the UN spring counteroffensive, which ended on July 8, 1951, negotiations began for an armistice. In September 1951, the UN forces launched a counteroffensive with the 24th ID at the center of the line; the Chinese attempted to counter this attack but were unsuccessful. It was at this point that both sides started serious truce negotiations, the UN forces settled down into a defensive line, and the front stabilized into trench warfare. The pace of the war now slowed, with small, localized actions replacing the earlier large-scale offensives. The Conflict became one of grinding, brutal fighting, as each side fought for a small advantage over the other. The conflict continued for more than two years, and military strongpoints were designated officially by their height in meters but known popularly by colorful or poignant nicknames bestowed by the Americans who fought over them — The Hook, Old Baldy, Pork Chop Hill, and Heartbreak Ridge. Along and to the north of the 38th Parallel, UN forces, S Koreans, Chinese, and N Koreans dug in to defend their positions. Across the entire peninsula, a system of trenches appeared. Tunnels and bunkers were built by engineers in the hillsides and sandbags were used to line the trench walls. Barbed wire was deployed in front of the defensive trenches and laced with tripwires that activated mines and set off phosphorus grenades that would reveal Chinese night attacks. Phosphorus is light in weight, which makes it suitable as a filling for hand grenades and provides illumination of terrain and targets. UN reconnaissance patrols went out nightly to counter night attacks. From the summer of 1951 until the ceasefire in 1953, the front became a fixed line just north of Seoul, crossing the peninsula just north of the 38th Parallel in very hilly terrain.

The 24th ID suffered over 10,000 casualties in 18 months of fighting. Upon returning to Japan, the 24th ID, with the 52nd Field Artillery, were stationed at Camp Younghans, near the small town of Jinmachi, Northern Honshu, located approximately 40 miles from the east coast of Japan. On July 1, 1953, secret orders alerted the 24th ID for immediate shipment to Korea. In mid-July of 1953, the entire division returned to Korea for a second time and took over the responsibility of guarding and repatriating thousands of Chinese Anti-Communist prisoners of war. In early February 1954, the division received orders to move north of the 38th Parallel to the position held by the 45th ID, which was returning to the US. The 24th ID continued to serve during the Cold War, the Gulf War, Operation Desert Shield 1990, and Desert Storm 1991, and was inactivated February 15, 1996, at Fort Riley, Kansas.

CHAPTER 11

US AIR FORCE STRATEGIC AIR COMMAND AND FAR EAST COMMAND

B-29 Superfortress Strategic Bomber

US Air Force General (Gen) Curtis R. Lemay was the head of the US Air Force Strategic Air Command (SAC) during the Korean conflict and carried out MacArthur's orders. It was the first major bombing campaign for the US Air Force since its inception in 1947 from the United States Army Air Forces. The USAF flew the B-29 Superfortress a four-engine, propeller-driven heavy bomber and took off from bases in Japan and Okinawa. The B-29 was conceived as a state-of-the-art, high-altitude strategic bomber. Despite the effort that went into developing the B-29's central fire control gun tracking system (12-.50 Caliber Browning remote-control machine gun turrets and one 20-millimeter cannon) the appearance of MiG fighters in the Korean skies signaled the end of the aging defense system. Though Superfortress gunners shot down 33 enemy aircraft, including 16 MiG 15s, gunners had trouble keeping up with the speed of the MiG. The B-29 had a maximum speed of 365 miles per hour at 31,850 feet. The Mikoyan Gurevich MiG-15 was a single-seat, single-engine aircraft built by the USSR and made its debut on November 30, 1950. The Soviet MiG-15 was specifically designed to shoot down the B-29 and would lead to limited daylight bombing missions. A Superfortress attacking an air base in N Korea was lightly damaged by a fighter that overtook the bomber too fast for the attacker to be identified, much less for the remote-control guns to fix it in the sights of the gun tracking system. The MiG had sufficient power to dive at supersonic speeds, but lack of a fully movable stabilizer "all-flying" tail (which serves the functions of stability, control and stick force) diminished the ability to control the aircraft. As a result, pilots understood they must not exceed Mach

0.92 or 700 miles-per-hour (mph). MiG pilots were able to open fire about 2000 feet away, avoiding being hit, and at that distance they could ravage a B-29 formation.

The Boeing B-29 Superfortress American Four-Engine Propeller-driven Heavy Bomber details are described in the introduction—specifically, Table 8.

The bomber was used in normal strategic day-bombings, although N Korea had few strategic targets and industries. Those of value were quickly reduced to rubble. While N Korea's industry may have been broken, the country coped because most of its supplies came from China and Russian territories that were off limits to US aircraft. The role of the USAF can be broken down into four distinct phases. The first few months of the conflict, phase one, were largely characterized by the destruction of vital facilities in N Korea's major cities. Gen. Lemay used his leadership and expertise drawn from the fire-bombing campaign of Tokyo in World War II. On July 31, 1950, SAC and the US Air Force Far East Command (USAFEC) initiated a systematic strategic bombing campaign against N Korea. It called for UN forces to use incendiary bombs, destroying five major N Korean cities: Kaesong, (Kaesong was the ancient capital of Korea (918-1392), Pyongyang, Wonsan, Chongjin, and the port city of Rashin, located only 17 miles from the Russian border. It was believed such damage would have a psychological impact on the population, which in turn would destroy the nation's morale and resistance.

The second phase, which started in the fall 1950, involved close support to ground forces being attacked by Chinese and N Korean forces along with daytime raids. Unable to stop these types of raids, the N Koreans appealed to China and Russia. In September 1950, the USAF conducted a massive daytime raid on the N Korean town of Sinuiju. The raid, conducted by eighty B-29 heavy bombers, resulted in the greatest loss of life since the American atomic bombing of Nagasaki. The entire town, which was built from bamboo and wood, burned to the ground. More than 30,000 innocent civilians, including old people and children, were burned alive. At the end of October 1952, the B-29s crushed N Korea's industry. Using conventional bombs resulted in delaying the southward advance of the Chinese 4th Field Army, giving the 8th Army time to prepare defensives. UN bombers and fighter-bombers continued the interdiction campaign Operation Strangle, which the USAFEC had begun on August 15, 1951, against railroad tracks, bridges, and highway traffic.

In the third phase, carried out in late fall early winter 1951/52, the US started bombing bridges, railroads, and other lines of communication such as long-distance tactical communication sites and communication relay centers.

The fourth phase, at the beginning of 1952, US aircraft targeted N Korea's means of producing electricity. The war's highest-ranking US POW, MG William F. Dean, Sr. reported that most N Korean cities and villages he saw were either rubble or snow-covered wasteland. Dean was interviewed by William L. Worden (Viking Press 1954). He was forthcoming about what he saw.

China's entry into the war also led to a drastic change in the precision-bombing policy. On November 5, 1950, when the UN forces began suffering defeat after defeat in battles with the new enemy, MacArthur designated cities and villages in N Korea as "main bombing targets" and permitted the use of incendiary bombs, which had been used in attacks against Japanese cities during World War II. The USAF regarded N Korean cities and villages as their crucial targets as political and military occasions demanded. The US burned down just about every city in N Korea and S Korea. The commanding general of the 5th Air Force, Lieutenant General (Lt Gen) E. George Stratemeyer, ordered all aircraft under 5th Air Force control to destroy all targets, including all buildings capable of affording shelter. That same day, 22 B-29s attacked Kanggye and destroyed 75 percent of the city. "Air supremacy over Korea was quickly established." – Lt Gen E. George Stratemeyer, Far East Air Forces Commander during the first year of war. National Museum of the United States Air Force Teacher Resource Guide.

The MiG-15 with its three cannons, 700 mph speed, exceptional altitude capability, plus being flown by Russia's finest, delivered the final blow to the aging B-29 fleet. The MiGs with their cannons became the B-29s worst nightmare. Toward the end of the conflict (1953), B-29s were taken out of combat. The bombers were used as intelligence, reconnaissance, weather, and rescue aircraft. The B-29 "spook" aircraft were modified to carry electronic warfare-detection equipment. The B-29s used for reconnaissance and weather missions had their gun turrets removed. Lifeboats from the Sky B-29s, known as SB-29s, carried Edo A-3 lifeboats attached under the aircraft fuselage. SB-29s accompanied bomber formations to the coast of N Korea and circled there while the bombers hit targets inland.

If a returning bomber had to ditch in the ocean, a lifeboat could be dropped to save the crew. The boat could carry fifteen people. It was equipped with food and water for several days and had a small engine. The boat was self-righting, featured covers to keep out the sun, wind, and rain, and had a ladder for boarding. About 100 of these boats were made. Other B-29s were redesignated as Training TB-29, refueling/tanker KB-29, and Photo Reconnaissance (Recon) RB-29. On July 27, 1953, a Superfortress of the 91st Strategic Reconnaissance Squadron flew the last B-29 mission of the conflict. In the total Far East Air Forces Sorties, June 1950 – July 1953, 710,886 missions were flown. [43] The USAFEC lost 2,714 aircraft of several types including B-29 losses.

In late 1954, the B-29 was withdrawn from USAF service, except for some Photo Recon RB-29s.

When UN troops retreated from N Korea in 1950, the US Far East Air Force (FEAF) provided tactical interdiction. At sea, naval units of nine nations tightened their blockade of N Korea. Carrier-based planes blasted railroads, bridges, and boxcars; destroyers bombarded enemy gun emplacements and depots. In August 1950, the battleship USS *New Jersey* (BB-62) provided support for the UN forces ashore near Kan song, situated in Kang-Won-do, S Korea. The *New Jersey* for four days provided harassing fire by night and broke up counterattacks by day, inflicting a heavy toll on N Korean forces. In October and November, it went north up the coast, bombarding numerous cities and coastal targets with 16-inch guns almost in range of Siberia. The *New Jersey* fired three times more 16-inch shells in the first tour in Korea than were fired in World War II. The 16-inch guns could range 20 miles inland, outdistancing army artillery, demolishing targets that had survived air attacks. The *New Jersey's* 16-and-5-inch guns destroyed enemy bridges, tunnels, artillery positions, shore batteries, supply dumps, a dam, and an oil refinery. On November 13, the *New Jersey* completed its first tour of duty. She prepared and trained for a second tour and departed Norfolk, Virginia on March 5, 1953, and on April 12 arrived on station. On July 26, 1953, the *New Jersey* sailed for a mission at Wonson and then destroyed bunkers, caves, and trenches. Two days later, learning of the armistice ending the first Korean Conflict. S Korea's President Rhee came aboard to present the S Korean's Presidential Unit Citation to the 7th Fleet. On October 14 the *New Jersey* was homebound, arriving in Norfolk, Virginia November 15, 1953.

---

43   Source: USAF Operations Statistics Division.

The "strangulation" operations were to "strangle" the People's Army on the front by cutting the line of N Korea's logistics and reinforcements to the front near the 38th parallel. But their aim was not confined to this. They attempted to massacre the Korean people through "strangulation" operations. When the US imperialists came out with the "strangling" operations the bigwigs of the US Department of Defense described Korea as a test ground for the most effective use of their military force and arms and drove their men into a hecatomb in Korea, urging them to "kill as many people as possible."

The Moranbong Park in central Pyongyang contains several heritage structures built during dynastic Korea, such as Ulmil Pavilion, Chilsong Gate, and Pubyok Pavilion. These were destroyed by US carpet bombing during the conflict. Most have been reconstructed and are designated as national treasures.

(During the Koguryo period AD 39-668, a fortress and city wall were placed here for the defense of Pyongyang. The fortifications were the site of important battles and several wars in Korean history such as the Imjin War, and the first Sino-Korean War.)

"Besides, they dropped napalm, mine, explosive, time bombs and gasoline tanks day and night over Nampo, Raijin, Chongjin, Hamhung, Wonsan, Sinuiju and all the other towns and areas of N Korea including remote mountain areas to massacre peaceful inhabitants and demolish and burn indiscriminately dugouts, and other dwellings of the inhabitants and schools, hospitals and other establishments."

"But the US aggressors could not frighten the Korean people with any number of mass-destruction weapons and barbarous means or retrieve themselves from their successive defeats at the front."

"In 1953, with the armistice near at hand, the US air pirates undertook more vicious bombings against non-military objectives.

Beginning in the middle of May 1953, US planes bombed and destroyed the Sogam Reservoir in Sunan County, the Jamo Reservoir in Sunchon County, and many other reservoirs in N Korea. This was a beastly atrocity."

First Jet War over MiG Alley: Air-to-Air Combat MiG-15 versus F-86 Sabre

China's involvement inevitably drew Russian pilots, maintenance teams, anti-aircraft-artillery crews, medical personnel, and support troops into the conflict. While never openly admitting their role in the conflict, an estimated 72,000 Russian air force personnel served in China or N Korea at some point during the conflict. The history of these covert actions has been a long-buried secret. As early as April 1950, Joseph Stalin, leader of Russia, had no intention of entering the conflict in Korea. But as the American and Western armies under UN command threatened to overrun the entire peninsula, and seeing the quality and shortage of Chinese pilots, Stalin, in April 1951, made the decision to involve his air force in the conflict. Russian air force pilots flew under the markings of the Chinese People's Liberation Army Air Force (PLAAF) or North Korean Peoples' Army Air Force (KPAAF). Stalin died March 5, 1953, a few months before the end of the conflict.

"News of war on the Korean peninsula seemed like something very remote. Initially they reported that the Armed Forces of the People's Democratic Republic of Korea, having repulsed the invasion of the S Korean dictator Syngman Ree's army, had gone on the offensive and were successfully advancing southward.

There were reports that whole cities were burned by napalm bombs dropped from American bombers and that tens of thousands of civilians were dying." (Air Combat over the Eastern Front and Korea – A Soviet Pilot Remembers, Sergei Kramarenko)

Until 1950, no MiG-15 inceptor regiments were stationed in the Far East. In the spring of 1951, Russia sent in their latest MiG-15, flown by battle-hardened veterans of World War II.

The Russian pilots from the 64th Fighter Aviation Corps of 97th Fighter Aviation Division, 16th Fighter Aviation Regiment, and 148th Guards Fighter Aviation Regiment with combat experience were told the story about American atrocities in N Korea. They were informed the N Korean government had sent an urgent request to send fighter jets and volunteer pilots to save the N Korean people from annihilation. Russian pilots—along with anti-aircraft-artillery crews, and search light and radar teams—volunteered. In preparation, the MiG-15s were dismantled, including removal of the wings, and were loaded on flat railroad cars and covered with tarpaulins. The next morning, pilots and support personnel were loaded onto a train to China. While in transit, Chinese uniforms were provided with "Chinese People's Liberation Army" (PLA) symbols on the pockets. The pilots wore Chinese uniforms when flying, and the rules were prescribed to stop Russian pilots flying near the coast or front lines (where they might be captured if shot down) and from speaking Russian on the aircraft radio. The first rotation of Russian aviation units of the Corps had its red stars replaced by Korean People's Army Air Force roundels painted on the aircraft to identify them. On occasion, Russian aircraft were seen with a red star, usually conducting reconnaissance. Beginning in mid-September 1950 Russian pilots from two fighter divisions began their operations in the skies over N Korea.

On September 4, 1950, 11 days before the Inchon landings, four F4U-4B Corsairs (VF-53) from the USS *Valley Forge* (CV-45), over the Yellow Sea, southwest of the Soviet-occupied Port Arthur naval base in China and west coast of N Korea, came upon two A-20 twin-engine bombers displaying the red star. One Soviet aircraft had passed over a screening ship of a UN naval task force and opened fire on a UN fighter, which returned fire and shot it down. The remaining A-20 turned away and headed back to Port Arthur. The A-20s were part of the 36th Mine-Torpedo Aviation Regiment of the Red Pacific Banner Fleet on an armed reconnaissance mission when they were intercepted. (A-20 was a US-built twin-engine medium bomber provided to the Russians during World War II Lend-Lease.) The body of one crew member was recovered — he was an officer of the Armed Forces of the former Soviet Union. The *New York Times*, September 5, provided the US State Department a note announcing this incident. The note read: "A Soviet Air Force bomber was shot down off of the coast of N Korea by US Navy fighter planes, after reportedly firing at UN naval forces. All crew members on the downed aircraft killed were because of the incident while one bomber escaped." The recovered body was returned to the Russians in 1956. The Soviet bomber shot down was flying over the Korean Bay, and Moscow muted the incident to avoid committing Soviet forces to the fighting. The US was not inclined to press the issue, to avoid escalating tensions further. This reaction by the Soviet government is expanded in more detail in *Red Wings over the Yalu: China, the Soviet Union, and the Air War in Korea* by Xiaoming Ahang, published by Texas A & M University Press, 2003.

Near the end of October 1950, the Russian Air Force units, based in Northeast

China, trained Chinese airmen to fly the Mikoyan - Gurevich MiG-9, a first generation jet fighter and the first turbojet developed after the second world war, and MiG-15 jets were ordered by the Russian Ministry of Defense to conduct combat operations to defend airspace over both Northeast China and N Korea. The result was dramatic. The very first aerial battle between Russian and American planes over Korea happened on November 1, 1950.

The First Squadron of the Russian Seventy-2nd Guards Fighter Aviation Regiment launched from its base in Northeast China to meet incoming US planes south of the Yalu River with its MiG-15 jet fighters.

Thus, a new phase began that would last throughout the conflict. Russians shot down two Mustangs, while losing none of their MiGs. It was not long before the jets, guided by Russian ground-radar systems, began to shoot down US and allied bombers. The radar systems with Russian crews, in combination with the MiG-15, secured their advantage in MiG Alley. The MiG-15s were based in Antung, China across the Yalu River from the village of Sinuiju, located in Northwest N Korea. Everything changed on November 8 during a USAF attack on an airfield in Sinuiju; the MiG-15 joined the fight. A flight of four F-80 Shooting Stars from the 51st Fighter Wing raked Sinuiju, N Korea—on the Korean side of the border with China. Suddenly, 10 jet fighters streaking toward the US fighters crossed the Chinese border—MiGs were coming! This area became known as "MiG Alley."

Recently, through the publication of books by Russian and Chinese authors such as Sergei Kramarenko, Xiaoming Zhang, and Leonard Krylov, the extent of Russian participation became clear.

"American mastery of the Korean skies had come to an end" writes former fighter pilot Major General Sergei Kramarenko, retired 1981, in his book *Air Combat over the Eastern Front and Korea - A Soviet Pilot Remembers* (*The Red Air Force at War*). Details are described in the introduction, specifically, Table 9.

Sergei Kramarenko was a Russian fighter pilot, an ace, who fought in two wars—first against the Luftwaffe, then the US Air Force—and survived. On the Eastern Front in the bitter conflict with the Germans, he dueled with Messerschmitt 109s and Focke-Wulf 190s. Then, in Korea, flying a MiG-15, he came up against the

Americans, the British, and the Australians in the first fighter-against-fighter clashes of the jet age. He was the first "ace" of the jet era, shooting down 15 US and Australian jets. He was awarded the title of Hero of the Soviet Union (Russia) in 1951. [44] In over 10 years as a front-line fighter pilot, he took part in a revolution in the development of combat flying.

In mid-November, the first of several B-29 aircraft were shot down, and gradually, losses for the heavy bomber force began to rise, which was unsustainable. This forced the bombers to operate only at night if they could not obtain a jet fighter escort. The aircraft also incurred significant losses from N Korea's air defenses. Although more US bombers were lost once the MiGs entered the conflict, the losses never came close to those suffered during the war against Germany a few years earlier. Epic large-scale dogfights with UN aircraft unfolded in the skies over N Korea.

Most aerial combat was between Russian and American pilots, rather than Chinese or N Korean pilots in history's first jet war over MiG Alley. [45] Russians flying MiG-15s participated in battles around the Yalu River Valley on the Chinese-Korean border and in operations against UN "train busting" attacks in N Korea, with considerable success. Factors such as good training and superior technology would prove decisive. The MiG-15 could easily outpace, outfly, and outfight any US or British aircraft, including the innovative F-86 Sabre. The MiG was lighter than the F-86, which gave it superior lift and thrust. The MiG had a maximum effective speed of 700 miles per hour, and the F-86 maximum speed was 685 miles per hour. The USAF accelerated deployment of the F-86 Sabre jet fighter. It was the only fighter capable of taking up battle with the MiG-15. The MiG-15 and F-86 Sabre were post-war construction based on German research into arrow-shaped swept wings.

Adolf Busemann was a German aerospace engineer and influential Nazi-era pioneer in aerodynamics, specializing in supersonic airflows. He introduced the concept of swept wings.

The MiG enjoyed some performance advantages against early model F-86s, the improved F-86A entered combat in mid-December 1950, and quickly proved its worth. The 1950s Korean Conflict proved a breakthrough for jet-powered

---

44   *Korean War Aces,* by Robert F. Dorr published April 10, 1995, Elm Court, Chapel Way, Botley, Oxford, OX 9LP Osprey Publishing.
45   The Russians in MiG Alley-Air Force Magazine.
      http://www.airforce.com/MagazineArchive/Pages/1991/February%25201991/Russians.aspx.

combat aircraft, which provided a driving force for both development in technical and construction as well as tactics.

Russian pilots, though forbidden from communicating in any language other than basic Mandarin or Korean across their radios, often resorted to Russian when stressed or when swearing. This was picked up by American pilots. The first all-jet war during the conflict in Korea saw F-86 Sabres of the USAF take on MiG-15s of the Russian, Chinese, and N Korean air forces. Although the allied pilots were initially taken back by the ability of the communist fighters in combat, sound training and skillful leadership soon enabled Saber pilots to minimize the dogfight losses over the Yalu River. In the summer of 1951, the upgraded MiG-15bis began to arrive with a more powerful engine, a hydraulic aileron booster, and reinforced pneumatic brakes. These modifications dramatically improved the thrust-to-weight ratio, climb rate, and maneuverability. The Sabre had one advantage: it was heavier than a MiG, and for this reason it could dive faster, which provided for a fast dive when engaging the MiG. Overall, the Sabre and the MiG-15bis were relatively equal in a dogfight.

"The MiG-15bis was significantly superior to the American planes."

"We were not allowed to fly over the sea although the MiG-15s and pilots were indeed Soviet, the Soviet Union officially had no part in the war.

"The Soviet diplomats categorically denied the participation of Soviet airmen in the Korean War, and it worked. The Americans did not publicly declare that Russians were fighting in Korea. For this reason, we had been banned categorically not only from flying over the sea but from approaching the front line as well."

"Therefore, almost all aerial engagements took place over North Korean territory."

From November 1951 to the armistice, the communist air forces maintained between three and four Chinese air divisions, along with two Russian divisions and one N Korean air division, totaling 350 to 400 MiG-15s at the airfields on China's side of the Yalu River.

"The N Korean and Chinese pilots fought along with Soviet pilots against American planes. In the summer of 1951, the United Aerial Army (UAA)

comprising N Korean and Chinese units was formed. By the end of the conflict the UAA numbered seven air divisions which had nearly 900 planes, including 635 MiG-15s and MiG-15bis planes. UAA pilots claimed 271 victories, losing 231 planes and 126 pilots." (Air Combat over the Eastern Front and Korea by Sergei Kramarenko.)

Throughout the conflict, American and UN aircraft were restricted by the fact they could not operate north of the Yalu River. Leaders and commanders of UN forces would not risk a full-scale conflict with China, which could have been the consequence of territorial incursions.

This gave the North the advantage of being able to operate from bases in China without risk of escalating the fighting. Eventually, US leaders overlooked this, allowing some pilots and groups to cross the border and attack aircraft on both take-off and landing. The Russian and Chinese roles in 1950-1953 were kept quiet to prevent widening the Conflict. Russia supplied hundreds of MiG-15s to the air forces of N Korea and China. At peak strength, the communist forces had more than 900 MiGs in the theater. The USAF never had more than 150 Sabres there.

There were 52 Russian MiG-15 pilots, each downing five or more UN/USAF aircraft in air-to-air combat, and for these achievements they are regarded as the MiG-15 aces of the conflict. Pilots of the USAF were heavily outnumbered and flew an airplane that in many ways was inferior to the MiGs by their adversaries. However, US pilots built up an impressive combat record. In all, 39 F-86 pilots achieved ace status, and pilots were from the US Navy, Marine Corps, and Royal Navy. The US pilots are regarded as aces for many of the same reasons as their opponents. The Russian Air Force participation in the conflict began on November 15, 1950 and ended in December 1954. USSR involvement remained a secret until well after the end of the Cold War.

Soviet Operation to Steal USAF F-86 Sabre

The Russian MiG-15 and the USAF F-86 Sabre were in fact nearly evenly matched. Both sides wanted to capture and have their engineers evaluate these new aircraft. Russian engineers had their first opportunity in October 1951, when a USAF F-86 Sabre was shot down near the Yellow Sea and captured nearly intact. On October 23, 1951, a Russian pilot pursued a USAF F-86 Sabre, which had been operating in MiG alley. The pilot knew the Russians wanted the plane, and he made a desperate move to ditch it in the water.

The damaged aircraft made it to the coast but fell short of the Yellow Sea. The pilot crash landed the plane onto the beach. He was rescued, but attempts to destroy the plane failed because it was stuck in mud pools formed on the beach.

Overhead, a battle raged as MiGs fought to claim their prize while Sabres tried to fight them off. Then the tide started coming in. Hundreds of Chinese and N Koreans scrambled to disassemble the Sabre, beginning with its wings, before the sea swallowed it completely. Despite losing seven MiGs, the Russians got their prize and carted the pieces back to Russia in a convoy of trucks that traveled at night to avoid being located. Upon entering China, the convoy was attacked. The lead truck was fired upon but not hit. Along with the USAF F-86 Sabre taken to the USSR, a second aircraft may have been captured. During a 1990s period of cooperation with the US, the Russians admitted that other planes and prizes, such as US G-suits and radar gunsights, were also seized.

The Russians were experts at "reverse-engineering" — in other words, stealing and copying technology. Their Tupolev (Tu-4) strategic bomber that served the USSR Air Force from the late 1940s to mid-1960s was based on American B-29 Superfortress bombers obtained in World War II and was nearly a total replica. The MiG-15's engine was a British design.

Operation *Moolah* – MiG-15bis "Red 2057"

In the final weeks of the conflict, the US offered $100,000 cash and US citizenship to any Chinese, Russian, or N Korean pilot who landed a MiG-15bis intact at Kimpo Air Force Base. This action became known as Operation Moolah. Beginning in April 1953, a public relations blitz geared at enemy pilots was broadcast into N Korea from Japan by radio announcing the cash. There were mass leaflet drops on Chinese and N Korean air bases up and down the Yalu River.

The results were disappointing; not a single communist flier from the North had defected by the end of the conflict. However, the US got a technically advanced

MiG-15bis, upgraded variant of the MiG-15bis when a N Korean pilot defected with his jet, landing near Seoul. The upgraded MiG had the improved version of the RD-45 (imported British Rolls Royce Nene) turbojet engine and had better ground attack capability.

Early in the morning on September 21, 1953, Senior Lieutenant (Sr. Lt.) No Kum-Sok flew a MiG-15bis, number "Red 2057"; ("bis" is Russian for "revised"); of the 2nd Regiment, Korean People's Air Force, from Sunan Air Force Base, just outside Pyongyang, N Korea, and landed before 1000 hours (10:00 a.m.) at Kimpo Air Force Base (K-14) in S Korea. US ground personnel airmen hustled the MiG-15bis into a base hangar to protect it from prying eyes. The aircraft was disassembled the same day, loaded onto a C-124A Globemaster, and shipped off the next day to Kadena Air Base on Okinawa. Sr. Lt. No Kum-Sok, 21 years old, was unaware of Operation Moolah when he defected. When he learned of the $100,000 reward offered in the leaflet, he claimed it. He immigrated to the US, learned English, and became a US citizen. He took the name Kenneth Rowe. His boyhood dream to become an American citizen was realized. Then, from the University of Delaware, he earned degrees in mechanical and electrical engineering. He married an émigré from Kaesong, Korea. They raised two sons and a daughter. The sons graduated from college as engineers and the daughter as a lawyer.

After working for Boeing, General Dynamics, and Lockheed and in several defense-related industries, he ultimately retired as professor of aeronautical engineering from Embry-Riddle Aeronautical University in Daytona Beach, Florida.

During November 1957, the MiG-15bis was transferred to the US Air Force Museum, Dayton, Ohio, for public exhibition. The $100,000 check dated April 27, 1954, given to No Kim-Sok is also displayed at the museum, with his signature on the back.

The Defense Department POW/MIA Accounting Agency reports the USAF lost 4055 men killed, including missing combined, along with 306 wounded during the conflict. Thirty airmen who had been declared missing were eventually returned, along with 214 prisoners of war repatriated under the terms of the armistice agreement. The DPAA research identified potential locations of air losses during the 1950s Korean Conflict based on analysis of available records. Locations identified may represent documented crash sites, the last sighting of the aircraft before it went missing, or the last known radio/radar contact. Korean War Air Losses Updated_1.pdf (dpaa.mil).

CHAPTER 12

WAR CRIMES: ATROCITIES

The Pentagon turned the Strategic Air Command (SAC) loose with incendiaries on N Korea. The USAF SAC was authorized to bomb urban and rural N Korea and carried out its assignment brutally, burning out cities and breaking big agricultural dams, scouring out entire valleys of peasant villages and rice paddies. General Curtis E. LeMay said, "We went over there and fought the war and eventually burned down every town in N Korea, some way or another, and some in S Korea, too." The firebombing killed over a million civilian Koreans and drove several million more from their homes. It is estimated that the firebombing campaign killed 20 percent of the population. [46] [47]

"The UN Forces and the Syngman Rhee puppet army were completely driven out of the region of the northern half of Korea by December 24, 1950. In the half-a-year-long war, the US aggressors suffered huge losses militarily plus a serious politico-moral defeat. The myth about the mightiness of US imperialism was shattered to pieces and its prestige fell to the ground. Upon fleeing from Seoul in January 1951 the air pirates of US imperialism dropped 500,000 gallons of gasoline and petroleum and 23,000 gallons of napalm over Kimpo, reducing the Kimpo aerodrome and its surroundings into a barren land in a flash.

"In the latter half of January, they sprayed 8,000 gallons of napalm over wide areas with 26 villages northwest of Suwon. The two-legged beasts fired 247,000 heavy machine gun bullets into the sea of flames.

---

46   https://warisboring.com/the-korean-wars-brutality-turned-the-stomachs-of-americas-most-hardened soldiers/
47   https://www.atomicheritage.org/profile/curtis-lemay

"The UN Command 'scorched-earth' operation of burning and destroying every town and village conducted by the US Air Force while its reeling background force defied human imagination in bestiality. The Korean people and the beautiful land of 3,000 ri meant nothing to them. They were keen only to take every life and blow away everything to attain their ambition in the war. In this sense their 'scorched-earth' operation might have served for their 'Korea obliteration policy.'"

3000 ri roughly corresponds to 745 miles, the approximate latitude, north-south, span of the Korean peninsula.

"The words 'ghastly behavior' and 'moral defeat by communists,' of course, fail to condemn all that was done by the monstrous 'scorched-earth' operation of the US army.

"Yet these fragmentary reports might serve as evidence telling the world how shamefully the US troops were behaving in Korea."

The Sunchon Tunnel Massacre

In October of 1950, at Pyongyang, when the fall of that city appeared imminent, the communists loaded approximately 180 American war prisoners into open railroad cars for transport northward. These men were survivors of the Seoul-Pyongyang death march and were weak from lack of food, water, and medical care. They rode unprotected in the raw climate for 4 or 5 days, arriving at the Sunchon tunnel on October 30, 1950. Late in the afternoon, the prisoners were taken from the railroad cars in alternate groups of approximately 40 to nearby ravines, ostensibly to receive their first food in several days. There they were ruthlessly shot by N Korean soldiers, using Russian PPsH-41 submachine guns. (Soviet submachine gun chambered in 7.62×25mm and was best known for its distinctive sound produced by the high rate of fire led UN forces to dub it "the burp gun" with the 71-round drum magazine.) One hundred and thirty-eight American soldiers lost their lives in this atrocity; 68 were murdered at the tunnel, 7 died of malnutrition while in the tunnel, and the remainder died of pneumonia, dysentery, and malnutrition on the horror trip from Pyongyang. Private First-Class John E. Martin, formerly with the Twenty-9th (RCT), and one of the survivors of the Sunchon Tunnel Massacre, testified before the US congressional subcommittee on the atrocities and provided a detailed description of what happened. Private Martin's testimony was fully corroborated by Army Major General Frank A. Allen, Jr., who was assistant division commander (ADC) of the 1CD, and in command of the troops who discovered the bodies and survivors at Sunchon tunnel. Other massacres which occurred during the 1950s Korean Conflict: The Chaplin-Medic Massacre, July 17, 1950; Waegwan Execution, August 17, 1950; Taejeon Massacre, September 27, 1950; the Naedae Murders, October 13, 1950; the Bamboo Spear Case, December 1950, and the Treatment in Prison Camps. The Communist government in China is equally responsible and guilty as the communist government in Korea for war atrocities committed against Americans. Virtually every provision of the Geneva Convention governing the treatment of war prisoners was purposely violated or ignored by the N Korean and Chinese forces.

Subcommittee on Korean War Atrocities Charles E. Potter, Michigan, and Chairman published a record of hearings on 1950s Korean Conflict (War) Atrocities conducted by this subcommittee on December 2-4, 1953. The 83rd US Congress, Senate, 2nd Session Report Number 848, January 7, 1954, ordered the report to be printed January 11, 1954, with illustrations. The testimony revealed that more than 1800 cases involving many thousands of victims of communist war atrocities have been opened by the War Crimes Division in Korea. Army LTC Jack R. Todd, Chief of the War Crimes Division, testified the most accurate estimate of American troops who died because of war crimes was 5639 as of November 1953. Furthermore, the American fatalities figure does not represent the total number of American victims of atrocities, because many victims survived and were either repatriated or in some other manner found their way back to the lines. The conservative estimate of probable American victims as of June 1953 was 6113. [48]

In 1948, the United Nations General Assembly first recognized the need for a permanent international court to deal with atrocities of the kind prosecuted after the World War II.

"Scorched-Earth" Operation

At the request of the General Assembly, the International Law Commission (ILC) drafted two statutes by the early 1950s, but these were shelved during the Cold

---

48   Complete report details: https://www.loc.gov/rr/rfd/Military_Law/pdf.

War, which made the establishment of an international criminal court politically unrealistic. It is very unlikely that any Chinese or N Koreans will ever find themselves at The Hague, the location of the International Criminal Court located in the Netherlands, capital of the province of South Holland, or even named in an indictment. [49] The US shares responsibility for atrocities under the "scorched-earth" operation, using incendiary bombs ordered by MacArthur and carried out by US Air Force General Curtis E. LeMay. The firebombing killed over a million civilian Koreans.

During World War II, LeMay commanded the 21st Bomber Command and planned and originated the low-altitude incendiary-bombing tactics in Japan. His flyers piloted hundreds of B-29 Superfortress bombers at low altitude and dropped phosphorus, napalm, and magnesium bombs that burned out parts of Tokyo and several other Japanese cities, and millions died. It was a maximum-effort fire-bombing campaign to force the Japanese to surrender.

LeMay's attitude toward firebombing is documented in the 2003 documentary *The Fog of War*.

> "Killing Japanese didn't bother me very much at that time," LeMay admitted later. "I suppose if I had lost the war, I would have been tried as a war criminal." Reported by Robert S. McNamara in the 2003 documentary *The Fog of War*. As a lieutenant colonel, McNamara served under LeMay.

In turn, the N Koreans and Chinese committed atrocities against American POWs. On September 27, 1950, 60 American prisoners, who had been confined in Taejon prison, were taken into the prison yard in groups with their hands wired together. They were forced to sit hunched in hastily dug ditches and then were shot by N Korean troops at point-blank range, with their own M-1 rifles, using armor-piercing ammunition. In late December 1950 five American airmen in a truck convoy were ambushed by N Korean forces. Their bodies, discovered shortly after by a S Korean patrol, showed that the flesh had been punctured in as many as twenty different areas with heated, sharpened bamboo sticks. The torture was so fiendish that no one perforation was sufficient to cause death by itself. These examples illustrate the brutality of war by both the communist and American forces. [50]

---

49   UN Department of Public Information, December 2002. The International Criminal Court.
      https://en.wikipedia.org/wk/inyernational_Criminal_Court

50   https://www.b-29s-over-kprea.com/index.html#POWatrocities

First reports of war crimes committed by the N Korean armies during the conflict against captured UN military personnel began to filter into General Headquarters, United Nations Command, early in July of 1950. When the facts were disclosed, General MacArthur set up the process for the investigation of war crimes committed by the communists.

CHAPTER 13

GENERAL OF THE ARMY DOUGLAS MACARTHUR, SUPREME COMMANDER OF UN FORCES, RELIEVED

When the Chinese offensive stalled just south of the 38th Parallel in the spring of 1951, President Harry S. Truman began to work on a peace proposal. This would have re-established the original border, the 38th Parallel, between North and South Korea and removed all foreign troops from both countries. General Douglas MacArthur did not think a ceasefire was an appropriate solution. MacArthur had argued for expanding the conflict to China despite President Truman ruling out this action. In perhaps the most famous civilian-military confrontation in the history of the United States, President Truman relieved Douglas General MacArthur of command of the UN Forces in Korea. The removal of MacArthur on April 11, 1951, set off a brief uproar among the American public, but Truman remained committed to keeping the 1950s Korean Conflict a "limited war." Though the concept of a "limited war," as opposed to the traditional American policy of unconditional victory, was new and initially unsettling to many Americans, the idea came to define the US Cold War military strategy. On Tuesday afternoon, April 10, Paul Nitze, Director of the Policy Planning Staff of the State Department and his associate, Charles Burton Marshall, met with President Truman in his office. Also present was Mr. Joseph Short, Presidential Press Secretary, who was directed to prepare a news release announcing the removal. The Chairman of the Joint Chiefs of Staff, General Omar Bradley, subsequently assisted in the preparation of this announcement. President Truman drafted an order which was issued under General Bradley's signature [51] and was sent through ordinary Army channels to General Douglas MacArthur.

It read, "I deeply regret that it has becomes my duty as President and Commander-in-Chief of the United States Military forces to replace you as Supreme Commander, Allied Powers; Commander-in-Chief, United Nations Command; Commander-in-Chief, Far East; and Commanding General, US Army, Far East." Lieutenant General (LTG) Matthew B. Ridgway, then commander of the 8th Army, was named to replace him, and on April 11, 1951, Army General James A. Van Fleet took command of the 8th Army and UN Forces. On May 11, 1951, Ridgeway was promoted to full general, assuming command of all UN Forces in Korea.

MacArthur turned over his duties to LTG Ridgway and returned to Japan. General MacArthur left Tokyo on April 17, 1951 and landed in San Francisco. On April 19, General MacArthur, after fifty-two years of service, gave his farewell speech before the joint session of the US Congress closing with a quotation from an old Army ballad: "Old soldiers never die, they just fade away." In the end MacArthur did not question the right of the president to remove him or any other military officer. Shortly afterward, a joint senate committee was established to investigate the reasons for MacArthur's dismissal, and details of the general's star began to fall. Ten years later, in 1962, at age 82, MacArthur gave his last speech to the Corps of Cadets at West Point. Two years later, MacArthur died of liver failure.

A transcript of General MacArthur's address to Congress is available at the Harry S. Truman Library & Museum, Independence, MO 64050.

"Limited War" – US Cold War Military Strategy

President Truman believed that every effort must be tried to limit the Conflict to the peninsula. Truman's policy was for vital reasons: to make sure that the precious lives of our fighting men were not wasted, to see that the security of

---

51 President Truman fired him for making public statements that contradicted the official policies. of the United States Government. In a statement explaining this action, President Truman said, "It is fundamental...that military commanders must be governed by the policies and directives issued to them in the manner prescribed by our laws and Constitution. In times of crisis this consideration is particularly compelling." National Archives. Rechttps:// web.archive.org/web/201006131845432 http://digitalvaults.org/record/3392. Htmlords Center (St. Louis, Missouri), Records of the Army Staff.

our country and the free world was not needlessly jeopardized, and to prevent a third world war. Several events made it evident that General MacArthur did not agree with the policy. A few days later, MacArthur announced his own terms for ending the fighting. MacArthur ignored Truman's December 1950 directive requiring all military officers and diplomatic officials to clear with the State Department all but routine statements before making them public, and refrain from direct communications on military or foreign policy with public media. In a public statement, without getting any clearance to do so, he taunted the Chinese for failing to conquer S Korea. General MacArthur went on to threaten to attack China unless the Chinese gave up the fight. MacArthur's announcement was an ultimatum to China.

It completely torpedoed Truman's diplomatic efforts to negotiate a ceasefire. Truman was stunned. "By this act," he later wrote, "I could no longer tolerate his insubordination." The US Constitution makes the president the commander in chief of the military. Civilians head the US Department of Defense and the individual service branches.

The intercepting and decrypting diplomatic messages of friend and foe alike was a closely held secret in the 1950s. In March 1951, Truman learned the US Army Security Agency, Arlington Hall Station in Virginia, intercepted and decrypted several telegrams that MacArthur wrote to foreign ambassadors spelling out his intention to have complete victory in Korea. He wanted to bomb industrial sites and other strategic targets within China and wanted to bring Nationalist Chinese troops lead by President of the Republic of China Chiang Kai-shek from (Taipei) to fight in Korea. Finally, he wanted the Nationalists to invade weak positions on the Communist Chinese mainland. Chiang Kai-Shek assumed leadership of China. The content of these intercepts was known by only a very few of Truman's closest advisers, two being Paul Nitze, and his associate, Charles Burton Marshall. Truman considered General MacArthur's conversations to be outright treachery and concluded that he had to be relieved but was unable to act immediately because of MacArthur's political support and to avoid wider knowledge of the existence of the electronic intercepts of diplomatic messages.

Provoking China

In early April 1951, the Joint Chiefs of Staff drafted orders for General MacArthur, authorizing nuclear attacks on Manchuria and the Shantung Peninsula if the Chinese launched airstrikes from there against UN forces. On April 11, 1951, the destroyer USS *John A. Bole* (DD-755) approached the Communist China mainland and maintained a position just outside the three-mile limit near China's sensitive port city of Swatow (Shantou). The *Bole* began provoking the Chinese to surround it. The crew manned battle stations for nearly six hours as numerous armed motorized vessels approached from the port and in a threatening manner surrounded the destroyer. Two hours later, a reconnaissance/show-of-force patrol consisting of several US Navy aircraft from Task Force 77 with the carriers USS *Boxer* (CV-21) and USS *Philippine Sea* (CV-47) arrived and made threatening passes at the Chinese vessels and the port city of Swatow for a period of two hours.

The *Boxer* and *Philippine Sea* launched 63 sorties, including photo reconnaissance. Midway during the period on April 11, when the aircraft were on the scene, it was announced to the world that General Douglas MacArthur had been relieved of his commands.

An hour after the aircraft departed, the *Bole* departed to the east, carefully avoiding contact with the surrounding vessels without hostile action being initiated by the Chinese vessels or the *Bole*.

On March 29, 1952, Truman announced that he would not run for re-election. In January 1953, Truman retired to Independence, Missouri, where he wrote his memoirs and from time to time spoke out on public issues. He died on December 26, 1972, at the age of 88, in Kansas City.

As Paul Nitze stated in his memoirs, "It was clear that General MacArthur was headed in a most dangerous direction." Although President Truman, Secretary of State Dean Acheson, and Paul Nitze had learned from intercepts of diplomatic messages what MacArthur's intentions were, they, as do historians today, remained unaware of how General MacArthur intended to achieve his goals. The intercepted diplomatic messages remain classified to this day. [52]

---

52   Sources: *Department of State Bulletin*, 16 April 1951-
     https://historyhub.history.gov/thread/8056; Office of Joint History of the Chairman of the Joint Chiefs of Staff, Washington DC - 1998 National Policy Volume III 1950-1951 The Korean War Part One James F. Schnabel and Robert J. Watson; Action Report for the period 15 March through 30 May 1951, Commanding Officer, I.E. Hobbs USS *Philippine Sea* (CV-47). Action report declassified, June 16,1963, and "Harry S. Truman to Omar Bradley, with attachments." Harry S, Truman Library and Museum 6 December 1950. Retrieved November 1, 2021.

CHAPTER 14

1950S KOREAN CONFLICT: GROUND, SEA, AND AIR COMBAT

The US Congress directed the National Guard to have an opportunity to serve in combat. The 24th Infantry Division was replaced by the 40th Infantry Division 1952–1953. The 40th ID "Fighting 40th" was a California Army National Guard unit activated on July 25, 1950, after receiving deployment orders. The division consisted of the 160th IR and the newly organized 223rd and 224th IRs. On August 10, 1950, the division was placed into federal service and moved to its new home, the abandoned Camp Cooke, Santa Maria, California, to conduct advanced combat training. Basic and advanced training continued through the fall and winter until March 29, 1951, when the division's main body departed California for the Japanese island of Honshu.

The 40th ID trained there for months while senior Army commanders debated deploying the division in Korea as a unit or as individual replacements. Three days before Christmas the division was alerted for deployment, with the advance party leaving on December 26, 1951. The 40th ID was to relieve the battle-hardened 24th ID, which had been there since the day that the ill-fated TF Smith landed on the peninsula in 1950. Eventually, in January 1952 the first troops departed from Yokohama, Japan aboard US Navy troop ships bound for Pusan. The soldiers were told how cold it would be and many struggled into long johns (thermal underwear), olive drab (wool) shirts, and two pairs of fatigue pants, field jacket, and gloves with liners. When troop ships arrived in Korea, the temperature hovered around five degrees below zero. There was little left of Inchon as the troops loaded their gear into railroad boxcars and climbed into little Korean rickety and battered third-class coach cars. It was incredibly cold, with icy wind cutting through clothing, especially for those from warm states back home. Later, fur-lined parkas and "sno pak" overshoes plus fur-lined gloves with a trigger finger were issued. Many soldiers would recall this period in Korea as the coldest time of their lives.

In February 1952, the division relieved the 24th ID in place, assuming control of its positions and equipment. Arriving troops were immediately put into the front lines, and on January 13, 1952, officially launched its first action. The foreign smells were unforgettable. The smell of human excrement was mixed with the pungent odors of kimchi, the spicy dish made from pickled cabbage, peppers, and garlic that is unique to Korea. The landscape was barren; trees had been stripped by artillery, or by villagers for fuel.

By 1952, the Conflict had evolved into static defensive combat of trench and bunker warfare and small unit patrolling. The 40th ID fought mostly in platoon and company actions in the Kumsong and Kumwha Valley sectors. Though relatively minor compared to earlier battles in Korea, these small unit actions were often violent and intense. By April 1953, the 40th ID fought at the northern edge of the Punchbowl sector.

The battle was one of the last battles of the movement phase of the conflict. Later, the 40th ID replaced the 45th ID positioned in the Heartbreak Ridge Hill 931 and Sandbag Castle area of operation.

The last significant combat action occurred on July 27, just prior to the armistice going into effect. The enemy shelled the division positions for four hours with an estimated 4700 rounds of mortar and artillery. There were few casualties and only slight damage. Division artillery responded with approximately 11,000 rounds of artillery and mortar fire. The ceasefire went into effect that day, and the 40th ID prepared to withdraw to the Post Armistice Main Battle Position.

On May 8, 1954, the final review of the 40th ID in Korea was conducted. Distinguished guests included President Syngman Rhee, who awarded the division the Republic of Korea Presidential Unit Citation. General Maxwell D. Taylor, Commanding General of the 8th Army, thanked the division for their accomplishments. The 40th ID remained in Korea until late May 1954 and was returned to state control on June 30, 1954. The division's battle flags were officially returned to the US, and the next day the City of San Francisco hosted a welcome home ceremony and parade. The parade marshal was Army Major General William F. Dean Sr., who earned the Medal of Honor, was the Deputy Commanding General of the 6th United States Army at the Presidio of San Francisco in California at the time he participated in the parade.

Personal stories recall the good times and the not so good times, the laughs and the misery, the struggles, and the accomplishments. These firsthand accounts follow veterans from their hometown, through basic and advanced individual training, and combat. The realities of war are told from their personal views. First-person accounts offer the best perspective.

Private First-Class Samuel F. Masessa. Interviewed by William R. Graser, on November 11, 2010, and in a follow-up interview in January 2013, and November 2021. Masessa, now 90, spoke with the author in 2021, and said, "I am proud of Scott Masessa, my grandson, presently serving in S Korea as an Army medic.

"My father immigrated to the US by way of Ellis Island, NY, from Naples, Italy. I was the youngest of three siblings. During World War II, my older brother became a US Navy Seabee and served in the Pacific Theater, and my other brother landed in Normandy on D-Day June 6, 1944, at the age of 18. Each survived World War II and returned home and began a family.

"I was a native of Lawrence, Massachusetts, and was playing professional baseball in Orlando, Florida, when I received my greetings. I was drafted at age eighteen-and-half, at the beginning of 1952 and began basic and specialized training at Fort Indiantown Gap, Pennsylvania."

Additionally, Pfc Masessa learned how to operate machine guns, mortars, flamethrowers, grenade-launchers, anti-tank weapons, and other portable crew-served weapons used in a heavy weapons unit.

"During this training, I became a friend of a Greek fellow named John Mavronkis, who spoke extraordinarily little English. I helped him get through the ups and downs of the training, and we became buddies.

"After the weeks of training were completed, we shipped out of Seattle, Washington. I still remember the name of the ship, the *Ballou*. It is funny the things you remember. What was not funny was my constant seasickness. I was sick the whole trip, and on top of it they put me on kitchen patrol (KP)."

In-Country

"We were assigned to different units going to Korea and I arrived in mid-1952. After processing at the replacement depot near Seoul, I was assigned to Echo Company (Heavy Weapons), 1st Battalion, 223rd Infantry Regiment, 40th Infantry Division.

During the winter of 1952, the division participated in defensive and offensive operations. The weather was extremely cold, and men tried to keep warm by burning whatever they could find. The air temperature was as cold as 35 degrees below zero, made even more intense by a strong north wind. The cold became the enemy, and it was exceedingly difficult living outdoors for any serious length of time. The elements can quickly become problematic. Extreme frostbite was a real concern; wet socks would freeze and then your feet.

"I hesitated to expose my bare body to the elements, even to cope with bodily functions. Despite cold-weather clothing and insulated boots, the chill of the winter night could numb the senses. Usually, I stood the nighttime watch in a fighting hole for 30 to 45 minutes before warming myself in a nearby bunker.

"I was never that cold in all my life. It is a damp cold, and I had these nylon-type pants, so every time I walked there was a *swish, swish*. We weren't dressed for patrols because the fabric made noise when it rubbed together."

Once Masessa was sitting in the trench and suddenly, the American tanks that had dug in just behind his position opened fire. "We had to return fire; it got hairy sometimes," he said.

"I was left partially deaf from the sound of the main gun firing at Chinese positions. My ears were ringing when the Chinese attacked, bugles blaring, some without weapons, waiting to pick up rifles dropped by their fallen comrades. They were wearing quilted uniforms, like mover's blankets back home, tan in color, and were carrying rice, indicating they intended to stay when they captured our positions. Some had mortar rounds strapped to their legs. Their attack came in waves led by shock platoons with submachine guns. It seemed they were fanatical; in fact, some were convinced the Chinese were high on something. The tanks played a key role in breaking up the assault, and they proved deadly against the Chinese troops. My hearing came back, and the experience was very scary. When the attack ended, Chinese dead lay littering the ground. We searched the dead and collected documents and removed their automatic weapons and machine guns, ammunition, and rations. They did not wear underwear, which surprised me and my buddies. I went with other GIs from the 'heavy weapons platoon' and picked up flamethrowers. Just a few yards from the perimeter, many of the dead were piled upon each other, and we used the flamethrower to burn the bodies to prevent disease and eliminate the smell."

Masessa's first battle was in the Chorwon Valley. "They had trenches already dug," he said. "It was foggy. We could hear the enemy close by." He and others had to go through a minefield to get information about the positions of the N Koreans. "It was scary," he said. "The minefields were what we were most worried about." What was going through Masessa's head? "Survival," he said.

He continued, "We had cold food, cold feet, cold everything," Masessa said. "You needed boots so you wouldn't get frostbite." Rats were regular companions in the bunkers. "You would hear them go by, but you hated to shoot them because it would alert the enemy.

"Some days it was like the 4th of July. But I was now 19, so I felt invincible.

"I was truly fortunate to survive the war. One day after the ceasefire was declared in July 1953, I was assigned with my company to the 38th Parallel. A couple months later, I was surprised to get a visit from my Greek buddy, John. It was great to see him, and we had a nice visit discussing our harrowing experiences. Before he left to go back to his company, John stated that after his discharge he would like to go back to Greece and be with his family, whom he deeply missed. John thanked me very much for being a good friend and I responded likewise. It was a memorable moment, which I will never forget."

Masessa added, "I feel bad for the Vietnam guys; they had it rough." Masessa is pleased with the attention given to today's veterans, although he admits that war is still war.

Masessa returned briefly to baseball, sending his $75 per month salary to his family. "I was on top of the world," he said. One evening, after dancing at the Commodore Ballroom in Lowell, Massachusetts, he was hit by a drunken driver, which ended his baseball career. He worked for Western Electric Massachusetts and a natural gas company.

"I met my future wife, Ana, at the Dedham Ballroom, Dedham, MA and fell in love. We have been married for 59 years and raised two children and have two grandchildren, Scott, and Caroline. Ana is originally from Glasgow, Scotland, and decided to apply for a green card; she arrived in the US at the age of 21 and worked as a nanny in western New York. She has since become an American citizen. Ana is in her late 80s and I am 90, we thank the Lord every day for our blessings."

Private First-Class Samuel Masessa served from 1952 to 1954. He earned the Bronze Star Medal for meritorious service, National Defense Service Medal, Korea Service Medal with two battle stars, United Nations Korean Service Medal, Republic of Korea War Service Medal, Combat Infantry Badge, Republic of Korea Presidential Unit Citation, and in February 2018 he received the commemorative Ambassador for Peace Medal with Neck Ribbon from the Minister, Patriots and Veterans Affairs, Republic of Korea. The citation in part reads: "*It is a great honor and pleasure to express the everlasting gratitude of the Republic of Korea and of our people for the service you and your countrymen have performed in restoring and preserving our freedom and democracy.*"

The 25th ID "Tropic of Lighting" was on occupation duty on the Japanese island of Honshu when the N Korean Communist forces crossed the 38th Parallel, attacking S Korea on June 25, 1950. The division was alerted the first week in July to prepare for movement to Korea. On July 21, 1950, the 3rd Battalion, 14th IR was reassigned to Far East Command.

Private First-Class Gerald P. Page. Interviewed by William R. Graser, on November 11, 2010, and in a follow-up interview in February 2013.

Private First-Class Gerald P. Page, now 93, was assigned to A Company, 3rd Battalion, 14th Infantry Regiment, 25th ID and participated in numerous actions against N Korean forces and Communist Chinese troops in 1953. When peace negotiations stalled on May 5, 1953, the division assumed the responsibility to guard the approaches to Seoul. Then, just 23 days later, a heavy Chinese assault was hurled at the division's center being held by the 14th Infantry Regiment "Golden Dragons." The assault was repulsed; the brunt of the attack was absorbed by the regiment. By successfully defending Seoul, the division earned its second Republic of Korea Presidential Unit Citation. Again, negotiators moved toward peace.

"I was a native of Holyoke, Massachusetts and was already in the military serving in the active reserves of the newly created US Air Force at Westover Air Force Base in Massachusetts. When things got hot with Korea, my squadron was called in and disbanded," he said. "I was discharged from the Air Force and drafted into the Army."

Page knew from basic training that he was headed for Korea. "It was not," he said laconically, "anything I was looking forward to." His sergeant reinforced the feeling, telling his group at the end of basic training, "Take care of yourselves. Some of you will not be coming back."

"I shipped out of Seattle, Washington and vividly remember the townspeople who gathered to see the GIs off. They were waving handkerchiefs and flags," he said.

Page was 21 and said that he did not feel invincible. His prior military training had given him some awareness of what could happen. "But as much as you train for it, the real thing is different," he said.

In-Country

Once in-country, his unit took the train north from Pusan. Page took note of the armed guards on the train. "They were there to protect us from snipers," he said. He remembers his first battle, in part because it happened quickly. "I had just gotten assigned to the 14th Infantry Regiment A Company," Page recalled. A day later they received word that a Turkish brigade was under assault and moved out at night to relieve the Turks.

Upon arrival they were assaulted by artillery from the Chinese and N Korean forces. "I had never heard noise like that," Page said. He was hit with shrapnel in his face and temporarily deafened. "Some sergeant I didn't know dragged me into an abandoned bunker," he said. "We were in the bunker for two minutes and the front blew off." The sergeant, from another division, administered first aid and Page eventually found his way back to his own division.

"I rejoined my outfit with a bandage over my face," he said. "They didn't know who I was, and for a few days they called me 'Tape.'" Was he afraid? Page thought for a minute. "You get kind of numb," he finally said.

"There's so much going on. All you think about is your survival." On the front lines, they had little contact with the S Korean civilians. "I liked the Korean people I met," Page said. "They had a lot of hardship—dirt roads, plowing fields by hand, no indoor plumbing." Though there was a language difference, he also admired the S Korean soldiers.

"There were Korean soldiers assigned to our unit as ammo bearers and other duties while online and segregated from us off the line. They had their own unit and separate roll call and did not share our sleeping area or chow/eating. By all accounts the S Koreans were good soldiers." Korean soldiers, or "KATUSA's," were assimilated into each unit in great numbers. Americans got to know the soldiers with names like Kim, Chung, and Lee, and the language barriers were gradually stripped away.

In late May 1953, Page was part of a small observation team stationed at a hilltop bunker overlooking a no-man's land, with fighting forces on both sides. Page said, "I noticed the trees had been stripped by artillery." Pinned down all night, they emerged to find their observation equipment destroyed. Miraculously, their bunker had not been hit. Page said, "Boy, that was a surprise."

Armistice negotiations entered their final and decisive phase in May 1953; the enemy stepped up combat action. Pork Chop Hill 255, an 836-foot-high outpost, would become not only a battle but prove to the communists that the UN was determined to fight on if a ceasefire agreement could not be reached. The Chinese forces launched two major attacks against Pork Chop in 1953 to take the outpost; the first was in April and the second attack, starting on July 6, was the heaviest. The first battle began on the night of April 16, shortly before midnight, with a sudden infantry assault preceded by an intense artillery barrage. Chinese forces quickly overran Pork Chop, although pockets of US soldiers defended isolated bunkers.

On April 17 at 0330 hours (3:30 a.m.) King (K) Company, 31st IR 7th ID was ordered into an attack position, and at 0430 hours (4:30 a.m.) K Company reached the assault line and counterattacked to retake the hill. One hundred thirty-five men, some of them veterans, some of them had no combat experience, all headed for 17 hours of hell. By 0745 hours (7:45 a.m.) K Company had not advanced more than 200 yards in two hours, and the Chinese still held bunkers along the trench line. Reinforcements arrived during the night and by dawn reached the main trenches on top of the hill but suffered heavy casualties. In the early morning of April 18, Chinese forces assaulted the hill again, but after a bloody close-quarters fight, they were driven back by an arriving company of US reinforcements. At dusk, the Chinese finally conceded and withdrew. After 17 hours of steady combat, the remaining members started off the hill singly just after midnight of April 17–18 and withdrew without further losses.

The battle ended the afternoon of April 18. UN artillery had fired nearly 40,000 on Pork Chop Hill alone on April 18; the Chinese expended a similar amount.

On the night of July 6, under the cover of a heavy monsoon rainstorm, using tactics identical to those used in the first assault, the Chinese again attacked Pork Chop. The second battle involved many more troops on both sides and was bitterly contested. On both July 9 and July 10, the two sides attacked, and counter attacked. The 7th took heavy casualties and failed once again.

In mid-July, the 25th ID was moved to reserve status at Camp Casey, located near Dongducheon (also sometimes spelled Tongduchon or TDC) 30 miles south of the 38th parallel and 40 miles north of Seoul. Page and his company moved up online for an attempt to retake Pork Chop.

With the Chinese apparently determined to take the outpost at whatever cost and an armistice imminent, Army Major General Arthur G. Trudeau, commander of the 7th ID, ordered Pork Chop Hill abandoned. Through a clever ruse, while under fire the 7th ID removed its troops during the day on July 11 without any casualties. The second battle for Pork Chop ended.

The 25th was then placed in a support position.

"For years I was left to wonder about what might have happened had there been no change in plans. I learned later that Pork Chop Hill was being used as leverage by the N Koreans to accept a ceasefire on their terms," said Page. The hill had no tactical importance; it was fought to make political statements relevant to the armistice negotiations.

Less than three weeks after the smell of gunpowder on Pork Chop Hill cleared, the Korean Armistice Agreement was signed, thus creating the division between N and S Korea that exists today. While the Korean Armistice Agreement ended large-scale combat, military forces were still required in positions of readiness. A threat still hung over Korea. N Korea remained loyal to Beijing (China) and Moscow (Russia) while S Korea maintained a strong relationship with Washington (US).

In mid-August 1953 as the DMZ took shape, the 25th ID relieved the 7th ID in the newly established DMZ in the Taekwang-ni sector of the Imjin Valley, between the 1stMARDIV to the West and the 40th ID to the East. The following months were spent constructing new main battle positions and patrolling the DMZ.

In a follow-up interview, Page said, "After the truce was signed, agreement was DMZ to be patrolled by Military Police only."

"In August 1953 I was selected, along with 27 other infantrymen of the 14th IR, and given MP armbands. Day and night, from five barren outposts, we patrolled an area with hopefully marked land mines."

At the end of the conflict, both Masessa and Page spent time patrolling the new DMZ, or demilitarized zone, before coming home. The City of San Francisco hosted a welcome home for the 40th ID with a parade. There was no parade for the 25th upon arrival by ship in Seattle, WA along with Canadian troops. The division returned in late 1954 to its home base, Schofield Barracks in Hawaii.

Page's main reception came from his mother. "When I left for Korea, I was 172 pounds; when I came home, I was 148. The first thing my mother said was, 'You look terrible.' Page went to Boston College on the GI bill, moved to Boston, and stayed at the YMCA. "There were mice in my $8 per week room," he said. "It was just like Korea." Page eventually worked in the insurance industry.

Private First-Class Gerald P. Page served from 1952 to 1954. He earned the National Defense Service Medal, Korean Service Medal with two battle stars, United Nations Korea Service Medal, Republic of Korea War Service Medal, Combat Infantry Badge, and Republic of Korea Presidential Unit Citation.

Total US losses during the battles for Pork Chop Hill were 347 killed in action along with 1036 wounded in action and 9 captured. The Chinese losses, according to UN estimates, were 1500 killed in action, 4000 wounded in action. China reported 533 killed in action and 1242 wounded in action. Pork Chop Hill claimed the lives of soldiers not only from the US but Thailand, Colombia, and the Republic of Korea (ROK), as well as China, in an ongoing struggle that lasted longer than on any other single battlefield in Korea.

The human toll of the 1950s Korean Conflict was staggering. Although Chinese and N Korean casualties are unconfirmed, estimates put Chinese casualties at 600,000 military killed and over 716,000 wounded. N Korean losses estimate is 406,000 military killed, 1.5 million wounded, and 1.2 million civilians killed, which includes 282,000 civilians killed during bombing raids. (In the absence of reliable statistics from N Korea, estimates of war losses on the northern side have varied widely, and distribution has remained uncertain between military and civilians killed, and those who fled to the South.)

The UN Command peak strength was 972,334, of which 326,863 million were American and 602,902 S Korean. Total casualties (battle deaths, wounded, prisoners of war): US in-theater deaths 36,574, wounded not-mortal 103,284, and POWs 7563 (2849 died in captivity, 4714 returned). S Korean deaths were 137,899, wounded 450,742, and POWs 8343. Reference: Table 9. US Military Casualties – Korean Statistical Snapshot.

The US imperialists sustained great losses in manpower and material on the Korean front during the three years of war: 1,567,128 men including 405,498 US soldiers, 1,130,965 South Korean puppet troops, and 30,665 soldiers of their satellite states were killed, wounded or captured; 12,224 airplanes including "air fortress B-29" were downed, damaged or captured; 7,695 guns, 3,255 tanks and armored cars were lost; and 564 warships and vessels including the heavy cruiser Baltimore and the flagship of the 7th Fleet Missouri were sunk or damaged. The losses suffered by the US imperialists were 2.3 times greater than what they had suffered in the four years of the Pacific War during World War II.

It was an appalling loss and a serious military defeat unprecedented in the US history of war.

Propaganda and Agitation Department

US Military Casualties - Korean Statistical Snapshot

Korean Conflict Ground/Sea/Air 1950 – 1953
dcas.dmdc.osd.mil
(As of July 8, 2022)

Table 9. Casualties Analysis System and Statistical Snapshot Correlates with the book's introduction, Tables 1 through 4.

CASUALTY TYPE	TOTAL	ARMY	AIR FORCE	MARINES	NAVY
Killed in Action	23,613	19,715	209	3320	369
Died of Wounds	2460	1887	14	532	27
Missing in Action - Declared Dead	4817	3337	991	386	103
Captured - Declared Dead	2849	2792	24	29	4
TOTAL HOSTILE DEATHS	33,739	27,731	1238	4267	503
Missing - Presumed Dead	8	4	4	0	0
Other Deaths	2827	2121	310	242	154
TOTAL NON-HOSTILE DEATHS	2835	2125	314	242	154
TOTAL IN-THEATER DEATHS	36,574	29,856	1552	4509	657
WOUNDED NOT-MORTAL	103,284	77,596	368	23,744	1576

TOTAL IN-THEATER DEATHS: 36,574
Inclusive dates are June 25, 1950, to July 27, 1953.

When freedom and democracy were under threat on the Korean Peninsula...2 million Americans left their homes, put on our nation's uniform, and answered their country's call to duty. For complete details, visit Defense Casualty Analysis System Reports (DCAS) – Korean War Casualty Summary (osd.mil). DCAS is an application maintained by the Defense Manpower Data Center (DMDC). The data that DCAS contains is provided from multiple sources, the primary source being that of the military services themselves. For questions regarding the data: dodhra.dodc-mp.dmdc.mbx.dcas-helpdesk@mail.mil.

CHAPTER 15

PRISONERS OF WAR EXCHANGE - ARMISTICE SIGNED, FIGHTING ENDS

On the surface, the problem of prisoners of war seemed simple. By March 1, 1953, the negotiations had one outstanding issue: voluntary or forced repatriation. [53] Prisoner repatriation was one of the greatest obstacles in the long cease-fire negotiations between forces of the United Nations and those of China and North Korea. In early April 1953, an initial agreement was reached between the UN and communist negotiators to exchange prisoners. Operation Little Switch, an exchange of Allied and Communists sick and wounded prisoners, began on April 20. When it was completed in the latter part of the month, 484 UN prisoners including 296 Americans had been exchanged for more than 6000 Communists.

Nuclear Coercion

Subsequently, the Chinese and N Koreans kept in doubt the question about the exchange of the remaining prisoners. US officials attempted to send indirect hints that President Dwight D. Eisenhower might expand the war into China or even use nuclear weapons. The increase in conventional US military pressure during the spring of 1953 may have also had a great effect on the willingness of the Chinese and N Koreans to negotiate a settlement. After Joseph Stalin's death in March 1953, Soviet leaders who came to power worried about US escalation and pressed for an end to the war. On May 23, 1953, US Secretary of State John Dulles sent a message to the Chinese leadership via the Indian diplomatic corps. The Chinese were raising unnecessary barriers to an armistice agreement ending

---

53   https://history.army.mil/books/korea/truce/ch7.htm
     Chapter VII Prisoners of War (POW)
     https://history.army.mil/books/korea/truce/ch7.htm
     Chapter VII Prisoners of War (POW)

the conflict, said Dulles, and if peace was not forthcoming, the US would bring in atomic weapons. Within 11 days of receiving Dulles's message, the Chinese accepted the armistice plan, with minor changes. The barrier was the outstanding issue about the release of prisoners of war. Dulles claimed the breakthrough came when the US, as part of a carefully worked out plan, had discreetly dropped the word "atomic." Whether or not Eisenhower's threats of nuclear attacks helped, both sides eventually made concessions on the question of the repatriation of prisoners of war. In June 1953, the two sides agreed that no prisoner who did not want to return to their homeland would not be forced to do so.

Armistice Agreement July 27, 1953

General of the Army Dwight D. Eisenhower campaigned for president on a promise to end the conflict in Korea. Soon after his inauguration in January 1953, he moved to do so while the fighting raged on the central front. The negotiators at Panmunjom rapidly approached an agreement on armistice terms.

On July 19, agreement was reached on all points by both sides. All details of the armistice agreement and its implementation were completed in a week. The terms of the armistice included creation of a demilitarized zone, the DMZ, each side being 2200 yards from a center point. The DMZ is always patrolled by both sides. At 1000 hours (10:00 a.m.) on July 27, 1953, Army Lieutenant General (LTG) William Harrison, Jr.; N Korean General Nam IL; Marshal Peng Dehuai, Chinese People's Volunteers; and the UN signed the Korean Armistice Agreement ending "all acts of armed force" in Korea.

There were representatives present from Turkey, Thailand, the Netherlands, France, the United Kingdom and the Commonwealth countries, Colombia, Belgium, Denmark, Luxembourg, Ethiopia, Philippines, and Norway.

The 1950s Korean Conflict: Began on June 25, 1950, and the fighting stopped July 27, 1953.

On June 27, 1950, President Truman ordered US air and naval forces to S Korea to repulse the communist invasion forces of N Korea. This date marks the official beginning of US involvement in the 1950s Korean Conflict.

All fighting stopped at 2000 hours (8:00 p.m.); the Korean Conflict ended. The armistice, while it stopped hostilities, was not a permanent peace treaty, but rather, a ceasefire between the Koreas. (The signing of the armistice did not bring an end to the ideological conflict.)

Armistice Agreement for the Restoration of the South Korean State (1953)

The Armistice Agreement details are described in this chapter—specifically, Table 10.

The Republic of Korea abided by the armistice but refused to sign it because it was not a peace treaty; it was a ceasefire arrangement. S Korea wanted to keep fighting. The 1950s Korean Conflict had lasted three years, one month, and two days. Korea remained one of the political hot spots in the world, and a dividing line between democracy and the remnants of communism. President Eisenhower ordered the 1CD and 7th ID to remain in S Korea as insurance against renewed hostilities. As a result of the formation of the 1CD (Airmobile) at Fort Benning, GA., in 1965 for duty in S Vietnam, the existing 1CD in Korea took the title of the 2nd ID (Indianhead). The 2nd ID-ROK/US Combined Division is its designation and presently, 2022, based at Camp Humphreys, S Korea. The division is unique; its personnel strength has S Korean soldiers permanently assigned. The 7th ID was withdrawn in 1974, and presently, 2022, is at Joint Base Lewis-McCord, Tacoma, WA.

Operation Big Switch

In August 1953 "Operation Big Switch" began and 13,226 (7862 S Koreans, 4418 Americans, and 946 British) prisoners returned to the UN Command; and 75,723 Communist fighters (70,183 N Koreans and 5540 Chinese Communist prisoners) returned. The exchange took place in the Demilitarized Zone (DMZ). Of the known Americans captured (mostly in the first nine months of the conflict) approximately 2849 died in captivity, and 21 Americans and one British declined repatriation in favor of remaining in N Korea or China. Ultimately, more than 22,000 N Korean and 327 S Koreans soldiers refused repatriation. By December 23, 1953, all prisoners of war (POWs) from both sides, UN and communist forces returned to their homeland.

In the early morning of February 24, 1954, a train carrying the 21 American defectors crossed the Yalu River into China. The Chinese soon shipped some of the men off to study language and politics. Others went to mills, factories, and farms across Eastern China. The 21 Americans were dishonorably discharged. This had the unintended consequence of rendering them immune to court martial when they finally returned to the United States (which the majority eventually did), because they were no longer active-duty military.

One American, Corporal Clarence Adams of Memphis, Tennessee, made propaganda broadcasts for Radio Hanoi in N Vietnam from its Chinese office, telling African American soldiers not to fight:

> "You are supposedly fighting for the freedom of the Vietnamese, but what kind of freedom do you have at home, sitting in the back of the bus, being barred from restaurants, stores and certain neighborhoods, and being denied the right to vote? Go home and fight for equality in America." Clarence Adams.

The US Army Graves Registration teams searched the battlefields in the Republic of Korea (ROK) from 1951 to 1956. During Operation Glory in 1954, N Korea returned the remains of more than 3000 Americans. Concurrently, US Army Graves Registration teams recovered remains from S Korean battlefields.

The US identified thousands of these remains. In 1956, a total of 848 Americans who could not be identified were buried in Hawaii at the National Memorial Cemetery of the Pacific, known as the Punchbowl. One of the unknowns was interred in the Tomb of the Unknowns at Arlington National Cemetery near Washington, DC.

In July 2018, N Korea returned 55 boxes of remains and artifacts to the US. The Defense POW/MIA Accounting Agency (DPAA) identified 41 US troops among the remains returned. As of September 28, 2021, according to the DPAA, the estimated number of unaccounted (missing in action) US personnel is 7554, including 5300 believed to be north of the DMZ.

In addition to those missing from the 1950s Korean Conflict, more than one hundred Cold War losses are in the vicinity of the Korean peninsula. DPAA made "overtures" to return in 2021/2022, but Kim Jong-un and the N Korean Army have yet to agree. [54]

---

54   Progress on Korean War Personnel Accounting Defense POW/MIA Accounting Agency.

At the conclusion of the conflict, the US and S Korea signed a Mutual Defense Treaty on October 1, 1953, the foundation of a comprehensive alliance that endures today, and commits the US to help S Korea defend itself. The treaty also provided the legal authority to station US forces in S Korea.

On August 8, 1953, even before the ink of their signature to the Armistice Agreement had dried, the US and S Korea concluded the "ROK-US Mutual Defense Pact" with the puppet clique to perpetuate the occupation of S Korea by US imperialism. (It was formally "signed" in Washington, DC on October 1, and "ratified" in January 1954.)

Stipulated in this "pact" are the permanent occupation of S Korea by US troops and their right for military action against the northern half of Korea. It was therefore an aggressive "pact" allowing the US imperialists to launch war at any moment.

(1) The "ROK-US Agreement on Military and Economic Aid" initiated by the US imperialists and the S Korean puppet clique on November 17, 1954, and the "minutes of the ROK-US Talks" were supplements to the "ROK-US Mutual Defense Pact" which reaffirmed the permanent occupation of S Korea by US troops and provided for a tightening of the military, political and economic control of US imperialism over S Korea and the warlike preparations for the "conquest of the North."

(2) Under the "pact" and "agreement," the US imperialists not only perpetuated their occupation of S Korea; but worked hard to turn S Korea into a military strategic base commensurate with the preparations for a new war, extensively reinforcing the puppet army and illegally supplying material needed for war.

(3) With the aim of enlarging the S Korean puppet armed forces, the US imperialists had cooked up a "volunteer ordinance" and organized ten reserve divisions by July 1955. As a result, the puppet armed forces swelled to 31 divisions from 16 at the time of the ceasefire, and its numerical strength increased to 720,000 from 594,000.

(4) In the postwar period the US imperialists also attached great significance to converting S Korea into a powerful military base, so necessary for war preparations.

Table 10. Armistice Agreement for the Restoration
of the South Korean State (1953)

Armistice Agreement for the Restoration of the South Korean State (1953)
US National Archives & Records Administration 700 Pennsylvania Avenue NW, Washington, DC 20408

The Korean War, which began on June 25, 1950, when the North Koreans invaded South Korea, officially ended on July 27, 1953. At 10 a.m., in Panmunjom, scarcely acknowledging each other, US Army Lt. Gen. William K. Harrison, Jr., senior delegate, United Nations Command Delegation; North Korean General Nam Il, senior delegate, Delegation of the Korean People's Army and the Chinese People's Volunteers, signed 18 official copies of the tri-language Korean Armistice Agreement. It was the end of the longest negotiated armistice in history: 158 meetings spread over two years and 17 days. That evening at 10 p.m. the truce went into effect. The Korean Armistice Agreement is somewhat exceptional in that it is purely a military document—no nation is a signatory to the agreement. Specifically, the Armistice Agreement:

1. suspended open hostilities.

2. withdrew all military forces and equipment from a 4000-meter-wide zone, establishing the Demilitarized Zone as a buffer between the forces.

3. prevented both sides from entering the air, ground, or sea areas under control of the other.

4. arranged release and repatriation of prisoners of war and displaced persons; and

5. established the Military Armistice Commission (MAC) and other agencies to discuss any violations and to ensure adherence to the truce terms.

The armistice, while it stopped hostilities, was not a permanent peace treaty between nations. President Eisenhower, who was keenly aware of the 1.8 million American men and women who had served in Korea and the 36,574 Americans who had died there, played a key role in bringing about a cease-fire. In announcing the agreement to the American people in a television address shortly after the signing, he said, in part:

Soldiers, sailors and airmen of sixteen different countries have stood as partners beside us throughout these long and bitter months. In this struggle we have seen the United Nations meet the challenge of aggression—not with pathetic words of protest, but with deeds of decisive purpose. And so, at long last the carnage of war is to cease, and the negotiation of the conference table is to begin. . . . [We hope that] all nations may come to see the wisdom of composing differences in this fashion before, rather than after, there is resort to brutal and futile battle. Now as we strive to bring about that wisdom, there is, in this moment of sober satisfaction, one thought that must discipline our emotions and steady our resolution.

It is this: We have won an armistice on a single battleground—not peace in the world. We may not now relax our guard nor cease our quest.

Korean War Armistice Agreement, July 27, 1953; Treaties and Other International Agreements Series #2782; General Records of the United States Government; Record Group 11; National Archives. • 1-866-272-6272.

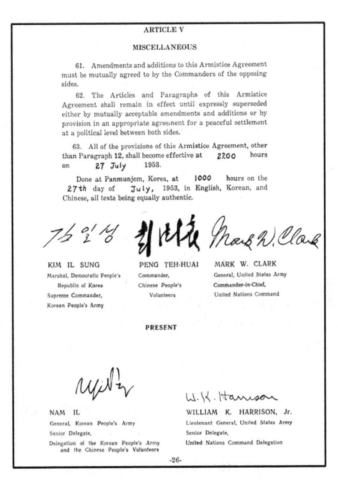

ARTICLE V

MISCELLANEOUS

61. Amendments and additions to this Armistice Agreement must be mutually agreed to by the Commanders of the opposing sides.

62. The Articles and Paragraphs of this Armistice Agreement shall remain in effect until expressly superseded either by mutually acceptable amendments and additions or by provision in an appropriate agreement for a peaceful settlement at a political level between both sides.

63. All of the provisions of this Armistice Agreement, other than Paragraph 12, shall become effective at 2200 hours on 27 July 1953.

Done at Panmunjom, Korea, at 1000 hours on the 27th day of July, 1953, in English, Korean, and Chinese, all texts being equally authentic.

KIM IL SUNG
Marshal, Democratic People's
Republic of Korea
Supreme Commander,
Korean People's Army

PENG TEH-HUAI
Commander,
Chinese People's
Volunteers

MARK W. CLARK
General, United States Army
Commander-in-Chief,
United Nations Command

PRESENT

NAM IL
General, Korean People's Army
Senior Delegate,
Delegation of the Korean People's Army
and the Chinese People's Volunteers

WILLIAM K. HARRISON, Jr.
Lieutenant General, United States Army
Senior Delegate,
United Nations Command Delegation

-26-

Signatories to the Armistice Agreement

Post Korean Armistice

The US bombing destroyed most of N Korea's industry, agriculture, transportation, and communications systems. Pyongyang, the capital of N Korea, was a pile of rubble, its buildings obliterated by an estimated 250,000 bombs.

Post armistice, the third-largest contributor of external assistance after the Russia and China was the Deutschland (German) Democratic Republic (DDR or GDR) communally referred to as East Germany (1945-1991), played a key role in the rebuilding of Hungnam, N Korea's second-largest city and an important industrial center. Hundreds of engineers, technicians, craftsmen, and their families were sent to Hungnam. The N Korean and East German governments declared the Hungnam project complete in 1962. The East Germans returned home.

In 1961, China and the Democratic People's Republic of Korea (N Korea)) signed a Treaty of Friendship, Cooperation and Mutual Assistance, an agreement that endures today, and commits China-N Korea immediate military and other aid in the event of an attack. The conflict also devastated S Korea, killing and injuring millions of people and scaring those who survived. The S Koreans emerged from that conflict as one of the poorest countries in the world. The scale of destruction made recovery seem like a distant dream. During the early years following the armistice, S Korea was entirely dependent on the US for food and consumer goods.

On July 11, 2021, leaders of China and N Korea vowed to strengthen ties. On the 60th anniversary of the 1961 signing of the China-DPRK Treaty the leaders of both counties, General Secretary of the Communist Party of China (CPC) Central Committee Xi Jinping and N Korea Chairman Kim Jong-un reaffirmed its provisions. Over the past six decades, China and N Korea have written a proud history of friendship through mutual support and help. China-N Korea ties go back to the 1930s, when Kim Il-sung, the grandfather of Kim Jong-un, led Korean guerrillas as they fought alongside Chinese soldiers against Japanese colonizers in northeastern China. In 1949, the two countries established diplomatic relations.

366th Engineer Aviation Battalion:
Special Category US Army with the US Air Force 1954-1955

Personal Story and Firsthand Account

Private First-Class Robert S. Messier. Interviewed by William R. Graser, on November 18, 2014.

Meisser said, "I was a radio operator with the 366th Engineer Aviation Battalion, Special Category Army with the US Air Force (SCARWAF), Daegu (English: Taegu), S Korea. I was drafted in 1953; Uncle Sam's expected greeting was in my mailbox.

"I went to Fort Jackson, South Carolina, for basic training and attended advanced individual training to become an immediate speed radio operator at Fort Knox, Kentucky. Upon completion, I was assigned to Fort Benning, Georgia, and completed the communications specialist course."

In-Country

"After a short leave, I found myself aboard a US Navy ship, and in October 1954 arrived in Taegu, S Korea. I was assigned to the 366th Engineer Aviation Battalion, as a radio and switchboard operator. The battalion was located at K-2 Air Force Base, Taegu and was a special US Army unit working with the US Air Force." USAF bases are still referred to by the "K" designation.

Example, Osan Air Force Base is referred to by its "K-55" airfield designation from the first Korean Conflict. The Far East Air Forces 5th Air Force had 57 air bases in Korea during the first conflict, and many of these were former Japanese airfields. The spelling of Korean locations on maps varied greatly, and villages had a Korean and a Japanese name. A "K" number identified individual air bases in both northern and southern Korea to prevent confusion among locations. The USAF suffered 1841 casualties, of which 1180 were killed in action. It lost 4053 aircraft to all types of causes. (USAF Statistical Digest for the years 1945 thru 1963 are unclassified in accordance with Executive Order 11652) All Army aviation engineer soldiers worked together with USAF troops. These soldiers were recruited, trained in communications and various engineer specialties, and assigned to Air Force units by the US Army. These troops were temporarily assigned, filling vacant Air Force personnel positions. Aviation engineer battalions-built facilities which Air Force units required to support jet fighters, bombers, and transports. The 366th Engineer Aviation Battalion operated a gravel pit, rock quarry, rock crusher, and asphalt plant; in addition, repair projects included fence lines, base drainage systems, road repair, runway and taxiway repair, rehabilitation of buildings and the petroleum depots.

With the creation of the USAF as a separate military branch, there was no longer provision for specialized semi-skilled and skilled troops to perform these sorts of tasks. Meisser added, "After a couple of months into my tour, I was assigned as the communications chief and remained in this capacity until I rotated home." Looking back, Meisser recalled seeing the destruction caused by the conflict, and the efforts to rebuild S Korea could be seen everywhere. Many cities were reduced to ruin and the Koreans were subjected to harsh conditions, including starvation and lack of medical care.

Meisser noted, "Today the S Koreans are anti-communist and in general pro-American, no matter what occasional frictions arise. I was then and still am proud to have served." In September 1955 Messier said, "I found myself aboard ship again, and returned to the states. On October 14, 1955, I was transferred to the army reserve and honorably discharged on November 30, 1961."

Private First-Class Robert S. Meisser earned the Good Conduct Medal, National Defense Service Medal, and Korea Defense Service Medal.

Historical Fact

Actual hostilities occurred from June 27, 1950, to July 27, 1953. However, the war period was extended to January 31, 1955, by the US Congress to define a period of eligibility for Veterans' Preference for federal employment in the wake of uneasy peace negotiations after July 27, 1953. Eligibility is based on dates of active-duty service, receipt of a campaign badge, Purple Heart, or a service-connected disability. Only veterans discharged or released from active duty in the Armed Forces under honorable conditions (honorable or general discharge) are eligible for Veterans' Preference. Data of Veterans of the 1950s Korean Conflict, June 2000. (va.gov) There were 6.8 million men and women who served during the Korean conflict period, June 27, 1950, to January 31, 1955.

Private First-Class Robert S. Meisser
Photo provided by the Veteran.

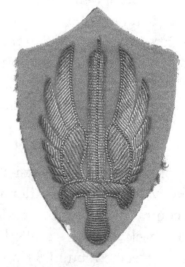

Organization Identification
Shoulder Patch
Provided by the Veteran

Stories and Firsthand Accounts by Private First-Class Samuel F. Masessa, Private First-Class Gerald P. Page, and Private First-Class Robert S. Meisser originally included along with 56 other stories and firsthand accounts in *Veterans' Reflections: History Preserved* by William R. Graser, retired soldier and author. These veterans served from World War II to the end of the Cold War, and one veteran participated in the Afghanistan War 2004.

"The appearance of US Department of Defense visual information does not imply or constitute DOD endorsement."

Images (including graphics, citations, maps, documents, and pamphlets) taken or made by members of the U.S. military or U.S. Department of Defense (DoD) during the person's official duties. Under United States copyright law, such images are public domain.

Official U.S. Military Photographs taken before 1982 repository is the: U.S. Military Images:

Still Picture Reference Special Media Archives Division College Park, MD. Archival Research Catalog (ARC) renamed the Inventory Entry Number (IEN).

Visual Information Record Identification Number (VIRIN). VIRIN is a unique identifier assigned by the United States Department of Defense to official still photographs and other media. Images are in the public domain.

Mass Communication Specialist US Navy (MCSN) during the person's official duties.

Under United States copyright law, images are in the public domain.

US Navy Photo Credit: Naval History and Heritage Command (NHHC) National Museum of the US Navy (NMUSN). United States copyright law, images are in the public domain.

US Army Military History Institute (USAMHI) US Army Heritage and Education Center (USAHEC) Carlisle, PA. United States copyright law, images are in the public domain.

With her brother on her back, a war-weary Korean girl tiredly trudges by a Medium Tank M46 Patton, at Hamangiu, Korea. June 9, 1951. US Army Korea - Installation Management Command NWDNS-80-G-429691. War and Conflict #1485.

Korean Conflict Montage

Korean Conflict Montage: Clockwise from top: A column of US 1st Marine Division's infantry and armor moves through Chinese lines during their breakout from the Chosin Reservoir; F-86 Sabre fighter aircraft; UN landing at Inchon harbor, starting point of the Battle of Inchon; US Marines, led by First Lieutenant Baldomero Lopez, USMC, leads the 3rd Platoon, Company A, 1st Battalion, 5th Marines over the seawall on the northern side of Red Beach, as the second wave lands, September 15, 1950, during the Inchon invasion; Korean refugees in front of an American Medium M46 Pershing tank.

Lt. General Walton H. Walker, Commander, US 8th Army (left) confers with Maj. General William F. Dean, Commander, Ground Forces in Korea, upon General's Walker's arrival at an advanced airfield. (Taejon, July 7, 1950) VIRIN 170117-D-XT155-001A.

T 34/84 N Korean tank, knocked out by MG Dean's soldiers on July 20, 1950, near the S Korean city of Taejon. US Army image 084615.

A 3.5-inch rocket launcher on a battlefield, July 20, 1950
NARA NAID Accession Number 67-7310.
United States Army/Harry S. Truman Library & Museum

Two American GIs holding a position overlooking the main bridge across
Kap-ch'on river near Taejon, August 8, 1950. Found in the Harry S. Truman
Library & Museum.
US Army Pusan Perimeter (https//dpaa-mil.sites.crmforce.mil)

General Douglas MacArthur (center), Commander-in-Chief of United Nations Forces, observes the shelling of Inchon on September 15, 1950.

Landing ships unload men and equipment on Red Beach one day after the amphibious landings. NARA Identifiers – 531373 and 5207772 US Navy photos. Accession number: 80-G-420027.

A Vought F4U-4B Corsair, of Fighter Squadron 113 (VF-113) from USS *Philippine Sea* (CV-47), flies combat air patrol over US warships and U.N. shipping in Inchon anchorage, South Korea, October 2, 1950. Wolmi-Do Island is in the right center distance, with Inchon city beyond to the right. USS *Missouri* (BB-63) is immediately below the Corsair. NHHC

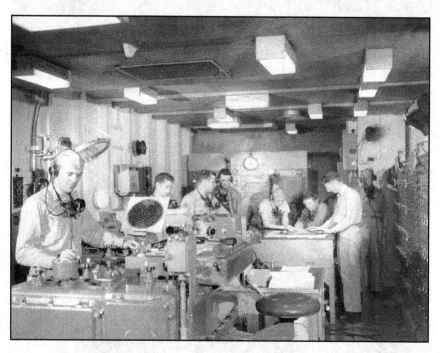

USS *Missouri* (BB-63). Scene in the ship's main battery plotting room, during operations off Korea, September 17, 1950. US Navy NAID 80-G-420319 and NHHC.

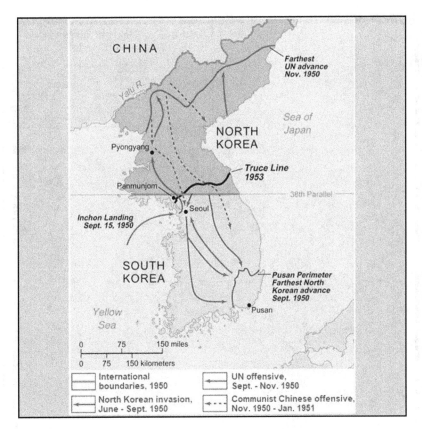

Overview Map - June 1950 to January 1951
Credit: Defense POW/MIA Accounting Agency
(https://dpaa-mil.sites.crmforce.mil.sites.crmforce)

On August 1, 1950, the 8th Army withdrew east of the Naktong River. Behind this river, US and South Korean forces set up a defense perimeter around the port of Pusan, an important logistical hub on the southeastern tip of the Korean peninsula. The Great Naktong Offensive launched by N Korea was one of the most brutal fights of the first Korean Conflict. Initially, the N Koreans did break through the Pusan perimeter at several places and were able to exploit their gains for a short time. There was a series of battles fought in August to mid-September 1950. The successful UN landing at Inchon on September 15, 1950, forced North Korean forces to withdraw north. On September 16, the 8th Army began its breakout and by September 23, the N Koreans were in full retreat, with UN Forces rapidly pursuing them north and recapturing lost ground along the way. The US defense of the Pusan Perimeter had stopped North Korea from capturing the entire peninsula and provided time for reinforcements to arrive.

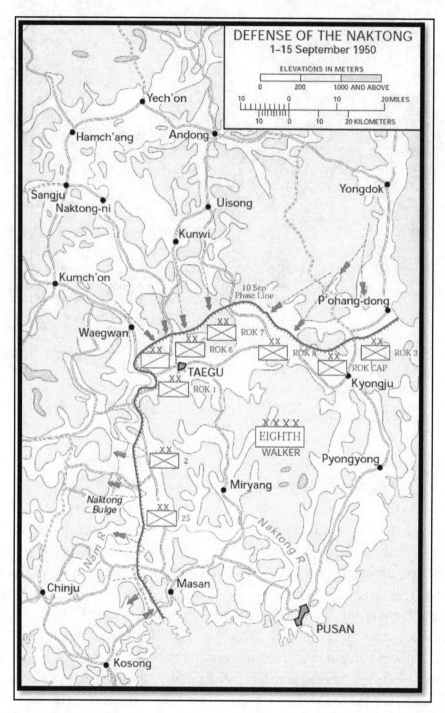

Map created by the US Army Center of Military History (USACMH)

Map is a work of a US Army soldier, taken or made as part of that person's official duties as a work of the US federal government; it is in the public domain in the United States.

Smell The Gunpowder

A North Korean POW captured by US Marines along Naktong Bulge, September 4, 1950. US Army/NARA FILE #: 127-N-A2122.

Men of the 7th Marine Regiment, US First Marine Division, wearing and carrying wintry weather gear, moving toward the Chosin Reservoir, North Korea, November 1, 1950.
US Marine Corps/NARA.

American .30 Caliber Machine Gun Position 2nd Infantry Division Battle of the Chongchon River on November 20, 1950. Image ID: H4H4JN US Army Photo/Alamy Stock Photo. License procured worldwide, start date March 10, 2022, duration in perpetuity from Alamy Inc Brooklyn, NY 11217.

Chinese soldiers taken prisoner by the US 7th Marine Regiment South of Koto-ri, N Korea, during the Battle of the Chosin Reservoir, December 9, 1950. USMC/ NARA Title No. 1231972. [55] rip103.

---

55   rip103.pdf (archives.gov) 39 series textual, still picture, motion picture, sound recording.

African American Battery A, 159th Field Artillery Battalion, firing a 105-mm howitzer, against N Korean positions 1950. US Army Heritage and Education Center 950 Soldiers Drive, Carlisle, PA, 17013. Permission Details: Alamy Inc., 20 Jay Street, Suite 848, Brooklyn, NY. License procured worldwide, start date March 5, 2019, duration in perpetuity. Alamy Stock Photo.
Credit: US Army/National Archives

A soldier from the 31st Infantry Regimental Combat Team, gunner crouching, fires a 75mm recoilless rifle during fighting near the Korean village of Outlook-tong, June 9, 1951.
US Army National Museum, Fort Belvoir, VA and NARA.

US Air Force 1950-1953
F-86 Sabre of the 51st Fighter Interceptor Wing "Checkertails" are readied for combat at K-13 Suwon Air Base, S Korea. Air Force National Engagement-NY. SAF/PAON airforcenyc@us.af.mil. https://dpaa-mil.sites.crmforce.mil.sites. crmforce

F-86 Sabre Air and Space Museum at Dulles International Airport
Washington, DC.
Photo: Wm Graser, Author.

MiG-15bis "Red 2057" National Museum of the US Air Force, Dayton, Ohio.
Photo: Wm Graser, Author.

US Air Force Douglas C-124C Globemaster
National Museum of the US Air Force, Dayton, Ohio.

MiG15bis "Red 2057" was transported to Okinawa in a C-124C Globemaster and later transferred to the museum in 1957. The story of the MiG-15bis on display; *Factsheets*. National Museum of the USAF. SAF/PAON.

On September 21, 1953, N Korean pilot "Red 2057" Senior Lieutenant No Kim-Sok, shown in his flight suit, defected to South Korea. National Museum of the US Air Force, Wright-Patterson Air Force Base Dayton, Ohio. SAF/PAON.

B-29 Superfortress American Four-Engine Propeller-driven Heavy Bomber Air Force National Engagement - NY SAF/PAON.

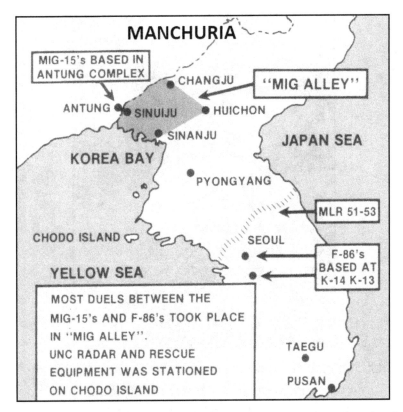

MiG-15s Based in China at the Antung Complex and in the shaded area,
Sinuiju, is the location of "MiG Alley" Northwest Korea

UN Command radar and rescue equipment were stationed on Chodo Island.
F-86's based at K-13 Suwon and K-14 Kimpo, South Korea
K-Sites identifies the bases that the Far East Air Force operated.

Air Force National Engagement-NY
805 3rd Ave Fl 9, New York, NY 10022
SAF/PAON airforcenyc@us.af.mil
Korean Air Battles (crmforce.mil)

US Navy Underwater Demolition Team 3 (UDT) rig
explosives to a pier at Hungnam.
Photo NHHC

USS *Begur* (ADP-127) high-speed transport lies off the port of Hungnam, N
Korea as 20 tons of demolition charges destroy port facilities and remaining
UN supplies at the conclusion of evacuation operations on December 24, 1950.
Photo NHHC. US Navy and collection of the NARA Catalog #: 80-G-K-11769.

Merchant ship SS *Meredith Victory* Port of Hungnam, North Korea

Photo Credit: US Navy Naval Transportation Service

Meredith Victory managed to board more than 14,000 Korean civilians and steamed south unescorted while navigating a minefield and dodging air attacks. Once in the open sea, it steamed for nearly 28 hours, reaching Pusan on Christmas Eve. The *Meredith Victory* earned the name "Ship of Miracles." In fact, five babies were born during the voyage.

Since thousands of refugees were already there, however, the ship was allowed to debark only its wounded and take on interpreters, along with a small supply of food and water. It then had to travel another 50 sea miles to take everyone else to Koje-Do Island.

The unloading of people there was completed on December 26. These evacuation efforts resulted in Leonard LaRue and his crew being awarded the Korean Presidential Citation by South Korean President Syngman Rhee in 1958. Two years later, *Meredith Victory* was given the title of "Gallant Ship" by a special act of Congress that was signed by President Dwight D. Eisenhower. This made *Meredith Victory* the only merchant marine ship serving in the 1950s Korean Conflict to receive such a designation. In addition, LaRue was awarded the Merchant Marine Meritorious Service Medal. Additional information is available online at the US Department of Transportation Maritime Administration.

Disclaimers:

"The appearance of the use of the imagery does not imply or constitute DoD endorsement."

"Use of released US Navy imagery does not constitute product or organizational endorsement of any kind by the US Navy."

UN delegate Lieutenant General William K. Harrison, Jr. (seated left), and Korean People's Army and Chinese People's Volunteers Delegate General Nam Il (seated right) signed the Korean Conflict armistice agreement at Panmunjom, Korea, July 27, 1953.
VIRIN: 530727-0-ZZ999-001.JPG .

Private First-Class
Samuel F. Masessa
Heavy Weapons Platoon
40th Infantry Division
Photo: Provided by the Veteran

Private First-Class
Gerald P. Page
Company A, 14th Infantry
Regiment
25th Infantry Division
Photo: Provided by the Veteran

Sergeant William H. Carney
Public Domain
Wearing his Medal of Honor, circa. 1901-1908
54th Massachusetts Colored
Infantry Regiment
July 18, 1864 - Fort Wagner on Morris Island, SC.
Presented the Medal of Honor May 23, 1900.
Oak Grove Cemetery, New Bedford, MA.
Story/photo courtesy of the US Army/181896

Sergeant William H. Johnson
Public Domain
"Harlem Hellfighters"
Awarded the Medal of Honor
Argonne Forest, France
May 14, 1918
Arlington National Cemetery
Story/photo courtesy of the US Army

Sergeant William H. Thompson
Company M, 24th Infantry Regiment
Posthumously
Received the Medal of Honor
August 6, 1950, Masan, South Korea
Credit: Photo Long Island National Cemetery

Author is the US Army - Public Domain

Staff Sergeant Cornelius H. Charlton
Company C, 24th Infantry Regiment
Posthumously
Received the Medal of Honor
June 2, 1951, near Chipo-ri, South Korea
Credit: Photo Arlington National
Cemetery

Author is the US Army - Public Domain

On July 18, 1863, the soldiers of Carney's regiment led the charge on Fort Wagner. During the battle, the unit's color guard was shot. Carney, who was just a few feet away, saw the dying man stumble, and he scrambled to catch the falling flag. Despite suffering several serious gunshot wounds, Carney kept the symbol of the Union held high as he crawled up the hill to the walls of Fort Wagner, urging his fellow troops to follow him. He planted the flag in the sand at the base of the fort and held it upright until his near-lifeless body was rescued. Carney lost a lot of blood and nearly lost his life, but not once did he allow the flag to touch the ground. His heroics inspired other soldiers that day. Carney was promoted to the rank of sergeant for his actions and for his bravery. [56]

Sergeant Henry Johnson, 369th Infantry Regiment, also known as the "Harlem Hellfighters." Born William Henry Johnson in Winston Salem, North Carolina

---

56   William Harvey Carney | US Civil War | US Army | Medal of Honor Recipient (cmohs.org).

About (Abt.) July 15, 1892. Awarded the Medal of Honor. Johnson died in July 1929, and is buried in Arlington National Cemetery, Arlington, Virginia. Sgt. Henry Johnson is "one of the five bravest American soldiers in the war." (Theodore Roosevelt Jr. in his book *Rank and File: True Stories of the Great War*.) Johnson was also awarded the French Croix De Guerre for bravery during an outnumbered battle with German soldiers on February 12, 1919.

Sergeant, then Private First-Class, William H. Thompson *Black Soldier, White Army: The 24th Infantry Regiment in Korea*, page 131. "Whatever the condition of the unit, some of its men were clearly willing to stand their ground. Pfc. William Thompson of Company M, for one, covered the retreating force with his machine gun. Hit repeatedly by enemy grenade fragments and small-arms fire, he refused to withdraw and continued to lay down covering fire until his company was clear of the area, and he was mortally wounded. But for him, casualties that day might have been far worse." [57] On June 21, 1951, at the Pentagon his mother received the Medal of Honor from Chairman of the Joint Chiefs of Staff General Omar Bradley. Thompson's battalion commander, Lieutenant Colonel Blair, initially refused to submit a recommendation until January 4, 1951, five months after the action. Thompson initially received a Silver Star Medal for the action, but after Blair changed his mind, he began pushing the paperwork through, personally locating witnesses who could attest to Thompson's valor.

Sergeant Cornelius H. Charlton, *Black Soldier, White Army: The 24th Infantry Regiment in Korea*, page 256. "Pfc. Ronald Holmes recalled what happened. Charlton was wounded in the chest, Holmes said, but he refused to be evacuated. He got the rest of the men together, and we started for the top. The enemy had some good emplacements . . . we couldn't get to him. Grenades kept coming at us and we were chased back down. Again, we tried, but no luck. Sgt. Charlton said he was going to make it this time and he yelled, 'Let's go,' and we started up again. We reached the top this time. I saw the Sergeant go over the top and charge a bunker on the other side. He got the gun but was killed by a grenade." Charlton caused heavy casualties among the enemy and saved many lives among his own men. Cargo transport SNS *Charlton* (T-AKR-314) proudly bears the name of US Army Sergeant Cornelius H. Charlton. [58]

---

57   https//:www.army.mil/africanamericans/timeline.html.
58   Cornelius H. http://www.cmohs.org/recipient-detail/3094/charlton-cornelius-h.php.

Major General William F. Dean, Sr.
Commander 24th Infantry Division
Photo: Author US Army Created January 1, 1950

Major General William F. Dean, Sr., was awarded the Medal of Honor for his actions on July 20 and 21, 1950, during the Battle of Taejon. The medal was received from President Truman by his wife Mildred Dean, son William Dean Jr., and daughter Marjorie. General Dean was still listed as missing in action. General Dean had no contact with the outside world until his interview-on December 18, 1951, by an Australian, Wilfred Burchett, who was a correspondent for *Le Soir*, a French left-wing newspaper. This was the first time that anyone had any idea General Dean was alive since reported missing in action. In late December 1951, the N Koreans finally announced that they were holding Dean as a POW.

The reason the N Koreans waited so long to announce Dean's capture has never been determined. He remained a POW in N Korean custody near Pyongyang for the remainder of the war. After the July 27, 1953 Armistice Agreement, he remained in N Korea as a POW for several more weeks while the armistice was worked out. He was returned to the UN forces at the Peace Village, Panmunjom during Operation Big Switch on September 4, 1953.

Three months after his return from Korea, Maj. Gen. Dean was assigned as the Deputy Commanding General of the 6th US Army at the Presidio of San Francisco in California. He retired October 31, 1955, after 32 years of Army service. Dean was awarded the Combat Infantryman Badge for his front-line service in World War II and Korea. General Dean died August 24, 1981 at the age of 82 and is buried at the United States national cemetery, the Presidio of San Francisco.

Major General William F. Dean, Sr.
Medal of Honor Recipient

Born: 1 August 1899, Carlyle, Illinois
Rank: Major General, Commanding General, 24th Infantry Division
Place and date: Taejon, Korea, 20 and 21 July 1950
Authority: Department of the Army General Order No. 7, 16 February 1951

Citation

Major General Dean distinguished himself by conspicuous gallantry and intrepidity at the repeated risk of his life beyond the call of duty. In command of a unit suddenly relieved from occupation duties in Japan and yet untried in combat, faced with a ruthless and determined enemy, highly trained and overwhelmingly superior in numbers, he felt it his duty to act which to a man of his military experience and knowledge was clearly apt to result in his death.

He personally and alone attacked an enemy tank while armed only with a hand grenade. He also directed the fire of his tanks from an exposed position with neither cover nor concealment while under observed artillery and small-arm fire.

When the town of Taejon became overrun, he refused to ensure his own safety by leaving with the leading elements but remained behind organizing his retreating forces, directing stragglers, and was last seen assisting the wounded to a place of safety.

These actions indicate that Maj. Gen. Dean felt it necessary to sustain the courage and resolution of his troops by examples of excessive gallantry committed always at the threatened portions of his front lines. The magnificent response of his unit to this willing and cheerful sacrifice, made with full knowledge of its certain cost, is history.

The success of this phase of the campaign is in large measure due to Major General Dean's heroic leadership, courageous and loyal devotion to his men, and his complete disregard for personal safety." This was the first Medal of Honor received for valor in the first Korean Conflict. [59]

Medal of Honor Recipient (cmohs.org)

By the end of the battle, the Americans counted 1128 men killed and 228 wounded with almost 2400 missing, including Dean. In December 1951, the North Koreans finally announced that they were holding Dean as a prisoner of war. The reason why the North Koreans waited so long to announce Dean's capture has never been determined.

Medal of Honor

Captain Lewis L. Millett, Sr., Korea 1951
"Red"
Photo: Author US Army

Citation

Capt. Millett, Company E, distinguished himself by conspicuous gallantry and intrepidity above and beyond the call of duty in action. While personally leading his company in an attack against a strongly held position, he noted that

59   History Center Korean War:
      https://armyhistory.org/ordeal-of-the-walking-general-mg-william-f-dean-in-korea

the 1st Platoon was pinned down by small-arms, automatic, and anti-tank fire. Capt. Millett ordered the 3rd Platoon forward, placed himself at the head of the two platoons, and, with a fixed bayonet, led the assault up the fire-swept hill. In the fierce charge, Capt. Millett bayoneted two enemy soldiers and boldly continued, throwing grenades, clubbing and bayoneting the enemy, while urging his men forward by shouting encouragement. Despite vicious opposing fire, the whirlwind hand-to-hand assault carried to the crest of the hill.

His dauntless leadership and personal courage so inspired his men that they stormed into the hostile position and used their bayonets with such lethal effect that the enemy fled in wild disorder. During this fierce onslaught, Capt. Millett was wounded by grenade fragments but refused evacuation until the objective was taken and firmly secured.

The superb leadership, conspicuous courage, and consummate devotion to duty demonstrated by Capt. Millett was directly responsible for the successful accomplishment of a hazardous mission and reflected the highest credit on himself and the heroic traditions of the military service.

Action took place in the vicinity of Hill 180, Soam-Ni, Korea. On February 7, 1951, Colonel Millett, then a Captain, commanded Company E, 2nd Battalion, 27th (IR) 25th Infantry Division. For his leadership during the assault, Millett was awarded the Medal of Honor.

The MOH was formally presented to him by President Harry S. Truman in July 1951. He was also awarded the Army's second-highest award for valor, the Distinguished Service Cross, for leading another bayonet charge the same month.

In the mid-1960s, he commanded the US Army Security Agency (ASA) Training Center and School, at Fort Devens, Massachusetts. Colonel Millett retired in 1973, and later stated he retired because he felt the US had "quit" in Vietnam.

He died on November 14, 2009, one month short of his 89th birthday. His funeral was held December 5, 2009, at Riverside National Cemetery in Riverside, California.

Medal of Honor Recipient (cmohs.org)

Historian S.L.A. Marshall described the attack as "the most complete bayonet charge by American soldiers since the 1864 Civil War "Battle of Cold Harbor" Mechanicsville, Virginia.

US Army Military History Institute (USAMHI), Collection: Marshall, S.L.A.

– Carlisle.army.mil.

American troops of the 25th Infantry Division 27th Infantry Regiment advance past dead Chinese soldiers, south of Seoul during Task Force "Punch," February 1951.
Photo (#957568) US Army.

US Navy/Marine Corps and Naval History and Heritage Command
Mass Communication Specialist US Navy (MCSN) Photo # NH 96876
September 15, 1950

First Lieutenant Baldomero Lopez, USMC, leads the 3rd Platoon, Company A, 1st Battalion, 5th Marines over the seawall on the northern side of Red Beach, as the second assault wave lands, 15 September 1950, during the Inchon invasion. Wooden scaling ladders are in use to facilitate disembarkation from the LCVP that brought these men to the shore. Lt. Lopez was killed in action within a few minutes, while assaulting a North Korean bunker. Note M-1 Carbine carried by Lt. Lopez, M-1 Rifles of other Marines and details of the Marines' field gear. The President of the United States, in the name of Congress, takes pride in presenting the Medal of Honor (Posthumously) to First Lieutenant Baldomero Lopez, United States Marine Corps, for conspicuous gallantry and intrepidity at the risk of his life above and beyond the call of duty on 15 September, 1950, as a Marine platoon commander of Company A, 1st Battalion, Fifth Marines, First Marine Division (Reinforced), in action against enemy aggressor forces during the landing at Inchon, Korea. With his platoon, First Lieutenant Lopez was engaged in the reduction of immediate enemy beach defenses after landing with the assault waves. Exposing himself to hostile fire, he moved forward alongside a bunker and prepared to throw a hand grenade into the next pillbox whose fire was pinning down that sector of the beach. Taken under fire by an enemy automatic weapon and hit in the right shoulder and chest as he lifted his arm to throw, he fell backward and dropped the deadly missile. After a moment, he turned and dragged his body forward to retrieve the grenade and throw it. In critical condition from pain and loss of blood, and unable to grasp the hand grenade firmly enough to hurl it, he chose to sacrifice himself rather than endanger the lives of his men and, with a sweeping motion of his wounded right arm, cradled the grenade under him and absorbed the full impact of the explosion.

His exceptional courage, fortitude, and devotion to duty reflect the highest credit upon First Lieutenant Lopez and the United States Naval Service. He gallantly gave his own life for his country.

National Medal of Honor Museum

In December 2021, the National Medal of Honor Museum Foundation announced that the Arlington (Arlington, Virginia) Entertainment District had been selected by the Foundation's Board of Directors as the site for the future National Medal of Honor Museum. The museum, which is set to open in 2024, will showcase the Medal of Honor recipients and their stories of valor and inspiration in the face of impossible odds.

The National Medal of Honor Museum (NMOHM) will inspire and teach.

3527 total Medals of Honor awarded
66 living receipts
19 recipients honored twice
1 medal awarded to a woman, Mary Edwards Walker
2468 medals awarded to members of the Army
300 medals awarded to members of the Marine Corps
749 medals awarded to members of the Navy
19 medals awarded to members of the Air Force
1 medal awarded to a member of the Coast Guard

NMOHM will host public programs and events featuring living Medal of Honor recipients, noted authors, veterans, and experts in every field.

This museum helps fill the hole, inspiring and educating youth of the splendor of America – why it is worth preserving, and why it is worth fighting for. NMOHM.

Any links to external web sites and/or non-MHOH information provided on MHOH pages, or returned from MHOH search engines, are provided as a courtesy. They should not be construed as an endorsement of the content or views of linked materials. https://miltaryhallofhonor.com/

Doctor Mary Edwards Walker, Wearing her Medal of Honor
Civil War Surgeon

Based on the recommendation of Major Generals William Tecumseh Sherman and George Henry Thomas, President Andrew Johnson signed a bill on November 11, 1865, to present Walker with the Medal of Honor for Meritorious Service. The only woman to receive the Medal of Honor.

The first and only woman recipient was Mary E. Walker, a contract surgeon with the US Army during the US Civil War. Presentation Date & Details: November 11, 1865. Medal issued in 1865; Walker's Medal of Honor rescinded following the 1916-1917 Review of Army Medal of Honor Awards as she was a civilian at the time of her valor; restored to the Medal of Honor Roll in 1977. Location of medal: Pentagon Women's Corridor (Medal presented in

1977), Arlington, VA; Richardson-Bates House Museum (original medal), her Hometown, Oswego, NY.

Ensign Jesse L. Brown
US Navy F4U-4 Corsair USS *Leyte* (CV-32) Fighter Squadron VF-32

The first African American to complete US Navy flight training and the first African American naval aviator in combat and to be killed in combat. On December 4, 1950, on the way to Chosin Reservoir with his squadron, Brown announced over the radio, "I think I may have been hit. I've lost my oil pressure." He crash-landed his Corsair on the side of a mountain in the snow. Unable to safely recover his body, Brown's shipmates instead decided to honor him with a warrior's funeral. On December 7, 1950, seven aircraft loaded with napalm and piloted by Ensign Brown's friends made several low passes over his downed Corsair. The top of Brown's head was still visible with snow on his hair when they dropped the napalm on his plane while reciting The Lord's Prayer. Ens. Brown posthumously received the Distinguished Flying Cross. For his twenty missions over N Korea, he also earned the Air Medal and the Purple Heart for his actions. He was also honored with a ship bearing his name: USS *Jesse L. Brown* (DE 1089), a KNOX Class-Frigate. Korean War Movie 'Devotion' an Epic Story of Friendship and Courage. "Devotion," a movie drama released in September 2022, is about the real-life friendship between Navy aviators Jesse Brown and Tom Hudner. Tom passed up Harvard to fly for his country. Jesse became the navy's first African American carrier pilot.

MCSN USN # 1146845, circa 1950, NHHC and the NMUSN.

PART THREE
2ND KOREAN CONFLICT

CHAPTER 16

POLITICAL TURMOIL: 1960S

The Republic of Korea experienced political turmoil under years of autocratic leadership by President Syngman Rhee, which was ended by student revolt in 1960. Throughout his rule, Rhee sought to take additional steps to cement his control of government. The increasingly authoritarian rule of Rhee, along with government corruption and injustice, added to the discontent of the people.

The elections of March 1960, in which Rhee won a 4th term, were marked by widespread violence, police brutality, and accusations by Rhee's opponents of government fraud. A student protest in April 1960, in which 125 students were shot down by the police, triggered a wave of uprisings across the country. The government capitulated, and Rhee resigned and went into exile.

Under the leadership of Dr. John M. Chang (Chang Myung), a new government was unable to correct the economic problems or maintain order, and in May 1961 the S Korean armed forces seized power in a bloodless coup.

Thus a "military coup" was staged on May 16, 1961, by the military gangsters represented by pro-American and pro-Japanese stooge Park Chung Hee, under the backstage manipulation of US imperialism.

Under the criminal "ROK-Japan treaty" and "agreements" concluded on June 22, 1965, under the wire pulling of US imperialism the S Korean puppets were tied up with the Japanese militarists, and the US imperialists became still more flagrant in their scheme to put up the Japanese military force as the "shock brigade" for aggression on Korea and other regions of Asia.

The US imperialists' preparations for a new war and their military provocations reached a graver stage in Korea following the rigging up of the military fascist dictatorial regime and the conclusion of the criminal "ROK Japan treaty" and "agreements."

Keeping pace with the war rackets of their master, the S Korean puppet clique cried ever louder for a north-south showdown by force, putting up the slogan of "reunification through domination over communism" instead of "reunification through a northward march."

The military junta under General (President) Park Chung-hee established tight control over civil freedoms, the press, and the economy, somewhat relaxing restrictions as its power solidified. Park was elected president in 1963, reelected in 1967, and following a constitutional amendment permitting a third term, again in 1971. Park's government was remarkably successful in fighting graft and corruption and in reviving the economy.

Successive five-year economic development plans, first launched in 1962, brought dramatic changes. Between 1962 and 1972, manufacturing was established as a leading economic sector and exports increased dramatically. By the time of Park's death in 1979, life was still difficult, but it was getting better.

On June 22, 1965, The Treaty on Basic Relations between Japan and the Republic of Korea was signed to establish basic diplomatic relations between Japan and S Korea. This diplomatic agreement established "normal" diplomatic relations between two East Asian neighbors.

The original documents of this agreement are kept respectively by Japan and Korea. The treaty is drafted using English, Japanese, and Korean, and each is considered authentic. In case of a "divergence of interpretation," the English-language version shall be deemed authoritative and prevailing. The 1965 treaty also declared that all treaties or agreements concluded between the Empire of Japan and the Empire of Korea, on or before August 29, 1910, are already null and void. The Treaty of Portsmouth formally ended the Russo-Japanese War and was signed on September 5, 1905, and it affirmed the Japanese presence in Korea. The years of colonization by imperial Japan (1910-45) humiliated Korea. The treaty became void after Japan surrendered at the end of World War II. There are no provisions to form a Japanese military force as the "shock brigade" for aggression on N Korea and other regions of Asia.

After a long lull following the Korean armistice, N Korea became more aggressive. During the late 1950s, each side carefully fortified its respective positions. In June 1959, the S Korean Army repelled several large-scale infiltration attempts by N Korean army units in the DMZ. The N Korean soldiers would deliberately provoke the Joint Security Area (JSA) security guards, and fistfights were common. The situation did not improve during the early 1960s. N Korean probes continued.

On October 3, 1962, a soldier from the 1CD was murdered by an unknown assailant. He was shot with rounds from a submachine gun while he was on guard duty. This was a grim milestone. Before this, the N Korean infiltrators engaged only S Korean forces. Over the next several months, more US soldiers were killed by infiltrators, some as far as 35 miles south of the DMZ, near the capital city of Seoul. N Korea clearly demonstrated its forces had no problems slipping agents into the interior of S Korea and had a support system in place to carry out its operations. On April 27, 1965, two N Korean MiG-17s attacked a USAF RB-47 Stratojet, a reconnaissance plane above the Sea of Japan, 50 miles from the N Korean coast. The aircraft was damaged but managed to land at Yokota Air Base, Japan. During this same time, a small naval battle occurred when a S Korean naval vessel sank a N Korean patrol boat in international waters.

A call to battle sounded from the convention of the Korean Workers Party (KWP) in Pyongyang in October 1966 at which Kim Il-sung announced a campaign of hostile acts aimed at the "liberation" of S Korea and the unification of South and North. The seeds for the 1960s Korean Conflict were planted. The significance of his speech was underestimated at the time, but in effect this was N Korea's declaration of war on UN Command forces in S Korea. This was followed by a dramatic rise in N Korean infiltration, terrorist incidents, and firefights along the DMZ. Between 1966 and 1967 incidents increased tenfold.

The Korean peninsula provided the background for a military confrontation that included guerrilla warfare, sabotage, and terrorism directed against the people of S Korea and the Americans serving there. The situation tested the willpower and resolve of the US and S Korea. As US involvement in the Vietnam conflict escalated, the tempo of incidents and violations of the Korean armistice also increased. Though it was not readily apparent at the time, there was speculation regarding a connection between the war in Southeast Asia and hostile acts committed by the N Koreans. N Korea became the third country to recognize North Vietnam (N Vietnam) in 1950, after China and Russia. President Ho Chi Minh traveled to N Korea in 1957 for an official summit with Kim Il-sung. During the Vietnam conflict, N Korea provided substantial economic and military aid to N Vietnam. In early 1967 N Korea sent a fighter squadron to N Vietnam to back up the N Vietnamese. It stayed through 1968; 200 pilots were reported to have served. In addition, at least two anti-aircraft artillery regiments were sent as well. Kim Il-sung told his pilots to "fight in the conflict as if the Vietnamese sky were their own."

Throughout the 1960s, N Korea enjoyed a healthier economy than N Vietnam. A rice-for-weapons program was established, with Vietnam receiving various modern armaments and N Korea pledging to assist in the conflict against the United States. From 1968, however, relations between Pyongyang and Hanoi started to deteriorate for various reasons. Anxious to keep the US bogged down in Vietnam, N Korea disagreed with N Vietnam's decision to enter peace negotiations with the US, and reacted negatively to the Paris Peace Accords.

During the period November 2, 1966, to December 3, 1969, American soldiers assigned to units positioned on and near the DMZ participated in combat actions against the N Koreans. This duty was shared between the 2nd and 7th US Infantry Divisions. These divisions were essentially due north of Seoul and provided security for an 18-mile sector of the DMZ. S Korea divisions manned the remaining 132 miles of the DMZ, also known as the Zone, or the Z. Small arms and artillery fire became commonplace along the 38th Parallel. This period is referred to as the 1960s Korean Conflict, Korean DMZ Conflict or as the "Quiet War." There was a series of armed clashes among N Korean, S Korean, and US forces.

The United States' Other "DMZ"

The point man gripped his M-16 rifle tightly as he pushed through the underbrush. Carefully looking for booby traps along the trail, he strained his ears, listening for the slightest sound ahead of him. It was dark as the patrol inched its way forward through the valley far below the guard posts on the hills of the DMZ. A branch snapped somewhere in the darkness. The point man turned to signal the patrol to stop as a shot rang out, hitting him in the chest. Grenades exploded, sending blinding flashes along with shrapnel into the night sky in all directions.

The young sergeant leading the patrol ran forward in a low crotch as his men automatically started shooting and fanned out along the sides of the trail. As he approached the small rise separating the main body from the point man, a burst of fire caught him in the shoulder, knocking him to the ground. He fought to remain conscious as he crawled toward the body of the point man. He yelled, but there was no answer.

Meanwhile, as the radio operator grabbed the hand mike of the radio and called back to the command post for help, the assistant patrol leader shouted for covering fire and slithered forward. Everyone was shooting, and the dull "thud" of the M79 grenade launcher was answered by a "kaboom" as it exploded on the far side of the rise. The sergeant's voice could be heard between the shooting as he yelled for a medic, and the specialist four (SP4), now in charge, had only one thing on his mind — to get the wounded out of the line of fire. He shouted back to the men in the rear to move around the hill to a position where they could put more fire on the enemy; but as quickly as it had begun, the shooting stopped. The radio squawked to life and asked for a situation report and location as the survivors regrouped and prepared for a counterattack.

The battle scene described above was Korea in the mid-1960s. It was the US' other DMZ. A nearly forgotten place where soldiers from the 2nd Infantry "Indianhead" Division and the 7th Infantry "Bayonet" Division were engaged in combat operations on a smaller scale, but no less deadly, than the operations faced during the same period by fellow "grunts" in Vietnam.

(Korea DMZ Part 1 Military Review Published by US Army Command and General Staff College Volume LXVIII – May 1988 – No 5 pp 32-43.)

Citation: Vandon, Jenerette, US Army (Ret) 1967-1991
Jenerette <vandoniii@aol.com>

CHAPTER 17

2ND KOREAN CONFLICT 1966 — 1969

The 1960s Korean Conflict was both a civil war on the Korean peninsula and the second military clash of the Cold War between Russian forces and its communist ally, China, and the US and its allies. The armistice ended America's first experience with the Cold War concept of "limited war." As part of the first conflict ceasefire agreement, a cap of no more than 1,000 personnel from each side would be authorized within the DMZ at any one time. Automatic and/or crew-served weapons would be banned from within the DMZ. The N Koreans broke these rules almost immediately with deadly results, along with attacks on UN Command, US Army, US Air Force, and US Navy aircraft.

The hostilities and hazards continued beyond the 1950s conflict and led to direct action against American soldiers patrolling the DMZ. The incidents described below are examples of N Korean actions.

On February 5, 1955, a UNC aircraft was attacked by four Chinese MiG-15s over the Yellow Sea. An air-fight resulted between eight US Air Force F-86 Sabre fighters and 12 MiGs. One MiG was damaged and two shot down.

On August 18, 1955, an unarmed US T-6 trainer plane converted for observation was shot down by N Korean groundfire near Panmunjom, killing the pilot, and the copilot was listed as missing in action.

On March 6, 1958, a US Air Force F-86A Sabre fighter was shot down over the DMZ by ground fire.

On April 20, 1961, a US pilot was fired upon by N Korean planes; the pilot crashed in an attempted emergency landing south of Seoul, and the pilot died.

On October 1, 1962, one US soldier was killed in the DMZ, the first time since the armistice ceasefire.

On May 17, 1963, an 8th Army OH-23 Raven, a light observation helicopter, was shot down in N Korean territory and two crewmen were captured. They were released a year later.

Accordingly, from the armistice in 1953, danger, violence, and death typified American military service along the demilitarized zone.

In 1965, S Korea was alarmed by the US plan to move two of its military divisions stationed in S Korea to S Vietnam, and the possible ramifications of this move on S Korea's security, especially against N Korea.

S Korea — and for that matter, the American — commitments to S Vietnam were made, understanding they created heightened risks to the security of S Korea. The N Korean government in Pyongyang took note and was emboldened by this prospect and began a gradual increase in hostile actions along the DMZ and the offshore islands. These areas had been hot zones since the 1953 armistice. Cross-border conflict and occasional sea battles occurred.

The descriptions of the 1960s Korean Conflict, casualties, frequency of violent incidents, and statistical summaries are in the introduction — specifically, Tables 5 and 6.

Infiltration by N Korean agents increased, and these were the realities of living adjacent to a hostile N Korea. During the Vietnam Conflict years, the N Koreans stepped up their harassment to extremely dangerous levels. Ultimately, the US decided not to send the 2nd and 7th Infantry Divisions to S Vietnam; however, these divisions were not at full strength and lacked the authorized number of officers and non-commissioned officers (NCOs). In time, these personnel shortages were rectified. In return, President Park Chunghee reached an agreement with the US regarding sending S Korean forces to S Vietnam. The S Korean government sought concessions, including combat pay for its soldiers (at American expense), military equipment for S Korean reserve units, and a guarantee of American force levels in Korea. American authorities agreed to the terms, and on August 19, 1965, the S Korean assembly authorized the deployment of combat troops to S Vietnam. From 1965 to 1973, S Korea sent more than 320,000 troops to S Vietnam. S Korean participation was made possible because the US was willing to underwrite [60] the entire Korean military and civilian operations in the country. S Korean units were as tough and professional as any in the US Army or Marines and came to be justly feared by the N Vietnamese military and the Viet Cong the guerrilla force that fought against S Vietnam (late 1950s-1975) the United States and its allies. More than 5000 died in the conflict. They fought hard. S Korea participated in the war along with other allied countries—S Vietnam, Australia, New Zealand, Thailand, and the Philippines.

In N Korea, the departure of the Chinese People's Volunteer Army by October 1958 gave N Korea leader Kim Il-sung a free hand to do things his way. His goal, simply stated, was "the fortification of the entire country" as a base for reunifying Korea by force.

> Weapons are tools of ill omen.
> -Sun-tzu, Chinese military theorist, ca. 350 BC

A new kind of conflict was on the horizon. Prior to the renewed N Korean infiltration in 1966, only eight US soldiers died along the DMZ in isolated, uncoordinated exchanges of gunfire. Sporadic combat mainly involved S Korean forces along their sections of the DMZ. In multiple small-scale engagements along the east, central, and western sections N Koreans killed 28 S Korean soldiers in a series of raids. In September 1966, in a country few Americans knew much about, events were in motion that would change the destination for thousands of US soldiers. For some, these events would change their lives forever; for others, these events would mean a rendezvous with death in a frozen rice paddy far from ("the world," the United States) home and far from Vietnam in a place called Korea. As US involvement in the Vietnam Conflict continued to escalate, the tempo of incidents and violations of the Korean armistice also increased.

---

60   S Koreans were allowed to shop at the Post Exchange (PX) stores in S Vietnam where they could use their per diem and bonus pay to buy hi-fi stereos, color televisions and other consumer goods. Initially, the Koreans were being paid before American troops, which created a shortage problem. This was reversed once the problem surfaced.

Though it was not readily apparent at the time, there was speculation regarding a connection between the war in Southeast Asia and hostile acts committed by the N Koreans. The Korean peninsula provided the perfect background for a military confrontation that included guerrilla warfare, sabotage, and terrorism directed against the people of S Korea and the Americans serving there. The situation tested the willpower and resolve of the US and S Korea. Premier Kim Il-sung in his speech to the Korean Workers Party (KWP) Conference on October 5, 1966, gave warning that the status quo since 1953 between North and South Korea was about to change, and the overall strategy would be to destabilize S Korea, linking military action to the conflict in Vietnam. N Korea was an active ally of North Vietnam. The Vietnam conflict was seen as an opportunity, and by late October 1966 violence along the demilitarized zone increased. N Korea began to attack both S Korean and US soldiers stationed in and near the DMZ. N Korea sent combat patrols probing the DMZ. Booby traps were set along familiar US and S Korean patrol routes; wooden box mines were buried along the inter-Korean border in streams and rivers. The ATM-74 wooden box mine used was a copy of the anti-personnel Soviet mine that was used during World War II. It consisted of a wooden box packed full of explosives and a pressure fuse. The mine was detonated when pressure was applied to the box or when someone tried to pry it open. The wooden box mine was designed to cause serious injury, usually the amputation of one or more limbs, rather than death. It had the minimum amount of metal components, making it extremely hard to detect using conventional mine detectors. Because the mines were buoyant, they were easily washed down from the hills and mountains in the frontlines to shorelines and riverbanks by torrential rains. They continue to be a constant threat to civilians and soldiers working inside and near the DMZ.

(In 2015, two S Korean soldiers were injured by two wooden box mines inside the DMZ. In August 2020, S Korean soldiers successfully removed two wooden box mines found on the inter-Korean border swept away from N Korea because of heavy rain. A new fully localized mine detector that can be used for sweeping and mapping minimum-metal land mines such as the wooden box land mines, was developed through a joint project led by Hanwha Systems, a major defense contractor in S Korea. The new detector began to be deployed in 2022.)

In addition to an anti-personnel mine, anti-vehicle mines and explosive devices concealed under or on the ground were placed on trails patrolled by Jeeps and armored personnel carriers and were detonated as a combatant vehicle passed over or near it, destroying or disabling the vehicle. Mortar and antitank fire sometimes accompanied ground probes by N Korean soldiers, either as distractions or in direct support of an attack.

This open show of force started the 1960s Korean Conflict, also known as the Korean DMZ Conflict, which resulted in US, S Korean, and N Korean casualties. By the time it sputtered to an ill-defined end more than three years later, N Korea had challenged the UN forces in every category of conflict and failed. First, unlike the 1950s Korean Conflict, the conflict in Korea during 1966-1969 was not a conventional stand-up fight. During 1966, N Korea positioned eight infantry divisions along its side of the DMZ. Eight additional divisions, three motorized infantry divisions, the 105th Armored Division, and various infantry and tank brigades were on standby. In addition to conventional forces, the 17th Foot Reconnaissance Brigade and the 124th and 283rd Special Forces Army Units. (On July 2, 1950, the 105th Armored Division faced off against American forces for the first time in the Battle of Osan. Today, the division remains a military unit of the North Korean People's Army.)

The 1960s Korean Conflict is the story of a wrong war that turned out right. The "right place" was Southeast Asia. American commanders in Korea faced the difficult prospect of defending their area without daring to start a second major Asian war. During most of the two decades after the 1953 armistice, both N and S Korea continued to press claims for reunification under their respective flags. *Smell the Gunpowder* is intended to be both informative and reflect on the veterans who served in Korea on land, sea, and air.

In mid-October, weeks before President Lyndon B. Johnson's scheduled visit to S Korea, N Korean infiltrators had attacked two S Korean patrols south of the DMZ, killing 17 soldiers. S Korea had promptly retaliated by sending an attack team north of the DMZ, which killed 30 N Korean troops. In late October, the N Koreans began attacking again and again S Korean forces and prepared to ambush American troops. President Johnson departed Washington DC on October 17, 1966, visiting six nations in Asia and the Pacific. Alarmed by the steady increase in violent incidents, the UNC raised the alert status of all forces in the weeks prior to Johnson's arrival. S Korea was the last stop and President Johnson arrived October 31, 1966, meeting in Seoul at the Blue House, the presidential residence, with President Chung Hee Park and Prime Minister Key Young Chung. The two presidents acknowledged the need to ensure that the forces of aggression do not again menace the peace and tranquility of the Republic of Korea. President Johnson reaffirmed the readiness and determination of the US to render prompt and effective assistance to defeat an armed attack against S Korea, in accordance with the Mutual Defense Treaty of 1954. President Johnson was sleeping at Walker Hill Resort near Seoul when N Korean commandos ambushed the United Nations (UN) patrol. It happened just a few hours before he was to leave Seoul for home at the end of his Asian journey. UN Command forces remained ready, but N Korea made no move against Johnson, and he departed S Korea as scheduled.

The first battle involving American soldiers was fought in early November 1966. The year 2022 marks the 56th anniversary of the beginning of the 1960s Korean Conflict.

First Major Incident:

Ambush United Nations Command Patrol

The N Koreans favored the dry ground, longer nights, and fog of early fall before the snow came. The months of September, October, and the first two weeks of November became prime infiltration times.

The first battle of this new phase of the 1960s Korean Conflict was fought on November 2, 1966. In the early morning at 0300 hours (3:00 a.m.), with the light of the full moon providing good illumination, two four-man squads, which included one S Korean KATUSA [61], left their home base located adjacent to the north side of the Imjin River, and about half-mile below the southern boundary (South Tape) of the demilitarized zone.

The camp was basically just a small collection of Quonset huts, a lightweight prefabricated structure of corrugated galvanized steel having a semicircular cross-section to house the men in between their guard shifts and patrol duty. The camp housed one company of infantrymen.

---

61   Korean augmentation to the US Army (KATUSA) is a branch of the Republic of Korea Army and consists of Korean drafted personnel who are assigned to the 8th United States Army. KATUSA members are equipped with standard US Army issues, and live and work with the US enlisted soldiers.

The patrol was a mix of volunteers and draftees ranging in age from 17 to 20, and two were barely out of high school. They were lightly armed with M-14 rifles, an M-79 grenade launcher, and two short-range radios. The squads crossed the line of departure to conduct a patrol north of the Imjin River.

They had the misfortune of patrolling the South Tape—the edge of the southern buffer zone. The men belonged to A Company, 1st Battalion, 23rd IR, 2nd ID. S Korean soldiers were embedded with the 2nd Infantry Division beginning in early 1950 during the first Korean Conflict. KATUSA members lived and worked with US enlisted soldiers. Shadowing the patrol were members of the elite N Korean 17th Foot Reconnaissance Brigade. They quietly moved ahead of the patrol and set up an ambush near the north side of the Libby Bridge spanning the Imjin River, just outside the village of Changpa-ri in the division's area of responsibility along the 18-mile sector. The two squads were forced to combine because one of their radios malfunctioned. It proved a fateful decision, one that allowed the N Koreans to concentrate their fire on the unsuspecting squad. The ambush began at 0315 hours (3:15 a.m.); it was over in a matter of minutes. Not content to merely kill the soldiers, the N Koreans fired bullets into their bodies, smashed in their heads, bayoneted them, and mutilated the dead. The N Koreans drew first blood. Six American soldiers and one S Korean of a UN Command patrol were killed. At the same time of the attack, a S Korean patrol was ambushed, killing two soldiers. Both attacks were well timed and well executed. The story of what happened was left to be told by the only survivor, Private David L. Bibee, a 17-year-old from Ringgold, Virginia who had been in-country for only three weeks. Wounded by 48 grenade fragments in his leg and shoulder, he survived by playing dead when a N Korean yanked his wristwatch off. This was the gravest incident involving American troops since the armistice in the series of clashes along the DMZ. The infiltrators ("line crossers") escaped back across the Military Demarcation Line (MDL) into N Korea. After spending about a month in the hospital, Bibee was assigned to a unit in the Seoul area. He never returned to DMZ duty to serve again as an infantryman. The ambush signaled the start of the 1960s Korean Conflict. During the 12 months that followed, more than two dozen Americans were killed, and scores more were wounded in combat.

In October 1966, President Lyndon B. Johnson flew into S Korea and inspected the area around the Military Demarcation Line. The Korean situation thereafter became so grave it resembled the situation on the eve of the first Korean Conflict

(Korean War) that had been created in June 1950, after Dulles' inspection of the 38th parallel.

Draws a comparison between Dulles and Johnson's visit to S Korea that ignited the first and second conflicts, respectively. Echoes of the Korean War.

Korea went from a cold war to a hot war overnight. Incidents of violence along the DMZ and in the interior of S Korea increased dramatically. The N Korean regime was launching attacks to test US resolve to defend S Korea during the Vietnam Conflict and create uncertainty in S Korea. N Korea pressed its attacks with increasing ferocity in 1967 and 1968; the outcome was unclear. Service north of the Imjin River, the geographical boundary for the American sector of the DMZ, became a nerve-fraying and sporadically lethal business.

In January 1967, Army General Charles H. Bonesteel, commander of the combined US and S Korean forces, focused on stemming the tide of N Korean infiltration. The combined forces established an innovative and enduring infiltrator "net" in the DMZ. The net consisted of four parts: forward patrols, integrated guard posts, an improved physical barrier along the DMZ, and pre-position-quick-reaction-forces. Forming the patrolling portion of the net, squad-and-platoon-sized elements went out for up to twenty-four-hour periods, with each company within the areas assigned to American forces along the DMZ always having a patrol out. They moved during daylight and established ambushes at night. The improved physical barriers consisted of a line of obstacles — tanglefoot and anti-personnel mines; a ten-foot-tall chain-link-fence with razor-sharp triple-strand concertina wire along the top remained formidable; and a line of guard towers and foxholes interconnected by landline and radio. A raked sand path on the southern side highlighted any infiltrator foot traffic. Engineers cleared grounds and installed searchlights and sensors increasing visibility between guard posts. Another innovation came from the Army importing buckwheat, the white blooms of the grain making thermal signatures more detectable when using night versions. Bonesteel emphasized the physical barriers and was not meant to stop infiltrators but rather hinder them and alert forces of intrusions for rapid application of the reaction forces to catch them.

In the wake of the November 2 ambush, the rules of engagement were loosened in January 1967 to allow the use of artillery and mortar fire against known N Korean elements in or south of the DMZ and against N Korean firing from north

212

of the Military Demarcation Line (MDL). The MDL is the land border and goes through the center of the DMZ and indicates where the battle front was when the armistice was signed. Spring 1967 witnessed a dramatic increase in losses due to ambushes, sabotage, and mines. One of the biggest battles of the conflict occurred in April when a reinforced N Korean platoon, more than 100 soldiers, slipped across the MDL and attacked a S Korean position within the DMZ. During the six-hour battle, the S Koreans were forced to call in artillery to repel the N Koreans. This was the first time artillery had been used in the DMZ since 1953.

At dusk on May 21, 1967, a N Korean heavily armed sapper team (commandos) slipped through the American-patrolled area. The sapper team covered their bodies with charcoal dust and grease that made them almost invisible in the dark. They were carrying explosives that were intended to be used for the express purpose of bombing an American barracks. The most common weapons in a field sapper's arsenal included AK-47 assault rifles, hand grenades, and TNT satchel charges. Prior infiltrations with the purpose of killing American soldiers had centered on small-arms ambushes near the DMZ. This attack was going to be different and intended to send a message to the Americans that not even in their barracks away from the frontlines were they safe. The N Koreans infiltrated three miles behind the American lines before coming upon Camp Walley. The N Koreans were so skilled at infiltration that they were able to creep around the camp and investigate the different buildings and determine which ones had the most people in them before blowing them up. Unfortunately for the men of First Platoon, A Company, 1st Battalion 23rd IR, their barracks were chosen. The saboteurs set their explosives on two different barracks and fled. At dawn, the explosives went off destroying the two buildings. The bombing killed two soldiers and wounded 17 others. The soldiers were killed in their beds while they slept.

In response to the urgency of the situation, US Army Special Forces teams, based in Okinawa, were inserted into the rugged mountain areas of S Korea and fought against the N Koreans during the summer of 1967. During the nine-month period from May 1967 through January 1968, in the US sector of the DMZ alone there were more than 300 reported hostile acts during which 15 US soldiers were killed and 65 wounded.

In June, a 2nd ID barracks was dynamited. By mid-1967, US patrolling along the DMZ became extremely serious. The N Korean-Army "hunter-killer" squads sought Americans. Losses in 1967 increased dramatically in comparison to previous years.

In accord with Kim Il-sung's new intent, Americans suffered some especially sharp reverses both on patrols and in their rear areas, with 16 killed and more than 50 wounded. S Korean casualties also climbed to over 100 killed and more than 200 wounded. To bolster defensive capability, two heavily armored M 48 "Patton" tanks, with a 90mm anti-tank gun from the 1st Tank Battalion 73rd Armor, Camp Beavers, were positioned overlooking the southern boundary line.

The N Koreans follow-up was a rapid acceleration of military attacks, amphibious landings by commandos, sabotage and guerrilla actions that would test US resolve to honor its commitment to the security of S Korea.

The skies above the DMZ saw North and South Koreans jets sparring, and the seas along the coast saw engagements between the two small-boat navies, resulting in increased casualties between the two sides without US involvement.

On August 10, 1967, a work detail from the US 13th Engineer Battalion was repairing a section of fence and clearing vegetation that might conceal N Korean infiltrators. Near noon, a light rain began, and the detail departed the worksite aboard two trucks headed back to their home base for lunch. Four men on each truck were armed with M-14 semi-automatic rifles, while the rest were unarmed. As the lead truck downshifted about halfway up a steep hill, N Korean infiltrators jumped out of the underbrush and lobbed grenades onto the truck's hood and open bed. At least eight grenades landed on or near the truck. One of the first landed on the right side of the hood near the windshield, killing the detail leader and seriously wounding the driver. With its driver disabled, the truck rolled back down the muddy slope and jack-knifed, overturning the water trailer it was towing. Other N Koreans opened fire with automatic weapons, including a heavy machine gun. One American soldier was killed by a grenade that landed in the crowded truck bed and another was killed by automatic weapons fire. September saw two S Korean trains blasted, one carrying US military supplies. In October, N Korean artillery fire sounded when more than 50 rounds were fired at a S Korean army barracks. By late 1967, it was clear that the N Koreans were attempting to develop a full-scale insurgency in S Korea.

On September 26, 1967, the anti-infiltration fence in their 18-mile sector was completed. One battalion of 7th ID joined the 2nd ID to start a new rotation system that placed four maneuver battalions on the DMZ and a 5th in reserve as a quick reaction force.

In 1976, in now declassified minutes, US Deputy Secretary of Defense William Clements told Henry A. Kissinger, Secretary of State under President Richard M. Nixon, that there had been 200 raids or incursions into N Korea from S Korea, though not by the US military. Details of only a small number of these incursions have become public, including at least three retaliatory cross-border raids in late 1967, using small teams of converted N Korean defectors. The raids killed 33 N Korean soldiers and sabotaged about 50 N Korean facilities. On September 27, 1967, S Koreans raided N Korea again with six converted N Korean agents after crossing the Imjin River near Gungjeong-ri encountered 15 N Korean soldiers south of the DMZ laying wooden-box landmines, and quickly eliminated the soldiers. (Minutes of Washington Special Actions Group Meeting, Washington, August 25, 1976. Office of the Historian, US Department of State, Washington, DC. [62])

During 1967-January 1968, N Korea infiltrated S Korea 566 times, killing 122 UN soldiers and wounding another 279 along with 22 S Korean police officers. Civilians were also killed, along with 53 others wounded during the incursions. US forces suffered 15 casualties and 65 injuries. However, these actions were only a prelude to more violent and drastic attacks yet to come. The N Koreans were putting one crisis on top of another.

> *From the outset of 1967 the US imperialists were crazy for military provocations. Up to January 18 they daily infiltrated dozens of warships and armed vessels into the coastal waters of the DPRK, and on January 19 their armed spy boat, patrol craft escort PCE-56, was sunk by self-defense measures of the Korean People's Army while committing provocative acts in the territorial waters of the DPRK. Echoes of the Korean War Booklet published in N Korea.*

Throughout the mid-1960s, the N Koreans continued their covert attempts to destabilize the government of S Korea. N Korean infiltrators continued to probe the DMZ, and N Korean spy rings were continually discovered in the South. N Korean attacks increased along the DMZ, and a 120-man commando team landed on S Korea's east coast. All the infiltrators were eventually killed or captured, but only after the loss of many civilian lives.

---

62   Foreign Relations of the United States, 1969–1976, Volume E–12, Documents on East and Southeast Asia, 1973–1976 - Office of the Historian.
    https://history.state.gov/./historicaldocuments/frus1969-76ve12/d28

During 1968 alone, 1245 N Korean agents/infiltrators were captured in the South. [63]

Casualties 1960s, described in the introduction—specifically, Table 5. The 2nd Korean Conflict DMZ Incidents: Statistical Summary described in the introduction—specifically, Table 6.

North Korean Special Operation Force – "Blue House" Raid

In 1966, the Korean People's Army (KPA) started training Unit 124 for the express purpose of assassinating S Korean President Park Chung-hee. The mission's secondary purpose was to create chaos throughout S Korea, and with assistance from clandestine N Korean supporters, launch a guerrilla campaign against the S Korean government to create a regime collapse. The soldiers selected for this mission were handpicked and trained for two years, including the last two weeks at a full-scale model of the Blue House near Wonsan.

The soldiers received intensive training on infiltration and exfiltration methods, weapons, land navigation, hand-to-hand combat, and concealment. The intense training resulted in numerous injuries; at the end, only 31 soldiers made the cut for the mission. The 124th N Korean Special Operations Force, led by 27-year-old Lieutenant Pak Jae-gyong, left Wonsan on January 16, 1968 and headed for the N Korean section of the DMZ. Each team member had dark overalls, tennis shoes, a cap, a submarine gun, a pistol, eight grenades, an antitank mine, a dagger, and a rucksack with other supplies. On the night of January 17-18, the soldiers infiltrated across the 2nd ID section of the DMZ, near Yeoncheon, in six different teams. The KPA chose the US sector because its personnel were known to operate under more restrictive rules of engagement than the S Koreans and, if the assassination was successful, S Korea might have blamed the US for the security failure. The teams had cut the wire on the south fence by 2300 hundred local time (11:00 p.m.) and, by 0200 hours (2:00 a.m.), the six teams had assembled at camp sites near Morae-dong and Seokpo-ri. The unit remained at these campsites until crossing the frozen Imjin River wearing white bedsheets at 0500 hours (5:00 a.m.) on January 19 and subsequently creating a single campsite on Simbong Mountain to hide in during daylight hours.

---

[63] Incidents in the relatively bloody 1960s were mostly isolated shooting encounters along the DMZ. There continued to be violent incidents in the DMZ through the 1970s and 1980s, although fewer took place relative to the 1960s.

At 1400 hours (2:00 p.m.), four S Koreans searching for firewood stumbled across the campsite and were captured. The team members debated whether to kill them but decided instead to convert them to their communist ideology. After several hours of indoctrination and threats by the KPA soldiers, the S Koreans promised not to give them away. After being released, however, they immediately alerted the police of what had happened.

After releasing the S Koreans, the team broke camp and traveled crossing Nogodan Mountain and arriving at Bibong Mountain on January 20 at 0700 hours (7:00 a.m.) S Korean forces immediately started a search for the N Koreans on Simbong and Nogodan Mountains, but the N Koreans had long departed those areas. The S Korean authorities increased security around Seoul, including at any high-value targets. After spending the rest of the day and most of the night on Bibong Mountain discussing what to do since they had been detected, they devised a new plan. The unit broke into teams of two to three soldiers and continued to infiltrate to a rally point at the Seungga-sa Temple, located on the northern side of the Seoul suburbs less than eight miles from the Blue House. They removed their overalls—revealing a S Korean Army uniform of the local S Korean 26th Infantry Division.

The Unit 124 soldiers openly marched in a platoon formation along Segeomjeong Road toward the Blue House, passing several S Korean police officers and army units. Whenever questioned by authorities, the N Korean leader would say they were a S Korean platoon on a break from the search operation.

At 2200 hours (10:00 p.m.) January 21, the unit approached the Segeomjeong-Jahamun checkpoint, less than 100 meters (110 yards) from the Blue House, President Park's residence, before being discovered and attacked, resulting in a large-scale firefight. The heavily armed Capital Garrison Command protecting the presidential residence [64] responded immediately, and an intense firefight ensued with the well-trained N Koreans. Unit 124 suffered grievous losses. Most of its members were killed in the opening minutes of the assault or in the shootout that followed. One was captured and another member of the unit, Lieutenant Pak, made it back to N Korea and was hailed as a hero. Pak Jae-gyong went on to become a general in the Korean People's Army, and a Vice Minister

---

64   In August 1974, S Korean President Park Chung Hee's wife was killed during another attempt on his life. An agent of a pro-N Korean group in Japan who entered Seoul disguised as a tourist fired several shots at Park at major public function; Park escaped unhurt, but the First The lady was hit by stray bullets and died several hours later. The agent, Mun Se-gwang, was tried and convicted and executed.

in the Ministry of People's Armed Forces. In September 2010, he was appointed as a member of the Central Committee of the Workers Party Korea (WPK). At the age of 76, he became a senior military and political official, surviving three generations of N Korean leaders. The year 2022 marks the 54th anniversary of the raid. Pak Jae-gyong was present at the Singapore Summit 2018 between former US President Donald J. Trump and N Korean leader Kim Jong-un.

Although the unit was believed to have been disbanded after the raid, it was succeeded by KPA's special battalions, part of the reconnaissance agency, formed to conduct intelligence gathering, espionage, terrorism, and abduction operations in S Korea. N Korean propaganda sought to depict the commando raids as a S Korean guerrilla movement akin to the Vietnamese Viet Cong.

President Park and his cabinet ministers grasped the enormity of this latest outrage. They insisted on retaliation against N Korea. Leaders in the South urged Park to "go north" with or without US support. S Korean generals bragged openly of their inclinations to interpret rules of engagement to permit hot pursuit all the way to the Yalu River.

The US restrained President Park from acting by reminding him that it controlled the ammunition, bombs, and fuel needed for such an action and said that the United States-Republic of Korea Mutual Defense Treaty, which only obligated support in the case of an external attack, would not apply. Fortunately, cooler heads prevailed, and a more limited response resulted. President Park ordered his armed forces to retaliate in kind. Accordingly, S Korean assassination squads were organized to carry out strikes on N Korea and the communist leader Kim Il-sung.

The Blue House incident raised tensions along the DMZ to their highest point since the armistice. The raid occurred on the same day that the Battle of Khe Sanh started in S Vietnam on January 21, 1968, making any US support for S Korean retaliation unlikely. Before the night was over, 92 S Koreans had become casualties of the firefight. Four American soldiers were also killed and three were wounded. However, the deadly attack would be overshadowed by yet another crisis, which took place two days later January 23, 1968: the USS *Pueblo* (GER-2) capture.

The Blue House Raid and the *Pueblo* incidents both served to raise the profile of the conflict being fought in S Korea and finally brought in the resources needed to fully implement the joint US-S Korea counterinsurgency strategy.

On April 1, 1968, the Department of Defense, on the recommendation of UNC General Bonesteel, declared the DMZ-Imjin River area a hostile fire zone. As the situation continued to deteriorate along the DMZ, the UNC Commander was given a mandate to defend S Korea from a N Korean conventional invasion and defend against a N Korea-sponsored insurgency. Bonesteel was ordered to restrain the understandably angry S Koreans from launching a war against N Korea.

Thousands of Vietnam-destined (US) troops were diverted to Korea in the first months of 1968. The 2nd ID was reinforced, and tours extended for some of those already stationed there. Throughout the year, firefights became part of the routine. Some 700 hostile actions were recorded. In the late-night darkness on April 14, 1968, one of the deadliest incidents occurred. Two Americans and two S Koreans lost their lives after N Koreans ambushed their truck. About 20 bullet holes shattered the front windshield and both headlights were shot out. At least 40 rounds ripped through the truck's rear canvas cover. Two soldiers survived the attack but were wounded. In another action on April 21, a patrol from B Company, 2nd Battalion, 31st IR, engaged a force of up to 75 N Koreans south of the DMZ. It was perhaps the largest US fight of the border war. The dead and wounded were taken by helicopter to the 121st US Army Evacuation Hospital, Yongdung-po, southwest of Seoul.

Northernmost Outpost Camp Alamo

Attacks such as these led to improving the 1967 barrier defense system. Combat duty became a routine part of life along the DMZ for Americans in base camps scattered north of the Imjin River. Camp Alamo was one the bases and home to B Company (Fwd) First Platoon 508th US Army Security Agency Group. The eight-acre camp was situated close to the south barrier fence and made defense preparations in case they were attacked. During 1966-67, the author was assigned to Camp Alamo. Camp Alamo was home to 42 soldiers and one of several small outposts situated on the DMZ. The Alamo located in the Chorwon valley near Yongchon-Chorwon consisted of 6 Quonset huts, motor pool, operations hut, and a barracks building on 8 acres of land, and was a small, isolated camp north of Seoul. Living conditions were below standards. However, there was improvement when a new barracks building was constructed, providing two-man rooms and hot and cold water. At the time, the Alamo was the US Army's northernmost outpost in S Korea. It was less than two miles from the southern barrier fence, and 18 miles north of the 38th Parallel. In 1966 the barrier fence nearest "Camp Alamo" was marked with white tape and strands of barbed wire, and the fence was made from wood.

(The Alamo was not mentioned in the agreement between the US and S Korea Land Partnership Plan in 2002 or its amendments in 2004, suggesting that it closed sometime between 1999 and 2001. [65])

There were ongoing propaganda campaigns between the North and South, such as loudspeaker broadcasts across the DMZ. Giant amplifiers set up on the DMZ played hits by S Korean singers, pro-democracy messages, and propaganda. N Korea had its own (outdated) speakers and could not reach further than the DMZ. N Korean speakers broadcast martial music or military music, traditional peasant fare, and praises to the country's rulers. The South responded with popular music and lectures on freedom and democracy. At night, soldiers standing in watchtowers or sitting in foxholes listened to the blare of N Korean loudspeakers. In spring and summer, large weather balloons with a basket filled with propaganda leaflets were released north of the DMZ. Depending on wind direction and altitude, the balloons found their way south, spreading the leaflets with the common theme demanding US forces leave S Korea.

Further to the south, in the 7th ID area of operations around Tongduchon, foot and airmobile patrols conducted counterguerrilla operations to secure the area. These patrols ranged in duration up to several days. Isolated radio relay sites, occasionally the targets of N Korean probes, were reinforced by ad hoc security detachments made up of scouts, cooks, supply clerks, and medics. The peak years of infiltration were 1967 and 1968 accounting for 743-armed N Korean agents sent to attack vital S Korean installations and kill government officials. The number of incidents dropped significantly in 1969-71.

The trenches dug and bunkers built during the first Korean Conflict were maintained by S Korean soldiers from the ROK 21st Infantry Division. The trenches were modified with sandbags to prevent the dirt walls from collapsing and reinforced bunkers were built. The defense system was maintained as a precaution should hostilities resume.

---

65   Alamo ASA (globalsecurity.org)

Personal Story and Firsthand Account

Specialist Harry F. Fraser

Specialist Four Harry F. Fraser, who served in Korea from 1966-1967, was interviewed by the author in June 2014, and his story and firsthand account is about what happened along the DMZ.

"My great-grandfather immigrated to the US by way of Ellis Island, NY from Stuttgart, Germany. I was born in Gloucester, Massachusetts, the second oldest of six siblings. Two of my brothers and one sister served in the US Armed Forces. My oldest brother served in the US Navy (Seabee); my younger brother served in the US Army, and my oldest sister served in the US Navy. My father served with the US Merchant Marines during World War II."

"I was a native of Gloucester, Massachusetts and was recruited by the US Army Security Agency (USASA) in 1965. Most enlistees who joined the Army with me did so for a period of three years and that was my intention, too. However, after taking the ordinary battery of tests given to new recruits, I and two others in my group were called aside and taken to a room to speak to the USASA field representative. He told us that our high scores on pre-enlistment tests qualified us to join an elite group of soldiers in the Army Security Agency (ASA).

"Of course, we had never heard of the ASA and when we asked questions, he seemed quite evasive, saying only that it was so secret that he could not tell us much about it, but he used the words top secret several times. It sounded very 'cloak and dagger.'

Then he said, one more thing—because the ASA schooling is considerably more extensive than most other military occupational specialties (MOSs)—many take from 6 to12 months—the required period of enlistment is four years instead of the usual three. We thought about it for a moment, but it did not deter us. We signed up and took the oath of enlistment. On July 6, 1965, I began basic training at Fort Dix, New Jersey. Upon graduation, I transferred to Fort Devens, Massachusetts, home of the US Army Security Agency (USASA or ASA) Training Center and School for specialized training."

The summer of 1965 was a transitional season for the US Armed Forces because the focus on a war in Europe against Russia was replaced with a conflict in Southeast Asia (Vietnam/Laos), and the opponent was North Vietnam. The Korean peninsula was also viewed as a dangerous place because N Korea supported the communist efforts in Vietnam and began to increase its own military pressure on S Korea and American forces.

"It was during this time I attended a 10-day tactical training course (TTC) preparing Army Security Agency (ASA) troops for duty in Vietnam or Korea." In 1965, the ASA Tactical Training Center (TTC) was developed and constructed by Colonel (then Lieutenant Colonel) Lewis E. Millet, Sr.,[66] who received the Medal of Honor for leading a bayonet charge during the 1950s Korean Conflict. He was the first commandant of the ASA Training Center and School at Fort Devens in the mid-1960s. He was concerned that ASA troops were not fully prepared to operate and fight in a combat environment. Lacking funding to create what he envisioned, Millet and his training staff ingeniously used available resources, including lumber from razed barracks, and wood from his own farm in Maine to build an authentic-looking Vietnam village in the Fort Devens training area. Millet also procured used and no-longer-serviceable flight suits from the US Air Force, Pease AFB, Newington, NH., to outfit soldiers playing the role of the aggressor. To add realism, Colonel Millet recruited within ASA Vietnamese-speaking soldiers and Hawaiian Asian-Americans to play the part of the Viet Cong (VC). These soldiers played the key role of VC aggressors wearing black clothing typical of the enemy at the time. These soldiers played this part in John Wayne's 1968 movie the *Green Berets*.

The TTC would boast two Vietnamese villages: one friendly and one hostile. The former had a Buddhist shrine, rice paddies, and a sapling fence, while the latter had a tunnel system and spider holes. The 10-day training cycle was divided into two phases. During the first phase, soldiers trained on the weapons and equipment of an ASA company that directly supported a combat division. During driver training, they practiced blackout driving as well as ambush drills. Weapons training on the rifle, machine gun, and grenade launcher culminated with live firing. More importantly, the soldiers learned to perform patrolling, establish perimeters, and other squad tactics.

---

66   Colonel Lewis E. Millett, Sr., received the Medal of Honor during the first Korean Conflict for leading the last major American bayonet charge at the time. He served in World War II and the Vietnam Conflict, retiring in 1973. He was 88 at the time of his death on November 14, 2009, and buried at Riverside National Cemetery, Riverside, California.

Throughout the phase, the TTC instructors stressed the six-paragraph code of conduct. During the second phase of TTC, the tactical scenarios became more intense for the students.

They received Army-mandated training on the geography, history, and politics of Vietnam, the Communist strategy and threat, and the US mission there. This was done in the friendly Vietnamese village of Mot Dong.

Between tactical squad exercises and rehearsals, the TTC instructors trained the soldiers on emergency destruction of equipment and information, along with a nighttime compass course, as well as escape and evasion techniques. On the ninth day of the training, the students prepared for their final exercise.

In the scenario, the student company was ordered to move from its defensive position to a more secure area. It began in a tactical convoy, but VC guerilla bands ambushed the convoy and destroyed its vehicles with land mines or grenades. Employing the newly trained ambush drills, the students repulsed the final assault but were forced to continue on foot. Upon approaching the enemy village of Hai Dong, they received orders to sweep the village and its subterranean tunnel complex. The students fought their way into the village and then defended it against a counterattack. At this point, the TTC instructors told the students that they needed to organize into groups of two or three and exfiltrate to friendly lines. Each soldier would say their name to the instructors before climbing down the ladder into the tunnel. Crawling through the tunnel to the exit outside the village perimeter near a river, students would then make their way to the hooch of the friendly farmer. If successful, the students were debriefed by the intelligence officer and taken to the TTC administrative area.

Not all students were successful in making their way back to friendly lines, and some were captured by VC patrols. Those students underwent simulated, but surprisingly harsh interrogation. The simulated capture and interrogation gave the soldiers an opportunity to practice and apply the Code of Conduct. After 15 to 20 minutes of interrogation, the students were allowed to escape and rejoin their comrades. The next morning, the students struck their bivouac and cleaned and turned in their weapons. While most of an ASA soldier's training concentrated on the technical skills of the collection and analysis of signals intelligence, the TTCs training gave basic soldier skills needed to successfully perform their mission on the battlefield where the combat zone was ill-defined. The details regarding the ASA TTC, Fort Devens, MA are described in the Tactical Training Brochure, Appendix H—specifically, depicting the number of ASA and Non-ASA that graduated through May 1966.

"I learned how to operate, assemble, disassemble, and clean the M-60 machine gun, M-14 rifle, M-79 grenade launcher, and the M1911 .45 caliber pistol used for close combat.

"Unknown to me at the time, my personnel record reflected that I qualified with the grenade launcher. After the two weeks of training were completed, I transferred from Fort Devens, Massachusetts and arrived in S Korea in mid-April 1966 for a 13-month tour. I had a direct assignment and after processing at the replacement depot near the capital city of Seoul, I was picked up and transported to the 508th ASA Group headquarters in Yongdung-po, on the south side of the Han River outside of Seoul. Ultimately, I was assigned to the 1st Platoon, Company B (Forward), Camp Alamo, a 42-man platoon located in the demilitarized zone, and I learned quickly the DMZ was still an active combat zone.

"The 1950s Korean Conflict never ended, and the documents signed only provided for a ceasefire. The conflict was moving into a phase that was hazardous without a traditional fight, and often overshadowed by events elsewhere," Fraser said.

Fraser continued, "At the time, the Alamo was the US Army's northernmost outpost in S Korea and was one of three camps in the US 7th ID sector of the DMZ."

The other two were home of the DMZ Military Police (DMZMP), and the 24th Psychological Warfare Site B five miles east of the Alamo. The DMZMP patrolled the DMZ to monitor violations of the ceasefire agreement. The DMZMPs were always composed of infantry units and were only allowed to carry small arms for self-defense.

"Intelligence operations were housed in huts mounted to various-size trucks, and each vehicle was elevated atop wooden blocks, thus keeping the tires off the mountain surface. The entire site sat on a hill overlooking N Korea and the

Chorwon Plain, site of one of the bloodiest battles of the first Korean Conflict, the Battle of Baengma-goji or White Horse. From our vantage point we could see Pork Chop Hill, Old Baldy, Whitehorse Mountain, and on a clear day, Heartbreak Ridge, the locations of some of the heaviest fighting in the Korean Conflict. On most days, N Korean soldiers could be seen patrolling and maintaining their side of the fence."

"On the other end of the hill was the Ground Surveillance Radar team, non-ASA unit."

As a result of the ceasefire agreement signed at Panmunjom in 1953, Pork Chop Hill found itself in the demilitarized zone between North and S Korea.

"Because of the tactical training course I completed, including being proficient with the M-79 grenade launcher, my personal weapon was the M-79. Duties included maintaining the armory and the ammunition bunker. The M79 grenade launcher was a single-shot, shoulder-fired, break-action grenade launcher, and looked like a sawed-off shotgun. The length of the barrel was 15 inches and the bore diameter, 40mm. It fired a wide variety of 40mm grenade rounds, including explosive, anti-personnel, smoke, buckshot, and illumination. The launcher was loaded like a shotgun by feeding the round in the back of the barrel. A high-explosive (HE) fragmentation round had a kill radius of 15 feet. The M79 was a mid-range small arms weapon. Its minimum range was just beyond the distance of a thrown hand grenade. The maximum effective range was approximately 1000 feet. The round would spin to arm itself."

It was not long before a combat experienced-officer was assigned to the Alamo. He began by establishing defensive positions within the camp. Fraser said, "I was assigned the responsibility of being the machine-gun operator along with two other soldiers. Over a period of two weeks, each man learned his defensive position in the event something big should happen." Fraser continued, "We were authorized to use lethal force, and maintained a heightened level of awareness from that point on."

It was during this time that a group of combat engineers arrived to assess the condition of the minefields that had been there since 1953. Anti-personnel mines and razor-sharp triple concertina wire were placed, and the layout revised around both the Alamo and the hilltop operation site. A concrete bunker had been built pre-1966 on the north end of the site to serve as the base of operations to engage infiltrators.

(The engineers built a bunker that was eight feet wide and 10 feet long and the height was about five feet. The walls were made of sandbags that supported a log roof, and more sandbags covered the roof. Dirt was shoveled on the sides and the roof for more protection. A small opening was in the back that served as an entrance. The rear entry accessed a 25-foot trench dug in both directions to create firefight positions. Stored in the bunker were ammunition, water, and medical supplies. The engineers placed a surprise in front of the bunker, a 55-gallon drum filled with napalm and diesel fuel (FUGAS). There was a small charge in the bottom of the barrel with a wire that ran from the charge to the bunker and connected to a detonator switch. The barrel was buried at a 45-degree angle facing north. The explosive barrel was for defensive purposes in the event the site was overrun. A detonated barrel of FUGAS would rain a fiery, burning hell onto any infiltrators. S Korean soldiers were always assigned to the bunker. Bunkers on the reverse slope could be used for sleeping and warning should the need arise. Realistically, they were of no use except for shelter.)

Fraser said, "In early December, the situation was worsening as N Korean infiltrators began attacks near the Alamo. When daylight faded into night, the sounds of small arms fire and explosions from grenades could be heard most nights. There was a report circulating in headquarters that N Koreans might attack. The possibility had been passed to Lieutenant Johnson the detachment commander, necessary steps were taken. He ordered additional ammunition to be taken to the site. It was near 2300 hours (11:00 p.m.) on a very cold night when he asked for two volunteers to make the trip up the mountain. I put on my 'cold weather' boots along with insulated gloves and I volunteered along with another soldier, and we started out fully prepared for any event that may present itself. At the midway point, we passed through another S Korean guard post, and I recall how surprised they were to see us. They were not only standing guard, but some were sitting in foxholes scattered around the access to the dirt road that led up the mountain. When we arrived at the site, our arrival was communicated to the operations hut as was our departure. After unloading the ammunition, which included hand grenades, we started back down the hill after midnight. We arrived back at the Alamo just before 0100 hours (1:00 a.m.) and were met by the detachment commander.

"The winter months were extremely cold. It was the coldest place I have ever been. The other thing that sticks with me is standing on the hill at the site in January and looking over the DMZ into N Korea at night. It was dark, with a million stars, and a frigid wind was blowing down the Chorwon Valley from the Gulf of Wonson [pronounced Munch'on]. Our cold weather boots. 'Mickey Mouse Boots' were worn when outside for any length of time." (A rubber relic from the 1960s maintains foot warmth in temperatures down to 60 °F below zero and is still in service with both soldiers and Marines.)

Fraser recalled, "The weather never seemed to cooperate. It was hot and miserable in the summer months, muggy and wet during the monsoon season in May and June, and cold and wet in the spring and fall months. And then there was winter. It began in October and lasted until March. We endured freezing temperatures of 18 to 32 °F degrees and wind chill as cold as 35 °F degrees below zero. The extreme cold not only affected your personal comfort but the electronics necessary to complete the mission sometimes would not work properly and ice would build up on the antennas." Fraser concluded, "I rotated out of Korea in May 1967, and went on to serve with the USASA Security Company, Aschaffenburg, West Germany."

Specialist Harry F. Fraser earned the National Defense Service Medal, Armed Forces Expeditionary Medal, Korea Defense Service Medal, and the Republic of Korea Presidential Unit Citation for his service. Both the Armed Forces Expeditionary Medal and Korea Defense Service Medal were authorized for participation in operations in S Korea during the same timeframe between October 1, 1966, and June 30, 1974. The Korea Defense Service Medal (KDSM) is currently being awarded and an end date has not been established. The KDSM was established in December 2002 and first awarded in February 2004 (retroactive to July 28, 1954).

Thousands of American soldiers served in Korea during this period, but only a few served near or were in the DMZ. The Purple Heart Medal is awarded to those killed in action or wounded resulting from combat with N Korean forces.

Defoliants: Agents Orange and Purple

Defoliants Agents Orange [67] and Purple, were used to eliminate hiding places for N Koreans attempting to infiltrate or attack US or S Korean units. In 1968-1969 59,000 gallons of these toxic chemicals defoliated nearly 21,000 acres on the DMZ. Chemicals were used to keep the area on either side of the barrier fence clear of vegetation.

Recognition Awards and Combat Pay

In November 1966, the US Army leadership realized the obvious: there was a live fire/shooting conflict in S Korea in the mid-1960s. Yet soldiers were not authorized combat pay or recognition awards. On April 1, 1968, combat pay was approved, and before this date a soldier earned combat pay only if wounded or killed in action. Under the previous rules, a soldier could be under fire for days and still not be eligible for combat pay. After April 1, 1968, all soldiers near the DMZ and north of the Imjin River would be authorized combat pay. The Imjin River flows roughly parallel to the DMZ, just behind the forward US positions. The Armed Forces Expeditionary Medal was authorized October 1, 1966, and shoulder sleeve insignia-former wartime service was authorized April 1, 1968, for personnel receiving combat pay. (sleeve insignia commonly called "Combat Patch")

The Combat Infantry Badge (CIB) was also authorized. The AFEM was awarded until June 30, 1974. The Korean Defense Service Medal (KDSM) was authorized for the same timeframe as a Department of Defense (DoD) exception to policy. The Combat Infantry Badge (CIB) was authorized in accordance with US Army Regulation 600-8-22, and there are basically three requirements for award of the CIB. The soldier must be an infantryman satisfactorily performing infantry duties, must be assigned to an infantry unit during such time as the unit is engaged in active ground combat, and must actively participate in such ground combat. Campaign or battle credit alone is not sufficient for the CIB. There was a caveat for soldiers in S Korea. Americans in the DMZ would have to be judged by a higher standard than infantrymen serving in S Vietnam or other theaters of operation. To earn a CIB for combat operations within the DMZ, soldiers not only had to meet the requirements listed in the regulation, but after January 4, 1969, a soldier must have:

---

67   Veterans and Agent Orange, updated 2014: Contributors, National Academies of Sciences, Engineering, and Medicine; Committee to Review the Health effects in Veterans of exposure to Herbicides. ISBNs: Hardcover 978-0-309-38066-9 and eBook: 978-0-309-38069-0.
The National Academies Press: https://doi.org/10.17226/21845.

(1) Served in the hostile fire area at least 60 days and was authorized hostile fire pay.

(2) Been assigned to an infantry unit of company or smaller size and must be an infantry officer or enlisted soldier possessing an infantry military occupational specialty in the grade of captain or lower.

(3) Been engaged with the enemy in the hostile fire area or in active ground combat involving an exchange of small arms fire at least five times. In the case of a commissioned and warrant officer whose basic branch is other than infantry who, under appropriate orders, has commanded an infantry company or smaller size infantry unit for at least 30 days, the award may be made, provided all the requirements are met.

Chapter 18

SEABORNE SURFACE SIGNAL INTELLIGENCE COLLECTION

In 1964, the Director for Defense Research and Engineering, Department of Defense, proposed that the United States begin a program of seaborne surface signal intelligence collection using trawler-type vessels. Lacking sufficient funds to build a completely new trawler-type hull, the US Navy decided to convert several former World War II US Army small cargo ships. This was the beginning of the Auxiliary General Environmental Research (AGER) program. AGER denoted a joint Navy and National Security Agency (NSA) program. On October 7, 1965, Secretary of the Navy Paul H. Nitze expressed concern to Secretary of Defense Robert McNamara about acquiring up-to-date intelligence on the operating capabilities, tactical doctrine, procedures, and state of training of the Soviet Navy. To accomplish this task, Nitze stated an immediate requirement for additional ship platforms of the AGER type. In 1964 the USS *Banner* hull number GER-1 (hull number is a serial identification number) was already being outfitted as such and in October 1965 was ready for signal intelligence (SIGINT) operations. Later in 1965 the Department of Defense (DOD) approved funding for two ships, the USS *Pueblo,* and the USS *Palm Beach.*

The *Pueblo* a 906-ton vessel arrived at Puget Sound Naval Shipyard, Bremerton, Washington, on April 22, 1966; the ship's conversion began promptly on Jul 5, 1966. Members of all trades besieged the *Pueblo,* sandblasting its hull, removing cargo winches and boom, and testing the engines and machinery. The *Pueblo* would be configured like the *Banner,* that the antennas would be placed toward the bow to minimize interference from the transmitting antennas located aft of the main mast. The first ship converted, the *Banner,* conducted its initial operational patrol in the western Pacific. Operations in 1967-1968 were conducted off the coasts of the Soviet Union, China, and along the West Coast of N Korea. The *Banner* arrived in Yokosuka, Japan, on October 24, 1965. It was the initial GER vessel, and as its mission history illustrates, did not remain strictly in international waters, but crossed into Russia territorial waters to ascertain Russian reactions and collect additional intelligence. *Banner's* first assignment commenced on October 29, 1965. The *Banner* traveled up the East Coast of Japan and entered the Sea of Japan through the Tsugaru Straits between Hokkaido and the main island of Honshu. Twice, on November 13 and again on November 24, the *Banner* crossed into Soviet claimed waters near Vladivostok, home of the Soviet Pacific Fleet. The Russian Navy confronted the *Banner* with a guided missile destroyer and the *Banner* withdrew. In the second instance, the *Banner* was monitored by a Russian signal intelligence (SIGINT) trawler but was not challenged to withdraw. Both SIGINT vessels gave each other a thorough intelligence inspection, after which the *Banner* departed from its operational area returning to Yokosuka arriving on November 28. In early 1966, the *Banner* returned to the coast of Siberia, but entered the Sea of Japan from the South through the Tsushima Strait and conducted surveillance of N Korea. On the way, it loitered in the vicinity of Tongji Son-man Bay for two days. On the eastern edge of this bay was the small island of Mayang-Do, home of the N Korean submarine base.

The Central Intelligence Agency (CIA) had reported its concerns over the growing threat of N Korean aggression, and the mission included gathering information about the submarine base. During this operation, the *Banner* monitored the coast of N Korea but was unable to acquire additional intelligence. This is also the area where the *Pueblo* would be captured two years later. (Mayang-Do is off the coast from the City of Sinpo, east of Hamhung. The N Korean submarine fleet is still based there today, and images of submarines are clearly visible on Google Earth.)

Following the first four operations, the amount and quality of intelligence collected during the Click Beetle Signals Intelligence (SIGINT) Operations, plus the unprecedented close-up pictures and descriptions of Soviet naval activities in their home waters, caused the US intelligence community to realize the value of the program. During Operation Click Beetle Five, the *Banner* cruised the Belkin Coast of the Soviet Union from north of Hokkaido down to Vladivostok. The *Banner* was sighted by Soviet planes and naval vessels and on May 24, 1966, a Soviet signal intelligence (SIGINT) ship collided with the *Banner*, harassing it to depart the area. This was the first recorded instance of a Soviet and US ship collision. Operations six, seven, and eight were in the same area and concluded without incident. Operation Click Beetle Nine, conducted in 1967, was the first operation outside of the Sea of Japan. The NSA tasked the *Banner* with the first US overt ship intelligence patrol off the coast of Communist China in the Taiwan Strait. Due to the unknown reaction of the Chinese, the US 5th Air Force in Japan and the 313th Air Division in Okinawa were alerted, and US Navy destroyers at Keelung, Taiwan were put on alert. During the deployment off Shanghai, the *Banner* was surrounded and harassed by Chinese trawlers, but escaped the encirclement without incident, and the mission was successful. This would be the last complete mission before the capture of the *Pueblo*. US Navy records indicate the missions of the *Banner* were rough and confrontational.

United States intelligence users lacked complete information on N Korean military and naval targets, and the NSA believed that a more mobile seaborne platform would be able to access short-range communications for information needed to fill the intelligence gaps. The N Korean Army used manual Morse code, radio telephone, and radio printer for communications from the Ministry of National Defense through battalion and lower levels, especially for operational messages. Analysis of this traffic could illustrate impending military action.

USS *Pueblo* (GER-2) Commissioned

On May 13, 1967, the USS *Pueblo* GER-2 and *Palm Beach* GER-3 were commissioned. Rear Admiral William E. Ferrall, Commandant, 13th Naval District, read the Navy department orders to commission these ships. The *Pueblo* and *Palm Beach* were officially declared in service of the United States Navy with the Union Jack and the colors (American Flag) flying. Regular watches set under a duty officer and the constant humming of electrical machinery were very gratifying to the crews. The *Pueblo* joined the *Banner* in the western Pacific while the *Palm Beach* operated in the Atlantic and the Mediterranean. (The lower hull number implies an older vessel.) These AGER ships were manned by US Navy crews, communication/cryptologic technicians (CTs) from the Naval Security Group, and civilians from the US Naval Oceanographic Office.

Before the *Pueblo* embarked on its first mission, its commanding officer, Lieutenant Commander (LCDR) Lloyd M. Bucher, was briefed on what to expect. Unfortunately, the N Korean Navy began operating under new and violent rules of engagement. As early as the commissioning ceremony, the Navy knew that the *Pueblo* would be home-ported and operating out of Naval Base Yokosuka, located 43 miles southwest of Japan's capital city, Tokyo.

Sea Trials Completed

The great day came in the latter part of July 1967. With the Special Operations Detachment (SOD-hut) Hut professionally installed and a few additional improvements, the *Pueblo* was ready for sea trials. By the first week in September the *Pueblo* had completed its last sea trial and the crew was notified to be ready for departure. Once the "classified equipment" was installed below deck in the metal SOD-hut, [68] *Pueblo* departed Bremerton on September 11 for San Diego via San Francisco. On September 15, the *Pueblo* tied up at the docks of Treasure Island Naval Base, San Francisco, for a three-day liberty call. While there the captain learned he was selected for promotion to full commander, as had the captains of the other AGERs, *Banner* and *Palm Beach*. The *Pueblo* reached San Diego on September 22 and was berthed at the Navy's anti-submarine school's docks and came under the jurisdiction of the training command, Pacific, for a period of refresher and redeployment training. The hour of departing San Diego came on the misty morning of November 6, 1967. The *Pueblo* continued to Pearl Harbor, Hawaii, for a stopover before crossing the Pacific to Yokosuka, home port in Japan. Early on the morning of November 14, the *Pueblo* entered Pearl Harbor and tied up at the submarine base. The ship was refueled and resupplied. The captain attended briefings about the upcoming mission. At the end of the third day, the *Pueblo* cast off its lines and departed, turning on a westward course. As the *Pueblo* proceeded northwesterly, the temperature began to fall, and the weather turned foul. The heavy seas pitched the ship about and at times the ship experienced 52-degree rolls. The constant pitching and the crashing of the sea, combined with the extreme rolling, tried the will of the crew. Anything not secured was tossed about, and seasickness affected everyone. During the afternoon of December 13, 1967, 13 days out of Pearl Harbor, the *Pueblo* approached the main Japanese island of Honshu and arrived at Yokosuka, its assigned home port. The crew had been on board for over six months and were anxious to get underway and go into the operational area.

---

68   The SOD-hut was a mental compartment (room) below deck where communication technicians operated the surveillance gear to intercept and gather sonar, radar, and other types of signal communications. Thus, space was a "restricted area."

No one could have foreseen the storm that was coming—not just the onboard problems, but what waited off the coast of N Korea.

There were many onboard equipment problems, refitting delays, command, and control relating to officers and the enlisted crew along with other personal points of contention. Command and control of the various aspects of the *Pueblo's* mission, a straightforward matter on most naval ships, were obscure and fragmented. Personality differences and the command arrangement aboard the *Pueblo* were the cause of constant friction between the captain and the Officer-in-Charge (OIC) of the SOD-hut. The captain was responsible for command of the ship but was not in command of the SOD-hut even though the captain held a clearance for special intelligence.

The SOD space was a "restricted area," and only communication/cryptologic technicians (CTs) were authorized entry. The CTs operated the surveillance gear to intercept and gather sonar, radar, and other types of signal communications. The captain's command of the SIGNET detachment could be accomplished only through the OIC of the detachment. Top Secret with Sensitive Compartmented Information (SCI) is required, limits access to a need to know to include the captain.

(Personality clashes occurred between the captain and the executive officer too many times to include in this writing. To appreciate the personalities and life aboard the *Pueblo*, I highly recommend both *Bucher: My Story* by Commander Lloyd M. Bucher, Captain of the *Pueblo*, and 2nd *in Command* by Edward R. Murphy, Jr., its executive officer, and former lieutenant.)

At this point, the captain and the OIC of the SOD-hut were the only officers who knew the ship's real mission. The captain was not authorized to know the details of the intelligence being collected, only the destination. There were two especially concerning items still to be resolved. One concern was the lack of defensive guns. Task Force 96 (CTF 96) Commander Rear Admiral (RDML) Frank L. Johnson did not support arming the *Pueblo* or the *Banner* because visible armament would alter the basic premise of AGER operations and scientific research. Eventually, two 50-caliber machine guns along with 10,000 rounds of ammunition were authorized. To maintain the ship's cover as a scientific research vessel, the guns were stored below deck under a tarp. The concern was not totally resolved because no one aboard the *Pueblo* had any prior experience with this type of weapon except for one seaman, who had served in the Army, and knew something about the weapon. The captain decided most of the crew would receive orientation firing of the weapon. The second concern was emergency destruction devices. There were only two slow paper shredders, one hand-fed incinerator, hand tools, sledgehammers, and weighted sacks onboard to handle a significant number of classified documents, instruction manuals, and classified electronic equipment. The quantity of classified material accumulated made it imperative to find a means of emergency destruction. The weighted canvas bags on board were not a satisfactory answer because the depth of the water in the operational areas was usually too shallow for jettisoning the bags. The bags would be no help in destroying the machines in the SOD-hut. The captain was determined that before *Pueblo* left port, a solution would be found. In the interim, consideration was given to securing and storing TNT (high explosive) and its use as a last resort to scuttle the *Pueblo* in a hopeless emergency. The captain met with the task force commander, explaining his concern and possible solutions.

RDML Johnson had his chief of staff set up a meeting for the captain to discuss his concerns with the commanding officer (CO) of Yokosuka's supply depot, who listened and arranged for explosive experts to inspect the *Pueblo*. The officer in charge of Azuma Island Naval Ammunition Depot sent explosive and demolition experts to survey the situation aboard the *Pueblo*. The recommendation was to install thermite bombs in strategic locations, including the SOD-hut. This solution was not well received, and the reaction was one of doubt. An accidental ignition could be catastrophic. Thermite is a pyrotechnic composition of a metal powder and a metal oxide that produces an exothermic oxidation-reduction reaction known as a thermite reaction. Thermite usage is hazardous due to the extremely high temperatures produced and the extreme difficulty in smothering a reaction. Steel melts at 2500 degrees Fahrenheit. Thermite burns at 4000 degrees Fahrenheit once ignited.

Before leaving Japan, Bucher bought a commercial fuel-fed incinerator, dipping into the crew's recreation fund for the required $1300. [69] The *Pueblo* departed without an adequate means to destroy the classified documents, instruction manuals, and classified electronic equipment. In recently declassified documents, it was noted that prior to deployment, the task force Commander

69   https://www.usni.org/magzines/navalhistory/2014-08/*Pueblo*-scapegoat.

RDML Johnson failed to effectively verify the feasibility of rapid destruction of the classified materials and equipment.

During the last days of 1967, two civilian oceanographers, Harry Iredale and Dunnie Tuck, reported aboard. The unclassified reason for the two civilian oceanographers picked up in Japan was intended to reinforce the *Pueblo*'s cover story as a scientific research vessel. They would function solely as cover for the spying mission. They did play a vital part in the intelligence gathering. Their job was to collect oceanographic data to develop sound velocity profiles that could be useful for submarine operations. There is an underwater layer known as the thermocline, which detects sonar signals.

In the open ocean, the thermocline is characterized by a negative sound speed gradient, making the thermocline important in submarine warfare because it can reflect active sonar and other acoustic signals. Thus, a submarine can safely operate underneath this layer without detection from above. The tests conducted by the oceanographers would be for the purpose of pinpointing and mapping these layers, essential data in case of a future invasion. Both oceanographers had made previous trips on the *Banner.*

On December 18, mission orders were received and the order used the codeword ICHTHYIC [pronounced ik-three-ik to investagate/inquire] for the operation.

Mission Orders - Special Instructions

1) Determine the nature and extent of naval activity in the vicinity of N Korea ports of Chongjin, Songjin, Mayang-do, and Wonsan.

2) Sample electronic environment of the East Coast of N Korea, with emphasis on intercepting fixing of coastal radars.

3) Intercept and conduct surveillance of Soviet naval units operating in Tsushima Strait to determine the purpose of Soviet presence in that area since February 1966.

Secondly, the operation will be conducted to:

(A) Determine Korean Communist (KORCOM) and Soviet reaction, respectively, to an overt intelligence collector operating near KORCOM periphery and actively conducting surveillance of Russian aka Soviet (USSR) naval units.

(B) Evaluate the USS *Pueblo's* capabilities as a naval intelligence collection and tactical surveillance ship.

(C) Report any development of KORCOM/Soviet units that may be indicative of pending hostilities and offensive actions against US forces.

Mission estimate of risk: Minimal since *Pueblo* will be operating in international waters for the entire deployment. This order was declassified on December 31, 1968.

Of note is the estimated risk position of the 303 Committee, which gave civilian approval on behalf of the executive branch. The existence of the 303 Committee was a closely held secret. It was headed by a senior White House aide and was so named because it met in Room 303 of the Executive Office Building. It was composed of the Director of Central Intelligence (DCI); Under Secretary of State; Deputy Secretary of Defense; and National Security Advisor to the President, as the White House Representative. The assessment of the committee differed from the Navy assessment of minimal risk. The committee expected the *Pueblo* to be shadowed, bullied, and bumped, but there was no reason to expect capture on the high seas. In hindsight, in view of the 303 Committee assessment, the Navy should have had at least a minimum protective force available. Meanwhile, the NSA was concerned over the possibility of hostile action by the N Koreans toward the *Pueblo*.

On the morning of January 2, the Joint Reconnaissance Center (JCS) transmitted the approval of the *Pueblo's* mission to Hawaii. With this message, the events that would lead to the attack and capture of the *Pueblo* were set in motion. On January 3 two Marines, Sergeants Robert J. Hammond and Robert J. Chicca joined the crew. These Marines were ordered aboard the *Pueblo* as Korean-language experts to translate monitored N Korean radio broadcasts. Both studied Korean in language school in 1965 and neither had used it since. One of the Marines thought he might be able to catch a few words, if spoken slowly enough, but that was it. It was apparent the interpreters were not qualified in the Korean language. The interpreters came from Naval Security Group (NSG) Activity Kamiseya, Japan, a station primarily oriented to Soviet collection effort. The commander of NSG activity provided school-trained but not operationally qualified interpreters and believed, however, that these interpreters would improve with experience. The SOD officer in charge was disappointed, but there was nothing that could be done about it. The rusty language skills of two Korean linguists belatedly assigned to the ship's SIGINT detachment were not up to the job of rapidly translating fast-moving tactical traffic. At a tactical level, NSA observed that had the linguists been qualified they would have understood a full 20 minutes before the first shots were fired at the *Pueblo* that N Korean patrol boats were maneuvering to fire. The NSG at Kamiseya did the *Pueblo* a major disservice by failing to properly screen its personnel and consequently sending unqualified linguists on a sensitive collection mission. The lack of language skills was demonstrated on January 22, 1968, when two N Korean fishing trawlers approached the *Pueblo* at 3 knots and circled twice within 25 yards (75 feet). The linguists could not decipher the individual ship names, which appeared in large Korean characters. When asked by the captain to translate the Kongi Marks (Korean alphabet letters) on the bows of each ship, one of the linguists said, "I'll get my Korean dictionary and find out right away." A few minutes passed, and the linguist returned gazing intently and said, "One of them is *Rice Paddy 1* and the other is *Rice Paddy, 2*, Captain." [70]

On December 29, 1967, the end of a terrible year of violence along the DMZ, the NSA wired the *Pueblo's* operational orders to the director of Naval Security Group (DIRNAVSECGRU) through Operation Order 301-68. The US military believed that 1968 would bring added aggression from N Korea, and the NSA was working to ascertain how that violence would manifest itself. By the last week of December, the sailing order had been received.

Altogether there were 83 officers and men aboard, including the two civilian oceanographers. The enlisted crew was not trained, except for the communication technicians and cryptologists (CTs). The Navy seemed to put on board whoever happened to be available. The general services officers did not have an appreciation for the need to protect classified materials. The executive and operation officers of the ship received their signal intelligence (SIGINT) clearances in the last weeks before the ship sailed. Neither officer probably had any concept of the destruction problem in the research SOD spaces.

---

70   Source: *Bucher: My Story*, pages 164 and 165.

On January 4, 1968, Task Force 96 (CTF 96) Commander RDML Johnson inspected the *Pueblo*, and although some problems remained—still lacking adequate means of emergency destruction and serious doubts about the steering—the task force commander was generally satisfied. For administrative purposes, the *Pueblo* was assigned to the Service Force, Pacific Fleet, but for its reconnaissance mission, it was assigned to the operational control of CTF 96, who was also Commander, Naval Forces Japan. CTF 96 had only two ships, the *Banner*, and the *Pueblo*, along with a small staff assigned to the task force commander. Admiral Johnson ordered the captain to get underway on January 5 for Sasebo, Japan to be in position for the coming mission. The *Pueblo* departed Yokosuka on a brisk and blustery morning.

The formal plan for the *Pueblo's* operation on December 18 was contained in Combined Task Force (CTF) 96 Operation Order No. 301-68, which provided specific guidance and instructions for the assigned mission, including reporting instructions and operating and communications plans. The *Pueblo's* mission involved both Navy and National Security Agency (NSA) goals. The ship was charged with conducting a detailed survey of increasing N Korean naval activity, including assessing its potential fleet strength. Operation codeword ICHTHYIC (pronounced ik-thee-ik) further used the sophisticated cryptographic equipment below deck in the SOD-hut to intercept Soviet-N Korean communications and locate radar and radio stations inland. The Navy wanted intelligence on N Korean submarines and a new class of Soviet submarines thought to be operating in the area. The mission assigned by the NSA included intercepting SIGNET from Soviet ships in the Tsushima Strait between Japan and Korea and gathering intelligence on N Korean coastal radars and radio stations. The *Pueblo*—a specialized spy ship packed with advanced sensors and encryption equipment—was the right fit for the mission.

The sailing order issued January 5 augmented the operations order issued December 18, 1968, by including the following specific instructions:

a. Depart Sasebo about January 8 and attempt to avoid detection by Soviet naval vessels while proceeding via Tsushima Strait. [71]

---

71 Tsushima Strait is a eastern channel of the Korea Strait, which lies between Korea and Japan, connecting the Sea of Japan and the East China Sea.

b. Arrive in the operational area of Mars (secondary areas Pluto and Venus) about January 10. Conduct collection operations in areas designated Mars, concentrating on most productive areas.

c. Avoid detection and maintain emission control procedures except when establishing contact with Soviet naval units. Only then, break radio silence or emission control (EMCON) and transmit a daily situation report (SITREP).

d. The closest point of approach (CPA) to N Korea, the Soviet landmass, and offshore islands is 13 nautical miles (15 land miles).

e. Defensive armament (two 50-caliber machine guns) should be stowed or covered in such a way that they do not cause unusual interest by surveyed units. They should be used only in the event of a threat to survival per the provisions of Commander-in-Chief Pacific (CINCPAC) instructions regarding the rules of engagement and conduct in the event of a threat.

f. Depart the operation area on January 27 and, if not under surveillance, maintain strict radio silence or EMCON conditions.

Proceed south along the Korean coast to the vicinity of Tsushima Strait between Korea and Japan. Intercept and conduct surveillance of the Soviet Nasima Straits.

g. Termination of surveillance to arrive at Sasebo February 4, 1968. Earlier departures were authorized to ensure 10% on-board fuel upon return/ arrival at Sasebo.

Normally, the voyage from Yokosuka to Sasebo on the western coast of Kyushu Island, the third largest island of Japan, and most southwesterly of its four main islands, would have taken three days. However, because of stormy conditions, the *Pueblo* arrived on January 9, a day later than planned. During the trip to Sasebo, the electronic intelligence intercept receiver (WLR-1 ELINT) used throughout the fleet in the SOD-hut had broken down, and a new part was flown to Sasebo. While in port, the ship refueled and was resupplied. Repairing the WLR-1 took another day, thus delaying the *Pueblo's* departure until the predawn hours of January 11, 1968. The *Pueblo* headed northward through the

Tsushima Strait into the Sea of Japan to begin its mission, the surveillance of N Korea, the monitoring and recording of Korean coastal radars, and surveillance of Soviet naval units operating in the Tsushima Strait. (The Tsushima Strait is 60 miles long and 40 miles wide). On Tuesday, January 16 the *Pueblo* arrived at the northernmost limit of its operating area, just south of Vladivostok, the boundary separating N Korea and Russia. There were four areas of special interest to US intelligence — ports of Chongjin, Songjin, Mayang-do, and Wonsan. The ship was 25-to-30 miles from the coast, and it cruised to a point off Chongjin and came within 15 miles of shore, closer than any previous time. The captain used the "big eyes" (22-inch binoculars) and could see smoke coming from chimneys. Having arrived at the patrol's northern limit, the captain called the general crew together to brief them on the operations and advised them that they were on a classified intelligence operation. Nothing about the SIGINT mission was disclosed. After spending about two days stationed in Chongjin, the *Pueblo* deployed farther south under the cover of darkness on the night of January 17. By the next morning it had entered the VENUS operational area and was stationed off Songjin (now Kimchaek). The *Pueblo* began slowly working its way south down the N Korean coast toward the military base and port city of Wonsan (pronounced Munch'on). In January 1968, the N Korean Navy had four squadrons at Wonsan with 65 vessels consisting of Komar-class missile boats, patrol/torpedo (PT) boats, minesweepers, and subchasers. The N Korean Air Force 2nd Fighter Division at Wonsan had MiG-15s, fighters that could fly 767 miles-per-hour and MiG-17s high-subsonic fighter aircraft representing a total of 74 aircraft.

The *Pueblo* headed south on January 19 toward the next coastal target, the port of Mayang-do. This area was a major base for N Korea's small submarine fleet and Soviet naval units. The *Pueblo* arrived off Mayang-do during the night of January 19 and was operating some 14 to 15 miles offshore to ensure that it remained in international waters on the morning of January 20. The *Pueblo* was now in operation area MARS, the southernmost of the three operational areas. The *Pueblo* continued to operate off Mayang-do. On Saturday, January 20, the *Pueblo* was found dead in the water about 15.4 miles southwest of Mayang-do. At 1730 hours (5:30 p.m.), a N Korean SO-1 [72] modified Soviet-style submarine chaser (subchaser) passed within 4000 yards of the *Pueblo*. Near twilight on January 21 while maintaining radio silence, the *Pueblo* contacted another Russian

---

72 SO-1 is a 90-ton modified Russian-model submarine chaser, which was assembled starting in 1957, and became infamous as the main vessel involved in the capture of the *Pueblo*.

type subchaser that passed within 1600 yards doing about 29 mph. It emitted no radar or other radio electronic signals, nor were any crew seen. This ship was apparently headed for Wonsan and had no interest in the *Pueblo*.

The decision was made not to break radio silence to report the encounter. The *Pueblo* continued to receive transmissions but maintained radio silence to avoid detection. None of the transmissions mentioned North Korean provocations taking place in S Korea, and the *Pueblo* was alone off the N Korean coast.

There was no radio message (warning) sent to the *Pueblo* concerning the attempted assassination of President Pak Chung-hee in his residence, the Blue House, on January 21 by N Korean commandos. It was discussed at Headquarters, US Navy's 7th Fleet, and since the *Pueblo* had only one day remaining on its mission the decision was made not to inform the *Pueblo*. The captain proceeded with the final phase of his mission unaware that tensions between the two Koreas had just escalated dramatically. After a brief stay near Mayang-do Island, the *Pueblo* proceeded south, arriving at a point 15 miles east of Wonsan at 0700 hours (7:00 a.m.) on January 22 near the N Korean headquarters for the eastern fleet and port of Wonsan. The mission was considered rather dull and unproductive until that time. The *Pueblo* for weeks had moved along the N Korean coast, intercepting communication without incident until it was detected by two N Korean fishing trawlers which circled the *Pueblo* when it was 18-20 miles from the nearest land. The *Pueblo* was again conducting oceanographic activities in the area when it was detected at 1225 hours (12:25 p.m.) by the two trawlers. When the ships were within 1,500 yards, one changed course and passed close to the *Pueblo's* starboard beam at about 100 yards. Neither ship carried an ensign nor flew any flag. Both ships resembled Soviet Lentra-class intelligence collection trawlers. At 1500 hours (3:00 p.m.) both ships began another approach. The *Pueblo* remained dead in the water. Throughout the incident, the *Pueblo* was showing the international signal flag for hydrographic operations. The trawlers departed at 1600 hours (4:00 p.m.) without incident, and the *Pueblo* continued with the mission. Unknown to the *Pueblo*, the fishing trawlers relayed a report of an unidentified ship, and the N Koreans had been tracking the ship throughout most of the southern leg. (Days after its capture, the NSA was able to decipher and analyze the *Pueblo's* SIGINT data, and a month later the NSA learned the *Pueblo* had been acquired by the N Korean radar station at Kukchi-bong and that the N Koreans had labeled the *Pueblo* an enemy ship and sent N Korean naval vessels to intercept it. The *Pueblo* was also under surveillance from N Korean MiG-17s.

The *Pueblo's* senior ELINT analyst passionately believed that the N Koreans were always aware of the *Pueblo's* presence and so stated at his debriefing upon return to the United States.)

The N Koreans were aware that the *Pueblo* displayed characteristics like the *Banner*, which had been seen there previously. About noon, the captain concluded that the ship had been detected, and in accordance with the sailing order, prepared the first situation report. There were difficulties in locating compatible radio frequencies between the *Pueblo* and the NSG Activity, Kamiseya. After a delay of over 12 hours, communications were not established until late morning on January 23. The crew transmitted all its SIGINT data, but the log report stated only that the ship had been sighted by N Korean vessels. From that time, until the *Pueblo* crew destroyed communications equipment upon being boarded, communications were maintained to keep higher authorities apprised. During the night, the *Pueblo* moved out to sea to avoid drifting into N Korean claimed territorial waters. In the morning it moved at full speed toward Wonsan, arriving at a point slightly to the northwest of the position where it had been detected the previous day. This position was thought best for the collections of all types of intelligence on commercial and military operations.

The *Pueblo* began what was scheduled to be the final day of monitoring. It was a bright, brisk day with a temperature of 36 °F and a slight breeze.

At about 0700 hours (7:00 a.m.), the OIC of the SOD-hut reported to the captain that SIGINT activity was picking up and that this was going to be the most fruitful area in which the *Pueblo* had operated. The CTs sat before their consoles and concentrated on their intelligence-gathering mission.

After breakfast, the captain went to the cryptoroom to see if the message left the previous night had been transmitted. He discovered there had been problems with contacting NSG Kamiseya, and it was not until 1054 hours (10:54 a.m.) that cipher communications were finally established, and backlogged messages were transmitted. The first message announced that the *Pueblo* had been sighted and gave its position, with a detailed description of the N Korean vessels and their reaction. The second message was a detailed list of activity since the *Pueblo* entered the operational area, which included 18 contacts and the sighting of an orange flare, indicating intentions to revert to complete electronic silence, although he never did, and it was addressed only to a signal intelligence audience. The third message contained an operational summary and stated the captain felt the *Pueblo* was no longer under surveillance. RDML Johnson learned around noon on January 23 of the *Pueblo's* position and that, although it had been detected by N Korean vessels, the *Pueblo* was no longer under surveillance. Earlier, at about 0930 hours (9:30 a.m.), the OIC of the SOD-hut reported to the bridge, officer-of-the-deck (OOD), two submarine chaser radar emissions were picked up conducting normal radar sweeps and that there was some "chatter" on nearby N Korean communication frequencies. The OIC indicated it was probably routine radio chatter and was being recorded. The captain reflected on the linguists and their lack of proficiency to translate the recorded radio conversations without time-consuming playbacks and references to a dictionary. But he knew they would do the best they could with the training they had been given for the assignment.

The day was uneventful until lunchtime. At 1145 hours (11:45 a.m.), the OOD sighted a ship approaching at high speed from the south. The OOD reported the sighting to the skipper, who arrived on the bridge about noon. The approaching ship was flying its national ensign and was identified as a N Korean SO 1 class submarine chaser, hull number 35 (SC-35), at general quarters with guns manned and trained on the *Pueblo*. The *Pueblo* was dead in the water with no flags or signal shapes flying, in a calm sea, and with no hydrographic operations in progress. The submarine chaser circled at close range and all hands were ordered to remain below decks in order not to indicate the size of the crew. The operations officer was instructed to begin keeping a complete narrative of the incident. The senior oceanographer went to his winch and commenced a Nansen cast, lowering water bottles to obtain samples of seawater. The N Korean ship signaled, "What nationality" and in answer the captain ordered the national ensign (American flag of the United States) and the signal flags "India and Romeo for hydrographer" hoisted, indicating underwater survey [73] work. The captain considered this to be normal harassment and directed the operations officer to prepare an Operations Event / Incident Report (OPREP-3) and to report the event required by the Operation Order. The OPREP-3 reporting system permits any level of command to report significant events and incidents to the highest levels of command. He

---

73 Survey boats display the international maritime signal flags India and Romeo (with Flag India displayed above Flag Romeo). Together these flags mean: "I am engaged in submarine survey work (underwater operations); keep well clear at slow speed." A military hydrographer deals with the measurement, description, and mapping of the physical features of oceans, seas, and coastal areas, as well as with the prediction of their change over time, for the primary purpose of safety of navigation and in support of security and defense.

ordered the engines lit-off (prepare the engines for operation) and prepared to maneuver. About 1220 hours (12:20 p.m.) three additional motor torpedo boats were sighted approaching, and shortly thereafter the SC-35 signaled an alarming message, "Heave to or I will open fire on you." By this time, the captain of the subchaser was certain of its target nationality, hull number (GER-2) and knew its mission was electronic surveillance. The captain verified his position, which was 15.8 miles from the nearest land and ordered the signal "I am in international waters."

The captain released the first operations report. He discussed the possibility of scuttling the ship with the chief engineer. The engineer replied that scuttling would take considerable time but suggested that water-tight integrity (Condition ZEBRA) [74] be set. Three-motor torpedo boats, now identified as N Korean P-4 class torpedo boats, took station around the *Pueblo* at close range. A fourth torpedo boat soon joined the others, and they surrounded the *Pueblo*; that is, two forward and two aft.

The captain ordered the word passed to all hands to prepare for emergency destruction of classified electronic equipment and material. A short time later, 15 minutes later, a supersonic jet fighter and interceptor MiG-21 aircraft arrived flying overhead; SC-35 signaled, "Follow in my wake; I have a pilot on board." An armed boarding party had transferred from SC-35 to PT-604, and PT-604 was backing down on the *Pueblo's* starboard side bow with high-impact fenders rigged to prevent damage to either ship.

The captain prepared and released his second Operations Event/Incident Report at 1315 hours (1:15 p.m.), reporting these occurrences. (This official message was the last to leave the *Pueblo* prior to capture.) He ordered the signal, "Thank you for your consideration; I am departing the area," and ordered one-third speed and right rudder to depart the area in as dignified a manner as possible. The captain had considered and rejected the idea of going to general quarters and decided against manning the 50-caliber machine guns because he "... saw no point in senselessly sending people to their death." He wanted to appear as nothing more than an innocent hydrographic ship for as long as possible. The operations officer at Commander Navy for Japan (COMNAVFOR Japan) received the *Pueblo's* second Operations Event/Incident Report at 13:25

---

74   Condition ZEBRA provides the greatest degree of watertight integrity to the ship. It is the maximum state of readiness for the ship's survivability. The commanding officer can set this condition at any time it is deemed necessary.

hours (1:25 p.m.) and decided the *Pueblo* was in an extremely difficult situation. The communications operator on the *Pueblo* informed his counterpart at NSG Activity, Kamiseya, Japan, through informal operator chatter that "They plan to open fire on us now." This informal chatter continued throughout the remainder of the incident.

As the *Pueblo* settled on a course to leave the area, the torpedo boats began crossing the bow, coming as close as ten yards, and the SC-35 signaled again, "Heave to or I will fire." As the *Pueblo* picked up speed, the PT boats tried to force it in a more southerly direction. The PT boats running at 28-to-40 miles-per-hour crisscrossed the *Pueblo's* bow, often cutting as close as 10 yards. All PT boats had their machine guns trained on the *Pueblo*. The N Koreans probably did not wish to get caught aboard a US ship in international waters if there were a possible US rescue attempt. The *Pueblo* was being forced farther and farther south and eventually would be headed for land, thus bringing the *Pueblo* near the claimed N Korean territorial waters. After about five minutes, the *Pueblo* increased speed to a full 15 miles per hour, and the SC-35 closed at high speed, attempting to gain a position on the port quarter. Because of the unfavorable speed differential, the captain was forced to turn more to the south to present as small a target angle as possible. The SC-35 kept coming and reached a position just forward of the *Pueblo's* stern off the port quarter. At about the same time, the torpedo boats moved out from the *Pueblo*, and at 1327 hours (1:27 p.m.) SC-35 fired the first burst of 57mm (shells); simultaneously, the surrounding PT boats raked the *Pueblo* with machine gunfire. The first rounds struck the *Pueblo's* forward mast, knocking out one of the antennas, and shrapnel exploded all about the flying bridge, wounding the signalman and the captain. Fortunately, the wounds were not incapacitating. At this point the captain decided that the N Koreans were going to make a "...full-scale incident" and ordered the emergency destruction of classified material, publications, and electronic equipment. The first period of 57mm firing lasted about seven minutes, during which time approximately 15 bursts of 6-to-14 rounds were fired. Light machine gunfire from the motor torpedo boats commenced at the same time and continued sporadically throughout the incident. Within seconds, the subchaser fired additional 57mm salvos, and it became obvious that the Koreans were deliberately trying to knock out the *Pueblo's* command and control.

None of the N Korean gunfire from the 57mm hit the *Pueblo* near the waterline; all of it was directed at the superstructure. The N Koreans did not want to sink the ship but rather, capture it. The captain told the OOD not to go to general quarters because he did not want crewmen coming on the deck with helmets on, nor did he want the 50-caliber machine guns uncovered. The captain wanted to avoid any hostile appearance and did not want to give the N Koreans any excuse to open fire.

The captain wanted to appear as nothing more than an innocent hydrographic ship for as long as possible. It was interpreted by the crew to prohibit anyone from going topside—a factor preventing the SOD-hut personnel from using the ship's incinerator for burning documents or throwing weighted bags of classified materials overboard. Consequently, the weighted bags remained on the deck. It was now approaching 1320 hours (1:20 p.m.), about 80 minutes after *Pueblo* was first challenged by the subchaser. A short time later, the captain ordered the ship stopped, at which time the firing ceased. He also ordered the signal flag "protest" be hoisted. He decided that the destruction of classified material was progressing well and depending on the next moves of the N Koreans, he would surrender the ship. The captain then left the bridge for about three minutes to check his own cabin for classified material and noted that emergency destruction was progressing in the ship. Returning to the bridge, SC-35 was again signaling "Follow me; I have a pilot on board," to which he responded by ordering the ship ahead at one-third speed in a wide turn to follow the subchaser. 5th Air Force Headquarters in Japan at 1350 hours (1:50 p.m.) became aware of the *Pueblo's* predicament. The captain again stopped the ship just outside N Korean territorial waters to inspect the progress of emergency destruction. This action triggered a third period of 57mm fire, which resulted in several hits above the main deck, the fatal wounding of Seaman First Class Duane Hodges, [75] fireman, and the serious wounding of others. To stop the firing, the ship was ordered once again all ahead, and the captain conducted an inspection of the SOD-hut. While there, he dictated an informal message to describe the situation to NSG Kamiseya that he did not intend to offer any resistance. He also noted there were three wounded—one seriously—and there was a considerable amount of material remaining to be destroyed and ordered it done. In fact, only a small percentage of the total classified material was destroyed. Within a few seconds Kamiseya answered, stating it was doing what it could to coordinate a response. Then the teletype operator in the cryptoroom began typing the *Pueblo's* last words to Kamiseya: "Have been directed to come to all stop and be boarded. Four men were injured and one critically injured. Going off the air now and

---

75   One 53mm shell burst in Seaman Hodges' groin, virtually tearing his right leg off and ripping open his lower abdomen. He died en route to Wonsan.

destroying this gear." Kamiseya's repeated reply to "please transit in the clear" went unheeded. The Senior Chief Communications Technician began smashing the crypto gear to render it useless.

2nd Major Incident: North Korean Forces Board and Capture the USS *Pueblo*

January 23, 1968

The captain granted the SOD-hut OIC permission to inform NSG Kamiseya at 1420 hours (2:20 p.m.) that destruction would not be complete, then in response to orders from the N Koreans, ordered the ship stopped to allow the boarding party to board. (There was no assistance provided.) It was apparent that the N Koreans now intended to board the *Pueblo,* having reached a more satisfactory position immediately inside the claimed 12-mile territorial waters limit. The boarding took place at about 1432 hours (2:32 p.m.).

The Koreans who boarded looked more like ground soldiers than sailors, they did not hesitate in their actions.[76] On the port-side of the main deck, a crewman secured a line passed from the PT boat as it worked itself alongside. Two N Korean officers with pistols drawn stepped aboard the *Pueblo.* They were followed by eight enlisted men, each armed with a bayonet-tipped AK-47 automatic weapon. About an hour after the initial boarding, the N Korean officer on the bridge ordered the *Pueblo* "all stop" to receive another group of officers who had boarded from one of the PT boats.

In this party was a senior colonel, who was the officer in command of the N Korean force, and an interpreter. The senior colonel immediately ordered the captain to take him on a tour of the ship, including the research detachment spaces. Upon entering the crypto area, the N Koreans noticed that a few of the teletype machines were still clattering away and immediately began jerking out patch panel wiring and hitting power switches, but even then, they could not completely shut down the equipment. According to the captain when debriefing in San Diego, "the N Koreans' eyes really bugged open when they saw that shack in there. They just didn't know what the hell they had..." The second boarding party included a N Korean pilot who took the helm and steered the

---

76 The Naval Court of Inquiry noted in declassified documents that the captain should have increased speed, zig-zagged, and maneuvered radically. No boarding party could have come aboard had the ship so maneuvered.

ship toward the N Korean coast. The engine room remained manned by *Pueblo* crew members during the trip into Wonsan. During the trip (1500 hours or 3:00 p.m.), Seaman Duane D. Hodges died. Two hours after sunset, 2030 hours (8:30 p.m.), the *Pueblo* was moored to a dock about ten miles northwest of Wonsan. Prior to docking, there had been little mistreatment of the crew, except for the captain. At no time during the incident, nor during the boarding, were the ship's 50-caliber machine guns manned, small arms issued, or any resistance offered, except the attempt to maneuver the ship farther to sea.

Seaman First Class Duane D. Hodges was posthumously promoted to Petty Officer 3rd Class and awarded the Silver Star Medal [77], the third-highest US Navy decoration for conspicuous gallantry.

The Commander Pacific Fleet was first notified at 1430 hours (2:30 p.m.). The 5th Air Force and 7th Fleet reacted by attempting to come to the *Pueblo's* assistance; however, none could react in a timely manner. Whatever their intentions, the N Koreans had captured an American SIGINT collector, giving them unfettered access to equipment, documentation, and the crew's knowledge.

> *What was especially grave in the US maneuvers for the provocation of a new war was the intrusion of their armed spy ship Pueblo into the territorial waters of the DPRK on an espionage mission. As is widely known to the world, the US armed spy ship Pueblo, disguising itself as an "oceanic electron research ship," was seized by the naval vessels of the Korean People's Army on January 23, 1968, in East Korea Bay, the territorial waters of the DPRK, while engaging in espionage and hostile acts in 17 places of the DPRK territorial waters from January 15.*

> *At that time, the US imperialists schemed to extend this incident to the provocation of another Korean conflict (war). Echoes of the Korean War.*

---

77   The President of the United States took pride in presenting the Silver Star Medal (posthumously) to Duane D. Hodges, Fireman, US Navy, for conspicuous gallantry and intrepidity in action on January 23, 1969, while serving aboard USS *Pueblo*. When the *Pueblo* came under fire in the Sea of Japan by N Korean air and naval forces consisting of two aircraft, two patrol boats, and four torpedo boats, Petty Officer Hodges rendered invaluable assistance in the face of the intense hostile fire while participating in the unfamiliar task of destroying classified materials, and was mortally wounded.
http://www.koreanwar-educator.org/topics/dmz/p_dmz_awards.htm#SilverStar.

Detention of the Crew

The *Pueblo's* crew was about to begin its harrowing ordeal of detention.

By 2030 hours (8:30 p.m.) the *Pueblo* docked at Wonsan. The crew was paraded off, their hands bound and blindfolded, amid a crowd of shouting, spitting, and kicking N Koreans, who attempted unsuccessfully to attack them. After leaving the ship, the N Koreans returned the captain and the SOD-hut OIC to the ship individually in an unsuccessful attempt to have them open the secured door to the SOD-hut.

Prior to boarding the train for Pyongyang, several of the crew members were severely beaten, and en route to the first detention site everyone was mistreated: kicked, prodded with rifle butts, slapped, and punched by the guards. Immediately upon arrival, in the early morning of January 24, at the first detention site where the crew spent 41 days prior to being relocated at a permanent place of detention, intensive interrogation of the officers commenced. The officers were assembled in front of several N Korean officers, including a N Korean general. Commencing with the captain, each officer was asked by the general to explain why the *Pueblo* had been spying on N Korea. Following the example set by the captain, each man divulged only his name, rank, and duties aboard the *Pueblo*. After some 24 hours of concentrated beatings, harassment, torture, threats of death, and intimidation, culminating with a threat to be shot, the entire crew, commencing with the youngest member, the captain signed his first confession admitting intrusions into claimed territorial waters of N Korea for espionage purposes. Similar mistreatment was inflicted upon other officers, and some of the crew, until all confessed to the intrusions. Some of the communication technicians were interrogated on several occasions, and classified information was either disclosed or verified. A common method of torture was to force them to kneel on the floor, squatting backwards with a board or stick placed behind the knees, and holding a chair high above the head, with the body straight, being kicked or beaten if they wavered or fell. The more defiant crew members received harsher treatment throughout the detention period.

On March 5, the crew was relocated to a relatively new building near Pyongyang, where they remained until repatriation. During June, communication technicians were subjected to interrogations involving intelligence matters and were questioned by N Koreans.

In some instances, block diagrams and explanations of the captured KW-47 [78] encryption system and KL-7, a standalone crypto-transmitter/receiver, were provided. Information was also provided about the KL-7 machine being used in conjunction with the KW-47 system to provide a multi-channel broadcast. Confessions were extracted from the executive officer, the ship's navigator, with respect to alleged intrusions into claimed territorial waters. In early September, the total number of alleged intrusions increased from 6 to 17, and the navigator was forced to admit them. In addition to the daily attempts to indoctrinate the crew in communist ideology, in late September, when it appeared they were about to be repatriated, "cultural development" trips were conducted in and around Pyongyang. On one occasion the crew, except for the officers, was taken to another building for interviews with N Korean officers masquerading as civilians, who sought their ideas of socialism and inquired whether individuals would be willing to receive sympathizers in their home upon returning to the United States. Some were encouraged to return to N Korea. Following the guidance and lead of the captain, the men attempted to deceive and resist the N Koreans' propaganda efforts throughout the detention by injecting discrediting signs, gestures, and language into confessions, photographs, and press conferences, with a degree of success.

Some 11 months after capture, Army Major General (MG) Gilbert H. Woodward, the chief US negotiator, executed a document on behalf of the United States government to obtain the release of the crew.

Release of the Crew - December 23, 1968

The number of armed intrusions committed by the US imperialists and the S Korean puppet clique in the one year of 1968 against the northern half of Korea more than tripled as compared with the previous year, and over six times more men were mobilized than those mobilized in 14 years after the armistice. At the Panmunjom meeting on December 23, 1968, Gilbert H. Woodward, Major General of the US Army, on behalf of the US government apologized to the Korean people in connection with the Pueblo case: "...Shoulders full responsibility and solemnly apologizes for the grave acts of espionage committed by the US ship

---

78 Aboard the *Pueblo* were a wealth of intercept equipment and high-grade cipher machines such as the KL-47, US roto-based cipher machine and the KW-7, US roto-based cipher machine. The K-47 was based on the principle of the KW-7 and used the same cipher wheels, but was larger, and it incorporates a paper tape leader/puncher and a standard teletype keyboard. KL-7 was an electro-mechanical roto based off-line cipher machine, developed by the National Security Agency (NSA).

against the Democratic People's Republic of Korea after having intruded into the territorial waters of the Democratic People's Republic of Korea and gives firm assurance that no US ships will intrude again in the future into the territorial waters of the Democratic People's Republic of Korea."

The document contained admissions concerning both the mission of the *Pueblo* and intrusion into the claimed territorial waters of N Korea. The document provided N Korea with a propaganda win. N Korea stated that the *Pueblo* deliberately entered its territorial waters 7.6 miles away from Wonsan and Ryo Island and intruded several times. The crew was told by the General-in-Charge of detention on December 20 that they would be released. On Saturday, December 21, they were taken by bus to the train in Pyongyang and by train to the City of Kaesong, six miles from the DMZ. On December 23, 1968, exactly 11 months after their capture, the 83 crewmen, including the remains of Seaman Duane D. Hodges, were transported by bus to the border at Panmunjom where they were repatriated. The crew of the *Pueblo* crossed the "Bridge of No Return" between N and S Korea. Immediately thereafter, the US verbally retracted the admission and apology. The capture of the *Pueblo* was terrible for the United States. However, its mission was within the parameters set by the Navy and the NSA, and the *Pueblo* was there to collect information deemed vital to the US government.

Cold War tensions were extremely high, the situation in Vietnam was spiraling into chaos, and N Korea was seemingly moving toward ever-increasing hostility toward S Korea. The US could not be surprised as it had been on June 25, 1950 and needed the *Pueblo* to collect SIGINT intelligence on N Korea to confirm a crystallization of war on the Korean peninsula.

Unfortunately, the N Koreans found this intolerable, and disaster ensued. The capture of not only its crew included specialized signals intelligence (SIGNET) equipment, KL-7, a standalone crypto-transmitter/receiver, and highly classified documents. (In all, 10 encryption machines and thousands of pages of top-secret documents were seized from the ship.)

In the 1960s, data analysis took considerable time to complete, and it would be a month after the capture that the NSA used the *Pueblo's* own transmitted intercepts to illustrate its last fateful days. [79]

---

[79] Source: DOCID 3075778 REF ID: A632597 NO. 1099 (Excerpts used to tell the story.)

After the return of the crew of the *Pueblo*, the Commander-in-Chief, Pacific Fleet, on December 24, 1968, ordered the establishment of a court of inquiry relating to the capture of the *Pueblo*. The court was required to report findings of fact. The facts as identified by the court were not binding upon the next level of command. On January 20, 1969, at the Naval Amphibious Base on Coronado Island near San Diego, California, the Naval Court of Inquiry was called to order. The Naval Court of Inquiry consisted of four rear admirals and one vice admiral. Originally expected to last three weeks, it lasted almost two months. The court was charged to inquire into the circumstances relating to the capture of the *Pueblo* by N Korean Naval Forces, which occurred in the Sea of Japan. The commander and his crew appeared before the Naval Court of Inquiry [80] regarding the capture.

The court of inquiry noted for the record that the capture of the entire crew with their personnel records and many classified materials placed the *Pueblo* crew in a unique situation in which it would have been impossible to resist successfully. As a result, the N Koreans did obtain propaganda instruments of value, and some classified material was either disclosed or confirmed by the crew members. The destruction [81] classified material, publications, and electronic equipment was ineffective, particularly in the SOD-hut, largely because of poor planning and lack of firm supervision by the OIC of the SOD-hut. At the time the ship was boarded, there was no debilitating damage, and only one crew member was fatally wounded. On March 13, the skipper read his final statement to the court. It was brief. In part his statement said, "The overall conduct of the officers, enlisted men, and civilians assigned to the *Pueblo* was outstanding, and I commend every one of them."

After extensive testimony, a court martial was recommended for the captain and the officer-in-charge of the special operations detachment. The court also recommended the commander Task Force 96, and the *Pueblo's* executive officer be given non-judicial punishment in the form of a letter of reprimand, sometimes called a letter of admonition.

---

80   The captain learned during the Naval Inquiry that two days prior to the confrontation, January 21, the N Koreans had dispatched a cross-border raid into S Korea, where the mission was to assassinate President Park Chung-hee. This was the so-called "Blue House Raid." The raid was the most daring cross-border raid carried out in the next sixty-nine years (2022) since the end of the 1950s Korean Conflict.
The captain contended that if he had been informed, he would have operated the *Pueblo* further out from Wonsan, probably at least 30 miles from nearest land. He also learned the aircraft carrier USS *Enterprise* (CVN-65) had been at sea within 510 miles of the scene of the capture no more than one hour's flying time from an airstrike.
81   The destruction of such large a volume of materials and equipment called for the use of extraordinary measures by the crew. Axes and sledgehammers proved useless against the metal-encased equipment and the shredder became jammed with piles of papers shoved into it, and burning the documents in the waste baskets filled the cabins with smoke.

The *Pueblo* court of inquiry was over.

Newly appointed Navy Secretary, John Chafee, had to walk a fine line in his final disposition of the case. At a press conference in May 1969, he revealed his admirals' preference for a court martial, but announced that he was overruling their recommendation. "They have suffered enough." Charges were dismissed. Chafee candidly admitted that mistakes and miscalculations by the Navy had led to what he called the *Pueblo's* "lonely confrontation by unanticipatedly bold and hostile forces." [82]

On recommendations contained in the report of the Naval Court of Inquiry, the USS *Banner* and *Palm Beach* had dual 20mm gun mounts added to replace the two 50-caliber machine guns. Additionally, a ship-scuttling system was added, along with the installation of a destruction system for the SOD-hut equipment. The scuttling system consisted of a firing circuit and three explosive charges located in the engineering spaces. When detonated, the charges were designed to cause flooding of the auxiliary and main engine rooms, thereby causing the ship to sink within 15 minutes.

The circuit was fired electrically through key locked panels located in the pilot house and an alternate station in the commanding officer's cabin. Electrically ignited thermite equipment was installed to destroy all designated electronic equipment and classified cabinets and safes.

The *Banner* and the *Palm Beach* were decommissioned on November 14, 1969. Going forward, intelligence-collection duties would be performed by regular US Navy ships.

The NSA Cryptographic Damage Assessment constitutes a review of the cryptologic - cryptographic damage resulting from the N Korean capture of the *Pueblo* and the 11-month internment of the crew. The information used to prepare this report was derived from the debriefing of *Pueblo* crew members, which led to a determination of what sensitive information and equipment are, or are assumed to be, in the possession of, at least, the N Koreans. The complete Assessment of the USS *Pueblo* incident is described in the introduction — specifically, Table 12 Appendix K DOCID 3997434, and Freedom of Information Act Case 40722.

---

82   Source and further details: https://www.usspeublo.org/Court_of_Inqiry/SecNav_Chafee.htmpl.

This report is a final overall review of the cryptologic-cryptographic damage resulting from the N Korean capture of the *Pueblo* and crew. Details about the experiences of the crew. [83] This assessment also provides complete details about the entire *Pueblo* incident. Starting with the background about the AGER program, it includes the risk assessment for the mission and the *Pueblo* mission specifics. Details about the Security Group Detachment include its organization, chain of command, funding, and physical configuration of the detachment. The most important detail is about the emergency destruction of classified materials, publications, and equipment. The assessment continues with the seizure and the reactions by the various commands along with an explanation/finding about damage, casualties, destruction of classified material, and the extent of hostilities by the N Koreans. The assessment concludes with the detention of the crew, interrogation, mistreatment, resistance, indoctrination attempts, and repatriation.

In 1990, the Pentagon awarded the Prisoner of War Medal to the entire crew. Until then, the US government maintained they were detainees rather than POWs because the US and N Korea were not at war.

The *Pueblo* officially remains a commissioned vessel.

The story you have read about the USS *Pueblo* and its crew is true, based on declassified documents (top secret and below), with influence from *Bucher: My Story* by Commander Lloyd M. Bucher, USN, Captain USS *Pueblo* with Mark Rascovich along with *Second in Command* by its Executive Officer, former Lieutenant Edward R. Murphy, Jr., with Curt Gentry.

Among the most significant compromises in the history of American military intelligence, the capture of the technically advanced spy ship was a source of embarrassment for all those involved.

The details remain the subject of controversy and speculation even now, fueled in part by the vastly different perspectives of the *Pueblo's* commander and his executive officer, both of whom published lengthy books about their experiences. The events described in this writing are accurate, but it is the personalities of both Bucher and Murphy that tell the story behind the incident. They give two

---

83   https://www.history.navy.mil/research/library/online-reading-room/titlr-list-Alphabetically/s/
some-experiences-reported-crew-uss-*Pueblo*-american-prosoner.

completely different descriptions of events as they unfolded, from refitting the *Pueblo* to its capture and the imprisonment of its crew.

Commander Lloyd M. Bucher continued his naval career and went on to serve five more years, and his last assignment at sea was to help clear US mines from North Vietnam's Haiphong harbor. He retired in 1973. Commander Bucher, 76, died January 28, 2004, and is buried at the Fort Rosecrans National Cemetery, San Diego Harbor Coronado. He was a veteran of World War II, the 1950s Korean Conflict, the 1960s Korean Conflict, and the Vietnam War. The executive officer, Lieutenant Edward R. Murphy, Jr., resigned his commission [84] and returned to civilian life. Commander Bucher, Captain of the USS *Pueblo,* and Lieutenant Murphy, Executive Officer, and second-in-command, received the Purple Heart Medal for wounds inflicted during the capture and the Prisoner of War Medal.

Tourist Destination Victorious War Museum, Pyongyang – USS *Pueblo* (GER-2)

Today the *Pueblo* is a tourist destination at the Victorious War Museum or Fatherland War of Liberation Museum along the Pothong River in Pyongyang.

A television movie, *Pueblo*, was released on March 29, 1973, starring Hal Holbrook as Commander Bucher, Ronny Cox as a signalman, and Andrew Duggan as a congressman. The Cold War incident, told in flashback sequences, tells the story of the capture of the USS *Pueblo* by N Korean naval units. It won five Primetime Emmys; it was directed by Anthony Page and written by Stanley R. Greenberg. This made-for-TV film is done semi-documentary style with certain parts resembling a stage play.

Additional source documents released are described in the introduction — specifically, Table12.

Appendix D, Risk Assessment of the USS *Pueblo* Mission

Appendix K, Cryptologic/Cryptographic Damage Assessment USS *Pueblo*

---

84   Prior to the capture of the *Pueblo*, Lieutenant Murphy had decided to leave the Navy. He had given thought to his decision to resign, realizing that at the time he made it, he had lost perspective. Source: *2nd in Command*, Chapter 31, last paragraph, pp 388/99.

Appendix M, Inquiry into the USS *Pueblo* and EC-121 Plane Incidents by the United States Congress

USS *Pueblo* National Security Agency

Release Summary on November 20, 2012

What is being released?

The National Security Agency (NSA) is releasing a rich collection of many types of documents relating to the USS *Pueblo* incident. This released collection includes internal memoranda, disseminated Executive Branch materials, and intelligence products. The release of these intelligence products and communication intercepts are significant. In support of the President's Openness and Transparency Initiative and the National Declassification Center's priorities, NSA is releasing the most complete and authoritative communication intercept on the capture of the USS *Pueblo* and the imprisonment of the crew.

This release also includes intercepts of possibly relevant activity before and after the actual event. This is a unique release that follows the National Archives and Records Administration's, National Declassification Center theme of "Releasing All We Can, Protecting What We Must."

What is new in this release?

Scholars will be able to study the original materials directly. Much of the content in the public domain is administrative documents and memoranda. Prior releases were summaries of the contents of these documents, but now original sources are released.

Also included in this new release is the 1992 NSA's Center for Cryptologic History study on the incident with more previously classified material now declassified and released under FOIA. This 1992 study includes a lengthy analytic view of the incident and its aftermath to include details on the interrogation during the crew's captivity as well as the US debriefing upon the crew members' return.

The capture of the *Pueblo* has been a controversial matter since it occurred. These new releases may not settle any of the questions debated publicly about the *Pueblo* incident, but they will assist in a more informed discussion.

What was the USS *Pueblo* Incident?

On January 23, 1968, 14 miles from the N Korean east coast, the USS *Pueblo* was attacked and captured by overwhelming N Korean forces. The crew was detained and interrogated until released on December 23, 1968.

Despite the crew's valiant efforts to destroy classified materials on board, much was still undestroyed and fell into N Korean hands when the ship was captured.

What events lead to the USS *Pueblo* Incident?

In the 1960s, the US cryptologic community, composed of NSA and the Service Cryptologic Components, conducted communications intercept via specially configured ships. These vessels, known as "technical research ships," or TRSes, could respond quickly to crises and provide needed intercept coverage in global regions where there were unanticipated needs for intelligence information.

In 1967, after more than a decade in which conflict on the Korean peninsula had been relatively muted, N Korea became increasingly aggressive toward S Korea. In fact, at the time the mission of the *Pueblo* was being conducted, N Korean commandos were on a mission to assassinate S Korea's president.

The United States had a mutual defense agreement with S Korea but was heavily involved in the war in Southeast Asia. US military leaders sought additional information on the DPRK to assist their decision-making in this renewed conflict in Northeast Asia.

The intelligence community judged that use of TRSes was an effective way to respond quickly. The *Pueblo*, a converted World War II supply ship, was one of the vessels assigned this collection mission. Although arguably not seaworthy, the *Pueblo* was refitted for a SIGINT mission, sailed to Japan in late 1967, and then to the East Coast of the DPRK.

For its mission, the *Pueblo* was instructed to be scrupulous about staying in international waters, which the United States interpreted as twelve miles from land, the international norm at that time. N Korea, however, claimed a boundary of two hundred miles for its national waters.

What happened to the crew of the *Pueblo*?

One member of the crew died because of injuries sustained during the ship's capture. The N Koreans detained and interrogated the ship's remaining 82-member crew for eleven months. Many among the crew were highly experienced in US SIGINT operations. On December 23, 1968, a US military representative signed a formal apology for intruding into DPRK waters–a statement he repudiated verbally immediately after signing it, after the crew was returned. The *Pueblo* is still located in N Korea. Upon the crew's return, they were questioned by experts to determine the extent of compromises of classified documents, equipment, and other information.

In addition, reflecting the high emotions prevalent at the time, the crew was frequently tarnished with unfair blame for the incident. Today history views the crew's valiant efforts as courageous. All crew members, including the civilian oceanographers who were held prisoner, were authorized the Prisoner of War Medal. All military crew members were authorized the Armed Forces Expeditionary Medal and the Combat Action Ribbon. The crewmembers are true American heroes.

Why does the NSA have documents related to the *Pueblo* incident?

The *Pueblo* mission was undertaken at the request of the US Navy, and the *Pueblo* was subordinate to the Naval Security Command, the service's cryptologic component. NSA's role was, and still is, to be a technical advisor to such missions. Also, prior to the mission, NSA was asked for its advice on the strategy for the *Pueblo* mission.

These documents show that NSA "signed off" on the mission, but also forwarded a warning statement about the growing aggressiveness of N Korea and expressed reservations about the value of conducting this sort of mission in the winter, when less N Korean activity might be expected. With the known risks, the dangerous mission proceeded.

As the central organization for US communications intelligence (COMINT) activities, NSA became a repository for administrative documents related to the *Pueblo* as well as much of the intelligence produced by and about the mission.

Why are they being released now?

NSA is committed to openness and transparency. NSA recognizes that this release will contribute to the study of a unique event important both to the history of NSA and the history of our nation.

On occasion, the N Koreans have attacked US reconnaissance aircraft. One incident occurred just after the 1953 armistice concluding the 1950s Korean Conflict. N Korean anti-aircraft in August 1953 shot down an unarmed trainer US Air Force (USAF) T-G on an intelligence mission near Panmunjom, resulting in the death of the pilot and one crewmember listed as missing in action.

On April 27, 1965, N Korean fighters from Sendek (English: Sunchon) Air Force Base attacked and severely damaged a USAF RB-47 aircraft conducting an electronic intelligence (ELINT) mission. Two MiG-17s fired on the aircraft over the Sea of Japan, eighty miles off the coast. The plane was able to return to the base. ELINT [85] is a coined word for the process of electronic intercept and analysis of electronic intelligence. The RB-47 was eventually phased out and replaced with the U-2 High-Altitude Reconnaissance and SR-72 Blackbird spy planes. [86] The Lockheed Martin SR-72, referred to as "Son of Blackbird," a hypersonic aircraft with top speed more than Mach 6, or just over 4500 miles-per-hour, is intended for intelligence, surveillance, and reconnaissance. First proposed in 2013, it is expected the test vehicle could fly by 2025, with the aircraft entering service in the 2030s.

---

85 ELINT pertains to all enemy electronic devices, including airborne intercept devices used by guided missiles, guided missile launchers, fighter aircraft, long-range and short-range navigational aids, ground-controlled intercept height finders, anti-aircraft, and aircraft fire control radar, blind bombing devices, electronic radiations emanating from scientific laboratories or production plants.

86 The U-2 was finally withdrawn in 1974, and the Blackbird was retired by the US military almost 30 years ago; its successor was anticipated. The hypersonic SR-72 spy plane, also known as the Son of Blackbird, could be operational soon.

CHAPTER 19

AIRBORNE SIGNAL INTELLIGENCE COLLECTION

Incidents between N Korea, S Korea, and the US continued, and in April 1969 a N Korean MiG fighter shot down a US Navy EC-121 Warning Star Surveillance Aircraft Call Sign: *Deep Sea 129*. The airborne signal intelligence-collection reconnaissance aircraft was on a routine mission off the N Korean coast in the Sea of Japan.

The N Korean MiG-21 Fishbed-Fs, supersonic fighter/interceptor of the N Korean Air Force (NKAF) First Fighter Division, flew to Homerun Air School on March 28 from Pukchang-ni Airfield near the city of Sunchon. The Joint Sobe Processing Center (JSPC), located at Torii Station, Okinawa sent a message on Sunday, March 30, 1969, to all Far East military commands and SIGINT sites, which indicated that this *first* radar reflection of Fishbed-F type aircraft at Hoemun near the northern city of Chongjin was probably related to pilot training. There was no known NKAF tactical unit located at Homerun. On the morning of Tuesday, April 15 two MiG-21s remained at Homerun and raised the question—why? Such was the initial warning of the coming crisis.

In the early morning of April 15, Lieutenant Commander (LCDR) James H. Overstreet, US Navy, met with members of the crew and 15 trainees for a preflight briefing. Nine of the crew, including one Marine non-commissioned officer (NCO), were communication/cryptologic technicians (CTs) and linguists in Russian and Korean. The routine briefing did contain a warning. The commander discussed three messages in the briefing, including one from the Commander of US Forces in Korea, General Bonesteel III, to the

Commander-in-Chief Pacific, Admiral John S. McCain, Jr., on Friday, April 11, 1969. The message warned of unusually vehement and vicious language used by the N Koreans in recent Military Armistice Commission (MAC) meetings held at the JSA, Panmunjom in the most sensitive area of Korea's demilitarized zone. While the crew members prepared for the mission, they were unaware of the unusual activity at Homerun. Although the communications were not directed toward the US Navy's Fleet Airborne Reconnaissance Squadron One (VQ-1), it was told to be alert and prepared to abort at the first indication of any serious reactions by the N Koreans. As a precaution, however, the flight was to approach no closer than 50 miles from the Korean coast. The Navy reconnaissance squadron had flown the route and orbit for two years, and the mission had been graded as being of "minimal risk." During the first three months of 1969, nearly 200 similar missions had been flown by both Navy and US Air Force reconnaissance aircraft off N Korea's East Coast without incident.

The Beggar Shadow mission was an EC-121 Warning Star [87] airborne early warning and control radar surveillance aircraft radio call sign *Deep Sea 129*. The commander taxied to the runway and took off from Atsugi Naval Air Station near Tokyo, Japan at 0700 hours (7:00 a.m.) Korean standard time Tuesday April 15 to begin the mission. The aircraft bore the tail code "PR 21."

The code name Beggar Shadow was used to describe the late-1960s Cold War reconnaissance program by the US Navy that collected intelligence about and communications among Soviet Bloc nations while remaining safely (at least according to international laws) in international waters. According to a declassified National Security Agency (NSA) history of the shootdown, the EC-121 would normally have been staffed by a crew of 10-to-15 Navy personnel.

But there were 31 individuals on the plane that day, including 15 trainees for the mission. The plane was fitted with a fuselage radar, so the primary tasks were to act as a long-range patrol, conduct electronic surveillance, and act as a warning device. Once the aircraft reached its cruising speed and altitude, the crew began preparing for the mission. The classified electronic equipment was tested to ensure working order. The trainees onboard settled in and began learning the routine and how to operate the equipment. The

---

87 The EC121M was the predecessor to the E-3 Sentry AWACS. The E-3 airborne warning and control system (AWACS) role was to carry out airborne surveillance, and command, control and communications (C3) functions for both tactical and air defense forces. US aircraft carry the designation E-3 AWACS. A total of 332 aircraft were constructed for both the US Air Force and US Navy.

scheduled flight duration was eight and a half hours; from Atsugi, the flight was to fly northwest over the Sea of Japan (East Sea of Korea) until it came to a point off the northeastern coastal city of Chongjin, near N Korea's border with Manchuria. The plane was then to fly two and a half orbits along a 120-mile elliptical path parallel to the coast of N Korea before continuing to Osan Air Force Base, near Seoul, S Korea, with a projected arrival time of 1530 hours (3:30 p.m.) Korean standard time. Except for the beginning and ending legs over Japan and S Korea, the entire flight was over international waters. The flight plan included flying no closer than 50 miles to the N Korean coast, a safe distance from N Korea's claimed territorial waters and airspace twelve 12 miles from its coast.

The EC-121 was a "slow and lumbering" plane that was once a familiar sight to trans-Atlantic air travelers, the Super Constellation, a major commercial plane before the jet age. The unarmed aircraft carried nearly six tons of electronic equipment with a bulbous radome on top to pick up radar signals and antennas under the belly to monitor radio communications. The plane contained a communications position and included secure voice (KY-8) and secure teletype (KW-7) equipment. Friendly radar was available during part of the flight from Japan and S Korea. The aircraft had a maximum speed of 253 miles per hour with a maximum altitude of 10,000 to 20,000 feet. Before the flight, the Navy provided a complete flight path and times to monitoring stations. One of the signals intelligence sites that supported the EC-121 flight was responsible to track the flight and coordinate via an operational communications (OPSCOM) circuit with USA-58. USA-58 was the SIGINT designator for the 6918th Security Squadron of the US Air Force Security Service and was interfaced with the US Army Security Agency (ASA) Station at Hakata, Kyushu, Japan. The ASA communications interception station at Osan Air Force Base (AFB) listened to N Korean air defense radio traffic.

The key role in the entire episode was played by ASA. Osan AFB is located near Songtan Station in the City of Pyeongtaek S Korea, 40 miles south of the capital city of Seoul. Collected information was passed to appropriate command and control facilities for possible action, such as a fighter launch. In the case of such a launch, ASA was to contact units of the 5th Air Force, the 5th Air Force Advanced Echelon (ADVON), and the 314th Air Division Warning Center (ADWC) located at Osan AFB, through secure voice and teletype. (ASA was from 1945 through 1976 the US Army's electronic intelligence branch.) The

Naval Security Group (NSG) facility USN-39 at Kamiseya, Japan, was to serve as another relay point in the SIGINT network, but communications problems would put it out of the picture until well after the shoot down occurred. NSG provided seven of the nine communications technicians (CTs) aboard *Deep Sea 129*, and their mission was also to intercept Soviet Air Force search radars.

Because of its proximity to Airborne Reconnaissance Squadron One, NSG had control over manning the onboard positions of the flight. The crew was in direct contact with NSG USN-39 during the early hours of the flight. At the very beginning of the mission, the commander (pilot) called Kamiseya for a ground check. This was acknowledged by the NSG several minutes later. An hour and a half later, chatter took place between the plane and the NSG to correct some minor communications difficulties; these problems were cleared up and 20 minutes later, the last direct contact occurred between the plane and NSG, Kamiseya.

At that time, the crew had some activity on a radiotelephone position and informed the NSG that no further transmissions would be forthcoming while this took place. The reason for this action was to prevent the loss of intercept which sometimes occurred during secure teletype KW-7 transmissions. The plane would simply acknowledge any transmissions from the ground by sending three short sync pulses on the KW-7 circuit. The plane was initially reflected by friendly radar over the Sea of Japan at 1035 hours (10:35 a.m.) Korean standard time approximately 150 nautical miles (73 statute miles) southeast of Vladivostok, not far from Russia's borders with China and N Korea. The city is the home port of the Russian Pacific Fleet and the largest Russian seaport. N Korea reacted to the presence of *Deep Sea 129*, but not in a way that would jeopardize the mission. The pilot was informed of unfavorable Soviet reaction and responded sending three short pulses on the K-7 circuit and continued to fly on a northwesterly path to a point about 90 nautical miles (103 statute miles) southeast of Vladivostok, also representing the closest point to Soviet territory at 60 nautical miles (69 statute miles). Shortly after, *Deep Sea 129* acknowledged the hourly radio check, providing location and distance from Soviet territory. Later the National Security Agency (NSA) would use this information to repudiate claims by the Soviets that *Deep Sea 129* violated its airspace. The Soviets changed their readiness posture believing the EC-121 violated their airspace. The 6918th Security Squadron was unable to assist at this critical point.

ASA station Hakata informed Osan that it was reflecting an Air Force Airborne Communications Reconnaissance Platform (ACRP) mission in the Vladivostok Bay area, but not *Deep Sea 129*, the EC-121. (The USAF Security Service flew several large intelligence gathering aircraft including C-47 Skytrain, and RC-135 Strarolifter sharing airspace with US Navy aircraft.)

Fact tracking was extremely sparse after its radar reflections several hours earlier. No warning was issued to the pilot at the time. Shortly thereafter, *Deep Sea 129* began its long elliptical track to the southwest. The 6918th USA-58 informed Osan that ASA Hakata had no reflections of the plane. At that point, Osan lost contact with ASA Hakata when its operation-command (OPSCOM) circuit went out for about 19 minutes. However, the NSG continued to track the plane throughout the next crucial hour. The OPSCOM circuit with ASA Hakata was restored, and Osan now seemed convinced that it was reflecting the correct aircraft. While reflecting the plane on the radar at the beginning of this elliptical orbit, ASA Hakata reported that it had tracked fighters over the water. The fighter radar reflections, however, were far to the southwest, over the Tong-son Bay, and seemed non-threatening. Hakata subsequently reported the fighters were heading back toward the Korean landmass. For the next half hour, *Deep Sea 129* continued its southwest leg, reaching the southernmost point of the orbit area at about 1100 hours (11:00 a.m.) Korean standard local time. The ASA circuit was quiet. The crew at this point was performing the assigned mission. As the reconnaissance plane approached the southern limit of its elliptical track, the final transmission from the plane occurred. Shortly after 1100 hours (11:00 a.m.) Korean standard time, the aircraft responded to the hourly communications check by NSG Kamiseya. It was still being tracked by radar and reflected a course compatible with the planned flight route.

Third Major Incident: Call Sign: *Deep Sea 129* US Navy EC-121M Warning Star Intelligence Collection Aircraft Shot Down

As the aircraft approached the northern part of the elliptical orbit at 1234 hours (12:34 p.m.) roughly six hours into the mission, the ASA and radars in S Korea detected the takeoff of two N Korean Air Force MiG-21s interceptor fighters launched from Homerun Air School, East Tongchong-nee near Wonsan. These fighters had appeared in late March at the Homerun Air School. The jets were tracked as they took off across the waters of the Sea of Japan in what appeared to be a carefully calculated maneuver in response to the mission of *Deep Sea*

129. In the meantime, *Deep Sea 129* filed a scheduled activity report on time at 1300 hours (1:00 p.m.) and did not indicate anything out of the ordinary. Twenty-two minutes later, the radars lost the picture of the MiGs and did not reacquire it until 1337 hours (1:37 p.m.), closing with *Deep Sea 129* for a probable intercept. The communications that this activity generated within the national security network were monitored by the EC-121's parent unit, Navy Reconnaissance Squadron One (VQ-1), which at 1344 hours (1:44 p.m.) sent *Deep Sea 129* a "condition 3" alert by radio, indicating it might be under attack. The commander acknowledged the warning and complied with procedures to abort the mission and return to base.

One of the jets from Homerun Airfield performed a defensive patrol over the Sea of Japan, with a position 65 nautical miles (74 statute miles) west of the EC-121 at the closest approach. The other jet, armed with 23-millimeter (mm) cannons and AA-2 toll missiles, continued an eastward track at supersonic speed, merging with that of *Deep Sea 129*. The time of the shootdown was probably 1347 hours (1:47 p.m.), an estimated 69 nautical miles (80 statute miles) west of the N Korean coast. The ASA noted the separation of the tracks at 1349 hours (1:49 p.m.) and by 1351 hours (1:51 p.m.), radar ceased to reflect the aircraft. However, ASA continued to reflect the fighters as they headed west over the Sea of Japan back toward Homerun. Immediately following the attack, the N Korean forces assumed a state of high alert.

Their media broadcast its version of events two hours after the incident. In their final few minutes, the crew did not acknowledge the warning that MiGs were rapidly closing on them. If it did receive the warnings, the pilot probably would have begun diving for the sea to gain speed and to drop below enemy radar coverage being used to vector (direct) the MiG against it. At a minimum, the aircraft would have made an easterly turn away from the fighters and the N Korean coast to avoid provocative action in accordance with the 7th Fleet directive.

At first, it was thought that the crew might have survived and just dove the aircraft below radar coverage as a defensive maneuver. Overstreet never radioed that he was under attack. Unlike their US Air Force counterparts, Naval SIGINT aircraft did not carry communications gear that would automatically receive messages, so investigators of the event could not determine if they had received them. In the Air Force planes, advisory warnings were automatically received in the form of a data burst transmission that set off a light on a ground console. In the Navy plane, a series was done in a remarkably fast manner, but slower than the automatic system. The Navy would subsequently install communications datalinks aboard its reconnaissance aircraft because they were faster and automatically acknowledged warnings. In retrospect, the N Korean planes were scrambled at a time that allowed minimum flight time over water, to intercept a plane that was flying on a previously known reconnaissance track. The initial reflections of the MiG-21s were picked up at 1234 hours (12:34 p.m.) and after a second plotting to determine the validity of the tracking ASA noted that the fighters were reflected within 51 to 55 nautical miles (58 to 63 statute miles) of the reconnaissance aircraft. By 1420 hours (2:20 p.m.), the ASA station at Osan had become increasingly concerned.

ASA first sent a FLASH message (a high-priority intelligence message to be actioned within six minutes) indicating that *Deep Sea 129* had disappeared, and then at 1444 hours (2:44 p.m.), an hour after the shootdown, sent a CRITIC (critical intelligence) message (the highest message priority, to be processed and sent within two minutes) to six addresses within the National Command Authority, including President Richard Nixon and National Security Advisor Henry Kissinger. President Nixon regarded the attack as a total surprise and remained at a loss to explain it. His administration assumed that N Korea would behave within the standards of international law. Similar to the *Pueblo* incident, Pyongyang took action against the EC-121 plane despite the aircraft being located well outside of N Korean territory. President Nixon's initial reaction was to seek military options.

The International Date Line, also known as just the date line, is an imaginary line on the surface of the Earth going from north to south in the Pacific Ocean. The date becomes one day later as one travels across it in a westerly direction, and one day earlier as one travels across it in an easterly direction. Therefore, the shootdown occurred at 1347 hours (1:47 p.m.) Sunday, April 15 Korean standard (local) time. It was 2347 hours (11:47 p.m.), Monday, April 14, 1969, Eastern Standard Time.)

The operations-command (OPSCOM) direct service tipoff was sent to the 314th Air Division Warning Center (ADWC), and several minutes later issued an initial SPOT report (STOPREP) that two N Korean fighters were probably responding to the Beggar Shadow mission.

The STOPREP was not sent to VQ-1 Atsugi Naval Air Station near Tokyo or the NSG facility at Kamiseya, Japan; the commands were solely responsible for operation and communication intelligence (COMINT) manning of the aircraft. This oversight would later be cited in congressional hearings as an example of the command control breakdown that existed during the shootdown. Although the specific cause for this lapse was never revealed, it certainly represented a lack of communication between the Navy units solely responsible for SIGINT information. The ADWC sent a follow-up to the direct service tipoff; the ADWC cited that the merged positions of the EC-121 and a fighter aircraft at 1347 hours (1:47 p.m.) was the probable shootdown time. Then the commander of the ADWC at Osan became aware of the tipoff report; he immediately ordered the launch of two F-102 Delta Darts all-weather interceptors to be placed on a combat air patrol (CAP) orbit 140 nautical miles (161 statute miles) from the S Korean city of Kangnung, also spelled Gangneung (Gangwon), in northeastern S Korea on the Sea of Japan about 100 nautical miles (115 statute miles) south of the incident area. This was in the vicinity of the planned path of the mission craft as it headed on its final leg to Osan. The F-102s were to proceed to this area to search for the aircraft and rescue it from harassment or attack if it were still in flight. Unfortunately, the launch time of 1354 hours (1:54 p.m.) occurred about seven minutes after the 1347 hours (1:47 p.m.) assumed shootdown time.

The SIGINT field sites spent two hectic hours trying to determine the fate of the aircraft. As the expected arrival time at Osan 1530 hours (3:30 p.m.) came and passed, US officials became convinced that the plane was lost. Within the hour, reports of a radio broadcast that came from Pyongyang further substantiated these fears. The Foreign Broadcast Information Service (FBIS) reported that at 14:55 hours (2:55 p.m.) a N Korean language broadcast came from the Pyongyang Domestic Service announcing the shootdown of a US reconnaissance plane when it intruded "into N Korean airspace." The FBIS monitored a N Korean Central News Agency report in English.

The shootdown was further described as a "brilliant achievement" by the N Korean Air Force in downing "with one stroke at a high altitude" a reconnaissance plane of the "US imperialist aggressor troops." Any retaliation, it was further announced, would be met with "hundredfold revenge."

Joint US – USSR Search and Rescue Operation

Although the 314th ADWC scrambled fighters within 17 minutes after receiving the alert, no unit-initiated search and rescue operations lasted over an hour after the shootdown. This did not occur until VQ-1, the operating unit of the reconnaissance plane, learned of the probable shootdown from the NSG. Within 10 minutes, VQ-1 contacted the 5th Air Force Combat Operations Center at Fuchu, Japan, and requested the initiation of search and rescue operations. The 5th Air Force informed VQ-1 that an HC-130 Hercules was airborne from Tachikawa Air Base outside of Tokyo, with F-106 fighters scrambled from S Korea to serve as a combat air patrol (CAP). By the time the HC-130 reached the shootdown area several hours later, daylight was coming to an end. An initial report from the HC-130 of smoke flares and multiple survival beacons provided some early hope that there were survivors. Shortly thereafter, the first report was deemed erroneous.

Vice Admiral William F. Bringle, Commander of the 7th Fleet, on board the USS *Oklahoma City* (CLG-5), a light cruiser off S Vietnam, when informed by VQ-I of the critical situation, directed the vessels USS *Dale* (DD-353) and USS *Tucker* (DD-875), located at Sasebo, Japan to proceed to the area of the shootdown. An interesting aspect of the search and rescue operations was the participation of Russia. At the time of the shootdown, a Soviet Ugra (945) class submarine tender with two Foxtrot-class submarines was in the immediate area. Later, three Russian destroyers moved into the area as well. The first hard evidence of the shootdown was the spotting of debris by a Navy P-3 Orion rescue plane on the morning of April 16 northeast of the reported location. This debris consisted of uninflated life rafts and paper and dye markers. The Russian role in the search operations began later that day when the US rescue aircraft contacted two Russian ships in the shootdown area. These were Russian destroyers DD-429 and DD-580, and they began to pick up debris from the aircraft. Radio contact with one of the Russian ships, DD-580, revealed that pieces of the plane had been picked up, but there was no sign of any survivors. The Russians granted permission for an American plane to fly low over the ship to photograph the debris. A survival radio was also dropped to the Russian ship to establish communications.

In the early evening, two additional US ships arrived in the area, the destroyer USS *Henry W. Tucker* (DD-875) and the missile frigate USS *Dale* (DLG-19). There were no survivors. On the following morning, April 17 the waters of the Sea of

Japan yielded two bodies from the ill-fated mission. The victims were identified as Lieutenant (j.g) Joseph R. Ribar and Aviation Electronics Technician (ATI) Richard E. Sweeney. [88] They were the only bodies recovered of the 31 men on board and were found about 17 nautical miles (19.5 statute miles) north of the general shootdown area. The search operation continued throughout the day with two destroyers, one Hercules search and rescue aircraft, one Navy P-3 Orion search plane, and four F-106 Delta Dart all-weather interceptors from the 5th Air Force. On April 18, the *Tucker* rendezvoused with the Russian destroyer *Vodokhnovemmy* (DD-580) to receive debris recovered by the Russian ships during the rescue. Included in the transfer were the radio dropped to the Russian ship by the USAF rescue aircraft, a 20-man lifeboat, three leather jackets, body remains, a parachute, two exposure suits, a wheel, a ladder, some aircraft parts, and some of the plane's internal parts.

The *Tucker* then proceeded to Sasebo, Japan with the bodies of two crewmen recovered and 500 pounds of debris. This included a piece of the bulkhead containing the crew's positions, a radar antenna, a photograph, pages of a computer printout, and several pages of handwritten operator's notes found in the personal effects of ATI Richard E. Sweeny. From the wreckage recovered from the Sea of Japan, a joint US Navy-Air Force investigative team concluded that the EC-121 sustained major structural damage from the detonation of a fragmentation warhead of one (or possibly two) air-to-air missiles. It was probably of the infrared, heat-seeking (ATOLL) type, an exact copy of the US sidewinder missile. The Joint Chiefs of Staff officially terminated the search and rescue (SAR) at 1520 hours (3:20 p.m.) Korean standard time/Sea of Japan on April 19. No N Korean ships were sighted during the search and rescue exercise, and no classified material was in the exchange from the Russian destroyer DD-429 to the *Tucker*.

However, a few pieces of classified material were recovered by Dale and *Tucker*. The Joint US-Soviet Union Search and Rescue Operations (SAR) details about bulkhead debris, classified documents, and equipment recovered not turned over to the US Navy are available at the Naval War College Review 2020 Soviet Admiral Gromov's comments. [89]

---

88   Remembering the Crew:
      https://stationhypo.com/2017/04/15/remembering-the-crew-of-ec-121-beggar-shadow/
      Source: https://www.nsa.gov.
89   Soviet Navy Admiral Gromov's comments recorded in (2020) "Improbable Allies" — The North Korean Downing of a US Navy EC-121 and US-Soviet Cooperation during the Cold War," Naval War College Review: Vol. 73: No. 2, Article 9. Citation, Streifer, Bill and Sabitov, Irek.

US Congressional Subcommittee Inquiry and Findings

USS *Pueblo* (GER-2) and US Navy EC-121 Warning Star *Deep Sea 129*

Shortly after public announcement of the release of the crew of the USS *Pueblo*, ranking members of the House Committee on Armed Services were given a preliminary information obtained by Defense Department officials concerning the internment of the crew of the *Pueblo* and a preliminary estimate of the national security implications resulting from the loss of the *Pueblo*. These briefings occurred on Monday, January 6 and Tuesday, January 7, 1969.

The Chairman of the Committee on Armed Services, House of Representatives, the Honorable L. Mendel Rivers, on February 18, 1969, directed that a special subcommittee be established to, among other things, conduct a full and thorough inquiry into all matters arising from the capture and internment of the *Pueblo* and its crew by the N Korean government. On March 3, 1969, the subcommittee was charged with the responsibility of reviewing the national security implications resulting from the loss of the *Pueblo* [90] and ascertaining whether deficiencies existed in the command response to emergencies of this kind. On April 22, 1969, after the April 15, 1969, shootdown of the US Navy EC-121 [91] aircraft, the jurisdiction of the special subcommittee was extended to include its loss. On July 1, 1969, Otis G. Pike, Chairman, Special Subcommittee, provided its completed inquiry into these matters and submitted a report of findings and recommendations, together with the facts upon which it reached its conclusions. The report reflects the unanimous views of all nine members of the special committee. At the time of this report, as submitted, it contained information classified by the Department of Defense as "top secret."

The most critical findings of the subcommittee related to command control responsibilities details are described in the introduction — specifically Appendix M, DOCID 3997686, Table 12. Approved for release by NSA. The report consisted of 81 pages and was declassified and made available September 14, 2012, through the Freedom of Information Act (FOIA Case #40722). [92]

---

90 https://www.nsa.gov/news-features/declassified-documents/uss-*Pueblo*/assets/files/congressional/actions/Inquiry.
91 https://catalog.archives.gov/search USS *Pueblo* and EC-121 plane Incidents.
92 National Archives, College Park Maryland *Inquiry into the USS Pueblo and EC-121 Plane Incidents.*

The commanding officer of the Reconnaissance Squadron One (VQ-1) was the responsible operating commander of the EC-121 aircraft. However, for reasons that are unclear, the emergency circumstances confronting *Deep Sea 129* were never provided to VQ-1 but handled entirely by communication units in the field and the 5th Air Force.

It was only after VQ-1 received a copy of the critical message from Kamiseya that the commander was able to ascertain the precise status of the aircraft. Furthermore, because of the confused command and control situation, no effort had been made by any command to initiate search and rescue at the time of the shootdown. However, the commanding officer of VQ-1 did initiate efforts to obtain search and rescue assistance within eight minutes of his receipt of the lateral critical message. Again, as in the case of the *Pueblo*, the command and control of the aircraft, EC-121, in the emergency which arose reflected tremendous confusion and a lack of clear-cut command responsibility. Since ASA at Osan Air Base had detected N Korean aircraft reacting to the EC-121, there inevitably arose the question as to why protective aircraft were not immediately dispatched to protect *Deep Sea 129*.

The subcommittee unanimously concluded that serious deficiencies existed in the organizational and administrative command structures of both the Navy and the Department of Defense. According to the subcommittee, the *Deep Sea 129* incident again strikingly illustrated, as in the *Pueblo* incident the inability of the system to relay information in a timely and comprehensible fashion to those charged with the responsibility for making decisions. President Richard M. Nixon said, "When a war can be decided in 20 minutes, the nation that is behind will have no time to catch up." This concern was shared by the subcommittee. It was this consideration, as to the national security implications inherent in these two incidents, which overshadowed all others in the inquiry made by the subcommittee. According to the chairman of the special subcommittee conducting the inquiry into both the *Pueblo* and EC-121, incidents identified an unacceptable delay in initiating search and rescue efforts due to the apparent fragmentation of command responsibility and authority of the military units involved. The subcommittee recommended that the Joint Chiefs of Staff review the entire military reconnaissance program. The protection of the flights was another major concern of the subcommittee.

Representative Lucien N. Nedzi (Democrat, Michigan), a member of the subcommittee, questioned why this had not been done following the 1965 landmass incident involving the N Koreans. On April 27, 1965, two N Korean MiG-17s attacked a US Air Force reconnaissance plane above the Sea of Japan 50 miles from the N Korean landmass. The aircraft was damaged, but managed to land at Yokota Air Base, Japan. US Army Chairman of the Joint Chiefs of Staff General (Gen.) Earle G. Wheeler's response was that flights had indeed been escorted after that incident, but because of the expense and no further reaction from the N Koreans, had been discontinued. Since 1965, there had been only one instance of a N Korean fighter coming close to a US reconnaissance aircraft. Several days after the *Pueblo* incident, General Wheeler added, this escort was revived. A combat air patrol creating a protective plane barrier between the reconnaissance aircraft and the landmass from which hostile aircraft might come was in effect from April 1965 until July 1968. At the time of the EC-121, the policy for air reconnaissance missions off the coast of N Korea was an airstrip alert from an Air Force Base on the S Korean mainland for contingency protection. The consensus was to improve command and control communications in general.

Despite the testimony received from General Wheeler, which suggested that no serious problems in command and control existed during the EC-121 incident, some degree of confusion existed in the military command organization in respect to the EC-121 incident that occurred previously in the case of the *Pueblo*.

In the view of the subcommittee, the entire reconnaissance program must be restudied by the Joint Chiefs of Staff to establish clear and unmistakable lines of command and control so that the more obvious shortcomings of these incidents would not be repeated. The subcommittee concluded that protection for reconnaissance flights into sensitive areas required more coordination between the SIGINT community and Air Force operational commands with protective responsibility.

A specific recommendation called for integrating SIGINT information with operational information at command-and-control centers where decisions could be made based on all-source information. A command advisory function (CAF) system emerged.

President Richard M. Nixon's Administration Response

The shootdown of the EC-121 was the first major foreign crisis faced by President Richard M. Nixon, who had just taken office on January 20, 1969. He had repeatedly used the *Pueblo* incident in his fall election campaign to state the need for new leadership. He stressed that there would be no *Pueblo* during his administration, no incident in which a "4th-rate" power would show total disrespect for the US while a Congressional investigation into the previous year's *Pueblo* incident was continuing. The new Nixon Administration was forced to deal with the shootdown crisis. The shootdown dominated newspaper headlines for several days and remained a major news story for several weeks. The press described the Washington reaction to the EC-121 incident as a "cautious" one, with Nixon maintaining a "deliberate calm." Secretary of State William P. Rogers reflected this cautious response in his address to newspaper editors on April 16, when he said, "The weak can be rash; the powerful must be more restrained." President Nixon made no public statement on the shootdown until a press conference on April 18. Using information provided by the NSA, Nixon answered several questions about the shootdown at his press conference. He also revealed that he had ordered the resumption of reconnaissance flights and vowed to provide protection for the unarmed planes. Although he did not announce it at the press conference, the president also instructed the US Navy to assemble a task force of aircraft carriers, destroyers, and perhaps a battleship to rendezvous south of the Sea of Japan.

In defending his administration's actions and the reconnaissance flight, Nixon declared that, in contrast to the *Pueblo* incident, there was no doubt as to the plane's whereabouts before and during the shootdown. Nixon said that the US knew that the N Korean and Soviet radars identified (reflected) [93] the *Deep Sea 129* that day. He enhanced the account to include American radar as showing the exact same thing.

Nixon said that this information totally refuted the N Korean claim that the EC-121 violated its airspace. In addition to assembling a task force and the call for the resumption of reconnaissance flights, the Nixon Administration also responded unfavorably to the N Korean request for another Military Armistice Commission (MAC) meeting at Panmunjom.

---

93 Nixon's public statement concerning N Korean and Soviet radar reflections caused a major reaction at NSA. The Deputy Director, Louis Tordella, was greatly concerned over the release of such sensitive information and its possible impact on future intelligence successes.

The US simply delayed its reply; administration officials felt that another meeting would be a propaganda vehicle for the N Koreans and that a walkout by its delegation would probably occur before an American response. After several days, Nixon Administration officials made the decision to keep open the channels of communication with N Korea. US officials called for a 290th meeting of the MAC on the morning of April 18. The opening N Korean statement, made by Major General Lee Chon-sun, the senior N Korean representative, made no mention of reconnaissance flights, but accused the United Nations Command (UNC) of many ground violations along the DMZ. Army Major General James B. Knapp, the senior US member of the delegation, responded, accusing the N Koreans of an "unprovoked attack" upon an aircraft that was making a routine reconnaissance flight, like many flown since 1950. Using the NSA intelligence information then available, Knapp stated that at no time did the aircraft penetrate or closely approach the 12-mile airspace claimed by N Korea. He concluded with the remark that this was not an isolated incident, but only another in a long list of violations of international law. Following his prepared address, General Knapp led a walkout of his delegation after the N Koreans refused to respond. Details are described in the introduction—specifically, Table 12. Appendix L, The NSA and the EC-121 Shootdown for details to include airspace claimed by N Korea; Appendix N, Inquiry into the EC-121 Plane Incident by the US Congress, and Appendix P, Recommended Reading: EC-121 Crisis, and the N Korean Perspective.

As the National Security Council discussed possible administration responses to the N Koreans and favored a moderate approach, Kissinger and President Nixon favored strong retaliatory measures. Task Force 71 (TF 71) [94] led by the USS Enterprise (CVN-65) that Nixon had ordered into the Sea of Japan was a compromise measure, and with its 250 available warplanes left open an assault for retaliation. As originally conceived by the US policymakers, the task force left open the possibility that Washington would respond with military force to the shootdown. US policymakers did not expect Russia and Chinese (CHICOM) forces to intervene. The battleship USS New Jersey (BB-62) was sailing from Yokosuka, Japan for the US when she received orders on April 15 to come about

---

94 The deployment included three attack carrier strike groups under the nuclear-powered USS Enterprise (CVN-65), the USS Ticonderoga (CVA-14), and USS Ranger (CVA-6); an anti-submarine carrier support group under the USS Hornet (CVS-12); an air defense group under the guided missile cruiser USS Chicago (CG-11) that also included the four vessels that participated in the search and recovery operations, USS Sterett (DLG-31), USS Dale (DLG-19), USS Mahan (DLG-11), and USS Tucker (DD-875); and a surface action group that included the cruisers USS Oklahoma City (CLG-5) and USS St. Paul (CA-73). On that same day, April 16, the Commander of the 7th Fleet, Vice Admiral William P. Bringle issued a call for SIGINT support. The most urgent request was for technical support.

and steam for Japan. The *New Jersey* arrived once more at Yokosuka and put to sea in readiness by nightfall, arriving April 22 off the coast of N Korea. The *New Jersey* joined TF 71, already on station. The ships of TF 71 came mostly from Southeast Asia (Vietnam) duty. Ultimately, President Nixon declined to retaliate, and four days later, *New Jersey* was released and continued her voyage, anchoring on May 5 at Long Beach, California (CA). The only response to the assembling of the task force was that Russian naval units continuously shadowed the major US ships and Russian Badger aircraft reconnoitered the task force. There was also a mild diplomatic rebuke by Soviet Ambassador Dobrynin to the Department of State.

He urged the Americans to act with "reasonableness and restraint" in connection with the Korean incident, stressing that the Russians could not help but look cautiously upon the large American force off their coast. The Department of State countered that the Russians were able to moderate tensions through contacts with N Korea, the perpetrator of the incident. By April 26 Task Force 71 began to depart from the Sea of Japan. On that day, the JCS directed Commander-in-Chief-Pacific (CINCPAC) to redeploy most of the task force to normal 7th Fleet operations in Southeast Asia. By May 1, only the destroyers USS *Sterett* (DLG-31) and USS *Radford* (DD-746) remained off the east coast of Korea, having been directed to assume duties as seaborne ground intercept (GCI) platforms. Ultimately, the US decided against military action.

Summary Second Korean Conflict: Began October 5, 1966, and Ended December 3, 1969

The 1960s Korean Conflict officially began October 5, 1966, ending December 3, 1969, resulting in scores of Americans killed and wounded, and was an unqualified success. The US, with its allies, have held N Korea at bay (1953–2022) for more than 69 years. Because of this, S Korea is a thriving democracy, economic powerhouse, and military titan. The S Koreans went from a country receiving aid to one that provides it. Most people have never heard of the 1960s Korean Conflict, which included the ambush of seven Americans and one S Korean conducting a UNC patrol on November 2, 1966, along the south side of the DMZ, followed by the capture of the USS *Pueblo* (GER-2) in January 23, 1968 while operating in international waters off the coast of N Korea, and the April 15, 1969 shootdown of a US Navy EC-121 Warning Star Surveillance Aircraft code name *Deep Sea 129* over the Sea of Japan. On December 3, 1969, Army

Captain David Crawford, Warrant Officer Malcom Loepke, and Specialist Herman Hofstetter were shot down in August after straying into N Korea; their return marked the end of the conflict. Though open hostilities had ceased by the end of 1969, combat pay and combat awards were not withdrawn until 1973.

The 1960s Korean Conflict cost 102 American lives and 111 wounded in action. S Korea suffered 299 killed in action and 553 wounded in action. The N Korean losses were 427 killed in action and 12 soldiers and 2462 agents captured; an unknown number were wounded. S Korean Special Forces units crossed the DMZ on at least 50 separate occasions, attacking military targets. One such action was when S Korean soldiers mounted a raid on October 26, 1966, a week before the November 2 attack, against N Korea. The S Korean team penetrated through the DMZ to execute the raid, claiming 30 casualties on the N Koreans. The total number of S and actual N Korean casualties resulting from the separate attacks is unknown. The Silver Star Medal was awarded to Private Ernest D. Reynolds, 17, who had been in Korea only 17 days, for gallantry in action on November 2, 1966, while engaged with an armed patrol of the N Korean Army. Reynolds was serving with Company A, 1st Battalion, 23rd Infantry Regiment, 2nd Infantry Division. Reynolds was a member of a patrol operating near the southern boundary of the Demilitarized Zone when his patrol was attacked near the Liberty Bridge and overrun by N Korean forces. The patrol attempted to fight back, but they were quickly killed by the infiltrators.

Reynolds, who posted to the rear security and was safely concealed, made a split-second decision. He broke cover and charged the infiltrators, firing his M14 rifle, only to be cut down in a hail of gunfire. The sole survivor of the patrol was Private First-Class David L. Bibee, who told the story of Private Reynolds and the action he took. Bibee himself was blown off a hilltop when a grenade exploded and was bleeding from 48 fragment wounds. He played dead while the N Koreans mutilated and looted the dead for weapons and trophies. The N Koreans also fired several rounds into the bodies. The attack lasted four violent minutes. [95]

Danger and bravery typified service along the Korean DMZ. American soldiers served resolutely, facing the ever-present threat of violence and death in an isolated location far from home. During their duty, these soldiers displayed

---

95   Reynolds Silver Star Medal "Valor award for Ernest D. Reynolds". *Military Times.*

discipline, doing dangerous work without official combat recognition. The Defense Department awarded the Armed Forces Expeditionary Medal [96] for service in Korea from October 1, 1966, until June 30, 1974, and the Korean Defense Service Medal from July 28, 1954, to a future undetermined date. [97] In the early 2000s, The US Army altered its position; it retroactively made the requirements the same across Army service for time spent along the violent and dangerous DMZ and all combat zones. On May 18, 2000, authorized combat awards and combat patches. (Army Regulation 670-1, *Wear and Appearance of the Uniform.*)

Casualties suffered by US, S Korean, and N Korean forces are detailed in the introduction — specifically, Table 5. Casualties 1960s Korean Conflict and Table 6. 1960s Korean Conflict DMZ Incidents: A Statistical Summary DMZ Incidents of Violence Frequency.

The 1960s Korean Conflict drifted into obscurity and became a footnote to the Vietnam era.

(The Forgotten DMZ - Major Vandon E Jenerette (korean war.org) and, Subject: Korea DMZ

Part 1 Military Review Published by US Army Command and General Staff College Volume LXVIII - May 1988 - No 5 pp 32-43.) [98]

North Korean commando captured during the Blue House Raid, 1968.

---

96 President John F. Kennedy established the Armed Forces Expeditionary Medal, per Executive Order 10977 dated December 4, 1961, for operations on or after July 1, 1958. Awarded for participation in operations in the Republic of Korea from October 1, 1966, to June 30, 1974.
97 Korean Defense Service Medal awarded as recognition for military service in the Republic of Korea (S Korea) and surrounding waters after July 28, 1954, and ending on such a future date as determined by the Secretary of Defense.
98 The Forgotten DMZ - Major Vandon E Jenerette (koreanwar.org). Subject: Korea DMZ Part 1 Military Review Published by US Army Command and General Staff College Volume LXVIII - May 1988 - No 5 pp 32-43.

Specialist Wm. R. Graser
ASA TC&S Ft. Devens, MA
1966
Photo: Wm. R. Graser, Author

US Army Security Agency Command Shoulder Sleeve Insignia (patch).
US 7th Infantry Division Shoulder Sleeve Insignia (patch).

To minimize ASA's exposure, troops were not allowed to wear the insignia patch (image above left) in Korea. The patch worn was determined by location; for example, ASA troops in the 8th US Army and the US 2nd Infantry Division areas wore the respective organizational patches. All soldiers assigned to Camp Alamo wore the US 7th Infantry Division (Bayonet) patch.

Tactical Training Center Fort Devens, Massachusetts 1966
Photo: US Army
Vietnam Village training area located on the backside of Moore Army Airfield at Fort Devens, MA. Fort Devens closed as an active-duty installation, March 31, 1996.

Menehune ("Little People") Platoon of Hawaiian Asian-Americans Aggressors at the TTC
The Menehune's played the part of the VC in the John Wayne movie "Green Berets"

Pictured ASA role players, 1966 at Fort Devens, MA. / Source: http://www. asalives.org/ Note: Caption has several errors, cannot be edited.

Retired United States Army Colonel Lewis L. Millett Sr.
Credit: US Army and Medal of Honor Society

Salutes the flag at a memorial service commemorating the charge he led up Bayonet Hill in 1951. The service was held during the joint U.S/South Korean 1985.

Former Commandant of the US Army Security Agency Training Center and School, Fort Devens, MA. Founder of the ASA Tactical Training Center (TTC) 1965.

Army Security Agency (ASA) Group Headquarters, Yong Dong Po, near
Seoul, Circa 1975.
Photo Credit: ArmySecurityAgency.net

Company B (Fwd) 1st Platoon 508th
Army Security Agency Group
Camp Alamo located near the Korean DMZ, 1966-1967
Photo: Wm. Graser, Author

View looking toward the front gate

Typical thatched huts, or "hootch"
(slang used to describe dwellings in South Korea) 1966-1967
Photos of the "hootch" and sign Camp Alamo The US Army Northernmost
Outpost; Wm. Graser, Author.

The view is from a hill near Camp Alamo, looking Northeast into North Korea.
"Pork Chop Hill": note the road near the base of the hill.
Photo: Wm. Graser, Author

A sandbag trench twists its way through Korea's hills along the DMZ, where American soldiers keep a watch for North Koreans troop activities, February 8, 1968. Credit: AP Photo. AP License No: LIC-01458571 procured worldwide, start date September 7, 2022, duration in perpetuity.

Truck struck road "land mine" in the live-fire training
area near the DMZ Winter 1966
Centered in the picture is a truck towing a trailer carrying tank ammunition that struck a land mine planted by North Korean infiltrators eight miles south of the DMZ. Local South Korean civilians are seen walking along the road.
Photo: Wm. Graser, Author

On April 14, 1968, a United Nations Command (UNC) vehicle was ambushed
by North Korean infiltrators, killing four UN soldiers and seriously
wounding two soldiers.
Photo: US Army

Checkpoint at Camp Red Cloud, Uijeongbu, South Korea. Photo: US Army

Main access road through Uijeongbu, South Korea 1966
The village is located 15 miles north of Seoul.
Photo: Wm. Graser, Author

Ship Badge – Designed by the crew

USS *Pueblo* (AKL-44) moored pierside,
June 18, 1966, before designation (GER-2)
Puget Sound Naval Shipyard, Bremerton, Washington

Photo: Naval History and Heritage Command
National Museum of the US Navy
(NHHC and the MNUSN)

USS *Pueblo* (GER-2) Commissioned May 13, 1967

NHHC and the NMUSN

Smell The Gunpowder

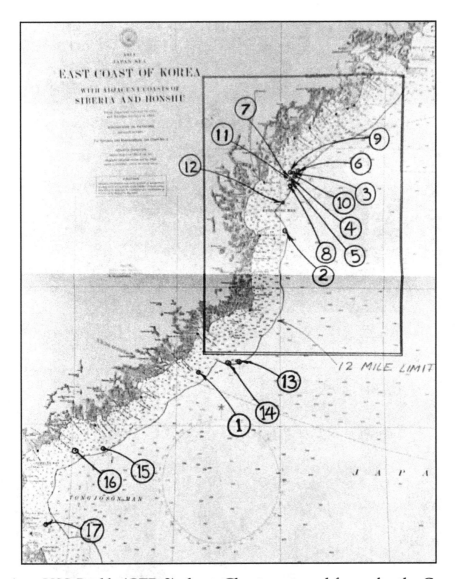

Caption: USS *Pueblo* (GER-2) chart. Chart prepared for us by the Court of Inquiry on the capture of *USS Pueblo* (GER-2). The chart shows the alleged 17 points of violation on the territorial waters claimed by the North Koreans during the period of capture on January 15-24, 1968. Captain Lloyd M. Bucher, Commanding Officer of *Pueblo*, denied each alleged violation, January 1969.

Official US Navy Photograph, now in the collections of the National Archives. (2017/05/23). Photographed from a reference card. Accession #: 428-GX-USN-1140171.

Naval History and Heritage Command National Museum of the US Navy

NHHC and the NMUSN

Lieutenant Commander James H. Overstreet, Pilot
The photograph is the work of a Mass Communications Specialist Navy

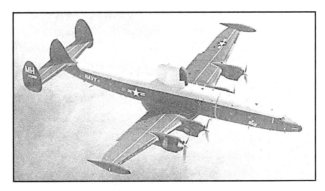

Airborne Signal Intelligence Collection Radio Call Sign: *Deep Sea 129*
Fleet Airborne Reconnaissance Squadron 1 Atsugi, Japan.

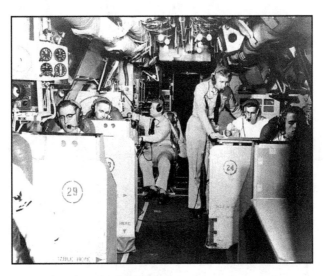

Exterior/Interior view of an EC121M Warning Star - Operators Monitoring
Intelligence Collection Intelligence Collection Equipment. US Navy Photos
Courtesy of National Naval Aviation Museum and NHHC.

PART FOUR
PREPARATIONS FOR WAR

Chapter 20

NORTH KOREA PREPARES FOR WAR

The military commanders of North Korea's KPA, the Chinese People's Volunteers, and the United Nations Command signed the armistice that ended the fighting and created a 6562-foot-wide demilitarized zone (DMZ) on either side of the then-current unit disposition, also known as the military demarcation line. Since the armistice was signed, N Korea has broken it many times with incursions into the DMZ and S Korea by land, sea, air, and even underground by tunnel. The N Koreans also kidnapped citizens of S Korea and Japan to better train its spies in S Korean and Japanese culture. This was done so that DPRK spies could learn to pass themselves off as either S Korean or Japanese. In addition, N Korea continued to infiltrate agents via seaborne insertion. Since the armistice, violence and death has typified American military service along the demilitarized zone. At the end of 1969, quiet returned and after a short period of adjustment, N Korea again prepared for conflict. After 1969, incidents continued, and throughout the 1970s and into the 2000s N Korea pursued covert attempts to destabilize the S Korean government. N Korean infiltrators continued to probe the DMZ, and communist spy rings were continually discovered in the South.

Tunnels of Aggression

A new dimension emerged with the first discovery of a North Korean infiltration tunnel. The first was discovered on November 15, 1974; a second tunnel was discovered in March 1975; a third was discovered in October 1978; and in March 1990, a fourth tunnel. A North Korean device, properly a land mine, exploded in the first tunnel complex that had been discovered the previous day. The explosion killed US Navy Commander Robert M. Ballinger and his South Korean counterpart as well as injuring five other Americans. In the early 1970s, Kim Il-sung ordered his divisions along the DMZ to dig and maintain tunnels that infiltrated S Korea. The first major tunnel discovered in the west-central sector of the DMZ stretched 2 miles in length. The tunnel was a mere 18 inches below the surface. It is located northeast of Korangpo in the DMZ, extending .62 mile past the official border and just 40 miles from the S Korean capital, Seoul. The walls, which are nearly 4 feet high and slightly more than 3 feet wide, are reinforced with concrete slabs. It has electric power, weapons storage, sleeping areas, and even narrow-gauge rails with carts and is lit with lamps connected to 220-volt power lines. The tunnel had the capacity to move two thousand soldiers per hour through the cramped space. In 1974, after the death of Kim Il-sung, his son Kim Jong-il continued digging tunnels under the border. The second tunnel found, in March 1975, was 8 miles north of Chorwon, which stretched .65 miles south of the heavily fortified border. The tunnel runs for 2 miles at a depth of 524 feet and is 8 feet high and 7 feet wide. The third tunnel was uncovered after a tip-off from a N Korea defector in October 1978. It runs for .65 miles, some 239 feet below the surface, just south of Panmunjom and 27 miles from Seoul.

After it was built, coal dust was smeared around the entrance so it would be disguised as an abandoned coal mine.

The last tunnel was uncovered in March 1990, it runs for .63 miles and was almost identical to tunnels two and three in size and structure.

The S Korean government believes there could be 20 more undiscovered tunnels. Tunnels are much less effective because now that N Korea has long-range artillery and missles.

In the decades since their discovery, some of the tunnels have found new life as tourist destinations.

Thousands of Koreans and foreign visitors explore these odd relics each year. The second tunnel is 1640 feet long and is open to travelers as part of an official tour group. Due to tunnel three's subterranean characteristics of 239 feet below

Smell The Gunpowder

ground, visitors with heart and respiratory conditions are not permitted to enter the tunnel.

N Korea has a long history of using earth to conceal its weaponry. It is believed as many as 12,000 artillery guns and 2300 multiple 12-tube, 5.8-inch rocket launchers are hidden. Many are dug into the rear slopes of hills and mountains just north of the DMZ to avoid detection. Even Pyongyang itself leverages underground protection; at 360 feet deep, its subway system is far deeper than it needs be. There can be little doubt that it is intended to serve as shelter from any attack by S Korea or its US ally — including a nuclear blast. N Korea built hundreds of bunkers at the DMZ even as the previous S Korean governments pursued the sunshine policy of opening to N Korea. In 2004, Pyongyang ordered the construction of between 800 and 1200 underground bunkers for troop concentrations near the DMZ. These underground storage sites contained enough gear to equip 1500 to 2000 soldiers. Even though some of the bunkers were intended to be decoys, the total number remains unknown.

Hostile Threats

The following historical information and examples of hostile threats that occurred during 1970-2022 could have triggered a military response between N Korea, S Korea, and the United States.

In April 1970, a clash left three N Korean infiltrators dead and five S Korean soldiers wounded; in June 1970, the N Korean Navy seized a broadcast vessel from the South in the Yellow Sea (West Sea) near the Northern Limit Line (NLL) [99]. Twenty crew members were captured.

On August 18, 1976, in the Joint Security Area (JSA) [100] Panmunjom located in the DMZ, two US Army officers were part of a work party cutting down a

---

99   The Northern Limit Line (NLL) is the disputed maritime boundary between N Koreas (Democratic People's Republic of Korea – DPRK) and S Korea (Republic of Korea – ROK) in the Yellow (West) Sea that was drawn sometime after the Korean War by the United Nations Command (UNC). Soon after the signing of the armistice on July 27, 1953, it became clear that a maritime boundary was needed, in part to ensure that S Korean Navy and fishing vessels did not stray too far north and restart hostilities. As a result, on August 30, 1953, UNC Commander General Mark Clark promulgated the NLL as a military control line in the West Sea.

100 The Joint Security Area (JSA) is the only portion of the Korean demilitarized zone (DMZ) where N and S Korean forces stand face-to-face. It is often called the "Truce Village" in both the media and various military accounts. The JSA is used by the two Koreas for diplomatic engagements.

poplar tree in the JSA that partially blocked the view of UN observers. They were assaulted and killed (murdered) by N Koreans, who claimed that the tree was planted by Kim Il-sung. This incident became known as the Panmunjom Axe Murder Incident.

In 1976, the US provoked the "Panmunjom incident" and kicked up a full-scale war racket under that pretext. Excerpt from Echoes of the Korean War Booklet published in N Korea.

Three days later, American and S Korean forces launched Operation *Paul Bunyan*, an action that cut down the tree with a show of force to intimidate N Korea into backing down, which it did. N Korea then accepted responsibility for the earlier killings.

On July 14, 1977, a US Army CH-47 Chinook helicopter was shot down after straying into the North over the DMZ. Three airmen were killed, and one was briefly held prisoner. This was the fourth of six such hostile incidents since the armistice was signed.

In May 1980, N Koreans engaged US/ROK Outpost Ouellette on the DMZ in a firefight. One N Korean was wounded in action. The US Army named this outpost in honor of Private First-Class Joseph R. Ouellette, recipient of the Medal of Honor (posthumously) for his actions near Yongsan from August 31 to September 3, 1950.

In June 1981, a N Korean spy boat was sunk off the coast of Sosan and Chungcheong-Namo, S Korea; nine agents were killed, and one was captured.

In July 1981 three N Korean agents were killed trying to cross into S Korea in the upper stream of the Imjin River.

In August 1982, police in Canada uncovered a N Korean plot to assassinate S Korean President Chun Doo-Hwan during his visit. In February 1984, two Canadians, Charles Yarnover and Alexander Gerol, testified in a Canadian court that N Korean agents hired them for $600,000 to assassinate President Chun. They were convicted and sentenced to prison terms of one to two years. The assassination was to take place during Chun's visit to the Philippines in July 1982.

On October 9, 1983, N Korean agents targeted the venue of a visit by S Korean president Chun to Burma, killing more than 20 people including four S Korean cabinet ministers. The president escaped. This was the second attempt on his life by N Korea.

In November 1984, three N Korean and one S Korean soldier were killed, and one American soldier was wounded, in a firefight that broke out after a Russian defector fled across the DMZ into S Korea.

In November 1987 one American soldier and two N Korean soldiers died, and one American soldier was wounded, during the firefight that erupted when a N Korean security detail confronted a sniper detail across the MDL into the southern-controlled sector of the JSA. The only portion of the DMZ where North and South Korea soldiers stood face-to-face.

On June 15, 1999, the First Battle of Yeonpyeong took place after N Korean gunboats crossed the Northern Limit Line (NLL), prompting a S Korean high-speed board to ram a N Korean torpedo ship, causing it to sink. S Korean also destroyed five N Korean patrol boats, killing 20 N Koreans, and injuring thirty. S Korean losses totaled nine injuries and minimal damage to the hulls of a patrol boat and a high-speed boat. The battle was the first naval clash of the two Koreas since the ceasefire of the 1950s Korean conflict. The victory became a source of great pride for the S Korean Navy. After the battle N Korea announced that the armistice would no longer be valid and that safety of vessels in the area could not be guaranteed.

Subsequently, there were numerous NLL clashes between the two Koreas over the disputed Yellow Sea (West Sea) islands, killing dozens and sinking vessels. On June 29, 2002, the 2nd Battle of Yeonpyeong between North and South Korean patrol boats led to the deaths of six S Korean sailors and nineteen wounded, causing some 38 casualties on the N Koreans, after the S Korean Navy high-speed patrol boat *Cham Suri* (357) was sunk by N Korean counterpart *Dengue Sangoi* (CCP-684).

The two Yeonpyeong naval battles reflect the illusion of the so-called "Sunshine Policy," also known as "Comprehensive Engagement Policy" of rapprochement with N Korea advocated by President Park Young-sam (1993-1998). Critics of the policy contended that rather than increasing the chances of reunification or undermining the regime in N Korea, it was used as a disguise to increase preparedness. They pointed to continuing provocations by the North, such as the 2002 2nd Battle of Yeonpyeong that left several Korean sailors dead.

"Sunshine Policy," also known as "Comprehensive Engagement Policy"

The Sunshine Policy emerged largely in the context of the growing economic gap between the two Koreas; the South was moving in the path of strengthening its nation power by the economic prosperity achieved from President Park Chung-hee's administration in the 1970s throughout the 1990s, while the North was falling into severe economic decline. The main aim of the policy was to soften N Korea's attitudes toward S Korea by encouraging interaction and economic assistance. The policy resulted in greater political contact between the two Koreas and some historic moments in inter-Korea relations such as several high-profile business ventures, and brief meetings of family members separated by the 1950s Korean Conflict. The culmination was the 2000 Inter-Korean summit when S Korean president Kim Dae-Jung visited N Korean leader Kim Jong-Il in Pyongyang. Both leaders signed the June 15 North-South Joint Declaration, in which both sides promised to seek peaceful reunification.

The European Union's Policy Toward North Korea: Abandoning Engagement

The Sunshine Policy, instituted by S Korean President Park Young-sam in 1993, was a watershed moment in inter-Korea relations. It encouraged other countries to engage with the North, which allowed Pyongyang to normalize relations with several European Union (EU) states and contributed to the establishment of joint North-South economic projects. The EU presence in N Korea started to grow after 1994 as part of a New Asia Strategy. In 1995, the EU was involved in aiding some of the most vulnerable communities. Activities mainly oriented toward support for the agricultural sector and projects are implemented by European teams working with partner organizations. In May 2001, the EU established diplomatic relations with N Korea, and most EU members established diplomatic relations with Pyongyang. The EU became N Korea's third-largest trading partner. The main objective was to help Pyongyang develop a healthy economy, thus ending the humanitarian crisis and establishing a basis for sustainable growth. The year 2003 became a turning point in the EU's approach to North Korea. All dialogue with N Korea was suspended, economic assistance was cut, and humanitarian aid was significantly reduced. After 2003, the EU abruptly disengaged from N Korea. Trade ties rapidly dissipated. The International Journal of Korean Unification Studies (Vol. 28, No. 1, 2019, 33-62) written by Lordanka Alexandrova, reads that the new EU foreign strategy prescribed disengagement from N Korea because if its commitment to oppose the proliferation (rapid increase) of Weapons of Mass Destruction (MD) on a global scale. [101] https://www.kinu.or.kr/

Regardless of S Korea's appeasement policy, or whatever it does, N Korea continues the aim of unifying the Korean Peninsula by military force. With thousands of N Korean artillery pieces little more than 30 miles away, Seoul established a vast underground network of air-raid shelters across the sprawling city with a population in 2022, of nearly 10 million.

South Korea has nearly 19,000 bomb shelters throughout the country. They include more than 3200 shelters in Seoul. Most of the civil defense shelters across the city are hiding in plain sight. These shelters are not built to protect against nuclear, chemical, or biological attacks. Shelters are mostly in subway stations, or basements and parking garages in private apartments and commercial buildings designated as shelters. Jaded by nearly 70 years of tension and threats from N Korea, locals rarely consider where they shop, take a train, or park their vehicles, which also serve as a subterranean defense infrastructure.

In July 2006 N Korea launched seven missiles into the Sea of Japan, and in October 2006 it tested a nuclear bomb. Before the N Korean missile and nuclear tests, S Korea suspended aid and shipments to the North and put their military on high alert status.

> If the US imperialists, oblivious of the lesson of history, are tenacious enough to provoke a new conflict (war) of aggression in Korea, turning a deaf ear to the just demand of the Korean people and going against the current of the times, they will eventually perish in the flames of war once and for all, suffering a still greater, miserable defeat than they suffered in the past two Korean conflicts."
> Echoes of the Korean War Booklet.

---

101 https://www.kinu.or.kr/.

On October 4, 2007, S Korean president Rho Moo-Hyun (2003-2008) signed the 2007 Inter-Korean summit as an eight-point peace agreement. The summit was held in Pyongyang between Rho and the leader of N Korea Kim Jong-Il, and both sides announced a declaration for development of Inter-Korean relations peace and prosperity. However, relations worsened when S Korean president Lee Myung-bak (2008-2013) adopted a more hardline approach altering the S Korean government's approach in the wake of increased provocation.

On March 26, 2010, a S Korean naval vessel, the ship *Cheonan*, a destroyer, in a deliberate act of violence, was sunk by a N Korean torpedo near Baengnyeong Island in the Yellow Sea (West Sea). The *Cheonan* (PCC-772) was split in half by the explosion and sank in the darkness with the loss of 46 sailors. A rescue operation recovered 58 survivors. A S Korean-led international investigation group concluded that the sinking of the warship was in fact the result of a N Korean torpedo attack. N Korea denied involvement. The UN Security Council made a presidential statement condemning the attack, but without identifying the attacker. In November 2010, N Korea launched yet another unprovoked conventional artillery attack on the S Korean Yeonpyeong Island. N Korea unexpectedly fired scores of artillery shells at Yeonpyeongdo, killing at least four (two soldiers, two civilians) wounding 18 more, destroying several houses, and setting numerous fires in one of the most serious clashes between the two countries. S Korea responded by firing 80 artillery shells of its own at N Korea. N Korean casualties are unknown.

In August 2015, N Korea denied planting wooden box anti-personnel mines on the southern side of the DMZ, wounding two S Korean soldiers near their guard post. As a reaction, S Korea resumed playing propaganda on loudspeakers near the border. N Korea threatened to attack those loudspeakers and fired a rocket and shells across the border. S Korea responded by firing shells back at the origin of the rocket. There were no reports of injuries on either side.

Following threats of war from the North, and various troop movements by both sides and the US, an agreement was reached that N Korea would express sympathy for the landmine incident; in return S Korea deactivated the loudspeakers.

In August 2016, N Korea installed anti-personnel mines to prevent the defection of its front-line border guards around the Bridge of No Return, situated in the JSA. The UNC protested this move, as it violates the Armistice Agreement which prohibits armed guards and anti-personnel mines.

On May 10, 2017, Moon Jae-in's inauguration was held, and he entered the office of President of S Korea. Following the election of Moon in 2017, S Korea began reconciling with N Korea once more, thus beginning a revival of the Sunshine Policy. Moon Jae-in's effort in improving the inter-Korea relationship resulted in three summits in a year, including two summits held in the JSA (April 2018 and May 2018), Panmunjom and in September 2018 in Pyongyang. In recognition of Moon's endeavor in inter-Korea relations his version became known as "Moonshine Policy." As president, Moon achieved international attention for his meetings with N Korean Chairman Kim Jong-un at inter-Korean summits, making him the third S Korean president to meet their N Korean counterpart. There was much concern regarding how S Korea can maintain a cooperative policy toward the North when provocative acts continued to occur. Nonetheless, the government of S Korea insisted that at least some aspects of the 1993 Sunshine Policy, including the Kumgangsan Tourist Region and the Kaesong Industrial Region will continue.

On September 3, 2017, N Korea successfully tested a thermonuclear bomb, also known as a hydrogen bomb. Corresponding seismic activity like an earthquake of magnitude 6.3 was reported by the US Geological Survey. The test was reported to be a perfect success. Kim Jong-un continued the North's hard line regarding using nuclear weapons as a threat to the world.

On November 13, 2017, a N Korean soldier defected to S Korea by crossing the demarcation line in the JSA. The elite soldier stationed at the heavily guarded Demilitarized Zone was shot by other N Korean soldiers and was found about 55 yards from the demarcation line. S Korean soldiers rescued the defector, and he was taken to a hospital for treatment of gunshot wounds. The wounded N Korean soldier survived.

In October 2018, North and South Korea officials agreed to clear the JSA of all landmines, weapons, and guard posts. On November 6, 2018, it was announced that the UNC would transfer primary guard duties of the new demilitarized

JSA to both North and South Korea. This transfer was completed on October 25, 2018, and the JSA now contains 35 unarmed security guards.

On November 30, 2018, a N Korean soldier fled across a heavily fortified border to defect to S Korea. S Korean soldiers escorted the defector to safety after finding him moving south of the eastern side of the military demarcation line. This defection came as N and S Korea pushed to reduce tensions between the Koreas.

On June 30, 2019, President Donald J. Trump and S Korean President Moon Jay-in visited the DMZ together prior to meeting with N Korean Leader Kim Jong-un. Trump met Kim for a third time, becoming the first sitting US president to step foot in N Korea. The two met in the building on the S Korean side known as Freedom House for about one hour before Trump escorted Kim back to N Korean territory. It was announced that the two countries would look to revise stalled talks.

In May 2020, a S Korean guard post inside the DMZ was hit by multiple bullets coming from N Korea, prompting S Korea to broadcast a warning and return fire twice. Afterward, S Korea activated the inter-Korean communication channels to prevent further incidents.

In September 2020, S Korean official (Lee Dae-jun) of the Ministry of Maritime Affairs and Fisheries disappeared from his patrol boat that was six miles south of the maritime boundary, Northern Limit Line (NLL), in the Yellow Sea (West Sea). He was found wearing a life jacket by a N Korean fishing boat, which was ordered to shoot him and burn his body. N Korean leader Kim Jong-un apologized to S Korea's leader President Moon Jae-in for killing the S Korean official.

In January 2022, N Korea conducted series of seven missile tests to include launching two hypersonic missiles, two short-range missiles from a railway-mobile (train) missile system, and its largest missile test since 2017, the Hwasong-12 an intermediate-range ballistic missile, taking N Korea closer to resuming long-range testing.

The preceding historical information and incidents of hostile threats 1970-2022 could have triggered a military response between N Korea, S Korea, and the United States.

Nearly 30,000 N Koreans have defected, mostly traveling via China, to S Korea since the end of the 1950s Korean Conflict. The Office of the Historian, Bureau of Public Affairs, US State Department estimates 1000 flee Kim Jong-un's regime each year. Beginning in 2020, there was a spike in illegal border crossing because of a food shortage and the grim economic situation made worse by coronavirus controls. In response, Pyongyang tightened border security and rolled out a series of aggressive measures to block access to the rugged 880-mile-long border. N Koreans seeking work in China or escaping onward to S Korea were facing dangerous obstacles. In mid-2021, frontier guards and special forces soldiers were ordered to shoot anyone within six-tenths of a mile of the border. The border area was beefed up with the latest type of anti-personnel landmines in border regions that had never been mined in the past, which was a sign that earlier measures had not stopped desperate citizens. In 2022, the border area remained heavily guarded to prevent border crossings and the shoot-to-kill order remained in force.

On May 21, 2021, President Joe Biden welcomed S Korean President Moon Jae-in to the White House for their first face-to-face meeting. Moon had N Korea high on the agenda. Moon and Biden spent a significant amount of time discussing N Korea and how best to reach out to N Korean Leader Kim Jong-un to find a diplomatic solution to end its nuclear weapons program and formally ending the 1950s Korean Conflict. Biden has previously signaled he is not necessarily keen to continue former President Trump's more open policy toward Pyongyang. The White House has made overtures to the Korean government, but those have gone unanswered.

North Korea and South Korea might agree to end hostile acts — in a peace deal or agreement — but an official peace treaty is another matter altogether. In the meeting, Moon discussed with Biden ending the 1950s Korean Conflict with a peace treaty. A peace treaty agreement would presumably replace the existing armistice, which introduces complications regarding which parties would be involved. The armistice was signed by military commanders, not by civilian government representatives. Dismantling the armistice would require involvement from the US and N Korea.

Diplomatic relations between China and S Korea were formally established in 1992. A peace treaty was also signed on August 24, 1992, declaring an official end of hostilities between S Korea and China. A formal peace treaty was needed because the Korean Conflict ended with only an armistice agreement. On September 3, 1994, China withdrew from the UN Military Armistice Commission established in July 1953 at Panmunjom. N Korea and the UN Command (US) are the remaining participants in the Korean Armistice Agreement. (S Korea never signed the agreement.)

It is unclear what role, if any, the United Nations would play in such a negotiation, particularly the 16 additional countries that contributed military forces to the US-led UNC during the conflict, known as the "sending states." South Korea and Japan, both US treaty allies, are not party to the armistice but would have significant national interests in the terms negotiated among other parties. The Russian Federation (formerly USSR) may also consider itself to have a strong national interest in the terms, as it borders N Korea.

In a joint statement, both Moon and Biden gave a nod to the 2018 Singapore Summit signed agreement between President Donald J. Trump and N Korean leader Chairman Kim Jong-un. Trump provided security guarantees to N Korea, and Chairman Kim reaffirmed his firm and unwavering commitment to complete denuclearization of the Korean Peninsula. Trump and Kim committed to cooperate for the development of new US-DPRK relations and for the promotion of peace, prosperity, and security of the Korean Peninsula.

Presidents Biden and Moon discussed the Singapore agreement and left open the possibility it may lead to a foundation for the Biden administration's policy toward N Korea. President Biden appointed a special envoy to N Korea after meeting with President Moon, declaring that both the US and the ROK are deeply "concerned" about the continuing threat of N Korea's nuclear missile programs.

In a breakthrough on July 27, 2021, the Koreas have announced measures to restore cross-border talks for the first time in more than a year; diplomacy could take hold in Korea. President Moon is committed to inter-Korean negotiations. Moon, since taking office, sees diplomacy as the only path to promote reconciliation for peace between the Koreas. Moon vowed in January 2022 to press for a diplomatic breakthrough with N Korea, despite public silence from Pyongyang. On May 10, 2022, Moon said he hopes the next administration continues to build on establishing a peaceful relationship with N Korea.

Pro-democracy Activities in the Republic of Korea

Democracy did not flourish in S Korea in the 1950s. The president, Syngman Rhee, used a national security law of 1949 to close newspapers and imprison critics. However, his administration was corrupt, and by 1960 it was facing growing economic problems. In 1960, riots by students forced Rhee to resign. Faced with inflation, unemployment, and continuing riots the army staged a coup in 1961. General Park Chung-hee became ruler. At first, the general declared martial law but in 1963 he held presidential elections and won. Nevertheless, his rule was repressive. He won a second election in 1967. The general won the third election in 1971 by only a small margin. Afterward, he drew up a new constitution which gave him more power. He was assassinated in October 1979.

Despite the repressive rule, S Korea's economy began to grow rapidly from the mid-1960s. General Park built roads and bridges and expanded education. A series of plans was drawn up and the government took a central role in running the economy. Industry became dominated by large corporations called Chaebol, with global multinational operations. After the assassination of General Park in 1979, the S Korean Army again stepped in to restore order. General Chun Doo-hwan took power in May 1980. In the 1980s, the Korean economy continued to grow, and the country climbed out of poverty. S Korea became an affluent society. Pro-democracy activities intensified in the 1980s, and S Korea began to transition to a vibrant, democratic system. In 1987, S Korea amended its constitution to provide for election of the president by direct, secret ballot, for a five-year term, with no possibility of re-election. The Constitution became effective on February 25, 1988, when Roh Tae Woo was inaugurated as president. Roh was a S Korean politician and an army general; he would be the last military-backed president. By the 1990s, Korea had become a rich nation and its people had a quite high standard of living. The government began to deregulate industry.

In 1998 the Olympics were held in Seoul, which brought S Korea into the international limelight. Kim Dae-Jung (1998-2003) became the first civilian to hold the office in over 30 years, ending military control and serving a single five-year term. His election marked the first time in Korean history that the ruling party peacefully transferred power to a democratically elected opposition winner. Then in 2013-2017, Park Geun-hye became the first woman president.

Over the past several decades, S Korea has achieved a remarkably elevated level of economic growth and is now the US' sixth-largest goods trading partner, with a trillion-dollar economy. Korea developed Korean Free Economic Zones (KFEZ) exclusively designated to improve business and living conditions for foreign countries that are investing in the Republic of Korea. Starting with the designation of the Inchon Free Economic Zone (FEZ), Inchon was recognized as the best business city in Northeast Asia in 2003, and now there are seven FEZs scattered throughout Korea. In 2016, S Korea invested $38.8 billion into the US, making S Korea the second largest Asian source of foreign direct investment into the US. South Korea has also become the major trade center of Northwest Asia. The US provides no development assistance to S Korea. Korea, a recipient of US aid in the years after the 1950s Korean Conflict, is now a development aid donor. Under the Special Measurement Agreement (SMA), S Korea has paid about half of the non-personnel costs of hosting US forces stationed in Korea since 1991. In 2014, S Korea paid $867 million dollars and in 2018, reached $890 million dollars. On February 10, 2019, S Korea's foreign ministry announced a $920 million dollar cost share for 2019/2020.

The Biden Administration concluded a new five-year burden sharing agreement in March 2021. S Korea agreed to pay about $1 billion annually as its cost share for stationing US forces in Korea. On March 10, 2021, the cost share was 1.03 billion dollars. There are about 28,500 American troops and civilian personnel assigned to US Forces Korea (USFK), although the number fluctuates during military exercises and when a new unit moves in to relieve another. Accordingly, the number of US troops can dip to about 27,000 or top off at 33,000. Most American troops are at the US Army Garrison Camp Humphreys in Pyeongtaek and Camp Walker at Taegu (Daegu). The US Air Force has two bases: Osan, only 40 miles away from Seoul, and Kunsan, located on the coast of the Yellow Sea in western S Korea. The US Navy operates from Pusan (Busan) and Jinhae on the southeast coast. The US State Department reported S Korea paid 92 percent of the $10.7 billion dollars to build the new facilities at Camp Humphreys. US Army Garrison Camp Humphreys is the headquarters of 8th Army and is located 55 miles south of its former base, Yongsan Garrison, in Seoul and about 60 miles from the DMZ. Camp Humphreys is the largest overseas base.

By relocating, the US military allowed more time to react to scenarios where every minute counts. On June 29, 2018, US Army soldiers fired cannons during an opening ceremony for the new headquarters building of the US Forces Korea. The opening of the new building, south of Osan Air Base, marked a historic milestone in the history of the UNC. The headquarters for US forces in Korea had been garrisoned in Seoul since 1957. The new headquarters building is home to US Forces Korea, the 8th Army, the Combined US-Republic of Korea Command, and the United Nations Command.

Communist Government in the Democratic People's Republic of Korea

After Russian troops occupied the north, a communist government was installed. Kim Il-sung was made a ruler. Like many dictators, he created a "cult of personality" by erecting statues of himself everywhere. School children were taught to see him as the font of all wisdom. In fact, he created a very repressive regime. Religious belief was outlawed, and the people strictly controlled. Today N Korea is the last Stalinist regime in the world. With a great deal of Russian aid, N Korea was transformed from a poor agricultural country into an industrial one. However, in the mid-1970s the economy began to stagnate. Furthermore, in 1991 North Korea was harmed by the collapse of the Soviet Union. Kim Il-sung died in 1994 and was succeeded by his son Kim Jong-il. In the late 1990s, a severe famine occurred in N Korea. There was unusually heavy rain and floods in 1995-96, followed by drought in 1997 and typhoon damage. Malnutrition became common, especially among children. How many people died in the famine is not known? Kim Jong-il died in 2011 and he was followed by his son Kim Jong-un. N Korea's economy is severely repressed and is ranked last among 40 countries in the Asia-Pacific region. Chronic structural problems beset one of the world's most centrally commanded and least open economies. In a country that lacks even the most basic policy infrastructure of a free-market economy, individuals and businesses lack any economic freedom whatsoever, both in principle and in practice. In 2020, the coronavirus pandemic resulted in N Korea closing its border with China and this action resulted in economic and social hardships to worsen. N Korea continued its policy of "Juche" adherence to self-reliance.

Promoting Peace and Stability on the Korean Peninsula and Beyond

For years, the US and the international community have tried to negotiate an end to N Korea's nuclear and missile development. In January 1994, the Central Intelligence Agency (CIA) estimated that N Korea may have produced one or two nuclear weapons. In October 1994, faced with N Korea's announced intent to withdraw from the nuclear Nonproliferation Treaty (NPT), which requires non-nuclear weapons states to not pursue the development and acquisition of nuclear weapons, the US, and N Korea signed the "Agreed Framework" in Geneva, Switzerland. To resolve US concerns about plutonium-producing reactors, N Korea once again agreed to freeze and ultimately dismantle its nuclear program in exchange for aid. The N Korean facilities subject to the freeze included the operational 5 MWe experimental graphite-moderated reactor, a partially complete reprocessing facility, and a 50 MWe power reactor under construction, all at the Yongbyon Nuclear Research Center, as well as a 200 MWe power reactor under construction at Taschen, N Korea.

N Korea also allowed IAEA to verify compliance through "special inspections," and it agreed to all 8000 spent reactor fuel elements to be removed to a third country. In return for North Korea's agreeing to freeze and ultimately dismantle its nuclear program, the US agreed to finance and construct in N Korea two light-water reactors (LWR) generating approximately 2000MW(e) of the Korean Standard Nuclear Power Plant model by 2003 and also to provide N Korea with an alternate source of energy in the form of 500,000 metric tons of heavy fuel oil each year for heating and electricity production until the first of those reactors is completed. The LWSs will be financed and constructed through the Korean Peninsula Energy Development Organization (KEDO), an international consortium.

KEDO was established March 9, 1995, when Japan, the Republic of Korea, and the United States expressed their common desire to implement the key provisions of the "Agreed Framework." As KEDO's founding members, these three countries constituted the Organization's Executive Board. On August 7, 2002, KEDO held a ceremony to mark the pouring of the concrete foundation for the first LWR. In November 2002, following reports that N Korea was engaged in an underground program to enrich uranium, KEDO's Executive Board decided to suspend the supply of heavy fuel starting in December. The last shipment reached N Korea on November 18. Subsequently, N Korea expelled inspectors from the IAEA from Yongbyon at the end of 2002; announced its withdrawal from the Non-Proliferation Treaty (NPT) of nuclear weapons in January 2003; and resumed operations at Yongbyon. The "Agreed Framework" collapsed.

Several diplomatic initiatives emerged seeking to resolve these nuclear issues. The most notable of these were the US-DPRK-China three-party talks in April 2003, and at three rounds of six-party-talks in August 2003, February 2004, and June 2004 that, in addition to the above-mentioned countries, included Japan, the Republic of Korea, and the Russian Federation. Throughout 2003,

Smell The Gunpowder

KEDO's Executive Board members held meetings to assess the implications of these events for the ongoing construction of the LWR project. On November 21, KEDO announced that because N Korea had not met the condition necessary for continuing the LWR project, it was suspending construction for a period of one year, beginning December 1. On November 26, 2004, KEDO's Executive Board decided to continue the suspension of the LWR project for another year, beginning December 1, 2004. In November 2005, KEDO's Board began discussions regarding terminating the project. On January 8, 2006, KEDO completed the withdrawal of all workers from the LWR project, and the Executive Board decided on May 31, 2006, to terminate the LWS project. The decision was taken based on the continued and extended failure of N Korea to perform steps that were required in the LEDO-DPRK Supply Agreement for the provision of the LWR project.

On April 27, 2018, N Korean leader Kim Jong-un and S Korea's President Moon Jae-in met in Pyongyang to discuss a nuclear free peninsula. During the day-long summit, N Korea and S Korea signed the Panmunjom Declaration for Peace, Prosperity and Unification of the Korean peninsula. The two countries committed to a nuclear-free Korea and held talks to bring a formal end to the 1950s Korean Conflict—69 years after open hostilities ceased. Because of the involvement of the United Nations Command, South Korea and the United States in the conflict would need to be signatories on an official peace treaty. At the summit, both S and N Korea leaders vowed to work with the US to bring an end to the "current unnatural state of armistice." Kim and Mood agreed to be committed to an era of no war. N and S Korea formed a plan to remove all threats that can cause war from the entire peninsula.

Beginning October 1, 2018, near Paju, northwest of the S Korean capital, Seoul, S Korean troops started removing some of the land mines at their heavily fortified border. Likewise, N Korean soldiers engaged in demining the northern part of the border. It is estimated that 2 million mines are inside the DMZ, and this mine removal is limited. The mine removal took place at the JSA in their shared border village of Panmunjom. The Koreas also removed 11 front-line guard posts. This meeting was the first in more than a decade in which leaders from both sides talked face-to-face.

The talks simply seem to be a means to an end—Korea reunification under Kim Jong-un's leadership. Pyongyang pursues dramatic political breakthroughs while Seoul prefers an incremental approach to dialogue, believing economic agreements and increased personal contacts provide an atmosphere more conducive to meaningful political agreements and a reduction in tension. However, the basic areas of contention remain unresolved. No dramatic reforms are likely in N Korea. Kim will go to any lengths, including war, to preserve what he and his family have created. North Korea is run by an oligarchy led by Supreme Leader Kim Jong-un. The Kim family has ruled the country since the end of World War II, and most military and civilian leadership consists of second-and-third-generation leaders who are family or close friends of the country's late founder, Kim Il-sung; his late son, Kim Jong-il; or his grandson, Kim Jong-un. This small group of people hold most or all political power. One of N Korea's major national policy goals is to remove US forces from the peninsula. Pyongyang believes the US military presence in S Korea directly impedes reunification. Most Koreans on both sides of the DMZ want to reunify, and N Korea's desire for reunification has consistently structured its proposals to ensure communist control.

Military Comparison

The S Korean military has 650,000 troops [102] with modern equipment, based on the 1953 Korean American Mutual Defense Treaty. All men in good health are expected to serve. Upon reaching 18 years old, military service is compulsory. However, enlistment does not have to begin immediately. It is possible to delay starting until age 28. Also, those who are not in good health are allowed to complete their military service through non-active duty. This could be through social work or other services for the government. Service time for the Army and Marines is 21 months, the Navy 23 months, and the Air Force is 24 months. By contrast, N Korea has 1.4 million military and paramilitary personnel, making it the world's fourth-largest standing army after China, India, and the United States. In February 1948, the draft constitution was adopted by the 4th Session of the People's Assembly, of which Article 98 provided for the formation of the Ministry of National Defense. The constitution was not adopted officially until early September 1948; however, for all practical purposes, the Ministry of National Defense was functioning and had been for some time under the guise of Voice Preservation Officers' Training Bureau, also known as Central Peace Preservation units. With the official announcement the N Korean Army

---

102 N Korea has 1.4 million military and paramilitary personnel who account for about 8% of its working age population. Only China, Russia, and India have larger standing armies. By comparison, S Korea, which has more than twice the North's population, and compulsory military service has fewer than half the armed forces.

(People's Army) was officially activated on February 8, 1948, and this action affirmed that the ministry was also, in effect, controlling the armed forces. The creation of a uniformed armed national military was viewed as an alternate means to accomplish the unification of Korea by force. Using battle-hardened Korean veterans of the Chinese Communist Forces as a core, they built a modern military force with its only glaring weakness being air power.

The striking comparison in organization, logistics, and tactics of the N Korean Army with those of the Soviet ground forces is attributable to the influence of the Soviet occupation army and the multitude of advisors which were left behind upon the Red Army's withdrawal from N Korea.

All men serve 10 years from the age of 17, representing about 40 percent of the populace (25,896,417 as of Aug. 1, 2021) in the regular armed forces, paramilitary, or defense-related industry and can be mobilized easily in time of war. The military and paramilitary account for about 8% of its working-age population and the remainder are in the defense-related industry. N Korean soldiers are mobilized to work at nearby military-run farms during the growing season. The use of military personnel to work on farms began in the early 1950s. The focus is on planting and harvesting rice, cabbage, and soybeans. Rice is N Korea's primary farm product; potatoes are considered a second-grade food item, but have become the main staple in rural areas, replacing rice. Since tensions have risen due to N Korea's recent missile tests and its development of nuclear weapons, N Korean soldiers have mobilized to work on farms near their military bases to maintain combat readiness. To help resolve their country's food shortages, Agricultural Management Committees provide extra food to these soldiers working on the farms. Living conditions in N Korea are characterized by deprivation. The elite ruling class enjoys basic benefits of modern life such as indoor plumbing, cars, meat, coffee, and a few luxury items.

The middle class receives sufficient food and occasional new clothes. Most people, however, struggle to survive. Half of the nation's 24 million people live in extreme poverty. For most people, meat is an unaffordable luxury. They subsist on fermented cabbage known as kimchi, rice, corn, and porridge. N Korea remains one of the most repressive countries in the world. Under the rule of Supreme Leader Kim Jong-un, the third leader of the 77-year Kim dynasty, the population remains fearful because of government threats of execution, imprisonment, enforced disappearance, and forced labor.

The era of N Koreans digging tunnels to invade the South is over. The North has been weakened by years of economic neglect since the collapse of Russia in 1991. China is now its largest trade partner. N Korea's economy is dwindling, and it is currently preoccupied with its survival rather than invading the South. Kim Jong-un's objective is to avoid the fate of regimes like that of Saddam Hussein's in Iraq and Moammar Gadhafi's in Libya. In October 2002, the US Congress passed the Iraq Resolution, which authorized the president to "use any means necessary" against Iraq. Saddam Hussein was captured and executed on December 30, 2006. Moammar Gadhafi, the deposed leader of Libya, was captured and summarily executed on October 20, 2011. The fear of an American-led invasion, well founded or not, is deeply ingrained in the mentality of North Korean leadership. S Korea, through diplomatic means, met with N Korean leaders and reached a signed military agreement pledging to cease all hostile acts against each other. Although a nuclear N Korea still is a serious concern, both sides are attempting to resolve this major issue. The US is actively participating as well to end the N Korea nuclear program. Peace and prosperity are the goals of the Koreas.

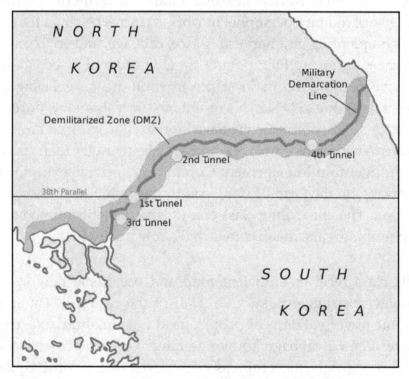

Locations of infiltration tunnels into South Korea
North Korean infiltration tunnels into South Korea - Credit: US Army Press
Department of Defense (DoD) Media

Smell The Gunpowder

PART FIVE
KOREA IN THE 21ST CENTURY

CHAPTER 21

POLITICAL GAMBLE OF THE 21ST CENTURY

The dawn of the 21st century made the international environment change considerably. With the election of President George W. Bush (2001) of the United States, his administration took several actions to set the tone. President Bush rejected S Korea's Sunshine Policy and the Agreed Framework simply because N Korea ignored the provisions of the agreements. His administration treated North Korea as a rogue state, while Pyongyang doubled down its efforts to acquire nuclear weapons to avoid the fate of Iraq. On March 7, 2001, after a working meeting with S Korean President Kim Dae-Jung at the White House, President Bush told reporters that he "looks forward to, at some point in the future, having dialogue with the N Koreans, but that any negotiation would require complete verification of the terms of a potential agreement."

On January 29, 2002, President Bush, in his State of the Union address, criticized N Korea for "arming with missiles and weapons of mass destruction, while starving its citizens."

The discovery in November 2002 of a N Korean hidden highly enriched uranium program set relations back into the deep freeze. Later, when Bush did engage N Korea, it was in the framework of the three six-party talks—including the Republic of Korea-S Korea, DPRK-N Korea, the US, Russian Federation and China—designed specifically to ensure that Pyongyang could not use provocations to secure their goal of direct talks with the US.

The Obama administration (2009-2017) considered N Korea to be the top national security priority for the incoming administration, a view he conveyed to then president-elect Donald Trump's transition team. Former president Barack Obama, in a policy of "strategic patience," refused to engage in high-level negotiations with N Korea. Instead, he waited for leader Kim Jong-un to show he was committed to abandoning his nuclear arsenal. Obama made little progress with relations with N Korea, and the development of Weapons of Mass Destruction (WMD) continued.

Throughout 2017, following Donald J. Trump's assumption of the presidency, tensions between the US and N Korea increased, and there was heightened rhetoric between the two, with Trump threatening "fire and fury." N Korea began threatening to test missiles that would land near the island of Guam. The island is a US territory and a keystone of American military strategy in the Pacific located 2100 miles from N Korea, and within range of Kim's missiles. President Trump vowed to stop the N Koreans and did not rule out using force if diplomacy failed. The US and its allies find N Korea a major threat to peace.

On November 2, 2017, Trump's National Security Adviser, former Army Lieutenant General H.R. McMaster [103] N Korea is a threat to the "entire world," calling on all nations to do more to counter the moves of Pyongyang.

Trump lashed out at the N Korean leader after the ballistic missile test conducted on November 28, 2017. The intercontinental ballistic missile (ICBM) was launched from Pyongsong. The N Koreans identified the missile as a Hwasong-15 with a range of more than 8000 miles, able to reach Washington, DC. The US called on N Korea to act on its long-time denuclearization pledge to dismantle its nuclear program. A series of summits took place between Kim Jong-un of N Korea, President Moon Jae-in of S Korea, and former President Trump.

On May 22, 2018, President Trump met with South Korea President Moon Jae-in at the Oval Office of the White House. President Moon encouraged President Trump to meet N Korean leader Chairman Kim Jong-un. Through diplomatic efforts, N Korea promised to shut down and destroy its main nuclear weapons test sites by the end of May 2018 and remove ground-based guard units—a

---

103 Herbert Raymond McMaster's book *Battlegrounds* is scheduled for 2020. The book will cover his 34-year military career and his time in President Donald J. Trump's administration.

significant symbolic gesture. On May 9, 2018 N Korea released three prisoners--Kim Hak-song, Tony Kim, Kim Dong-chul—all American citizens of Korean descent. This was the most tangible gesture of sincerity shown by N Korea's leader. On May 28, 2018, N Korea destroyed the Punggye-ri nuclear test site, including at least three nuclear tunnels, observation buildings, a metal foundry, and living quarters. These developments provided the opportunity for Trump to meet face to face with the Chairman Kim Jong-un. (Moon played a major role in brokering the meetings between Trump and Kim in Singapore.) These gestures eased tensions between the US and N Korea. Since taking office, Trump had been hoping to secure a deal with N Korea in which Chairman Kim would relinquish his nuclear weapons.

Singapore Summit June 12, 2018

The Singapore Summit was held on June 12, 2018, and President Trump and Chairman Kim shook hands to kick off the historic summit. The summit was the first time a sitting US president met with a leader of N Korea. N Korea's nuclear weapons program was discussed. The US offered economic help to impoverished N Korea if it gave up its nuclear weapons. In a joint statement by President Trump and Chairman Kim, President Trump committed to provide security guarantees to N Korea, and Chairman Kim reaffirmed his firm and unwavering commitment to complete denuclearization of the Korean peninsula. It was acknowledged that Kim sought security assurances that the US had no intention to attack or invade N Korea. Trump and Chairman Kim hoped to develop a lasting relationship between their respective countries that have had a long history of hostility. The US had suspended several military exercises with S Korea amid ongoing negotiations with N Korea. As a show of good faith, Trump announced that the US was canceling joint military exercises with S Korea that the North has traditionally called practice for an invasion.

The Pentagon announced that the annual Ulchi Freedom Guardian exercises, which usually took place in late August and involve about 50,000 S Korean and 17,500 US troops, were being canceled indefinitely. Presently, there appears to be no corresponding gesture by the N Koreans to reduce tension. The historic summit set the stage for future meetings to discuss nuclear weapons and trade sanctions.

The US, S Korea, Japan, and N Korea "share" a vision for the future of the Korean peninsula. President Trump believes there is a good chance that there will be other meetings in the future.

Trump has hailed the Singapore summit as a success; skeptics have questioned whether he achieved anything, given that Pyongyang, which has rejected unilateral nuclear disarmament, appeared to make no new tangible commitments in a joint written declaration.

Details are described—specifically, Appendix I: White House Press Release provides a readable version of the Joint Statement.

On June 13, Trump declared that N Korea is "no longer a nuclear threat" to the United States and regional allies. The true test of success is whether further negotiations can close the gap between the US and N Korea on the definition of denuclearization and lay out specific, verifiable steps that Pyongyang will take to reduce the threat posed by its nuclear weapons. Through the personal diplomacy of President Trump with N Korean Leader Kim and the partner diplomacy of S Korea's President Moon, a new relationship is at hand between the US and N Korea. To build on the new relationship, the US wants the return of the USS *Pueblo* (GER-2), captured on January 23, 1968, in international waters off the East Coast of N Korea.

In June 2018, the *38 North* website [104], which monitors N Korean activity, said commercial satellite imagery of N Korea's Sohae Satellite Launching Station showed no dismantlement activity of its rocket engine test stand. Presently, US intelligence does not believe N Korea intends to fully give up its nuclear stockpile.

Team Spirit (1976-1993) was suspended five times to provide N Korea the opportunity to work toward denuclearization. It was replaced with Foal Eagle, a military exercise involving 50,000 to 300,00 military personnel. After running for more than two decades, Foal Eagle ended in 2019, when it was replaced by a scaled-down version. In 2021, the field exercises are altogether gone, replaced with simulations. In mid-March 2021, the US and S Korea began conducting a joint military exercise. The nine-day exercise was a command post exercise, meaning it took place mainly via computer simulations.

---

104 Link to *38 North* Website: https://www.38north.org & https://en.wikipedia.org/wiki/38_North.

N Korea committed to recovering remains from the POW/MIAs of the 1950s Korean Conflict. However, N Korea was slow in providing information about returning Americans killed during the conflict. Donald Trump remained certain that N Korea is in the process of doing so following his summit with Kim Jong-un.

On July 5, 2018, the former US Secretary of State, Michael R. Pompeo traveled to N Korea for a third time in search of commitments and possible timetables from N Korea on denuclearization and the return of remains of US troops missing from the Korean Conflict. The Secretary told the Senate Appropriations Committee on July 18, that he is optimistic that the US will receive some remains.

The US military moved transfer cases to the border between N and S Korea in preparation. When a team from the UN Command, including US officers, showed up at the truce village of Panmunjom fully prepared to meet a N Korean team to discuss details about the return of remains, the N Koreans did not show up. The UN delegations waited in one of the buildings at the JSA, where the N Koreans called on a "hot line" they had not used for years. The message was they wanted talks not just between colonels on either side but between generals. This should not be a surprise, given N Korea's track record. In a concession, the US and N Korean officials met again to discuss the return of remains. It was the first time in nine years that US and N Korean generals held talks. The agreement at Panmunjom was between a US team led by US Air Force Major General Michael Minihan, Chief of Staff of the United Nations Command, and a N Korean military delegation. N Korea agreed, after two days of talks with the US military, to return 50 to 55 sets of remains. Also, an agreement was reached to resume joint field activities to search for the remains of Americans. Joint US-N Korea military search teams collected 229 sets of US remains from 1996 to 2005. But efforts to recover and return more remains stalled for more than a decade as the US and N Korea clashed over N Korea's nuclear weapons program.

Presently, US intelligence does not believe N Korea intends to fully give up its nuclear stockpile.

On Friday, July 27, 2018, the 65th anniversary of the armistice that ended the fighting with the US and the UN, N Korea turned over what were believed to be the remains of 55 US service members who were killed during the 1950s Korean Conflict and included just one military identification tag (dog tag).

A US Air Force C-17 Globemaster cargo aircraft flew from Osan Air Force Base, in Pyeongtaek near the S Korean capital of Seoul, to Kalma Airport near Wonsan, N Korea to receive the remains. There was no ceremony for the initial handover of remains. The return took place about 0600 hours (6:00 a.m.) Friday, Korean standard time. The USAF jet departed N Korea at about 1100 hours (11:00 a.m.) transporting the remains to Osan Air Force Base, near Camp Humphreys, headquarters for the unified UN Command for Korea and US Forces Korea. US servicemen and a military honor guard lined up on the tarmac to receive the remains that were wrapped in the UN flag, the flag under which US troops fought during the conflict. The return of the US soldiers was one of the agreements reached during the summit with N Korean leader Kim in Singapore. On Thursday, July 26, 2018 (July 27, Korean standard time) the White House Office of the Press Secretary, released a statement on the repatriation of remains for N Korea. [105] [106] Events in N and S Korea occur 14 hours ahead of Eastern Standard Time.

The remains stayed at the Osan for several days to permit the initial DNA analysis along with review of documentation and the military identification tag returned. "There's no reason at this point to doubt that they do relate to 1950s Korean Conflict losses," said John Byrd, a forensic anthropologist working for the Hawaii-based agency in charge of identifying the remains. Forensic analysts could spend months, or even years, trying to identify the remains. [107] The remains were then flown to the identification laboratory run by Defense POW/MIA Accounting Office (DPMA) at Joint Base Pearl Harbor-Hickam, Honolulu, Hawaii.

(Deoxyribonucleic Acid [DNA] is the genetic code that determines all the characteristics of a living thing. Basically, an individual's DNA is unique "hereditary material.")

---

105 http://www.whitehouse.gov/briefings-statements/statement-press-secretary-repatriation-Remains-north-korea/, July 26, 2018.
106 https://www.whitehouse.gov/copyright/
     Pursuant to federal law, government-produced materials appear on the White House Web.
     Sites are not copyright protected.
107 Included with the 55 remains returned, just one military identification tag (dog tag). Military officials contacted the family of the service member referenced in the identifying tag. It was Emphasized that it was too early to confirm if that identity matched accompanying remains.

The official repatriation honor ceremony was held on August 1 at Joint Base Pearl Harbor-Hickam. Vice President Mike Pence, other dignitaries, and dozens of veterans gathered for a somber repatriation ceremony to receive the possible remains of 55 American soldiers. Officials in N Korea had no comment on the handover of the remains. N Korea celebrated July 27, 2018, as victory day ending the conflict with ceremonies at war-related memorials; the capital Pyongyang and other cities were decked out in national flags and bright red banners.

The process to return the remains took more time than President Trump expected, partly because of the extensive coordination with the N Korean government to authorize a USAF aircraft to fly into N Korean airspace and to prepare a dignified American repatriation of the remains. It was thought that US recovery teams could be on the ground in N Korea by the spring of 2019, to search for the remains of service members lost during the stalled conflict recovery operations. According to the DPMA, as of June 15, 2021, 7556 US troops remain unaccounted for from the 1950s Korean Conflict, and about 5300 of them are presumed to be north of the DMZ.

DPMA reported in February 2022 that 81 American troops have now been identified among the 55 boxes returned by N Korea. On February 17, 2022, DPMA Factsheet Progress on Korean War Personnel Accounting states the remains of 200 individuals are contained in the 55 boxes.

Master Sergeant (Master Sgt.) Charles H. McDaniel, 33; Private First-Class William H. Jones, 19; and Corporal Lloyd D. Odom, 19, are the first three identifications from the remains returned.

Master Sgt. Charles H. McDaniel, Sr.'s dog tag [108] was the only piece of identification included among 55 boxes of human remains that N Korea returned to US officials. Military officials contacted the family of the service member referenced in the identifying tag. Master Sgt. McDaniel was a medic and earned the Bronze Star Medal with V device, for valor, while saving a severely wounded soldier during an artillery barrage.

He served with the 83rd Infantry Division, European Theater of Operations (ETO), and participated in two campaigns: Ardennes (Battle of the Bulge) and

108 http://www.indystar.com/story/news/2018/08/14/dog-tag-belonging-indiana-man-charles-mcdaniel-re-turned-north-korea/946676002/.

Central Europe. In 1949, McDaniel was assigned to the First Cavalry Division with the occupation forces responsible for the Tokyo area, where his family joined him after the end of World War II. McDaniel was with the 3rd Battalion, 8th Regiment, 1st Cavalry Division, and deployed to S Korea in August 1950 from Japan. It is believed McDaniel Sr. was killed in the opening months of the Korean Conflict. McDaniel went missing in November 1950, during a battle with Communist Chinese forces at Unsan and Chongchon River Valley battle area, in Northwest Korea. The battle was the first major engagement between US and the Communist Chinese forces in N Korea and was a series of engagements that took place from October 25 to November 4, 1950. Unsan was one of the few access points into the Yalu River area. Scores of American soldiers were killed in action or listed as missing in action.

It would be 72 years before McDaniel Sr. 's identifying tag was returned from N Korea. Charles, Jr. 71, of Indianapolis, and his brother Larry, 70, of Jacksonville, Florida, were three and two years old respectively when their father was killed. His son, Charles, Jr., noted that his dad fought in the Battle of Unsan. During a ceremony in Arlington, Virginia the US Army presented McDaniel's dog tag to his son.

Master Sgt. Charles H. McDaniel, Sr. earned the Bronze Star Medal w/V device, Purple Heart Medal, Good Conduct Medal, America Defense Service Medal, European Africa Middle Eastern Campaign Medal with two battle stars, World War II Victory Medal, Army of Occupation *Germany* Medal, National Defense Service Medal, Korean Service Medal with two battle stars, United Nations Korea Service Medal, Republic of Korea War Service Medal, and US Army Combat Medical Badge (CMB). [109]

To: Sergeant First Class William R. Graser, USA (Ret)

"You have my permission to use my father's picture, the picture of the dog tag, and his brief bio. Thank you for your interest and for doing this important work of remembrance. Thank you for your service as well my fellow soldier. We know how important this is to remember our lost comrades."

---

109 The Combat Medical Badge (CMB) is awarded to any member of the Army Medical Department, ranked Colonel or below, assigned to a medical unit providing support to an infantry or Special Forces unit during any period in which the unit was engaged in active ground combat. The CMB was first created in 1945 but is retroactive to December 6, 1941.

Colonel Charles H. McDaniel Jr., Chaplin, US Army (Ret). Permission granted September 10, 2018. [110]

Private First-Class (Pfc.) William H. Jones remains identified September 13, 2018. Pfc William H. Jones was the second soldier identified. He left North Carolina as an 18-year-old boy from a small town in Nash County, 55 miles east of Raleigh-Durham, and went off to Korea to fight as an infantryman in the US Army.

He was reported missing on November 26, 1950, during the Battle of Unsan and Chongchon River Valley area. Jones was assigned to the 25th Infantry Division, E Company, 2nd Battalion, 24th Infantry Regiment. The Chinese Communist Forces' overwhelming size forced the 25th Division to embark on a fighting withdrawal from the area, and Pfc. Jones went missing in action during this movement. He was never reported as a prisoner of war, and his remains were not identified among remains returned to US custody immediately following the conflict. On December 31, 1953, the US Army declared him deceased and his remains non-recoverable. On June 20, 2019, Jones' remains finally returned to his North Carolina home. Jones's family traveled to Washington DC in August 2019 to bury his body in Arlington National Cemetery. Pfc. Jones was awarded the Purple Heart, the National Defense Service Medal, the Korean Service Medal, the United Nations Service Medal, the Korean Presidential Unit Citation, and the Republic of Korea War Service Medal. Pfc. Jones earned the Army Combat Infantryman Badge.

Corporal (Cpl.) Lloyd B. Odom's remains were identified September 12, 2019. Cpl. Lloyd B. Odom of Odessa, Missouri, was the third missing soldier identified. Odom was a member of the 7th Infantry Division, 31st Regimental Combat Team, and was reported missing in action on December 2, 1950, in the vicinity of the Chosin Reservoir. He was buried at Arlington National Cemetery. After his death, Cpl. Odom was awarded the Purple Heart, the Prisoner of War Medal, the National Defense Service Medal, the Korean Service Medal, the United Nations Service Medal, the US Presidential Unit Citation, and the Korean Presidential Unit Citation. Cpl. Odom earned the Army Combat Infantryman Badge.

---

110   Charles McDaniel cmcquest@aol.com. 7537 Timberfield Lane, Indianapolis, IN 46259.

Source: These abbreviations, Master Sgt., Cpl., and Pfc. DoD Visual Information Guide.

The Defense POW/MIA Accounting Agency reports there are still 1,700 service members missing from the Unsan and Chongchon River battle area and the Chosin Reservoir.

Hanoi Summit February 27 and 28, 2019

President Donald Trump and Chairman Kim Jong-un arrived in the capital city of Hanoi, Socialist Republic of Vietnam, on February 26 for a second summit and were greeted with flowers and giant portraits of Trump and Kim. The Vietnam, United States of America, and Democratic People's Republic of Korea flags were displayed throughout the city.

Chairman Kim Jong-un arrived in his personal armored train, painted military green with yellow trim, which pulled to a stop at Vietnam's Dong Dang railway station. This is the last station on the line before the Friendship Pass border crossing with Pingxiang, Guangxi in China. It is not possible for foreigners to board the International Train at the station; it can be boarded only in Hanoi. (On the Chinese side it is possible to disembark at Pingxiang or Nanning.) A beaming Kim Jong-un stepped out of his customized carriage onto a red carpet lined with bouquets of red flowers. The drive to Hanoi is 310 miles, and about three hours later he reached Hanoi's five-star Melia Hotel. President Donald J. Trump landed in Hanoi at the Noi Bai International Airport on Air Force One. The airport is 27 miles north of the city center. Four decades after fighting a long, bloody war, the US has forged a friendship with Vietnam, an authoritarian state with a booming, capitalist-oriented economy. The US and Vietnam came from war to peace and friendship. President Trump is quoted as saying: "Vietnam is thriving like few places on earth."

Trump tweeted February 27 on Wednesday morning, Vietnam time, that "North Korea would be the same, and very quickly, if it would denuclearize." (Quote source in part: *Los Angeles Times*.)

The high-profile June summit in Singapore resulted in only assurances from Kim to denuclearize, and no timeline to achieve it. Pyongyang has refrained from conducting further nuclear tests but made no progress on dismantling its nuclear facilities or producing a full accounting of its nuclear-related sites. President Trump committed again to provide security guarantees to N Korea.

Trump and Kim met at the French colonial Metropole Hotel, Hanoi's finest, for dinner and a one-on-one conversation that kicked off their summit. The historic Metropole Hotel was opened in August 1901 and was chosen as the best hotel in Vietnam'by Condé Nast Traveler Magazine (2007). It is unclear what steps Kim would take toward eliminating his nuclear arsenal or what concessions the US might offer in exchange. A full day was scheduled for Wednesday, February 27 with the goal of achieving sincere commitments going forward. The morning of February 28 began with talks between Trump and Kim, but later in the day the summit collapsed and was a dramatic turnaround from the optimism that surrounded the talks. The Hanoi summit failed for an amazingly simple reason: N Korea would not agree to eliminate its nuclear arsenal over the next months or years. N Korea's conduct of late and over the last year should leave no doubt about its intention to retain its nuclear arsenal. President Trump and Chairman Kim Jong-un departed the summit early because no agreement was reached regarding rolling back N Korea's nuclear program; consequently, sanctions remained in effect. Kim was seeking complete relief from economic sanctions without committing to eliminating its nuclear arsenal. The US remained firm to the position that N Korea remove its nuclear threat first before sanctions issues could be addressed. The summit ended without even an agreement on symbolic issues, such as declaring an end to the 1950s Korean Conflict or opening a US liaison office in Pyongyang, where the US does not have an embassy.

Expectations were high for concrete concessions from N Korea after the leaders' first summit in Singapore that produced only vague commitments from Kim to denuclearize, with no details or a timetable. Trump would not commit to holding a third summit after two high-profile meetings had failed to produce a concrete agreement.

But even after the summit ended, and in the absence of a sign of any agreement, Trump praised Kim's commitment to continue a moratorium on nuclear and ballistic missile tests now in its 16th month, and those diplomatic negotiations would continue. No deal does not mean there will not be one in the coming months. It is Kim's decision whether to abandon hopes of a quick and easy deal and authorize serious working-level negotiations to complete an agreement that he and Trump can sign at a third summit.

President Trump said, "This wasn't a walk away like you get up and walk out. No, this was very friendly. We shook hands. Kim and I thought, and Secretary Pompeo felt, that it was not a good thing to be signing anything, sometimes you must walk. This was just one of those times."

Before leaving Vietnam, Trump tweeted a thank you to Vietnam President Trọng and Prime Minister Phuc for hosting the summit and the wonderful people of Vietnam. His motorcade departed the Metropole hotel about 1325 hours (1:25 p.m.) Vietnam Time. At 0351 hours (3:51 a.m. Eastern Standard Time), Air Force One departed Noi Bai International Airport more than an hour earlier than originally scheduled for the return to Andrews US Air Force Base, Maryland. (Hanoi is 12 hours ahead of Eastern Standard Time)

By walking away from the table in Hanoi, President Trump kept the door open to continue negotiations. Trump made clear that he is prepared to continue the freeze on major joint US-South Korean military exercises and meet with Kim for another summit if it would be productive. [111]

For S Korea, the result of the Hanoi summit hurt S Korean President Moon Jae-in's prospects of re-starting some inter-Korean projects that had been stalled by the sanctions. The South planned to connect railways and roads across the inter-Korean border and reopen the jointly run industrial park at the North's border city of Kaesong. These projects were suspended in consideration of the US and its sanctions on N Korea. Neighboring Japan has a different set of concerns. With the failure of the summit to provide a substantial outcome, N Korea continues to have a nuclear arsenal that includes missiles capable of reaching Japan. [112]

Kim Jong-un remained in Vietnam for a two-day official state visit following the summit. Kim laid a wreath at the mausoleum of Vietnam's founding

---

111 On March 1, the US announced it was permanently canceling the spring large-scale US-S Korean military exercise. Timing of the decision raised the question whether Trump gave away a major piece of leverage over N Korea, which it has denounced the exercise as provocative, and failing to receive anything in return.
Smaller-scale training and annual exercises were not affected.

112 The S Korean President Moon met with Kim three times last year. Their meeting in April was the first time in more than a decade that leaders from both sides talked face-to-face. President Moon also played a major role in brokering the meetings between Trump and Kim in Singapore and Vietnam.

president, Ho Chi Minh, and met Prime Minister Nguyen Xuan Phuc before leaving Vietnam. His train left the Vietnamese border station of Dong Dang for the 2,800-mile return trip to Pyongyang.

In March 2019, N Korea demolished its inter-Korean liaison office in the border city of Kaesong, S Korea's Ministry of Unification (MOU) officer and N Korean state media confirmed. The joint Inter-Office Liaison Office opened on September 14, 2018, between the Koreas. The 24-hour, year-round communication channel between Seoul and Pyongyang is no more. The office was opened following an agreement between Seoul and Pyongyang at their historic Panmunjom summit. The decision to pull out may have been intended to signal the US that tensions are about to return to the Korean peninsula. The fact that N Korea is not happy with the current state of diplomacy on the peninsula, and the sudden pull-out, could be connected to how the US has ramped up sanctions since Hanoi. The border town of Kaesong had for years been a symbol of the fragile relationship between the Koreas. In 2003, it also sprang to life as the site of an industrial zone – the Kaesong Industrial Complex – set up between the North and South.

At its peak, it saw more than 120 factories, employing more than 50,000 N Koreans and hundreds of managers from the South.

"There is growing evidence that tough new sanctions imposed on N Korea to stop its nuclear weapons and missile programs have begun to bite, and bite hard. Factories have closed because of a lack of raw materials, fishermen have deserted their boats, and military units are resorting to charcoal-engine vehicles and even ox-driven carts for transport." Source: The *New York Times*, April 20, 2018.

Shortly after the end of the summit, N Korea conveyed displeasure over the breakdown of negotiations between its leader Kim Jong-un and President Trump. It continued rebuilding the Sohae rocket site it had promised to close. The rebuilding activities demonstrate how quickly N Korea can reverse any steps taken toward scrapping its Weapons of Mass Destruction (WMD) programs. N Korea is also operating "uranium enrichment facilities" at its Yongbyon nuclear complex. In late spring 2019, N Korea ratcheted up its military displays with rocket and missile tests. Relations between the US and N Korea have deteriorated sharply since the breakdown of the Hanoi summit. Nevertheless, Trump continued to insist that a deal was possible.

In a related issue, recovery of remains of American service members lost during the 1950s Korean Conflict evaporated after the Hanoi summit collapsed. The US Defense POW/MIA Accounting Agency (DPMA) reported its counterparts in the Korean People's Army have stopped communicating—and that it had given up hope of organizing joint recovery operations. It was thought that US recovery teams could have returned to N Korea in early 2019. In May 2021, the DPAM suspended efforts to recover remains of US service members.

Political Gamble "Status Quo"

The Singapore and Hanoi summits gave rise to optimism on the Korean Peninsula. The US assurances and N Korea's agreement to dismantle its nuclear weapons were a political gamble. With the failure of the summits to provide a substantial outcome, N Korea continued to have a nuclear arsenal; the status quo remained in effect. Pyongyang has signed five denuclearization agreements in the past but reneged on all of them.

After the 2019 G20 Osaka Summit held on June 28-29, the 14th meeting of the G20, a forum of 19 countries and the European Union (EU), Trump traveled to Korea. (The G20s primary focus is the governance of the global economy.) On June 30, 2019, a one-day summit was held at JSA Panmunjom between N Korean Chairman Kim Jong-un and President Donald Trump, and S Korean President Moon Jae-in. The meeting was intended to convey a political message without raising expectations. During the meeting held in the Inter-Korean House of Freedom, Trump set foot on N Korean soil marking the first time a sitting US President had done so. The meeting was strong on optics, weak on substance. Behind the scenes, working-level discussions had continued until nuclear talks held in Stockholm, Sweden in October 2019 broke down without an agreement.

In early December 2019, N Korea carried out major tests of its long-range missile engine. Kim indicated he would seek a "new path" if the US persists with sanctions and pressure. In late December 2019, N Korea repeated its assertions that the Trump Administration is running out of time to salvage nuclear negotiations. Kim set a deadline for the end of 2019, for the US to offer terms of a nuclear deal. In response to threats, the US sent surveillance planes over and around the Korean Peninsula. The action followed reports that N Korea warned of a possible missile launch or nuclear test for late December

2019, amid stalled nuclear negotiations. Trump had said N Korea risks losing everything if Chairman Kim resumes hostility. The last week in December 2019 ended without a major incident. Still, N Korea is a global threat, and the nuclear threat is not the only concern. N Korea has a longstanding chemical weapons program with the capability to produce nerve, blister, blood, and choking agents, and likely possesses a large chemical weapons stockpile. This includes the highly toxic sarin and VX chemical agents. VX nerve agents are the most toxic of the known chemical warfare agents. It is yellowish, tasteless and odorless. N Korea is not a signature to the Chemical Weapons Convention, which is an arms-control treaty that outlawed the production, stockpiling, and use of chemical weapons. N Korea possibly has weaponized anthrax or smallpox that could be mounted on a missile for use against US, S Korea, or Japanese targets in the region. The US with its allies, the Republic of Korea, and Japan are ready to meet any challenge posed by N Korea. Japan's Self-Defense Force created a Rapid Deployment Brigade, its first marine unit since World War II to counter invaders from occupying Japan. Japan and N Korea are as far away as ever from establishing anything resembling "normal relations," let alone official diplomatic ties. Japan is the world's third-largest economy and a major US ally. The US, S Korea and Japan will continue addressing security challenges including N Korea's weapons programs. Historically, post-World War II, Japan's Constitution Article 9 Japan renounced its right to wage war and maintain military forces. Today, due to external threats from N Korea and China the constitution was amended to allow a Self-Defense Force and the national flag of Japan officially called the *Nisshoki*. It embodies the country's sobriquet; Land of the Rising Sun.

In August 2021, the joint Inter-Office Liaison Office in Kaesong hotlines were restored for the first time in over a year. The liaison office allows officials from the North and South to communicate regularly and is staffed by up to 20 people from each side. The US State Department welcomed the reopening of the inter-Korea's communication lines as a "positive step."

With the dawn of 2022, concerns about N Korea and its intentions remain at a high level since the end of the 1950s and 1960s Korean Conflicts. N Korea ramped up its missile testing to bolster its defenses against the United States, S Korea and Japan. On January 5, 2022, a hypersonic missile was tested. It was the first major weapons test of the new year and on January 11 a second test was conducted. On January 14, N Korea test-fired two short-range ballistic missiles from separate trains. The test was to evaluate the response time and alert posture of its new railway-borne missile regiment. On January 17, 2022, two tactical guided missiles were test-fired within minutes of each other toward the ocean off its east coast of the Korean peninsula and traveled 186 miles reaching an altitude of 31 miles. On January 29, a Hwasong-12 mid-range ballistic missile was launched; this type of missile has an estimated range of 2796 miles with ability to carry a nuclear warhead and can reach the US territory of Guam. It last tested a ballistic missile in November 2017, a Hawasong-15 with an estimated range of 8077 miles that can reach Washington, DC.

The US, S Korean and Japan condemned the launch, which violated UN Security Council resolutions that bans N Korea from testing ballistic missiles and nuclear weapons.

These launches are N Korea's first known weapons tests since the October 19, 2021 launch of a missile from a Sinpo class submarine, a new class of submarine designed for N Korea's navy. As of January 30, 2022, N Korea has carried out 165 tests of strategic missiles since its first such test in April 1984. There were 15 tests carried out under the rule of Kim Il-sung, 16 under Kim Jong-il, and Kim Jong-un, conducted 134 tests.

Economic Hardship and Coronavirus Pandemic

Impact on North Korea

Since January 2020, there have been multiple signs of economic hardship, at least in parts of the economy that rely on imports and exports. Without imported goods, or the ability to bring in hard currency through exporting goods, markets have suffered shortages and volatility. Emphasis on fish production and aquaculture, which predates the coronavirus disease border closure, suggests the regime is trying (unsuccessfully) to minimize the country's dependence on international trade for its basic food requirements. In 2020, weather contributed to worsening the situation. Severe drought was followed by a succession of typhoons and heavy rain in August and September which hampered food production creating an even more severe food shortage. The regime may have to offset food shortages by releasing reserves of rice (from military reserves) as a way of overcoming market shortages. Living conditions are characterized by deprivation; half of the nations' 26 million people live in extreme poverty and subsist on fermented cabbage, known as kimchi, rice, corn, and porridge.

On January 21, 2020, N Korea became the first country to shut its borders in response to the coronavirus pandemic (COVID-19). N Korea's border closure is likely to have long-term effects until it reopens border trade. N Korea resorted to increasingly strident campaigns to deal with food and fuel shortages. UN sanctions regarding fuel sales have North Korea in a difficult position. The sanctions ban sale of fuel to N Korea. The United Kingdom's frigate HMS *Richard*'s deployment in the East China Sea has been taking part in UN sanctions enforcement operations and collected evidence of multiple ships breaching UN sanctions. The sanctions, adopted in 2017, ban the supply of fuel or refined petroleum products. By January 21, 2021, the borders have been closed for one year. According to S Korean analysis, trade with China in 2021 had fallen 90 percent from 2019 before the pandemic. In March the impact was noticeable when N Korea decided not to participate in the 20th Summer Olympics held in Tokyo due to concerns over potential exposure to the coronavirus.

In February, UNICEF, also known as the United Nations Children's Fund, a UN agency responsible for providing humanitarian and developmental aid to children worldwide, reported ten million N Koreans are considered food insecure and 140,000 children under the age of five suffer acute malnutrition.

In April, Russian diplomats in Pyongyang indicated that North Korea's total restrictions are unprecedented in their severity. Later that month, Kim Jong-un said his country is facing its worst-ever situation, referencing the economic downturn. American activist Reverend Tim A. Peters, a humanitarian aid worker living in Seoul, S Korea, operates Helping Hands Korea. Rev. Peters believes there are signs of "enormous stress on the N Korean population" due to the coronavirus and associated restrictions. He suspects the COVID-19 is spreading within the country despite the lack of confirmed cases.

In July 2021, N Korea rejected shipments of around two million doses of the Oxford-AstraZeneca vaccine, citing concerns over side effects. Russia also offered to supply the country with its own Sputnik V vaccine on multiple occasions. In September 2021, the country rejected three million doses of the CoronaVac, also known as the Sinovac COVID-19 vaccine, developed by the Chinese company

Sinovac Biotech. It was offered under the COVID-19 Vaccines Global Access (COVAX) program, a worldwide initiative aimed at equitable access to the coronavirus vaccine. UNICEF procures and transports vaccines along with supplies such as syringes, safety boxes for their disposal, and a low temperature-controlled cold chain, such as vaccine refrigerators. (An unbroken cold chain is an uninterrupted series of refrigerated production, storage and distribution activities) The full extent of the coronavirus disease is unclear. Although N Korea may have the capacity to implement a national vaccine strategy based on existing immunization programs, the regime instead opted to implement "our style" in epidemic prevention — essentially, heavy restrictions on internal movement and strict quarantine measures. The World Health Organization said that N Korea prior to May 2022, has not reported any coronavirus deaths. Experts widely doubted the claim that there has not been a single case of the virus, given its poor health infrastructure and porous border with China.

On May 10, 2022, N Korea reported its first COVID-19 outbreak and ordered a lockdown. An Omicron variant was detected in the capital, Pyongyang. N Korea sent aircraft to China to pick up medical supplies after it confirmed the outbreak. On August 11, 2022, N Korea declared victory over COVID-19 and ordered the lifting of maximum anti-epidemic measures.

Details are described in the introduction — specifically, Coronavirus Pandemic Cases, Deaths, and Population statistics regarding S Korea, N Korea, US, and Mainland China, Table 11.

N Korea is facing one of the worst economic crises in its 77-year history, amid shortages of fuel, food, and medicines and warnings of rising unemployment and homelessness. Kim Jong-un is facing the biggest domestic test of his 11 years in power. Pre-COVID-19, N Korea did not produce all the food it needs every year and heavily relies on China – its main ally and aid donor to meet its food requirements. N Korea dramatically reduced imports of staple foods and medicine from China in August and stopped almost all imports in October. N Korea is now trying to rebuild its economic lifeline with China, including the resumption of a cross-border cargo train service. The UN Food and Agriculture Organization estimated in a 2021 report that N Korea will be short about 860,000 tons of food. N Korea was hanging on by a thread before COVID, and now is taking severe measures to take control of the food shortage. Authorities told schools, factories, and businesses to grow food and raise fish and other animals to increase self-sufficiency. Ordinary people who are caught hoarding food could face execution.

Following Kim Jong-un's acknowledgment of the COVID-19 outbreak, and the extreme food shortages and necessities, he is signaling the need for outside help before the shortage turns into famine, raising speculation that the S Korean and US governments may undertake humanitarian efforts. The severe situations in N Korea may give rise to opening diplomatic discussion to formally end the decades-long 1950s Korean Conflict.

In early December 2021, S Korea, US, and N Korea, agreed in principle on a declaration to mark a formal end to the 1950s Korean Conflict.

On December 14, 2021, speaking at a joint press conference with Australian Prime Minister Scott Morrison after bilateral summit talks in Australia, former S Korean President Moon said he believes that an end-of-war declaration will assist in reviving talks between North and South Korea, as well as between North Korea and the United States.

The new year, 2022, N Korean leader Kim Jong-un called for solutions to economic hardships and development of military prowess in his speech to the Workers' Party's central committee.

Kim Jong-un vowed to bolster his military forces while addressing food shortages, domestic hardships, and despite pandemic-related difficulties. His speech indicates the country will press ahead with plans to modernize its nuclear and missile arsenals rather than return to disarmament talks anytime soon. The missile-tests in January were in line with Kim's intention to continue enhancing its capabilities.

On September 12, 2022, N Korea announced it is ruling out denuclearization with a new law adopting a more aggressive nuclear position. Its nuclear policy states it would preemptively strike the US or S Korea if an attempt to remove Kim Jong-un from power was initiated.

Short of an escalation in military action by N Korea there was little or no chance of talks between the US and N Korea in 2022, partly because of US midterm elections held in November 2022.

Formally Ending the 1950 – 1953 Korean Conflict

South Korean President Moon Jae-in in a speech to the United Nations General Assembly on September 21, 2021, urged his country, the United States, North Korea and possibly China to formally reach a peace agreement ending the decades-long 1950s Korean Conflict. President Joe Biden in his own UN speech said the US sought "serious and sustained diplomacy to pursue the complete denuclearization of the Korean Peninsula" in order to "increase stability" in the region. (On August 24, 1992, S Korea and China signed a peace treaty at a ceremony declaring the official end of hostilities.)

On September 23, 2021, the US announced it is open to discussing the possibility of formally ending the 1950s Korean Conflict and it was restarted in December 2021 by former S Korean President Moon. The US remains committed to achieving lasting peace on the Korean Peninsula through dialogue and diplomacy. For the last 30 years, the US has tried to force N Korea to unilaterally denuclearize. While there have been some agreements, these eventually collapsed, and over time both sides increasingly hardened their positions. The term "peace agreement" means an international legal instrument that solemnly, bindingly, and permanently ends the state of war. The difference is that the 1953 armistice merely imposed a ceasefire but did not end the state of war. N Korea rejected the calls for a peace treaty officially ending the 1950s Korean Conflict prematurely so long as US policies remained unchanged.

The Workers' Party Central Committee Vice Department Director Kim Yo-jong, sister to Supreme Leader Kim Jong-un, said N Korea is open to ending the war with the South "if conditions are met" — her comments were made after S Korea's president Moon suggested a new attempt at peace talks.

However, any work toward a permanent peace agreement would require the South to stop the "hostile policies" against N Korea. "Only when such conditions are met, would it be possible to sit face to face and declare the significant termination of war." She added that "an inter-Korean summit could take place, but only if mutual respect and impartiality are guaranteed."

S Korea's Unification Ministry is carefully reviewing Kim Yo-jong's statement as S Korea continues its efforts to restore ties with the North.

Smell the Gunpowder: The Land of the Morning Calm attempts to tell the story of Korea in a way that is informative and reflects on veterans who served in Korea. This writing makes no pretense of providing the complete account of the undeclared, unconventional struggles that gripped Korea since 1945, although this effort may serve to refocus attention on a most intriguing chapter in the annals of American and Korean history.

Just a short distance south of the DMZ, the Republic of Korea (S Korea) remains a free nation and one of the strongest and wealthiest countries in Asia. S Korea hosted the 23rd 2018 Olympic Winter Games in Pyeongchang. N and S Korea delegations marched together under one flag at the opening ceremony promoting hope and peace. History is still being made daily by the Koreans and the United States. To ensure the future of S Korea, N Korea, and the United States, finding common ground to promote peace on the Korean Peninsula is critical.

The American servicemen and women, who are serving or have served in the Republic of Korea since 1945 to the present day, made it possible for S Korea to remain free.

The Smell of Gunpowder lingers over The Land of the Morning Calm

Someone to Watch - Kim Yo-jong, age 34
Head of the Propaganda and Agitation Department
Workers' Party Central Committee Vice Department Director

Who is Kim Yo-jong? KimYo-jong is the youngest child of former N Korean leader Kim Jong-il (1994-2011) and Ko Yong Hui.

She is the sister of the current leader Kim Jong-un. Her grandfather was North Korea's first leader, Kim Sung-il. In recent years the younger sister of Kim Jong-un has emerged as a powerful ally. From 2014, Kim Yo-jong's main job is to protect her brother's image, taking up a key role in the party's propaganda department. In 2017, she was elevated to an alternate member of the politburo, although her main role remained in propaganda. In 2018, she shot into the international spotlight when, at the Winter Olympics, she became the first member of the Kim family to visit S Korea. Her continued rise shows she has gained the deep trust of her brother.

In April 2021, with Kim's disappearance prompting questions about his health, Yo-jong was mentioned as a possible successor.

In mid-August 2021, she has been responsible for delivering several strongly-worded messages against S Korea – and has emerged as N Korea's new point person on inter-Korean affairs, according to N Korean media. She oversees policies toward the US and S Korea and is the head of the propaganda and agitation department.

Recently she also served as the Workers' Party's Central Committee first vice department director. The position grants her greater power over the party and by extension the country. It is hard to gauge how much power – or how much of her own political network – the 34-year-old might have. Kim Yo-jong ripped S Korea for proceeding with military exercises with the US she claimed are invasion rehearsal and warned that the North will work faster to strengthen its preemptive strike capabilities.

Her statement came after S Korea media reported the allied militaries will begin four days of preliminary training before holding computer-simulated drills on August 16-26, 2021. Kim said she was delegated authority to release the statement.

She said continuing the drills exposed the hypocrisy of the Biden administration's offer to resume dialogue over the North's nuclear weapons program. She said there won't be stabilized peace on the peninsula unless the US withdraws its troops and weapons in S Korea. The US has kept about 28,000 troops in S Korea to help deter potential aggression from N Korea. Their US presence has long irked N Korean leader Kim Jong-un. The US insists the drills are "purely defensive in nature" to maintain S Korea's security. Kim said the drills held between the US and S Korea military forces were unwelcome and set back progress in improving inter-Korean relations. The US and S Korea would face a more serious security threat by ignoring N Korea's repeated warnings about these dangerous war exercises. N Korea's reaction to the drills threaten to upend previous efforts by former S Korean President Moon Jae-in to hold another summit as part of efforts to restore relations.

Who would succeed Kim Jong-un in N Korea? Look to Mount Paektu, N Korea's sacred mountain. Kim has reportedly ascended the mountain several times by horseback accompanied by mounted special forces troops in the past, often before making big announcements. Kim Yo-jong, sister, and confidante of the dynastic family's dictator, is believed to be a top candidate due to her bloodline. Only those from the "Mount Paektu bloodline," or those with a direct lineage to the country's founder Kim Il-sung, are deemed legitimate successors. Mount Paektu holds a special place in the country's identity. An active volcano, it is feted as the birthplace of Kim's father Kim Jong-il and served as a key military base for his grandfather Kim Il-sung—N Korea's founding leader. The peak of the mountain, lying on the border with China, is considered a sacred place in Korean folklore. It is said to be the birthplace of Dangun, the founder of the first Korean kingdom more than 4000 years ago.

US Service Members Repatriated

Vice President Mike Pence, Indo-Pacific Commander US Navy Adm. Phil Davidson, and Defense POW/MIA Accounting Agency Deputy Director Rear Adm. Jon Kreitz render salutes during an honorable carry ceremony at Joint Base Pearl Harbor-Hickam, Hawaii, August 1, 2018.

The United Nations Command recently repatriated 55 transfer cases from N Korea that contain what are believed to be remains of American service members lost in the 1950s Korean Conflict. VIRIN 18081-F-AN072-0046.

Flagged draped transfer cases, containing the remains of US service members.
VIRIN 180801-F-ZZ999-0131

Master Sergeant Charles H. McDaniel, Sr.
Undated Photograph Department of Defense POW/MIA Accounting Agency
Identification Tag (dog tag) Courtesy of Colonel Charles H. McDaniel, Jr., US
Army (Ret)
Pictured as a Staff Sergeant
VIRIN: 18123-A-ZZ111-003

Master Sgt. McDaniel was an Army medic from Indiana who disappeared in a battle with Chinese forces during the Korean War in 1950. His dog tag was the only piece of identification included among 55 boxes of human remains that North Korea returned to US officials on July 27, 2018.

Corporal Lloyd B. Odom
Updated Photograph: Department of Defense POW/MIA Accounting Agency
Remains identified September 12, 2019
VIRIN: 191024-A-ZQ077-03

Corporal (Cpl.) Odom was an infantryman from Missouri and was reported missing in action on December 2, 1950, in the vicinity of the Chosin Reservoir. Cpl. Odom was a member of the 31st Regimental Combat Team, 7th Infantry Division. He was taken prisoner of war and died as a prisoner on January 31, 1951. His remains were not recovered at the time.

Private First-Class William H. Jones
Updated Photograph: Department of Defense POW/MIA Accounting Agency
Remains identified September 13, 2018
VIRIN: 181217-A-ZZ111-016

Private First-Class Jones (Pfc.) was an Army infantryman from North
Carolina who was reported missing on November 26, 1950, during the Battle
of Unsan and the Chongchon River area. PFC Jones was a member of the 24th
Infantry Regiment, 25th Infantry Division. His remains were not recovered
at the time.

On August 2, 2018, the Defense POW/MIA Accounting Agency (DPAA)
announced the remains returned in July 2018 were possibly those of US Army
troops. N Korean officials indicated that the remains were recovered from the
village of Sin Hung-ri on the east side of the Chosin Reservoir and near Unsan.
The N Koreans handed over 55 boxes along with equipment associated with
the American military, such as boots, canteens, buttons, and buckles. Of the 55
boxes, 20 came from Unsan in November 1950 and 35 came from the Battle of
Chosin Reservoir in December 1950. It was estimated in 2018 that between 50
and 100 individuals could likely be identified, with about 80 of them expected
to be Americans and the others S Koreans fighting alongside US forces. In
September 2018, two soldiers were identified and in August 2019, 25 remains
were identified, and in October 2019, 41 more service members were identified
among the remains from N Korea.

On February 17, 2022, DPAA reported more than 7547 Americans still unaccounted for in N Korea. DPAA's Authoritative Data Mart (ADM) and Content Management System (CMS) updates data weekly, typically on Friday. Reference: dpaa.mil.

In February 2022, DPMA reported that 81 American soldiers have been identified among the 55 boxes returned by N Korea.

Major US Ground Forces Organizations Identification Shoulder Patch

8th *Army*   *I Corps*   *IX Corps*   *X Corps*

1st Cavalry Division   *2nd Infantry Division*   *3rd Infantry Division*   *7th Infantry Division*

11th Airborne Division   *24th Infantry Division*   *25th Infantry Division*   *1st Marine Division*

40th Infantry Division   *Army Security Agency*   *45th Infantry Division*
California National Guard   *Oklahoma National Guard*

Korean War Veterans Memorial Wall of Remembrance
On Patrol, Washington, DC.

Prisoner of War and Missing in Action Flag (Courtesy American Flag Clipart)

Major US Ground Forces Identification Shoulder Patch

8th Army; I Corps; IX Corps; X Corps; First Cavalry Division; 2nd Infantry Division; 3rd Infantry Division; 7th Infantry Division; Eleventh Airborne Division, (187th Regimental Combat Team); 24th Infantry Division; 25th Infantry Division; and the 1st Marine Division. The 40th Infantry Division, Army Security Agency, and the 45th Infantry Division.

Korean War Veterans Memorial

Wall of Remembrance

The National Park Service rehabilitated the 26-year-old memorial.

In March 2021, the construction project began to expand the memorial by adding names of 36,634 American and 7,174 Koreans, who served as advisors and interpreters of the Korean Augmentation to the US Army (KATUSA).

In December 2021, the first seven-ton panel with 450 names was placed at the Korean War Memorial. The panel was one of 100 to be added to the site southeast of the Lincoln Memorial. The memorial remained open during construction, though some areas, including the Pool of Remembrance, were inaccessible.

On July 27, 2022, the Korean War Veterans Memorial Wall of Remembrance was officially dedicated in Washington, D.C.

Statues

The 19 statues were created by Vermont sculptor Frank Gaylord and represent an ethnic cross section of America. They include 14 soldiers, three Marines, one sailor and one airman. The troops wear ponchos covering their weapons and equipment which seem to blow in the cold winds of Korea. https://www.defense.gov/Multimedia/Experience/Korean-War-Memorial/

PART SIX
APPENDICES

APPENDIX A

GLOSSARY

AAA	Anti-aircraft artillery used to detect hostile aircraft and destroy them.
ACRP	Airborne Communications Reconnaissance Program - after the term was coined, "ACRP" often simply referred to the "Airborne Communications Reconnaissance *Platform*" — i.e., the actual aircraft, e.g., EC-121, RC-130 or RC-135 — depending on context.
AD HOC	In the military, ad hoc units are created during unpredictable situations, when cooperation between different units is suddenly needed for fast action.
AFB	Air Force Base or USAFB - United States Air Force Base.
AFEM	Armed Forces Expeditionary Medal - is a military award of the United States Armed Forces, which was first created in 1961, and is granted to personnel for their involvement in "any military campaign of the United States for which no other service medal is authorized." The AFEM is awarded to members of the Armed Forces of the United States who have been assigned, attached, or mobilized to units operating in eligibility for 30 consecutive or for 60 non-consecutive days. Criteria: given as recognition for military service in the Republic of Korea (S Korea) and surrounding waters for the period October 1, 1966 – June 30, 1974.

AFSS	Air Force Security Service - During and after World War II, a portion of Army COMINT assets was dedicated to support of the US Army Air Corps, and, when the independent Air Force was created in 1947, these cryptologic assets were subordinated to the new organization as the US Air Force Security Service (AFSS).
AGI	Auxiliary General Intelligence (Soviet Trawlers) - Cold War Russian spy ship specially equipped for a variety of intelligence missions. Visual and photographic, acoustic, electronic (radar, etc.) and communications intelligence.
AGER or GER	Auxiliary General Environmental Research (Ship) - Small unarmed or lightly armed intelligence vessels. Manned by general service US Navy crews, and specialized communications technicians (CTs) from the Naval Security Group. Provided an equivalent capability to Soviet trawlers. GER - General Environmental Research
AKL	US Navy Ship term "AKL." Auxiliary, Cargo, Light, ship originally built for exclusive US Army use basically as a coastwise freighter designed for logistic support of island and continental naval bases where no great distances are involved. Designation FS is for an Army vessel. FS/AKL ships that will live forever in history began their lives as FS 344, FS 217, and FS 345. These eventually became Navy ships and were. converted into USS *Banner* (AGER 1), USS *Pueblo* (AGER 2), and USS *Palm Beach* (AGER 3) "environmental research ships" (with a mission described as "electronic intelligence collection and other duties")
AMAG	American Military Advisory Group a.k.a. Korean Military Advisory Group (KMAG). On June 25, 1950, KMAG became the United States Military Advisory Group, Korea. It helped to train and provide logistic support for the Republic of Korea Army.
ASA	Army Security Agency (ASA), or US Army Security Agency, was the principal Army intelligence organization from 1945 through 1976. The ASA was tasked with monitoring

and intercepting military communications of the Soviet Union, the People's Republic of China, and their allies and client states (for example, N Korea) around the world.

BBGP	Bombardment Group, a unit of organizational command and control.
BEGGAR SHADOW	Code name for US Navy and Air Force program to collect intelligence.
BLUE HOUSE	Official residence of the President of the Republic of Korea. The term used to refer to the incident of January 21, 1968, wherein N Korean infiltrators attempted to assassinate the ROK President.
BRIG. GEN.	Bridger General (sometimes BG) in the United States Army, United States Air Force and United States Marine Corps, is a one-star general officer.
CAF	Command Advisory Function - uses integrated SIGNET information with operational information at command-and-control centers where decisions could be made.
CAP	Combat Air Patrol - applies to both overland and overwater operations, protecting other aircraft, fixed and mobile sites on land, or ships at sea.
CCF	Chinese Communist Forces entered Korea on October 19, 1950, and completely withdrew by October 1958.
CCP	Chinese Communist Party, also called Communist Party of China (CPC).
	The CCP was not formally constituted until its first congress in July 1921.
	It originated from political and literary groups that studied Marxism.
CDR	Commander - is a senior naval officer rank.

CHICOM	Chinese military forces. Short for Chinese Communist and sometimes Chinese communications.
CIA	Central Intelligence Agency - a civilian foreign intelligence service of the US federal government, tasked with gathering, processing, and analyzing national security information from around the world, primarily through the use of human intelligence (HUMINT).
CIB	Combat Infantry Badge - is awarded to Army enlisted infantry, or Special Forces officers in the grade of colonel or below, as well as warrant officers with an infantry or Special Forces military specialty. After December 6, 1941, recipients must have satisfactorily performed duty while assigned as a member of an infantry, ranger, or Special Forces unit during any period in which such unit was engaged in active ground combat.
CLICK BEETLE	Click Beetle - Code word for AGER operations. Canceled January 1, 1968 and suspended by "ICHTHYIC."
CINCPAC	Commander-in-Chief, Pacific - designating the headquarters of the officer commanding all US military areas of the Pacific and part of the Indian Ocean and representing the highest military authority within those areas.
CINCPACFLT	Commander-in-Chief, Pacific Fleets - designing the operational and administrative commander of all ships and naval bases within the Pacific Ocean. Subordinate to CINCPAC for operations.
CHICOM	Short for Chinese Communist and sometimes Chinese Communications (military intelligence - Chicom).
CO	Commanding Officer - is a commissioned officer who is in charge of a military unit.
COMNAVFOR	Commander, Naval Forces, Japan - designating the officer commanding all US Naval Forces and Naval Activities in Japan.
COMSERVPAC	Commander of Service Forces, Pacific Fleet.

COMINT	Communication Intelligence (COMINT) is the technical and intelligence information derived from foreign communications.
COMSEC	Communication Security - is the discipline of preventing unauthorized interceptors from accessing telecommunications in an intelligible form, while still delivering content to the intended recipients.
CP	Command Post-is a post at which the commander of a unit in the field receives orders and exercises command.
CPA	Closest Point of Approach - is an estimated point in which the distance between two objects, of which at least one is in motion, will reach its minimum value; abbreviated CPA. The estimate is used to evaluate the risk of a collision of two ships or closest point of approach (CPA) to shore e.g., N Korea, the Soviet landmass.
CPLA	Chinese People's Liberation Army-is the unified organization of China's land, sea, and air forces.
C-RATIONS	The C-Ration, or Type C ration-was an individual canned, pre-cooked, and prepared wet ration. It was intended to be issued to US military land forces when fresh food (A-ration) or packaged unprepared food (B-ration) prepared in mess halls or field kitchens was not possible or not available.
CRITIC	CRITIC (critical intelligence) message - is the highest message priority, to be processed and sent within two minutes to six addresses within the National Command Authority, including the president and national security advisor.
CRYPTOGRAPHIC	Cryptographic - pertaining to secure communications using ciphers and codes.
CRYPTOLOGIC	Cryptologic - pertaining to communications intelligence and communication security.
CT	Communication/Cryptologic Technician - an enlisted specialist in the fields of communications and electronic interception and analysis.

CTF	Commander Task Force-(usually includes numerals, e.g., Commander, Task Force 96) designating the officer commanding a force of naval vessels under his tactical and operational control for specifically assigned missions.
DCI	Director of Central Intelligence - was the head of the American Central Intelligence Agency from 1946 to 2005, acting as the principal intelligence advisor to the President of the United States and the United States National Security Council.
	The office existed from January 1946 to April 21, 2005, and was replaced on that day by the Director of National Intelligence (DNI) as head of the Intelligence Community and the Director of the Central Intelligence Agency (D/CIA) as head of the CIA.
DET	Detachment most often used terminology to organizationally describe a small military organization. Size depended on circumstances, equipment used, and mission.
DIA	Defense Intelligence Agency - first in all-source defense intelligence to prevent strategic surprise and deliver a decision advantage to warfighters, defense planners, and policymakers. DIA deploys globally alongside warfighters and interagency partners to defend America's national security interests.
DMZ	Demilitarized Zone - an area where, by international agreement or treaty, military operations are prohibited or limited, such as the zones separating N and S Korea and N and S Vietnam.
DMZMP	DMZ Military Police - composed of infantry units, patrol the Korean DMZ to monitor violations of the ceasefire.
DOCID	Document Identifier - identifies documents that can be used to retrieve items.
DOD	The Department of Defense - provides the military forces needed to deter war, and to protect the security of the United States. A.k.a DoD.

DPAA	Defense POW/MIA Accounting Office - is responsible for identifying the remains of servicemen and women and its laboratory is located at Joint Base Pearl Harbor-Hickam in Hawaii.
DPRK	Democratic People's Republic of Korea (N Korea)
ELINT	Electronic Intelligence - collections of operational intelligence from hostile electronic emission. ELINT pertains to all enemy electronic devices including airborne intercept devices used by guided missiles, guided missile launchers, fighter aircraft, long-range and short-range navigational aids, ground-controlled intercept-height finders, anti-aircraft and aircraft fire control radar, blind-bombing devices, electronic radiations emanating from scientific laboratories or production plants, and so on.
EMCON	EMCOM is used to prevent an enemy from detecting, identifying, and locating friendly forces and allows actions to go unnoticed. For radiomen, EMCON usually means full radio silence.
	The most secure communications methods during EMCON reduce, but do not eliminate, the possibility of identification. It is assumed that any electromagnetic radiation will be immediately detected, and the position of the transmitting ship will be fixed by an enemy.[113]
ENS	Ensign - is a US Navy Lieutenant (junior grade) commissioned officer.
ENSIGN	National Ensign - is the United States national flag originally adopted by the Continental Congress on June 14, 1777. The Ensign is flown on a vessel to indicate nationality.
E.O.	Presidential Executive Order 13526, Section 1.4 (c) (d) describes a uniform system for classifying, safeguarding, and declassifying national security information, including information relating to defense against transnational terrorism. The executive order reference is posted on

---

113 https://www.globalsecurity.org/military/library/policy/navy/nrtc/14226_ch3.pdf

classified pages within a document to include "Withheld from public release Pub, L. 86-36,"

EOTKW
Echoes of the Korean War - is a booklet written by no specific author about the First and 2nd Korean War (Conflict), Foreign Languages Publishing House, Pyongyang, (north) Korea.

EUSA 8th United States Army - an American field army which commands all United States Army forces in S Korea.

FEAF
Far East Air Force - was officially known as the US Far East Air Force during the Korean Conflict (June 25, 1950 – July 27, 1953).

FEBA
The forward edge of the battle area (FEBA) is a military term referring to the generally contiguous line of troops, or sensor and weapon.

FECOM
Far East Command - was a United States military command from 1947 until 1957, functionally organized to undertake the occupation of Japan. It was created on 1 January 1, 1947, and abolished, with functions transferred to Pacific Command, effective 1 July 1, 1957. FECOM had command authority during the Korean War 1950-53.

FLASH
Message - reserved for initial enemy contact messages or operational combat messages of extreme urgency. Brevity is mandatory. FLASH messages are to be handled as fast as humanly possible, ahead of all other messages, with in-station handling time not to exceed 10 minutes.

FOIA
Freedom of Information Act - a law that provides the right to access information from the federal government.

GEN
General in the United States Army, United States Marine Corps, and United States Air Force, general is a four-star general officer rank.

HF
High frequency signals - is the designation for the range of radio frequency electromagnetic waves (radio waves) between 3 and 30 megahertz (MHz).

Smell The Gunpowder

IAEA	International Atomic Energy Agency - is an international organization that seeks to promote the peaceful use of nuclear energy, and to inhibit its use for any military purpose, including nuclear weapons.
ID	Infantry Division - is a large military unit or formation, usually consisting of between 10,000 and 20,000 soldiers.
IR	Infantry Regiment – normally comprised two field battalions of about 800 men each or 8-10 companies.
ICBM	Intercontinental Ballistic Missile - is a guided ballistic missile with a minimum range of 3400 miles (5500 kilometers) primarily designed for nuclear weapons delivery (delivering one or more thermonuclear warheads).
ICHTHYIC	Code word for AGER operations in the Pacific after January 1, 1968. (Suspends "Click Beetle").
ISBN	The International Standard Book Number (ISBN) - is a 13-digit number that uniquely identifies books and book-like products published internationally.
ISCAP	The Interagency Security Classification Appeals Panel - provides the public and users of the classification system with a forum for further review of classification decisions. The protection of national security requires that some of the work of the US government be done outside the purview of its citizenry. To ensure an informed public while simultaneously protecting certain information, checks and balances are needed over the classification system. [114]
JCS	Joint Chief of Staff of the Republic of Korea.
JRC	Joint Reconnaissance Center - a focal point for military intelligence gathered by different intelligence organizations.

---

114 https://www.archives.gov/declassification/iscap.

JSA	Joint Security Area - is the only portion of the DMZ where N and S Korean forces stand face-to-face. It is often called the truce village of Panmunjom (the Truce Village; or simply, Panmunjom)
JSPC	Joint SOBE Processing Center - US Army Station "Torii Station" Sobe, Okinawa. This unit was shut down in 1971.
KATUSA	Korean Augmentation to the United States Army - a branch of the Republic of Korea Army that consists of Korean drafted personnel who are augmented to the 8th United States Army (EUSA). KATUSA does not form an individual military unit, instead small numbers of KATUSA members are dispatched throughout most of the 8th United States Army departments. They fill in positions for the United States Army enlisted soldiers and junior non-commissioned officers.
KCNA	Korean Central News Agency - the main, state-run news organization responsible for all news in N Korea.
KDSM	Korean Defense Service Medal - awarded to members of the Armed Forces of the United States who have been assigned, attached, or mobilized to units operating in eligibility for 30 consecutive or for 60 non-consecutive days. Criteria: given as recognition for military service in the Republic of Korea (S Korea) and surrounding waters after July 28, 1954, and ending on such a future date as determined by the Secretary of Defense.
KORCOM	Korean Communist - the Communist movement in Korea emerged as a political movement in the early 20th Century.
KPAAF	N Korean People's Army Air Force - during the First Korean Conflict soviet pilots flew MiGs under the markings of the KPAAF.
LST	Landing Ship Tank - is an ocean-going ship capable of shore-to-shore delivery of tanks, amphibious assault vehicles, and troops.

LCDR	Lieutenant commander - is a commissioned mid-ranking officer rank in the United States Navy.
LT	Lieutenant - is a junior commissioned officer in the armed forces. In the US Army, US Marine Corps, and US Air Force, a first lieutenant is a junior commissioned officer.
	It is just above the rank of second lieutenant and just below the rank of captain.
LTC	Lieutenant Colonel normally ranks immediately below colonel or above major. Commands a battalion or serves in operation or administration position.
LT. GEN.	Lieutenant General (sometimes LTG) normally ranks immediately below general and above general. Commands an army corps, made up of typically three army divisions, and consisting of around 60,000-70,000 soldiers (United States).
LTJG	Lieutenant Junior Grade or LTJG - the second commissioned officer rank in the US Navy and is equivalent to the rank of first lieutenant in other branches of the US Armed Services.[115]
MAC	Military Armistice Commission - Panmunjom supervises the truce between the Koreas.
MAJ. GEN.	Major General (sometimes MG) in the United States Army, it is a division commander's rank subordinate to the rank of lieutenant general and senior to the ranks brigadier and general.
MAJGEN	Abbr. MajGen US Marines Corps
1stMARDIV	1st Marine Division is a Marine Infantry Division of the US Marine Corps headquartered at Marine Corps Base Camp Pendleton, CA. Combat — Ready force of more than 19,000 men in 1950. Today, 2021, both men and women serve in the First Marine Division.

---

115 https://www.military-ranks.org/navy/lieutenant-junior-grade

MARS	Military Operational Area Designation Code name. USS *Pueblo* was assigned Specific Operational Order designation code name MARS for its 1968 mission off the N Korean (East Coast). The order included north longitude and south latitude boundaries.
MAW	Marine Aircraft Wing - is an aviation unit of the United States Marine Corps.
MDR	Mandatory Declassification Review - Requests for MDR at the agency level are addressed to the person(s) or office (s) responsible for the document to determine its declassification.
MOH	The Medal of Honor – It is the highest award for valor in action against an enemy force which can be bestowed upon an individual serving in the Armed Forces of the United States. Presented to its recipient by the President of the United States of America in the name of the Congress.
MSG	Master Sergeant - is a senior non-commissioned officer (NCO).
	A Master Sergeant is often specialized in a certain field or subject matter.
MiG-21	N Korean supersonic fighter/interceptor - MiG 21bis introduced in N Korea, 1950, was considered a superior aircraft compared to the USAF F-86 Sabre.
MOR	Memo of Record - used when the subsystems have the same classification by the National Security Agency (NSA).
MOVREP SYSTEM	Movement Report System – is a system established to collect and make available to certain commands vital information on the status, location, and movement of flag commands, commissioned fleet units, and ships under the operational control of the US Navy. Provides accurate positional data to operational commanders in the event of emergencies such as search and rescue

and evacuations. In the event of a storm, reports must be made at least once every 24 hours and a final report when the storm subsides.

MSR — The main supply route is the route or routes designated within an area of operations upon which the bulk of traffic flows in support of military operations.

NANSEN CAST — Fridtjof Nansen (October 10, 1861–May 13, 1930) was a Norwegian explorer, scientist, and diplomat. One of Nansen's lasting contributions to oceanography was his work designing instruments and equipment; the Nansen cast for taking deep water samples remains in use in the 21st Century. The Nansen cast is a method of oceanographic sampling in which NANSEN bottles are lowered (CAST) to take samples of water (seawater) at a specific depth where the changing density creates an effect called the thermocline, which acts as a barrier, causing sound energy to bend away. A canny submarine captain can use the thermocline to good effect, effectively shielding the submarine from view.

If a submarine is submerged at the layer of thermocline or immediately below the layer, the submarine (risk) will not be "captured" from the wave (market participants), and the submarine (risk) will stay undetected until it is too late.

NAS — Naval Air Station - a military air base that consists of a permanent land-based operations location for the military aviation division.

NCO — Non-Commissioned Officer - a military officer who has not earned a commission. The NCO corps usually includes all grades of corporal and sergeant.

NKA — The North Korean Army aka the Korean People's Army Ground Force (KPAGF) is the main branch of the Korean People's Army responsible for land-based military operations.

NKAF — North Korean Air Force or Korean People's Army Air Force (KPAAF) - the unified military aviation force of N Korea.

NKN	North Korean Navy - officially known as the Korean People's Army Naval Force. The N Korean Navy is considered a brown-water navy and operates mainly within 31 miles from shore.
N KOREA	North Korea - officially the Democratic People's Republic of Korea (DPRK), is a country in East Asia constituting the northern part of the Korean peninsula. Sometimes referred to as the North Korean Republic (NKR).
NLL	Northern Limit Line - the disputed maritime boundary between N Koreas and S Korea in the Yellow (West) Sea that was drawn after the first Korean Conflict in August 1953, by the United Nations Command (UNC).
	Ensured S Korean fishing vessels did not venture far enough north to spark clashes.
NM	Nautical mile - based on the circumference of the earth at the equator. So, the earth is ideally, by definition, 21,600 nautical miles. A nautical mile is a unit of measurement used on water by sailors and/or navigators in shipping. A nautical mile is 1852 meters, or 1.852 kilometers. In the English measurement system, a nautical mile is 1.1508 miles, or 6076 feet.
NSA	National Security Agency - a national-level intelligence agency of the United States Department of Defense, under the authority of the Director of National Intelligence.
NSC	National Security Council - the principal forum used by the President of the United States for consideration of national security, military matters, and foreign policy matters with senior national security advisors and Cabinet officials and is part of the Executive Office of the President of the United States.
NSG	Naval Security Group; also NAVSECGRU - under the command of the Chief of Naval Operations, performs cryptologic and related functions; provides, operates, and maintains an adequate NSG; approves requirements for the

use of existing NSG capabilities and resources; coordinates the execution of approved cryptologic programs.

Exercises command authority over, and is responsible for the primary support the shore activities of the Naval Security Group Command as a naval service-wide system; and provides such other activities and resources as may be assigned.

Naval Security Group Activities [NSGA] and Detachments [NSGD] under the Commander, Naval Security Group Command, perform Naval Security Group functions as assigned.

Naval Security Group Detachment Kamiseya, Japan, provides support to the Fleet Ocean Surveillance Information Facility - Western Pacific [FOSIF WESTPAC] in Kamiseya.

Note: In 2006, all NAVSECGRU Commands were renamed Navy Information Operations Commands (NIOCs).

NVA — North Vietnamese Army - circa 1960s and early 1970s, or the People's Army of Vietnam, also known as the Vietnamese People's Army (VPA), became the military force of the Socialist Republic of Vietnam.

OIC — Officer-in-Charge - often used to designate the person responsible for a special operations detachment or small unit otherwise without a commanding officer.

OOD — Officer-of-the-Deck - abbreviation for the watch-keeping officer in charge of the bridge and responsible directly to the captain for all shipboard operations. Another common but unofficial term is to "take the deck." The OOD is not necessarily a commissioned officer, but his competence must be such that he represents the captain who is always ultimately responsible for the ship's operations even when he is not physically present on the bridge.

OSD	The Office of the Secretary of Defense - is the principal staff element of the Secretary of Defense in the exercise of policy development, planning, resource management, fiscal, and program evaluation responsibilities.
OPREP-3	Operation Report - designated for rapid transmission and handling of information to the Department of Defense and intermediary headquarters. OPREP format is used to report any incident, which may cause international repercussions. Use of the numeral identifier reflects the number of parts to the report, i.e., OPREP-3 has three parts.
OPSCOM	Operations Communications - circuit ensuring that vital information on enemy contacts was disseminated quickly.
PARPRO	Peacetime Aerial Reconnaissance Program - reconnaissance flights began in 1946 along the borders of the Soviet Union and other Socialist Bloc states like N Korea. Strategic overflight reconnaissance in peacetime became routine US policy. Aerial reconnaissance was dangerous. Of the 152 cryptologists who lost their lives during the Cold War, 64 were engaged in aerial reconnaissance.
PAVN	People's Army of Vietnam/North Vietnam - circa 1960s and early 1970s or the People's Army of Vietnam also known as the Vietnamese People's Army (VPA).
PFC	Private First-Class (Pfc) - is the third-lowest Army rank. A Private First- Class should always be addressed by their full rank. The primary role of a PFC is to follow the orders issued by their superiors.
POLICE ACTION	Police Action - a euphemism for a military action undertaken without a formal declaration of war. (Example: The First Korean Conflict)
PRC	People's Republic of China - a unitary sovereign state in East Asia and the world's most populous country.
PL 86-36	Public Law 86-36, May 29, 1959: National Security Agency Act of 1959 – The Secretary of Defense (or his designee)

is authorized to establish such Positions, and to appoint thereto, without regard to the civil service laws, Officers and employees, in the National Security Agency, as necessary to conduct the functions of such an agency.

PX   A store on a military base that sells goods to military personnel and their families or to authorized civilians and foreign military personnel.

RCT   A regimental combat team (RCT) is a provisional major infantry unit. It is formed by augmenting a regular infantry regiment with smaller combat, combat support and combat support service units.

RDML   Rear Admiral - is a one-star flag officer naval commissioned officer.

RECON   Reconnaissance - military operations, reconnaissance is the exploration outside an area occupied by friendly forces to gain information about natural features and enemy presence.

RESEARCH
SPACES   Classified security group spaces Aka SOD-hut. Restricted access.

ROK   Republic of Korea - a sovereign state in East Asia, constituting the southern part of the Korean peninsula (South Korea).

ROKA   The Republic of Korea Army - also known as the ROK Army, is the army of S Korea, responsible for ground-based warfare.

ROKN   Republic of Korea Navy - also known as the ROK Navy, is the naval warfare service branch of the S Korean armed forces.

SAC   Strategic Air Command – US military command that served as the bombardment arm of the US Air Force and had a major part in the First Korean Conflict (1950-53).

SAR	Search and Rescue.
SAVIN	Retired SIGINT code word.
SCUTTLE	To sink a ship from within by intentional flooding.
SIGINT	Signal Intelligence systems that gather information from adversaries' electronic signals.
SITREP	Situation Report - an abbreviated report to higher headquarters transmitted concurrently with, or immediately after an event or action of special interest. A SITREP is supposed to contain essential information only to permit understanding and quick reactions along the chain of command.
SKA	South Korean Army - The Republic of Korea Armed Forces, also known as the ROK Armed Forces, are the armed forces of South Korea.
S KOREA	South Korea is also known as the Republic of Korea.
SO-1	A small, fast coastal Soviet-made submarine chaser escort of about 147 feet in length. Cannon-armed vessel.
SOD-hut	The special operations department restricted spaces aboard a ship where the communications specialists (CTs) work. Also called "Spook-Shack."
	Always a highly classified area that may be entered only by personnel with appropriate security clearance. Department head reports to the Commanding officer aka captain.
S VIETNAM	Received international recognition in 1949 as the "State of Vietnam" (1949–55) and later as the "Republic of Vietnam (RVN)" (1955–75). Its capital was Saigon. A unified S and N Vietnam became the Socialist Republic of Vietnam in 1976. Its capital is Hanoi.
TORPEDO BOAT	A small, fast boat equipped with torpedos.
UMBRA	TOP SECRET code word. UMBRA code word to inform the reader of a certain report that the *original source* for the intelligence was of the most sensitive category.

USAFIK	US Army Forces in Korea.
USNI	The United States Naval Institute (USNI), based in Annapolis, Maryland, is a private, non-profit (EIN:52-0643040), professional military association that seeks to offer independent, nonpartisan forums for debate of national defense and security issues.
USN-39	NSG Designator - National Security Group (NSG) Kamiseya, Japan.
USA-58	SIGINT designator 6918th Security Squadron, US Air Force Security
	Service and US Army Security Agency (ASA), Hakata, Japan.
USAF	US Air Force - the United States Air Force is the aerial warfare service branch of the United States Armed Forces. The US Air Force was officially founded on September 18, 1947.
USSR	Union of Soviet Socialist Republics, also known as the Soviet Union, Soviets and referred to as Russia, was a socialist state that existed from 1922 to 1991.
UN	United Nations - an intergovernmental organization tasked to promote international cooperation and to create and maintain international order. A replacement for the ineffective League of Nations, the organization was established on October 24, 1945, after World War II in order to prevent another such conflict.
UNC	United Nations Command - is the unified command structure for the multinational military forces, established in 1950, supporting, during and after the first Korean Conflict (War).
UNICEF	United Nations Children Fund - is a UN agency responsible for providing humanization and developmental aid to children worldwide.

US	The United States of America, commonly known as the United States or America, is a federal republic composed of 50 states.
USC	United States Code - The Code of Laws of the United States of America (variously abbreviated to Code of Laws of the United States, United States Code, US Code, USC., or USC) is the official compilation and codification of the general and permanent federal statutes of the United States.
VIRIN	Visual Information Record Identification Number is a unique identifier assigned by the United States Department of Defense to official still photographs and other media.
VQ-1	Fleet Air Reconnaissance Squadron VQ-1 is an aviation unit of the United States Navy established on June 1, 1955.
	In its role as aerial reconnaissance and signals intelligence, the squadron is nicknamed the "World Watchers" and is based at the Naval Air Station on Whidbey Island located near Oak Harbor, on Whidbey Island, Washington.
WMD	Weapons of Mass Destruction identified as nuclear, chemical, and biological weapons.
XO	Executive Officer - also referred to as "exec." The officer who is responsible directly to the captain of a US Navy ship for all administrative work and crew training. Is presumed to be able to take over command in case the commanding officer is incapacitated.
ZULU	Time is world time. It is commonly used in electronic communications.
	It is also known as UT or UTC (Universal Time (Co-ordinated)). There are no time zones for UTC. UTC also has no Daylight-Saving Time or Summertime. UTC is used in plane and ship navigation. The military is a big user of UTC. Information: https://www.navysite.de/what/zulu.htm
	UTC uses a 24-hour system of time notation. "1:00 a.m." in UTC is expressed as 0100, pronounced "zero one hundred."

APPENDIX B

OFFICE OF THE HISTORIAN UNITED STATES DEPARTMENT OF STATE

Revision of General Order No. 1 Surrender
to the Supreme Commander for the Allied Powers

All Japanese Forces by the Empire of Japan

General Order No. 1 referenced in the introduction presented here is a typed
copy of the original to facilitate ease of reading.

FOREIGN RELATIONS OF THE UNITED STATES: DIPLOMATIC PAPERS,
1945, THE BRITISH COMMONWEALTH, THE FAR EAST, VOLUME VI

SWNCC 21 Series

Revision of General Order No. 1

SWNCC 21/5

[WASHINGTON, August 11, 1945]

MILITARY AND NAVAL

I. The Imperial General Headquarters by direction of the Emperor, and
pursuant to the surrender to the Supreme Commander for the Allied
Powers of all Japanese armed forces by the Emperor, hereby orders all
of its commanders in Japan and abroad to cause the Japanese armed
forces and Japanese-controlled forces under their command to cease

hostilities at once, to lay down their arms, to remain in their present locations and to surrender unconditionally to commanders acting on behalf of the United States, the Republic of China, the United Kingdom and the British Empire, and the Union of Soviet Socialist Republics, as indicated hereafter. Immediate contact will be made with the indicated commanders, or their designated representatives, and their instructions will be completely and immediately carried out.

a. The senior Japanese commanders and all ground, sea, air and auxiliary forces within China, excluding Manchuria, Formosa and French Indochina north of 16° (degrees) north latitude shall surrender to Generalissimo Chiang Kai-shek.

b. The senior Japanese commanders and all ground, sea, air and auxiliary forces within Manchuria, Korea, north of 38° (degrees) north latitude and Karafuto shall surrender to the Commander-in-Chief of Soviet Forces in the Far East.

c. The senior Japanese commanders and all ground, sea, air and auxiliary forces within Thailand, Burma, Malaya, French Indochina south of 16° (degrees) north latitude, Sumatra, Java, Andamans, Nicobars, Borneo and the Lesser Sundas shall surrender to the Supreme Allied Commander, Southeast Asia Command.

d. The senior Japanese commanders and all ground, sea, air and auxiliary forces in the Celebes, Halmahera, New Guinea, the Banda Sea areas, Bismarcks, Solomons shall surrender to the Commander-in-Chief, Australian Imperial Forces.

e. The senior Japanese commanders and all ground, sea, air and auxiliary forces in the Japanese Mandated Islands, Bonins and other Pacific Islands shall surrender to the Commander-in-Chief, US Pacific Fleet.

f. The senior Japanese commanders and all ground, sea, air and auxiliary forces in Korea south of 38° north latitude shall surrender to the Commanding General, US Expeditionary Forces in Korea.

g. The Imperial General Headquarters, its senior commanders, and all ground, sea, air and auxiliary forces in the main islands of Japan, minor islands adjacent thereto, the Ryukyus, and the Philippines shall surrender to the Commander-in-Chief, US Army Forces in the Pacific.

The Japanese Imperial General Headquarters further orders its commanders.

The Japanese Imperial General Headquarters further orders its commanders in Japan and abroad to disarm completely all forces of Japan or under Japanese control, wherever they may be situated, and to deliver intact and in safe and good condition all weapons and equipment at such time and at such places as may be prescribed by the Allied Commanders indicated above. (Pending further instructions, the Japanese police force in the main islands of Japan will be exempt from this disarmament provision. The police force will remain at their posts and shall be held responsible for the preservation of law and order. The strength and arms of such a police force will be prescribed.)

The Japanese Imperial General Headquarters shall furnish to the Supreme Commander for the Allied Powers, within (time limit) of receipt of this order, complete information with respect to Japan and all areas under Japanese control, as follows:

a. Lists of all land, air and anti-aircraft units showing locations and strengths in officers and men.

b. Lists of all aircraft, military, naval and civil, giving complete information as to the number, type, location and condition of such aircraft.

c. Lists of all Japanese and Japanese-controlled naval vessels, surface and submarine and auxiliary naval craft in or out of commission and under construction giving their position, condition and movement.

d. Lists of all Japanese and Japanese-controlled merchant ships of over 100 gross tons, in or out of commission and under construction, including merchant ships formerly belonging to any of the United Nations which are now in Japanese hands, giving their position, condition and movement.

e.   Complete and detailed information, accompanied by maps, showing locations and layouts of all mines, minefields, and other obstacles to movement by land, sea or air and the safety lanes in connection therewith.

f.   Locations and descriptions of all military installations and establishments, including airfields, seaplane bases, anti-aircraft defenses, ports and naval bases, storage depots, permanent and temporary land and coast fortifications, fortresses, and other fortified areas.

g.   Locations of all camps and other places of detention of United Nations prisoners of war and civilian internees.

III.   Japanese armed forces and civil aviation authorities will ensure that all Japanese military, naval and civil aircraft remain on the ground, on the water, or aboard ship, until further notification of the disposition to be made of them.

IV.   Japanese or Japanese-controlled naval or merchant vessels of all types will be maintained without damage and will undertake no movement pending instructions from the Supreme Commander for the Allied Powers. Vessels at sea will immediately render harmless and throw overboard explosives of all types. Vessels not at sea will immediately remove explosives of all types to safe storage ashore.

V.   Responsible Japanese or Japanese-controlled military and civil authorities will insure that:

a.   All Japanese mines, minefields, and other obstacles to movement by land, sea and air, wherever located, be removed according to instructions of the Supreme Commander for the Allied Powers.

b. All aids to navigation can be reestablished at once.

c. All safety lanes be kept open and clearly marked pending accomplishment of *a* above.

VI. Responsible Japanese and Japanese-controlled military and civil authorities will hold intact and in good condition pending further instructions from the Supreme Commander for the Allied Powers the following:

a. All arms, ammunition, explosives, military equipment, stores and supplies, and other implements of war of all kinds and all other war material (except as specifically prescribed in Section IV of this order).

b. All land, water and air transportation and communication facilities and equipment.

c. All military installations and establishments, including airfields, seaplane bases, anti-aircraft defenses, ports and naval bases, storage depots, permanent and temporary land and coast fortifications, fortresses, and other fortified areas, together with plans and drawings of all such fortifications, installations, and establishments.

d. All factories, plants, shops, research institutions, laboratories, testing stations, technical data, patents, plans, drawings, and inventions designed or intended to produce or to facilitate the production or use of all implements of war and other material and property used by or intended for use by any military or paramilitary organization in connection with its operations.

VII. The Japanese Imperial General Headquarters shall furnish to the Supreme Commander for the Allied Powers, within (time limit) or receipt of this order, complete lists of all the items specified in paragraphs *a, b,* and *d* of Section VI, above, indicating the numbers, types and locations of each.

VIII. The manufacture and distribution of all arms, ammunition and implements of war will cease forthwith.

IX. With respect to United Nations prisoners of war and civilian internees in the hands of Japanese or Japanese-controlled authorities:

a. The safety and well-being of all United Nations prisoners of war and civilian internees will be scrupulously preserved, to include the administrative and supply services essential to provide adequate food, shelter, clothing, and medical care until such responsibility is undertaken by the Supreme Commander for the Allied Powers.

b. Each camp or other place of detention of United Nations prisoners of war and civilian internees together with its equipment, stores, records, arms, and ammunition will be delivered immediately to the command of the senior officer or designated representative of the prisoners of war and civilian internees.

c. As directed by the Supreme Commander for the Allied Powers, prisoners of war and civilian internees will be transported to places of safety where they can be accepted by allied authorities.

d. The Japanese Imperial General Headquarters will furnish to the Supreme Commander for the Allied Powers, within (time limit) of the receipt of this order, complete lists of all United Nations prisoners of war and civilian internees, indicating their location.

X. All Japanese and Japanese-controlled military and civil authorities shall aid and assist the occupation of Japan and Japanese-controlled areas by forces of the Allied Powers.

XI. The Japanese Imperial General Headquarters and appropriate Japanese officials shall be prepared, on instructions from Allied occupation commanders, to collect and deliver all arms in the possession of the Japanese civilian population.

XII. This and all subsequent instructions issued by the Supreme Commander for the Allied Forces or other allied military authorities will be honestly and promptly obeyed by Japanese and Japanese-controlled military and civil officials and private persons.

Any delay or failure to comply with the provisions of this or subsequent orders, and any action which the Supreme Commander for the Allied Powers determines to be detrimental to the Allied Powers, will incur drastic and summary punishment at the hands of Allied military authorities and the Japanese government.

Source: Office of the Historian, Bureau of Public Affairs, US State Department.[116]

---

116 Unless a copyright is indicated, information on State Department websites is in the public Domain and may be copied and distributed without permission.

APPENDIX C

UNITED NATIONS SECURITY COUNCIL'S REQUEST, JUNE 30, 1950

Harry S. Truman Presidential Library and Museum[117]

IMMEDIATE RELEASE   JUNE 30, 1950

At a meeting with Congressional leaders at the White House this morning, the President, together with the Secretary of Defense, the Secretary of State, and the Joint Chiefs of Staff, reviewed with them the latest developments of the situation in Korea. The Congressional leaders were given a full review of the intensified military activities.

In keeping with the United Nations Security Council's request for support to the Republic of Korea in repelling the North Korean invaders and restoring peace in Korea, the President announced that he had authorized the United States Air Force to conduct missions on specific military targets in Northern Korea wherever militarily necessary, and had ordered a Naval blockade of the entire Korean coast. General MacArthur has been authorized to use certain supporting ground units.

---

117 https://www.trumanlibrary.org/hstpaper/naval.htm.

APPENDIX D

THE CAPTURE OF THE USS *PUEBLO*
AND ITS EFFECT ON SIGNET OPERATIONS

Risk Assessment of the USS *Pueblo* Mission
Approved for Release by NSA on September 14, 2012

DOCID: 3997429   ~~TOP SECRET UMBRA~~

~~SECRET SAVIN~~

FROM: DIRNSA 29 DEC 67
TO: JCSIJRC
SECRET SAVIN LIMDIS NOFORN
ADP-541
PINKROOT OPERATION I (C)
CINCPAC 2302309Z NOTAL

1. REF STATES "RISK TO PUEBLO IS ESTIMATED TO BE MINIMAL, SINCE OPERATIONS WILL BE CONDUCTED IN INTERNATIONAL WATERS." 2. FOLLOWING INFO IS FORWARDED TO AID IN YOUR ASSESSMENT OF CINCPAC ESTIMATE OF RISK. SIGINT INDICATES: (1) THE NKAF HAS BEEN EXTREMELY SENSITIVE TO PERIPHERAL RECON FLIGHTS IN THIS AREA SINCE EARLY 1965 (THIS SENSITIVITY WAS EMPHASIZED ON 28 APRIL 1965 WHEN A USAF RB-47 WAS FIRED ON AND SEVERELY DAMAGED 35-40 NM FROM THE COAST), (2) THE NKAF HAS ASSUMED

AN ADDITIONAL ROLE OF NAVAL SUPPORT SINCE LATE 1966, (3) THE NKN REACTS TO ANY ROKN VESSEL OR ROK FISHING VESSEL NEAR THE NK COASTLINE (THIS WAS EMPHASIZED ON 19 JAN 67 WHEN A ROKN VESSEL WAS SUNK BY COASTAL ARTILLERY), AND (4) INTERNATIONALLY RECOGNIZED BOUNDARIES AS THEY RELATE TO AIRBORNE ACTIVITIES ARE GENERALLY NOT HONORED BY NK ON THE EAST COAST OF KOREA. BUT THERE IS NO SIGINT EVIDENCE OF PROVOCATIVE HARASSING ACTIVITIES BY NORTH KOREAN VESSELS BEYOND 12 NM FROM THE COAST.

3. THE ABOVE IS PROVIDED TO AID IN EVALUATING THE REQUIREMENT FOR SHIP PROTECTIVE MEASURES AND IS NOT INTENDED TO REFLECT ADVERSELY ON CINCPACFLT DEPLOYMENT PROPOSAL.

DOCID 3997429 ~~TOP SECRET~~ Declassified (DOCID - Document Identification Codes)

Link: US_Cryptologic_History--The_Capture_of_the_USS_*Pueblo*.pdf (gwu.edu)

Approved for Release by NSA on 09-14-2012, DOCID: 3997429 and FOIA Case # 40722

UMBRA   ~~TOP SECRET~~ Code word. UMBRA code word to inform the reader of a certain report that the *original source* for the intelligence was of the most sensitive category.

SAVIN   Retired SIGINT code word.

NSA   National Security Agency

APPENDIX E

COMBAT SERVICE UNIT INSIGNIAS, IDENTIFICATION BADGES, USS PUEBLO EMBLEM AND FLEET AIR RECONNAISSANCE SQUADRON 1 INSIGNIA EC-121M (VQ-1)

These insignias, badges, and emblems were worn by the veterans whose stories are featured in *Smell the Gunpowder: The Land of the Morning Calm.*

Combat shoulder sleeve unit insignias left to right: 40th Infantry Division; 25th Infantry Division; 7th Infantry Division and 2nd Infantry Division. Unoffical: US Navy ship badge USS *Pueblo*, and US Navy flight patch EC-121.

Personal earned combat
identification badge (CIB)

Combat Medical Badge (CMB)

Department of Defense (DoD) visual imagery (VI) non-DoD endorsement
disclosure
"This appearance of the use of the imagery does not imply or constitute
DoD endorsement."

Image source with permission: USA Military Medals, www.usamm.com.
Appendix E and F.

APPENDIX F

PERSONALLY EARNED SERVICE MEDALS, COMBAT ACTION RIBBON AND UNIT COMMENDATION CITATION

The medals and unit citation below were earned by veterans whose stories appear in *Smell the Gunpowder: The Land of the Morning Calm*. The images reflect the military service medals, combat service ribbon and unit citation.

National Defense Service Medal	Korean Service Medal	United Nations Service Medal	Republic of Korea War Service Medal

Armed Forces
Expeditionary
Medal

Korean Defense
Service Medal

Prisoner of
War Medal

US Navy and US Marine Corps
Combat Action Ribbon

Republic of Korea Presidential Unit
Citation

Department of Defense (DoD) visual imagery (VI) non-DoD endorsement
disclosure.
"This appearance of the use of the imagery does not imply or constitute DoD
endorsement."
Ribbons and Medals are not copyrighted.

APPENDIX G

US ARMY SECURITY AGENCY TRAINING CENTER & SCHOOL, FORT DEVENS, MA TACTICAL TRAINING COURSE BROCHURE

Depicts the number of ASA and non-ASA personnel who graduated through May 6, 1966.

TACTICAL TRAINING COURSE

THE UNITED STATES ARMY
SECURITY AGENCY
TRAINING CENTER & SCHOOL
FORT DEVENS. MASS.

The brochure depicts the number of ASA and non-ASA personnel that have graduated from the Tactical Training Course thru 31 December 1965. An updating of these data to 6 May 1966 shows:

Organization	Number
ASA	1,772
196th Light Infantry Brigade, Fort Devens (non-ASA)	1,500
20th Engineer Battalion (non-ASA) (now in RVN)	300
44th Truck Company (non-ASA) (now in RVN)	170
US Army Hospital, Ft Devens (non-ASA)	49
ROTC Cadets (from various colleges located throughout the New England area) (non-ASA)	154
Naval Construction Battalion (Seabees), Danville, Rhode Island (non-ASA)	48
TOTAL	3,993

ASATC&S has responded to scheduled and spontaneous requests made by Major General Charles S. O'Malley, Jr., Commanding General, Fort Devens, for the conduct of briefings and tours of TTC facilities for high ranking visitors to Headquarters, Fort Devens. Among the most recent visitors were the State Adjutant Generals and the civilian aides to the Secretary of the Army from each of the New England States and Major General Frank H. Britton, Deputy Commanding General, First US Army.

Consistent with continued emphasis on tactical training by the Department of Defense, it is anticipated that the number of personnel required to undergo the TTC will increase during fiscal year 1967.

APPENDIX H

A TRIBUTE TO THE VETERANS OF THE 1960S KOREAN CONFLICT

November 2, 1966 – December 3, 1969

"I appreciate these soldiers, sailors, and the United States Marines for their service, and I honor their sacrifice. They were honorable, selfless, courageous, and bold; please remember them as you grow old." (Poet unknown)

Korean Demilitarized Zone November 2, 1966

A Company, 1st Battalion, 23rd Infantry Regiment, 2nd Infantry Division

Killed in action

- Benton, Johnny Wayne, Vermont
- Burrell, Robert Wayne, Indiana
- Fischer, Morris Lee, Wisconsin
- Hasty, Leslie L., Palestine, Texas
- Hensley, James, Michigan
- Reynolds, Ernest, Missouri
- Myong, PFC Hwan Oh, KATUSA attached to A Co. 1/23 2ID Camp Young.

Of note is Private Reynolds, killed in action during the ambush. He was nominated for the Medal of Honor, but was awarded the Silver Star and the Purple Heart. He had been in Korea only 17 days.

Survivor, Private First-Class David L. Bibee, 17 years old. He was wounded but escaped death by playing dead. "The only reason I'm alive now is because I didn't move when a N Korean yanked my watch off my wrist." Company A 1st Battalion, 23rd Infantry Regiment, 2nd Infantry Division.

Source: Korean War Project - tbarker@kwp.org.

USS *Pueblo* (AGR 2) Sea of Japan

A Listing of the Crew Members:

CDR Lloyd Bucher	LT Stephen Harris	LT (jg) Edward Murphy
Lt. F. Schumacher	ENS Timothy Harris	WO-4 Gene Lacy
CTMCS Ralph Bouden	ENC Monroe Goldman	CTTC James Kell
CT1 Don Bailey	HM1 Herman Baldridge	CT1 Michael Barrett
EN1 Rushel Blansett	YN1 Armando Canales	SK1 Policarpo Garcia
CT1 Francis Ginther	EMI Gerald Hagenson	BM1 Norbert Klepac
QM1 Charles Law	CT1 James Layton	PH1 Lawrence Mack
CT1 Donald Peppard	CT1 David Ritter	EN1 Wm. Scarborough
CT1 James Sheppard	CT2 Michael Alexander	CT2 Wayne Anderson
BM2 Ronald Berens	SGT Robert Chicca	IC2 Victor Escamilla
SGT Robert Hammond	RM2 Lee Hayes	CT2 Peter Langenberg
SM2 Wendell Leach	CS2 Harry Lewis	CT2 Donald McClarren
ET2 Clifford Nolte	CT2 Charles Sterling	GM2 Kenneth Wadley
CT2 Elton Wood	CT3 Charles Ayling	CT3 Paul Brusnahan
BM3 Willie Bussell	RM3 Charles Crandell	CT3 Bradley Crowe
CT3 Rodney Duke	CT3 Joseph Fejfar	CT3 John Grant
CT3 Sidney Karnes	CT3 Earl Kisler	CT3 Anthony Lamantia
CT3 Ralph McClintock	QM3 Alvin Plucker	CS3 Ralph Reed
CT3 Steven Robin	CT3 John Shilling	CT3 Angelo Strano
EN3 Darrel Wright	Steward Rogelio Abelon	Seaman Earl Phares
Fireman Peter Bandera	Fireman Steven Woelk	Seaman Stephen Ellis
Fireman John Higgins	Fireman Richard Arnold	Fireman Richard Bame
Seaman Robert Hill	Fireman Howard Bland	Fireman Duane Hodges
Seaman Roy Maggard	Seaman Richard Rogala	Seaman Dale Rigby
Steward Rizalino Aluague	Seaman Larry Marshall	Seaman Ramon Rosales
Fireman Thomas Massie	Fireman John Mitchell	Fireman Michael O'Bannon
Seaman Edward Russell	Seaman John Shingleton	Fireman Norman Spear
Fireman Larry Strickland		

Civilian Oceanographers Harry Iredale and Dunnie Tuck

* Note: All crew members were authorized the Prisoner of War Medal, the Armed Forces Expeditionary Medal, Korean Defense Service Medal, and Combat Action Ribbon.

January 23, 1968, killed in action by Fireman (Petty Officer 3rd Class) Duane Hodges. Awarded the Silver Star Medal (posthumously).

Petty Officer Hodges was killed during the forced boarding of the USS *Pueblo* captured by N Korean sailors in international waters.

Crew released on December 23, 1968.[118]

United States Navy EC-121M Early Warning *Deep Sea 129*

US Navy Photograph Naval History and Heritage Command

On April 15, 1969, while on a routine intelligence mission, N Korean MiGs shot down an unarmed United States Navy surveillance aircraft over the Sea of Japan, resulting in the deaths of 31 crewmen.

---

118 https://www.nsa.gov/news-features/declassified-documents/uss-*Pueblo*/assets/files/release-Summary/USS_Pueblo_Release_20_Nov_2012.pdf

Crew *Deep Sea 129*

General Service Personnel

Overstreet, James H., LCDR, USN (pilot)
Gleason, Dennis B., LT, USN
Singer, James H., LT., USN
McNamara, Marshall H., ADRC, USN

Naval Security Group Personnel

Taylor, Robert F., LT, USN
DuCharme, Gary R., CT3, USN
Lynch, Hugh M., SSgt, USMC
Miller, John A., CT3, USN
Potts, John H., CT1 USN
Randell, Frederick A., CT2 USN
Smith, Richard E., CTC USN
Sundby, Phillip D., CT3 USN
Tesmer, Stephen J., CT2 USN

Other Military Personnel

Dzema, John, LT, USN
Perrottey, Peter P., LT USN
Ribar, Joseph R., LTJG USN *
Sykora, Robert, J., LTJG USN
Wilkerson, Norman E., LTJG USN
Balderman, Louis F., ADR2 USAF
Chattier, Stephen C., AT1 USAF
Conners, Ballard F., Jr. ADR1 USAF
Horrigan, Dennis J., ATR2 USAF
Graham, Gene K. ATN3 USAF
Greiner, LaVerne A. AEC USAF
Kincaid, Richard H., ATN2 USAF
McNeil, Timothy H., ATR2 USAF
Prindle, Richard T. AMS3 USAF
Roach, James L., ATN1 USAF
Willis, David M., ATN3 USAF
Colgin, Bernie J., AT1 USAF
Sweeney, Richard E., ATN1 USAF *
* bodies recovered.

Crew Job Specialties

Communication/Cryptologic Technician	USN	US Navy
Aviation Electronics Technician	USMC	US Marine Corps
Signals Intelligence Analyst	USAF	US Air Force
Cryptologic Language Analyst	ADRC	Aviation Machinist's

APPENDIX I

JOINT STATEMENT OF PRESIDENT DONALD J. TRUMP OF THE UNITED STATES OF AMERICA CHAIRMAN KIM JONG-UN OF THE DEMOCRATIC PEOPLE'S REPUBLIC OF KOREA AT SINGAPORE SUMMIT

THE WHITE HOUSE
Office of the Press Secretary

FOR IMMEDIATE RELEASE
June 12, 2018

Joint Statement of President Donald J. Trump of the United States of America and Chairman Kim Jong Un of the Democratic People's Republic of Korea at the Singapore Summit

President Donald J. Trump of the United States of America and Chairman Kim Jong Un of the State Affairs Commission of the Democratic People's Republic of Korea (DPRK) held a first, historic summit in Singapore on June 12, 2018.

President Trump and Chairman Kim Jong Un conducted a comprehensive, in-depth, and sincere exchange of opinions on the issues related to the establishment of new U.S.–DPRK relations and the building of a lasting and robust peace regime on the Korean Peninsula. President Trump committed to provide security guarantees to the DPRK, and Chairman Kim Jong Un reaffirmed his firm and unwavering commitment to complete denuclearization of the Korean Peninsula.

Convinced that the establishment of new U.S.–DPRK relations will contribute to the peace and prosperity of the Korean Peninsula and of the world, and recognizing that mutual confidence building can promote the denuclearization of the Korean Peninsula, President Trump and Chairman Kim Jong Un state the following:

1. The United States and the DPRK commit to establish new U.S.–DPRK relations in accordance with the desire of the peoples of the two countries for peace and prosperity.

2. The United States and the DPRK will join their efforts to build a lasting and stable peace regime on the Korean Peninsula.

3. Reaffirming the April 27, 2018 Panmunjom Declaration, the DPRK commits to work toward complete denuclearization of the Korean Peninsula.

4. The United States and the DPRK commit to recovering POW/MIA remains, including the immediate repatriation of those already identified.

Having acknowledged that the U.S.–DPRK summit—the first in history—was an epochal event of great significance in overcoming decades of tensions and hostilities between the two countries and for the opening up of a new future, President Trump and Chairman Kim Jong Un commit to implement the stipulations in this joint statement fully and expeditiously. The United States and the DPRK commit to hold follow-on negotiations, led by the U.S. Secretary of State, Mike Pompeo, and a relevant high-level DPRK official, at the earliest possible date, to implement the outcomes of the U.S.–DPRK summit.

President Donald J. Trump of the United States of America and Chairman Kim Jong Un of the State Affairs Commission of the Democratic People's Republic of Korea have committed to cooperate for the development of new U.S.–DPRK relations and for the promotion of peace, prosperity, and security of the Korean Peninsula and of the world.

DONALD J. TRUMP
President of the United States of America

KIM JONG UN
Chairman of the State Affairs Commission of the Democratic People's Republic of Korea

Pursuant to federal law, government-produced materials appearing on this site are not copyright protected.[119]

THE WHITE HOUSE

Office of the Press Secretary

FOR IMMEDIATE RELEASE

June 12, 2018 - Typed copy of the original to facilitate ease of reading.

Joint statement of President Donald J. Trump of the United States of America and Chairman Kim Jong-un of the Democratic People's Republic of Korea at the Singapore Summit.

President Donald J. Trump of the United States of America and Chairman Kim Jong-un of the State Affairs The Commission of Democratic People's Republic of Korea at the Singapore Summit (DPRK) held the first historic summit in Singapore on June 12, 2018.

President Trump and Chairman Kim Jong-un conducted a comprehensive, in-depth, and sincere exchange of opinions on the issues related to the establishment of new US-DPRK relations and building a lasting and robust peace regime on the Korean peninsula. President Trump agreed to provide security guarantees to the DPRK, and Chairman Kim Jong-un reaffirmed his firm and unwavering commitment to complete denuclearization of the Korean peninsula.

Convinced that the establishment of new US-DPRK relations will contribute to the peace and prosperity of the Korean peninsula and of the world, and recognizing that mutual confidence building can promote the denuclearization of the Korean peninsula, President Trump, and Chairman Kim Jong-un state the following:

1. The United States and the DPRK commit to establish new US-DPRK relations in accordance with the desire of the peoples of the two countries for peace and prosperity.

---

[119] https://www.whitehouse.gov/copyright/

2. The United States and the DPRK will join their efforts to build a lasting and stable peace regime on the Korean peninsula.
3. Reaffirming the April 27, 2018, Panmunjom Declaration, the DPRK commits to work toward complete denuclearization of the Korean peninsula.
4. The United States and the DPRK commit to recovering POW/MIA remains, including the immediate repatriation of those already identified.

Having acknowledged that the US-DPRK summit-the first in history-was an epochal event of great significance in overcoming decades of tensions and hostilities between the two countries and for the opening of a new future, President Trump and Chairman Kim Jong-un commit to implement the stipulations in this joint statement fully and expeditiously. The United States and DPRK commit to hold follow-on negotiations, led by the US Secretary of State, Mike Pompeo, and a relevant high-level DPRK official, soon, to implement the outcomes of the US-DPRK summit.

President Donald J. Trump of the United States of America and Chairman Kim Jong-un of the State Affairs Commission of the Democratic People's Republic of Korea have committed to cooperate for the development of new US-DPRK relations and for the promotion of peace, prosperity, and security of the Korean peninsula and of the world.

DONALD J. TRUMP
President of the United State of America

KIM JONG-UN
Chairman of the State Affairs Commission
Democratic People's Republic of Korea

APPENDIX J

AMERICAN CRYPTOLOGY DURING THE COLD WAR, 1945-1989

Chapter 10: SIGINT in Crisis, 1967-1969
Book II: Centralization Wins, 1960-1972
The USS *Pueblo*, specific pages 439-453
The Shootdown of the US Navy EC-121, specific pages 462-470
Declassified July 26, 2013, ISCAP No. 2008-021 - DOCID: 523682 No 1666

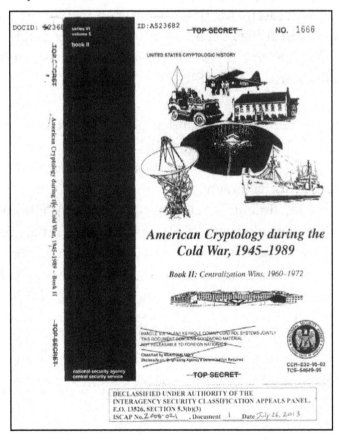

Excerpts from the American Cryptology during the Cold War, 1945-1989

Chapter 10: *SIGINT in Crisis,* 1967-1969, *Pueblo,* pgs. 439-453, US Navy EC-121, pgs. 462-470

Background

After the placid decade of the 1950s, the 1960s produced a series of international paroxysms unmatched in post-World War II history. Although cryptology participated in virtually all the events, four crises in the decade had an impact on the cryptologic business. The Arab Israeli War of 1967 was a defining moment in cryptologic contributions to the intelligence picture. The Soviet invasion of Czechoslovakia in August 1968, and the accompanying crisis concerning Romania, helped shape signal intelligence (SIGINT) production and reporting in later years. The other two events, the capture of the USS *Pueblo* in 1968 and the shootdown of the naval EC-121 in 1969, were uniquely cryptologic in their origins and implications, and they changed the way National Security Agency (NSA) and the cryptologic community have done business from that forward. The *Pueblo,* a 906 ton vessal, was first constructed in 1944, as an Army freight and supply vessel, and it was used to haul materials to South Pacific islands during the latter days of World War II. In 1966, the *Pueblo* joined the Navy and became the smallest version of the SIGINT ship, AGER 2.

Its new captain, Lieutenant Commander Lloyd M. Bucher, reported to take command in January 1967, while it was still undergoing refitting. The captain and his crew were mismatched from the start. Bucher resented being jerked out of submarines to the surface navy. He knew nothing of electronic espionage and apparently learned little in his courtesy stop at NSA. His autobiographical account of the visit revealed considerable distaste for the mission and the people involved in it. Once on board, he found it difficult to get along with his executive officer, Lieutenant Edward Murphy. Moreover, he resented the operational control that Lieutenant Stephen Harris, the NSG chief of the cryptologic space, had. To Bucher, not being in full control of his ship was intolerable. The cryptologic crew was ill-prepared for duty. Harris had a good background, including Russian language training and assignment on several NSG afloat detachments. But only two enlisted members had ever been to sea.

The two Marine linguists who were put aboard at Kami Seya (USN-391), Japan, were very green at Korean, and during the capture, they could not understand the N Korean voice transmissions discussing the impending fate of their vessel. NSG had placed a vessel in harm's way without an advisory warning capability.

On January 23, 1968, N Korea captured a small SIGINT trawler, the USS *Pueblo*. It was everyone's worst nightmare, surpassing in damage anything that had ever happened to the cryptologic community. In the end, however, the government had to sign a phony "confession" and apology at Panmunjom to get the crew back. On December 23, 1968, the crew was released, and they walked across the bridge at the truce village to freedom just in time for Christmas. The complete mishandling of the crew debriefing was emblematic of the entire *Pueblo* incident. Viewing it as an internal matter, the Navy kept NSA uninformed of arrangements for the debriefing and insisted that NSG represent the cryptologic community. NSA viewed the assessment of cryptologic damage as their business, and finally got the Joint Chiefs to intercede with the Navy so that NSA could take its proper role. [120]

---

120 A note from the author: To view and read the complete story Chapter 10: SIGINT in Crisis.
1967-1969, enter DOCID 523682 into the search engine on a computer.

APPENDIX K

CRYPTOLOGIC/CRYPTOGRAPHIC DAMAGE ASSESSMENT USS *PUEBLO*

Declassified Approved for release September 14, 2012

DOCID: 3997434 FOIA Case # 40722

DOCID: 3997434 ACCT # 24105 CBOJ 36

38

~~TOP SECRET~~
National Security Agency
Fort George G. Meade, Maryland

CRYPTOLOGIC/CRYPTOGRAPHIC

DAMAGE ASSESSMENT

USS PUEBLO

~~THIS DOCUMENT CONTAINS CODEWORD MATERIAL~~

Approved for Release by NSA on 09-14-2012, FOIA Case # 40722

(b) ((3) - P.L. 86-36

~~LIMITED DISTRIBUTION~~

- 50 USC 50
- 10 USC 798

~~NOFORN~~

~~TOP SECRET~~

DOCID 3997434

In port, circa 1967. This photograph was received by the Naval Photographic Center in January 1968.

Official US Navy Photograph. Catalog #: USN 1129296

Excerpts from the Cryptologic/Cryptographic Damage Assessment Document

Background

The USS *Pueblo* departed the Sasebo Naval Base at 2100 hours (9:00 p.m.) on January 10, 1968, for its first intelligence collection patrol, which was to be in the Sea of Japan, primarily off the East Coast of N Korea. The primary mission was to:

- Determine the nature and extent of naval activity in the vicinity of the N Koreans ports of Chongjin, Songjin, Mayong-do, and Wonsan.

- Sample the electronic environment of the East Coast of N Korea, with emphasis on intercepting/fixing of coastal radars. Intercept and conduct surveillance of Soviet naval units in the Tsushima Strait to determine the purpose of the Soviet presence in that area since February 1966.

- Determine the Communist reaction to an overt intelligence collector operating near the periphery of N Korea and the Soviet Union and conduct surveillance of their naval units.

- Report any deployment of N Korean/Soviet units which might indicate a change in the Western Pacific (WESTPAC) area of operations threat level.

- Evaluate the USS *Pueblo* (AGER 2) capabilities as a naval surveillance ship.

The USS *Pueblo* arrived at its station off the coast of N Korea at 1430 hours on January 12, 1968. From that date until capture on January 23, the USS *Pueblo* conducted an intelligence surveillance patrol off the N Korean coast.

However, from January 12-22, the USS *Pueblo* operated under radio silence and, therefore, did not report her position to any US Naval authority during this period.

The N Koreans capture occurred on January 23, 1968. After the capture, the crew of the USS *Pueblo* were detained for a period of eleven months in N Korean detention camps. During this eleven-month period, the N Koreans conducted extensive interrogations of the communications technicians assigned to duty aboard the USS *Pueblo*.

Cryptologic Damage Assessment

The volume and type of information acquired by N Korea represents an excellent cross-section view of the overall effort and success of the US cryptologic community. The estimates of this damage are obviously contingent upon a successful translation and interpretation of the information obtained. The Naval Security Group Detachments (NAVSECGRUACT) aboard the USS *Pueblo* possessed the signal intelligence (SIGINT) documentation and equipment considered necessary to accomplish their assigned mission.

DOCID 3997434 Cryptologic Damage Assessment (continued).

Although the mission was targeted against various entities in N Korea and the USSR, the NAVSECGRUACT material inventory included general cryptologic publications and technical support documents which relate to various aspects of the total national SIGINT effort. Additionally, on the date of the USS *Pueblo* capture, a record copy of the western Pacific navy operational intelligence (OPINTEL) broadcast for the period January 5-23 was on board. The information in this OPINTEL record pertained in depth to the US SIGINT efforts and successes throughout the Far East/Pacific area and contained a large amount of sensitive information relating to Southeast Asia SIGINT targets. Also, on board were some 90 DIA specific intelligence collection requirements (SICRs) which provided detailed background information (including intelligence successes) and SIGINT collection needs on various Soviet, N Korean, and Communist China SIGINT targets.

The SIGINT collection equipment operated by the NAVSECGRUACT personnel is not considered classified. However, the combination of several types of equipment into an intercept position configuration in conjunction with its assigned mission reveals specific SIGINT interests. As a result of the USS *Pueblo* capture and the verbal disclosures of her crew, all the intercept position configurations aboard the USS *Pueblo* are considered compromised. The potential damage inflicted on a given SIGINT target area (e.g., N Korea, USSR, etc.) varies relative to the amount of documentary or verbal information obtained. The volume and type of information acquired by N Korea represent an excellent cross-section view of the overall effort and success of the US cryptologic community. Consequently, effective exploitation and dissemination of this information could prompt costly communications security changes to signal methods and procedures by certain foreign countries (i.e., N Korea, Communist China, North Vietnam, and the USSR) for the next 10 years. The estimates of this damage are obviously contingent upon a successful translation and interpretation of the information obtained.

In summary, it can be concluded in all probability that at least the N Koreans are aware of:

a. The extent and positioning of US SIGINT collection and processing resources worldwide (particularly the Naval Security Group Stations)

b. The intensity and relative priority assigned to various SIGINT target efforts.

c. The depth of our understanding of SIGINT target techniques and capabilities.

d. Our ability to construct complex intercept equipment to collect sophisticated SIGINT target emissions.

e. Some of our successes against foreign cryptographic methods and.

f. Our ability to analyze and disseminate intelligence derived from SIGINT on a near real-time basis.

Cryptologic and Cryptographic Damage Assessment DOCID 3997434

Preface Reads

This report constitutes a review and assessment of the Cryptologic - Cryptographic damage resulting from the N Korean capture of the USS *Pueblo* (AGER-2) and the eleven-month internment of her crew. The information used to prepare this report was derived from the debrief of USS *Pueblo* crew members which led to a determination of what sensitive information and equipment is, or is assumed to be, in the possession of, at least, the N Koreans. *All previously published reports estimating the possible cryptologic and cryptographic damage resulting from the assumed compromise of information and equipment aboard the USS Pueblo are herewith superseded.* This report is a final overall review of the cryptologic and cryptographic damage resulting from the N Korean capture of the USS *Pueblo* and her crew. To view and read the entire document, enter DOCID 3997434 into the search engine of a computer or the website link below:

https://www.nsa.gov/news-features/declassified-documents/uss-*Pueblo*/assets/files/damage-assessments/Cryptologic-Cryptographic_Damage_Assessment.pd

TABLE OF CONTENTS

How serious was the intelligence loss from the *Pueblo?* According to long-secret NSA damage assessments obtained through the Freedom of Information Act, the capture of the ship and her eavesdropping gear was one of the worst intelligence debacles in US history.[121] Of the 539 classified documents and pieces of equipment onboard the ship, up to 80 percent had been compromised, the NSA reported. Only 5 percent of the electronic gear had been destroyed beyond repair or usefulness. NSA officials worried that the N Vietnamese might tighten their communications security, making their secret messages harder to crack and putting US servicemen in more jeopardy.

But the United States was lucky. NSA analysts concluded in a 1969 report that the N Vietnamese had gained no apparent advantage on the battlefield because of the ship's commandeered electronics. Nor has any evidence surfaced since then that US security interests were damaged because of the *Pueblo* incident.

---

121 Thomas R. Johnson, *American Cryptology during the Cold War, 1945–1989, Book II: Centralization Wins, 1960–1972,* (National Security Agency, United States Cryptologic History, 1995), page 439.

APPENDIX L

THE NATIONAL SECURITY AGENCY AND THE EC-121 SHOOTDOWN

(S-CCO)

DOCID 4047116 Declassified and Approved for Release by NSA, CIA, DIA,

the Joint Staff, NSC and OSD on 04-23-2013 pursuant to E.O. 13526, MDR Case #60085.

Excerpts from the National Security Agency and the EC-121 Shootdown Document

Tuesday, April 15, was a day of celebration in N Korea. The year was 1969, and the nation was observing the 57th birthday of its leader, Kim Il-sung. His birthday celebration had become the most important national holiday. The festive mood, however, changed radically when the crowds became aware of early evening bulletins announcing a "brilliant battle success." Birthday cheers were quickly replaced with familiar shouts of "Down with the US imperialism" and "liberate the South."

The incident that changed the mood of the holiday crowds was the shootdown of a US Navy EC-121 reconnaissance plane by a N Korean MiG-21 jet over the Sea of Japan off N Korea's East Coast. The shootdown occurred at 1347 hours (1:47 p.m.) Korean standard time. It was 2347 hours (11:47 p.m.), Monday, April 14, 1969, Eastern Standard Time and claimed 31 American lives. For the second time in 15 months, small, isolated N Korea (referred to as a "4th-rate power" by President Richard M. Nixon in his election campaign) had attacked a US intelligence vehicle.

This study traces the role the National Security Agency (NSA) played during the crisis and in the reevaluation of US intelligence activities which followed.

Prior to the shootdown, the NSA did not participate in the risk assessment process (to establish the likelihood of enemy hostile actions) on Navy flights. During the 20-year period dating back to 1950, US reconnaissance aircraft were subject to enemy attacks on 40 occasions. Most of these incidents, in which the US lost 16 aircraft, were attributed to the Soviet Union. On occasion, however, the N Koreans attacked US reconnaissance aircraft. One incident occurred just after the armistice concluded the Korean conflict. N Korean anti-aircraft fire in August 1953, shot down a USAF T-6 intelligence mission over the DMZ. Six years later, the N Koreans attacked a US Navy reconnaissance flight. The

Martin P4M-1Q Mercator, originally designed as a long-range bomber, had been modified in the late 1950s to take on a new role in electronic reconnaissance. On July 16, 1959, two N Korean MiGs shot at an ELINT Mercator flight. The incident occurred at 7,000 feet over international waters, nearly 40 miles off the Korean coast. The Mercator managed to escape by diving to sea level and, badly damaged, with a wounded tail gunner, limped back to a forced landing on a Japanese airfield. On April 27, 1965, N Korean MiG-17 So'ndo'k attacked and badly damaged another ELINT mission, a US Air Force (USAF) RB-27, over the Sea of Japan, 80 land miles (69 nautical miles) off the East Coast. In December 1967, the NSA issued a warning about N Korean dangers. Sent to aid in the risk assessment, the message cited the downing of the USAF RB-27 in April 1965, as an example of this N Korean sensitivity. The NSA message sent during the height of the holiday season was virtually ignored. It was routed as routine information to Commander-in-Chief Pacific and was not seen until after the capture of the *Pueblo*. The *Pueblo* capture was certainly a major reason for increased US intelligence efforts against N Korea.

The incident was still under investigation by a congressional subcommittee as Lieutenant Commander James Overstreet met with other members of an EC-121 crew for a preflight briefing. The routine briefing did contain a warning.

The message warned of unusually vehement and vicious language used by the N Koreans in recent military armistice commission meetings held at Panmunjom.

The message directed them to be alert and prepared to abort at the first indication of any serious reactions by the N Koreans. While Commander Overstreet and other members of the crew prepared for their mission, they were unaware of the unusual activity at an airfield on N Korea's East Coast. Homerun was the home base of the N Korean Air Force (NKAF) Air School's Jet Training element. While this school normally had only MiG-15/17 aircraft, two NKAF First Fighter Division MiG-21 aircraft flew to Homerun on March 28, 1969. On March 30, a message was sent from the Joint Sobe Processing Center (JSPC), located at Torii Station, Okinawa, to all Far East military commands and SIGINT sites which indicated that this was the first time MiG-21 aircraft were at Hoemun. There was no known NKAF tactical unit located at Homerun. On the morning of Tuesday, April 15, the two MiG-21s remained at Homerun. Such was the initial warning of the coming crisis.

The EC-121, codenamed Beggar Shadow, took off from Atsugi Naval Station, Japan, at 0700 hours (7:00 a.m.) Korean standard time. The crew consisted of nine officers, 22 enlisted electronic technicians, and Russian and Korean linguists. One of the enlisted crew was a US Marine, the rest US Navy. The scheduled flight duration was eight-and-a-half hours. As the EC-121 approached the northern part of its second elliptical flight path, two MiG-21s at Homerun launched at 1330 hours Korean standard time (1:30 p.m.) and took off across the waters of the Sea of Japan in what appeared to be a carefully calculated maneuver. There was no time to coordinate information, and over the next several minutes, the N Korean fighters were moving rapidly to overtake the EC-121 codenamed *Deep Sea 129*. One of the MiGs performed a defensive patrol positioned 74 land miles (65 nautical miles) west of the EC-121 at the closet approach. The other MiG continued eastward pursuing the EC-121 and when flight paths merged, the MiG fired two AA-2 toll air-to-air missiles destroying the US Navy EC-121, killing 31 American servicemen. The shootdown was at 0447Z, approximately 90 land miles (78 nautical miles) east of the N Korean coast. US monitoring sites noted *Deep Sea 129* was heading easterly away from the N Korean coast across the Sea of Japan before it was shot down.

The shootdown of the EC-121 caused a crisis at NSA headquarters at Fort Meade, Maryland. NSA officials and analysts played a major role in providing answers to questions raised by the Nixon White House, the Pentagon, other US intelligence agencies, Congress, and the press regarding the loss of the Navy intelligence aircraft.

The normal crew was between 10 and 15. Not only was NSA faced with dealing with the shootdown of a mission that was under-tasked but one that was considered overmanned.

Yet another major NSA role in the EC-121 shootdown crisis was to provide evidence to refute the N Koreans claim that the plane violated its airspace and that it had come within 12 miles (10 nautical miles) of the N Korean coast.

To refute that claim, NSA, in the days following the shootdown, reported detailed tracking information from radar reflections from Soviet, N Korean sites and a classified location. President Nixon used the NSA-supplied information (and caused some consternation at NSA when reporting the classified source) to refute the N Korean claim that the aircraft had callously intruded upon its airspace.

Studies of the EC-121 shootdown did show shortcomings in the command-and-control responsibility for air reconnaissance missions by the military units involved; however, the major problem was the Navy's extremely independent stance regarding its resources.

The Navy was a reluctant participant in an advisory warning program set up by the NSA for reconnaissance aircraft. Its planes lacked communication equipment that had become standard on USAF planes. This deficiency prevented US officials from determining whether the EC-121 received warning messages. A lack of Air Force-Navy communications cooperation also resulted in Navy units in direct control of the aircraft being left off the list of addresses of early warning reports issued by the Air Force field site. This caused a serious delay in the initiation of search and rescue operations following the shootdown. Military commands also called upon the NSA, following the shootdown, to help establish a better system for integrating SIGINT intelligence into general intelligence information at military commands control centers. Following the crisis, NSA also played an important role in helping the USAF establish a Command Advisory Function (CAF) system in which military commands could act more quickly upon information pertaining to reconnaissance missions, and as required, provide protective actions.

In short, NSA played a major role in providing the "whole story" of the shootdown to Washington policymakers. From this experience the National SIGINT Operations Center (NSOC) that remains today has a unique capability within the national intelligence community. The EC-121 shootdown crisis represented a conclusive case for convincing the NSA decision makers that the full potential of the SIGINT system could be realized only through the establishment of a central current operations and crisis-management center.[122]

Pyongyang Planned and Directed the Attacks

The N Koreans preparation suggested the possibility of a deliberate, nationally ordered attack. The SIGINT record points to the conclusion that the attack was

---

122 https://www.nsa.gov/news-features/declassified-documents/cryptologic-histories/assets/files/EC-121.pdf.

planned. The staging of high-performance MiG-21 fighters to a base close to the EC-121 track 18 days before the shootdown; the calm deliberation, timing, and precision characterizing the shootdown; and the lack of subsequent confusion in N Korean command and control likewise suggest prior planning and national oversight. Both the capture of the USS *Pueblo* and the shootdown of the EC-121 suggest it is unwise to count exclusively on defensive changes in an adversary's force posture as a signal of hostile intent.

The incidents also demonstrate that the few forces required to conduct a provocative act may not offer much of a warning. Pyongyang in neither instance ordered changes in its own alert status that would have cued intelligence analysts to an impending attack.

Despite having planned (or at least approved) the operation on short notice, the N Koreans evidently did not change the state of alert near Wonsan or raise general NKAF readiness posture before capturing the *Pueblo*. Similarly, a N Korean military alert did not precede the EC-121 shootdown.

Source: Extracts from Historical Crises in N Korea, Lessons from the Capture of the USS *Pueblo*, and the Shootdown of a US Navy EC-121 – 1968 and 1969, by Richard A. Mobley.

Studies in Intelligence Vol 59, No. 1 (Extracts, March 2015). The complete article is UNCLASSIFIED in its entirety. [123] [124]

NSA has posted documents in the collection on its website at www.nsa.gov.

---

123 Richard A. Mobley is a former naval intelligence officer and the author of *Flash Point Korea: The Pueblo and EC-121 Crises*. Publisher: Naval Institute Press, October 9, 2003.
ISBN-10: 1557504032
https://www.amazon.com/Flash-Point-North-Korea-*Pueblo*/dp/1557504032.
124 https://www.cia.gov/library/center-for-the-study-of-intellgence/csi-publications/csi-studies/studies/vol-59-no-1/pdfs/Studies-Extracts/pdf.

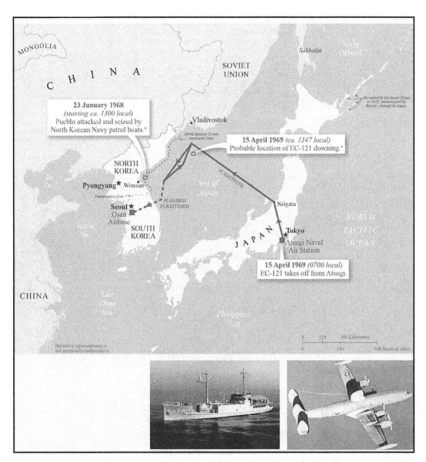

USS *Pueblo* and US Navy EC-121M mission course, location of captured/shootdown locations. US Navy Image Courtesy of Naval History and Heritage Command

APPENDIX M

INQUIRY INTO THE USS *PUEBLO* AND EC-121 PLANE INCIDENTS BY THE UNITED STATES CONGRESS

3997686   [H.A.S.C. No. 91—12]

INQUIRY INTO THE U.S.S. PUEBLO AND
EC–121 PLANE INCIDENTS

REPORT

OF THE

SPECIAL SUBCOMMITTEE ON THE U.S.S. PUEBLO

OF THE

COMMITTEE ON ARMED SERVICES
HOUSE OF REPRESENTATIVES
NINETY-FIRST CONGRESS
FIRST SESSION

JULY 28, 1969

[Pages of all documents printed in behalf of the activities of the House
Committee on Armed Services are numbered cumulatively to
permit a comprehensive index at the end of the Congress. Page numbers lower than those in
this document refer to other
subjects.]

U.S. GOVERNMENT PRINTING OFFICE
37–066   WASHINGTON : 1969

Approved for Release by NSA on 09-14-2012, FOIA Case # 40722

DOCID 3997686 [H.A.S.C. No 91-12] Inquiry into the USS *Pueblo* and EC-121 Plane

Incidents. Approved for Release by NSA 0n 09-14-2012, FOIA Case # 40722. US Congress, House of Representatives, Committee on Armed Services, Hearings Before the Special Subcommittee on the USS *Pueblo* — Inquiry into the USS *Pueblo* and EC-121 Plane Incidents, 91st Congress, First Session, 1969. (Washington, D.C.: Government Printing Office, 1969).

3997686

LETTER OF TRANSMITTAL

U.S. HOUSE OF REPRESENTATIVES,
COMMITTEE ON ARMED SERVICES,
Washington, D.C., June 30, 1969.

Hon. L. MENDEL RIVERS,
Chairman, Committee on Armed Services,
House of Representatives,
Washington, D.C.

DEAR MR. CHAIRMAN: I have reference to your letter of February 18, 1969, in which you established a special subcommittee to conduct a full and thorough inquiry into all matters arising from the capture and internment of the U.S.S. *Pueblo* and its crew by the North Korean Government.

I also have reference to your letter of April 22, 1969, in which you expanded the jurisdiction of that special subcommittee to extend its inquiry to include the loss of a Navy EC–121 aircraft.

As you will recall, you directed the special subcommittee to, among other things, ascertain the national security implications implicit in the loss of both the U.S.S. *Pueblo* and the EC–121, as well as the requirement for possible changes in the Code of Conduct for military personnel who are captured by hostile enemy forces.

I am pleased to report that your special subcommittee has now completed its inquiry into these matters and herewith submits a report of its findings and recommendations, together with the facts upon which it reached its conclusions.

I am also pleased to advise that the report reflects the unanimous views of all nine members of the special subcommittee.

The report, as submitted, contains information classified by the Department of Defense as "top secret." Therefore, the subcommittee was compelled to provide similar classification to the report as submitted to you. However, the subcommittee urges that the report be submitted to the Department of Defense for declassification at the earliest possible date so that it can be made available for public release.

Sincerely,

OTIS G. PIKE,
Chairman, Special Subcommittee.

Lucien N. Nedzi
Alton Lennon
Bill Nichols
Jack Brinkley

William G. Bray
Durward G. Hall
Robert T. Stafford
G. William Whitehurst

L. MENDEL RIVERS, *Chairman.*

Approved:
JULY 1, 1969.

(III)

Paragraphs one and two read: "Dear Mr. Chairman: I have reference to your letter of February 18, 1969, in which you established a special committee to conduct a thorough inquiry into all matters arising from the capture of the USS *Pueblo* and its crew by the N Korean government. I also have reference to your letter of April 22, 1969, in which you expanded the jurisdiction of that special committee to extend its inquiry to include the loss of a Navy EC-121 aircraft." Paragraph four reads: "I am pleased to report that your special committee has now completed its inquiry into these matters and herewith submits a report of its findings and recommendations, together with the facts upon which it reached its conclusions."

Preface

"The subcommittee, in pursuing its inquiry into the loss of USS *Pueblo* and the EC-121, found it necessary to examine many facets of the intelligence reconnaissance activity pursued by our Nation. This detailed examination was necessary to provide the subcommittee with the broad perspective essential to evaluating the actions taken on the *Pueblo* and EC-121 missions. Because of this detailed review, the report submitted by the subcommittee is somewhat lengthy. However, the summary which follows endeavors to present a brief summary of the principal findings and recommendations of the subcommittee on this matter."

Summary of Findings and Recommendations

General

- "The inquiry made by this special subcommittee into the USS *Pueblo* and the EC-121 incidents has resulted in the unanimous view that there exist serious deficiencies in the organizational and administrative military command structure of both the Department of the Navy and the Department of Defense. If nothing else, the inquiry reveals the existence of a vast and complex military structure capable of acquiring almost infinite amounts of information but with a demonstrated inability, in these two instances, to relay this information in a timely and comprehensible fashion to those charged with the responsibility of making decisions.

- As President Nixon recently said, "When a war can be decided in 20 minutes, the nation that is behind will have no time to catch up." This concern is shared by the subcommittee. It was this consideration, as to the national security implications inherent in these two incidents, which overshadowed all others in the inquiry made by the subcommittee.

- The reluctant but inescapable conclusion finally reached by the subcommittee is that because of the vastness of the military structure, with its complex division into multiple layers of command, and the failure of responsible authorities at the seat of government to either delegate responsibility or in the alternate provide clear and unequivocal guidelines governing policy in emergency situations – our military command structure is now simply unable to meet in emergency criterion outlined and suggested by the President himself.

- The absent or sluggish response by military commanders to the emergencies evident in the *Pueblo* and EC-121 incidents demonstrate the need for a complete review of our military-civilian command structure and its capability to cope with emergency situations. The subcommittee inquiry was not of sufficient scope to permit it to offer a proposed solution to the problem. It is evident, however, that a problem exists, and it has frightful implications.

- It is therefore recommended that the President establish a special study group of experienced and distinguished civilian and military personnel to approach this problem on an emergency basis and make such recommendations for changes in both the National Security Act [125] and the military structure itself that will provide our nation and its military forces with a genuine capability to respond quickly and decisively to emergencies of a national security structure."

A note from the author: The National Security Act was enacted by the 80th US Congress, and on July 26, 1947, President Harry S. Truman signed the National Security Act, which became one of the most important pieces of Cold War legislation. Most of the provisions of the Act took effect on September 18, 1947. The Act merged the Department of War (renamed as the Department of the Army) and the Department of the Navy into the National Military Establishment (NME), headed by the Secretary of Defense. It also created the Department of the Air Force and the United States Air Force, which separated the Army Air Forces into its own service. It also protected the Marine Corps as an independent service, under the Department of the Navy. The act was amended on August

---

125 https://www.dni.gov/index.php/ic-legal-reference-book/national-security-act-of-1947.

10, 1949, to ensure subordination to the Secretary of Defense. At the same time, the NME was renamed as the Department of Defense. The purpose was to unify the Army, Navy, and Air Force into a federated structure. The Joint Chiefs of Staff was officially established.

Aside from the military reorganization, the act established the National Security Council and the Central Intelligence Agency, the US's first peacetime non-military intelligence agency. [126] [127]

On June 30, 1969, Otis G. Pike, Chairman, Special Subcommittee, reported to the Honorable L. Mendel Rivers, Chairman, Committee on Armed Services, House of Representatives, Washington, DC., that the subcommittee completed its inquiry and advised that the report reflects the unanimous views of all nine members of the special subcommittee. The report was approved on July 1, 1969, by L. Mendel Rivers, Chairman.

The complete report is available to the public through the US Government Printing Office, Washington, DC.

126 https://www.history.com/topics/cold-war.
127 To view and read the entire document enter DOCID 3997686 into computer search engine.
    https://www.nsa.gov/news-features/declassified-documents/uss-*Pueblo*/assets/files/congressional-actions/
    Inquiry_into_the_USS_Peublo.pdf.

APPENDIX N

DISCIPLINARY ACTION RESULTING FROM THE *PUEBLO* INCIDENT. TRANSCRIBED FOR EASE OF READING

THE SECRETARY OF THE NAVY
WASHINGTON, D.C. 20350

6 May 1969

MEMORANDUM FOR THE CHIEF OF NAVAL OPERATIONS

Subj: Disciplinary action resulting from the PUEBLO incident

Encl: (1) Statement of the Secretary of the Navy, 6 May 1969

1. It is desired that you initiate action to dismiss all charges against officers arising from the PUEBLO incident in accordance with thoughts expressed in enclosure.

John H. Chafee

Then newly appointed Navy Secretary John Chafee had to walk a fine line in his final disposition of the case. A politically savvy former Rhode Island governor, he realized that public and media sympathy precluded a court-martial for Bucher. But the secretary, who had served as a Marine company commander in the Korean War, wanted to pay homage to the brass' strong disapproval of Bucher's surrender, and he understood the importance of maintaining the don't-give-up-the-ship ethos within the officer corps.

Chafee fashioned a shrewd compromise. At a press conference in May 1969, he revealed his admirals' preference for a court-martial, but announced that he was overruling their recommendation. Chafee candidly admitted that mistakes and miscalculations by the Navy had led to what he called the Pueblo's "lonely confrontation by unanticipatedly bold and hostile forces." Thus, the consequences of the ship's capture "must in fairness be borne by all, rather than by one or two individuals whose circumstances had placed them closer to the crucial event." Noting that Bucher and his men had endured a great deal of punishment in N Korea, the secretary said they'd face no further disciplinary action by the Navy. "They have suffered enough," Chafee said as reporters raced for the phones. His decision was widely praised for its wisdom and compassion.

On balance, Bucher did the right thing in preserving the lives of his men.

As for the crew members, they did not receive full recognition for their involvement in the incident until decades later; in 1988, the military announced it would award Prisoner of War [128] medals to those captured in the nation's conflicts. While thousands of American prisoners of war were awarded medals, the crew members of the Pueblo did not receive them. Instead, they were classified as "detainees." It was not until Congress passed a law overturning this decision that the medals were awarded; the crew finally received the medals at San Diego in May 1990.

---

128 Remembering the *Pueblo* and N Korea". *The San Diego Union-Tribune*. December 19, 2011. Retrieved October 18, 2014.

APPENDIX O

RECOMMENDED READINGS: WRITINGS RELATIVE TO THE CAPTURE OF THE USS *PUEBLO*, EC-121 CRISES AND N KOREAN PERSPECTIVE

Bucher, Lloyd M. *Bucher: My Story*. Garden City, New York: Doubleday & Co., Inc., 1970.

A very one-sided book written by Commander Bucher to explain and justify his actions during the attack of the USS *Pueblo* and while imprisoned in N Korea. He is very straightforward in his feelings about the men in his command. Some of the points he claims in the book, however, are not consistent with his statements at the Board of Inquiry.

Murphy, Edward R., Jr.; with Curt Gentry. 2nd *in Command*. New York: Holt, Rinehart, and Winston, 1971.

Lieutenant Murphy does not pretend to write from an unbiased point of view. He immensely disliked and distrusted the commanding officer. Portions of his book were written to counter what Commander Bucher wrote in *Bucher: My Story*. He justifies his actions during the event and explains why the actual capture of the USS *Pueblo* never should have happened. His description of the commander's actions before, during, and after the capture are extremely critical. He justifies the decision of the Secretary of the Navy to put the situation behind the country by not prosecuting any of the crew as a "whitewash" of the true facts. He explains in detail many of the events which happened during and after the capture, from his point of view. His book is well worth reading, especially if compared with *Bucher: My Story*.

Harris, Stephen R. *My Anchor Held*. Old Tappan, New Jersey: F. H. Revell Co., 1970.

Lieutenant Harris was the Officer-in-Charge of the Naval Security Group Detachment (SOD hut) on board the ship. The Board of Inquiry recommended that he be given a Letter of Reprimand; however, this was negated by the Secretary of the Navy. His book is written in defense of his actions on the USS *Pueblo* and while imprisoned. Overall, it is an interesting book and worth reading for personal information.

Schumacher, Frederick C. with George C. Wilson, *Bridge of No Return*: *The Ordeal of the* USS *Pueblo*. New York, Harcourt Brace, Jovanovich, Inc., 1971.

Lieutenant Schumacher was the Operations Officer of the USS *Pueblo*. He was commended by the House Hearing Committee for his actions while imprisoned. The book is basically his account of the ship's capture and the crew's imprisonment. The book contains many insightful passages about the psychology of the ship's crew.

Mobley, Richard A. *Flash Point North Korea: The Pueblo and EC-121 Crises*. Naval Institute Press, October 9, 2003. Author Richard A. Mobley is a retired commander of the US Navy and is a military intelligence analyst with the US government.

Kim Jun Hyok, *Democratic People's Republic of Korea (DPRK) - United States Showdown*, published by Foreign Language Publishing House, Pyongyang, Korea 2014. Published, May Juche* 103 Book on Politics No. 4835036.[129] This short book was written by Kim Jun Hyok and approved by the N Korean government. Its bias is obvious; however, this does not detract from the importance of the book and its understanding of how the N Korean government perceived the USS *Pueblo* capture and EC-121 shootdown incident. It is one of the few documents written on the subject from the N Korean point of view.

---

129 https://www.nknews.org/2014/09/dprk-us-showdown-a-book-review/

Ho Jong Ho, *The US Imperialists Started the Korean War* by Candidate Academician Ho Jong Ho, Doctors Kang Sok Hui and Pak Thae Ho. Published by Foreign Languages Publishing House (1993), Pyongyang, (north) Korea. The US imperialists set their huge propaganda machines in motion and strove to lay the blame for the war on the Democratic People's Republic of Korea, and no small number of the world public were, in fact, misled by their false propaganda. But this tampering with history was short-lived, and the truth could not be withheld indefinitely. As the days went by, the true colors of the criminal were exposed more clearly, and the cause of the Korean War and the objective of its provokers, too, became apparent.

Om Hyang Sim, *Understanding Korea (6) Culture,* published by Foreign Language Publishing House, Pyongyang, Korea Juche 106 (2017). Politics No. 7835010 [130]

Editor: Kim Ji Ho - Translators: Pang Song Hui and Yang Song Im. This short book was written by Om Hyang Sim and approved by the N Korean government. The Democratic People's Republic of Korea developed a socialist culture. Created and enjoyed by the masses including the working class. The culture of the DPRK comprises domains of the people's mental activities such as education, science, art and literature, public health, sports, and mass media. In a broad sense, it also encompasses the material wealth accumulated in the process of building socialism.

The Foreign Languages Publishing House (FLPH) is the central N Korean publishing bureau of foreign-language documents, located in the Potonggang-guyok of Pyongyang, N Korea. It employs a small group of foreigners to revise translations of N Korean texts to make those texts suitable for foreign-language publication.

The publishing house is under the control of the Propaganda and Agitation Department of the Workers' Party of Korea, which also makes decisions concerning its staff.

---

130 https://www.ebay.com/itm/232740068447

"Today the DPRK is advancing dynamically toward the peak of a thieving country under the helmsmanship of Marshall Kim Jong-un, supreme leader of the Party, the state and Army."

— Kim Jun Hyok

*Juche: The year 1912 is "Juche 1" (Juche translated: literally means self-reliance) in the N Korean calendar. The Christian calendar is used for years prior to 1912. [133]

131 http://www.korean-books.com.kp/en/search/?page=book
132 http://www.naenara.com.kp
133 The Juche ideology emphasizes N Korea's political, economic, and military self-reliance.

APPENDIX P

THE WHITE HOUSE

Office of the Press Secretary - Transcribed for Ease of Ready

FOR IMMEDIATE RELEASE

July 26, 2018

STATEMENTS & RELEASES

**Statement from the Press Secretary on the
Repatriation of Remains from N Korea**

FOREIGN POLICY

ALL NEWS

At their historic meeting in Singapore, President Donald J. Trump and Chairman Kim Jong-un took a bold first step to achieve the complete denuclearization of the Korean peninsula, transform relations between the United States and North Korea, and establish enduring peace. Today the Chairman is fulfilling part of the commitment he made to the President to return our fallen American service members. We are encouraged by N Korea's actions and the momentum for positive change.

A US Air Force C-17 aircraft containing remains of fallen service members has departed Wonsan, N Korea. It is accompanied by service members from United Nations Command Korea and technical experts from the Defense POW/MIA Accounting Agency. The C-17 is transferring the remains to Osan Air Base, where a formal repatriation ceremony will be held on August 1.

The United States owes a profound debt of gratitude to those American service members who gave their lives in service to their country, and we are working diligently to bring them home. It is a solemn obligation of the United States Government to ensure that the remains are handled with dignity and properly accounted for, so their families receive them in an honorable manner.

Today's actions represent a significant first step to recommence the repatriation of remains from N Korea and to resume field operations in N Korea to search for the estimated 5,300 Americans who have not yet returned home. Pursuant to federal law, government-produced materials appearing on this site are not copyright protected.[134]

---

134 https://www.whitehouse.gov/copyright/

APPENDIX Q

VETERANS' INTERVIEWS

Personal Stories and Firsthand Accounts

Private First-Class Samuel F. Masessa, interviewed by William R. Graser, on November 11, 2010, and follow-up interviews in January 2013, and November 2021.

Private First-Class Gerald P. Page, interviewed by William R. Graser, on November 11, 2010, and follow-up, in February 2013.

Specialist Harry F. Fraser, November 11, 2010, and follow-up, on August 2, 2018.

Private First-Class Robert S. Messier, interviewed by William R. Graser, on November 18, 2014.

Source: *Veterans' Reflections: History Preserved* by William R. Graser.

Permission to include stories and photographs originally provided to iUniverse self-publishing, December 2015. Revision date April 21, 2016.

iUniverse Self-Publishing
1663 Liberty drive
Bloomington, Indiana 47403
1.800.288.4677

Army Master Sergeant Charles H. McDaniel, Sr., 33, September 10, 2018

Source: Colonel Charles H. McDaniel, Jr., Chaplin, US Marines (Ret), granted permission to include his father's story, Department of Defense photograph, and the picture of his identification tag (dog tag). September 10, 2018.

Army Private First-Class William H. Jones, 19, Department of Defense photograph September 21, 2018

Army Corporal Lloyd B. Odom, 19, Department of Defense photograph September 12, 2019

Source: Defense POW/MIA Accounting Agency

APPENDIX R

ECHOES OF THE KOREAN WAR

Published by Foreign Languages Publishing House (1996),
Pyongyang, (north) Korea

Propaganda and Agitation Department

Echoes of the Korean War, an informational (propaganda) booklet published in 1996 by the N Koreans, explaining their side of the story in a scholarly discussion on the maneuvering of the great powers, including events within Korea between 1945 to 1950 that led up to the beginning of the 1950s Korean Conflict (War). Finally, an opportunity to explore the mindset of the "other side" the N Koreans, in the confused period between post World War II and the beginning of the 1950s Korean Conflict. *Echoes of the Korean War* is a softcover publication divided into four parts and is 106 pages long. The perfect read for anyone interested in the 1950s Korean Conflict (War).[135] [136] A set-up by US Imperialists and S Korean puppet i.e., Republic of S Korea.

---

135 Military and War Korean War (1950-53)
https://www.ebay.ca/itm/ECHOES-KOREAN-WAR-North-Korea-published-book-corea- DPRK-/232497689617?ha
   sh=item3621f13411
136 http://www.ebaystores.ca/NORTH-KOREA-IMPORTS - Item location: Beijing, Chaoyang
 District 100024, China.

Cover: Translation Reads "Here is 38 parallel. Let's Dash North."

APPENDIX S

THE US IMPERIALISTS STARTED THE KOREAN WAR

Propaganda and Agitation Department

The US imperialists set their huge propaganda machines in motion and strove to lay the blame for the war on the Democratic People's Republic of Korea, and no small number of the world public were, in fact, misled by their false propaganda. But this tampering with history was short-lived, and the truth could not be withheld indefinitely. As the days went by, the true colors of the criminal were exposed even more clearly, and the cause of the first Korean Conflict (War) and the objective of its provokers, too, became apparent.

In less than one year after the outbreak of the conflict, progressive-minded foreigners had already found inconsistencies in the US government's propaganda and began to suspect it. Despite unfavorable conditions prevailing at that time, they strove to clear up the truth through an unbiased comparison and analysis of the data and laid bare the true colors of the aggressors by their incisive pens. Among them were well-known American and Japanese journalists and scholars. Today, as a considerable amount of data has been dug up and a deep study made, it has been brought into bolder relief, as an unshakable fact, that the 1950s Korean Conflict was ignited by none other than the US imperialists.

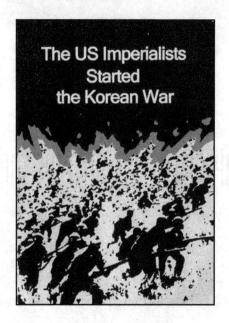

The US Imperialists
Started
the Korean War

Cover:

South Korean puppet army men going over to general armed attack against the northern half of Korea on the instruction of the US imperialists. By Candidate Academician Ho Jong Ho, Doctors Kang Sok Hui, and Pak Thae Ho.

Published by Foreign Languages Publishing House (1993), Pyongyang, (north) Korea.

APPENDIX T

ENEMY TACTICS, TECHNIQUES AND DOCTRINE - INFILTRATION AND GUERRILLA ACTIVITIES

Enemy Tactics monograph was compiled by personnel of the Historical Section, Headquarters Eighth US Army (EUSAK) and the Eighth Army Historical Service Department, released December 26, 1951. The enemy tactics described not only apply to the 1950s Korean Conflict, the basic principles were adopted during the 1960s Korean Conflict. Korean People's Army (KPA) infiltration units, sometimes referred to as line-crossers, were made up of two officers and three 10-man squads. A third of the unit was issued civilian clothes and performed in a semi-agent capacity in S Korea while others wore US and S Korean uniforms. Line-crossers infiltrated by land/sea to identify and mark the location of US and S Korean forces, artillery positions, and command posts. Infiltration units placed concealed wooden anti-personnel mines, sabotaged military infrastructure, and ambushed American and S Korean military personnel. Reconnaissance is particularly important to KPA military doctrine. The KPA will strive to conduct reconnaissance continuously at all levels to include the enemy's read area to achieve surprise when attacking and to prevent surprise when on defense. Each forward-deployed KPA infantry corps fields a reconnaissance battalion, and each infantry division contains an organic reconnaissance company. Each infantry regiment possesses a reconnaissance platoon and there are three independent reconnaissance brigades able to deploy anywhere on the battlefield for additional intelligence-gathering operations. Military Organization Order of Battle Structure.

Enemy Tactics, Techniques and Doctrine, a guide to point out techniques and tactics used by the enemy as evidenced by a year's experience in 1950s conflict, refer to introduction Table 2.

PART SEVEN
REFERENCES
RESOURCES
ABOUT THE AUTHOR

REFERENCE

Sources and Permissions

"The appearance of the use of the imagery does not imply or constitute Department of Defense endorsement."

I relied on many sources to conceptualize, prepare, and write *Smell the Gunpowder: The Land of the Morning Calm.*

- Personal interviews and photographs provided by veterans reprinted with permission.
- *Veterans' Reflections: History Preserved* by William R. Graser, US Army, (Ret). Published by iUniverse in 2016, and available in softcover and digital formats, and audio book. Author's Website: https://www.graser-vetsreflect.com
- USA Military Medals, LLC - Texas 4401 Swanner Loop, Killeen, TX 46543. Email: usamm_cs@usamm.com
- Naval History and Heritage Command

  history-navy.mil/usnhistory
- US Air Force National Engagement-NY, 805 3rd Avenue Fl 9, New York, NY 10022 airforcenyc@us.af.mil
- Alamy Inc., 20 Jay Street, Suite 848, Brooklyn, NY 11201. Image: US Army artillery crew firing a 105mm howitzer against N Korean positions during the Korean War 1950. License start date March 5, 2019, duration in perpetuity. Credit: World History Archive/Alamy Stock Photo.
- Associated Press, New York Office, NY 10281. Image: A sandbag trench twists its way through Korea's hills along the DMZ, where American soldiers keep a watch for North Koreans troop activities, February 8, 1968. Observation Post center top of image. License start date September 7, 2022, duration in perpetuity. Credit: AP Photo.

- Office of the Historian, Bureau of Public Affairs, US State Department.

- USS *Pueblo* (AGER-2) - Crypto Museum http://www.cryptomuseum. com/covert/cases/*Pueblo*/index.htm

- Records of the US National Archives and Records Administration https://www.archives.gov/ and www.nsarchive.org

- US National Archives, Information Security Oversight Office (ISOO), Presidential Executive Order (E.O.) 13526. https://www.archives.gov/ isoo/policy-documents/cnsi-eo.html

- Permission granted, September 10, 2018, by Colonel Charles H. McDaniel, Jr., Chaplin, US Marines (Ret), to include his father's story, photograph, and picture of the identification tag (dog tag). Master Sergeant Charles H. McDaniel, Sr.

  Email: Charles McDaniel at cmcquest@aol.com.

N Korea returned the remains of 55 US service members who were killed during the 1950s Korean Conflict and included just one military identification tag (dog tag): MSG Charles H. McDaniel, Sr.

- Billy Kobin, Reporter, IndyStar, Indianapolis, Indiana.

  Publication date August 14, 2018.

  I extend my sincere appreciation to Billy Kobin for his assistance in connecting me with Mr. Charles H. McDaniel, Jr. Without his assistance this important piece of history would have been missed.[137] https://www.indystar.com/staff/48781/billy-kobin/[138]

Sixty-nine years after first Korean Conflict, hundreds of US families are still searching for closure.

---

137 Permission granted, September 10, 2018, by Colonel Charles H. McDaniel's Jr., Chaplin, US Army (Ret), to include his father's story, picture, and the picture of the identification tag (dog tag).
138 https://www.indystar.com/staff/48781/billy-kobin/

RESOURCES

United States Army in the Korean War, South to Naktong, North to Yalu, Office of the Chief of Military History, Department of the Army, Washington, DC., 1961, reprinted 1966. Available for sale by the Superintendent of Documents, US Government Printing Office, Washington, DC., 20402-0001. (This is the first volume, 813 pages of five published in the series.)

Army Security Agency, http://www.armysecurityagencyveterans.com

Footnotes

Korean War Project, https://www.koreanwar.org/html/dmz_war.html. Ted Barker (214) 320-0342 (LL) Email: h.barker@lwp.org

Harry S. Truman Library & Museum, 500 W US Hwy 24, Independence, MO 64050

US Air Force Museum, 1100 Spaatz Street, Wright-Patterson, Air Force Base, Dayton, OH 45433

The *World Factbook* 2022. Washington, DC: Central Intelligence Agency, March 4, 2022.
South Korea and North Korea. (www.cia.gov/the-world-factbook/countries/korea-south and www.cia.gov/the-world-factbook/countries/korea-north).

Link: https://www.cia.gov/library/publications/the-world-factbook/index.html. The *World Factbook* 2022 is in the public domain. It may be copied freely without permission of the Central Intelligence Agency.

US National Archives & Record Administration: Interagency Security Classification Appeals Panel (ISCAP). Authorized by Executive Order (E.O.)

13526 (section 5.3) Establishment and Administration.[139] The ISCAP is composed of representatives of the Departments of State, Defense, Justice, NSC, ODNI and NARA. The ISOO Director serves as executive secretary.

American Cryptology during the Cold War, 1945-1989, Chapter 10, SIGINT in Crisis, 1967 – 1969, pages 425 to 486, declassified July 26, 2013, Book II - ISCAP No. 2008-021 - DOCID: A523682. Approved for Release by NSA 07-26-2013, including content pages. Reference: doc 4 2008-21 Burr Release. Document 2- Part A.pdf.

Appendix J: Document Cover Page.

> **Link:** DOCID 523682
> https://nsarchive2.gwu.edu/NSAEBB/NSAEBB441/docs.

Cryptologic/Cryptographic Damages Assessment USS Pueblo. Consists of five supplements and five sections. Approved for Release by NSA on 09-14-2012. Reference: Cryptologic-Cryptographic Assessment.pdf.
Appendix K: Document Cover Page.

> **Link:** DOCID 3997434
> https://www.nsa.gov/news-features/declassified-documents/uss-*Pueblo*/assets/files/damage-assessments/Cryptologic-Cryptographic_Damage_Assessment.pdf

NSA analysts concluded in 1969 that the N Vietnamese had gained no apparent advantage on the battlefield because of the *Pueblo's* commandeered electronics. Nor has any evidence surfaced since then that US security interests were damaged because of the *Pueblo* being captured.

The National Security Agency and the EC-121 Shootdown (S-CCO).
Declassified and approved for release by NSA, CIA, DIA, the Joint Staff, NSC and OSD on 04-23-2013 pursuant to E.O. 13526 MDR Case# 60085. Reference: EC-121. pdf

---

139 Resources
    https://fas.org/irp/offdocs/eo/eo-13526fr.pdf.
    The ISCAP is composed of representatives of the Departments of State, Defense, Justice, National Safety Council, Office of the Director of National Intelligence, and National Archives and Records Administration (NARA). The Information Security Oversight The Office Director serves as executive secretary.
    The ISOO is responsible to the president for policy and oversight of the government-wide security classification system and the National Industrial Security Program in the US. The ISOO is a component of the NARA and receives policy and program guidance from the National Security Council.

Appendix L: Document Cover Page.

> **Link:** DOCID 4047116
> https://www.nsa.gov/news-features/declassified-documents/
> cryptologic-histories/assets/files/EC-121.pdf

The Capture of the USS Pueblo and Its Effect on SIGINT Operations (S-CCO).
Declassified and approved for release by NSA on 12-20-2006 pursuant to E.O.
12958, as amended. MDR 42507.
Reference: Declassified NSA History_*PUEBLO*_incident.pdf

> **Link:** DOCID 3075778 http://www.uss*Pueblo*.org/Links_Legal/
> Declassified%20NSA%20History_*PUEBLO*_Incident.pdf

Appendix M: Document Cover Page

Inquiry into the USS *Pueblo* incident. *Report of the Special Subcommittee on the
USS Pueblo of the Committee on Armed Services, House of Representatives Ninety-
First Congress, July 26, 1969.* Includes inquiry into the EC-121 plane incident.
Approved for release by the NSA on 09-14-2012. [House Committee on Armed
Services H.A.S.C. No. 91-12]
Reference: Inquiry_into_the_USS_Pueblo.pdf.

> **Link:** DOCID 3997686
> https://www.nsa.gov/news-features/declassified-documents/uss-
> pueblo/assets/files/congressional-actions/Inquiry_into_the_USS_
> Pueblo.pdf

Findings of Fact, Opinions and Recommendations of a Court of Inquiry were
declassified on June 10, 1969. Referring to an inquiry into the USS *Pueblo* and
EC-121 Plane Incidents by the United States Congress.

Convened by Order of Commander-in-Chief, US Pacific Fleet to inquire into the
circumstances relating to the capture (aka seizure) of USS *Pueblo* (AGER-2), and
184 pages in six parts.

Court of Inquiry into USS *Pueblo* capture (aka seizure) January 23, 1968.
Download pdf files from the US Navy Judge Advocate General's Corps website.

http://www.jag.navy.mil/library/investigations/pueblo%20basic%20pt%201.pdf.

http://www.jag.navy.mil/library/investigations/pueblo%20basic%20pt%202.pdf.

http://www.jag.navy.mil/library/investigations/pueblo%20basic%20pt%203.pdf.

http://www.jag.navy.mil/library/investigations/pueblo%20basic%20pt%204.pdf.

http://www.jag.navy.mil/library/investigations/pueblo%20basic%20pt%205.pdf.

http://www.jag.navy.mil/library/investigations/pueblo%20basic%20pt%206.pdf.

Lessons from the *Capture of the USS Pueblo and the Shootdown of a US Navy EC-121 – 1968 and 1969,* by Richard A, Mobley.

N Korean Navy Voice Reflections of USS *Pueblo* Capture (aka seizure) February 1968.
https://www.cia.gov/library/center-for-the-study-of-intelligence/csi-publications/csi-studies/studies/vol-59-no-1/pdfs/Revisiting-*Pueblo*-and-EC121.pdf.

Studies in Intelligence, *Historical Crises in North Korea,* unclassified articles from March 2015. Lessons from the USS *Pueblo* and the Shootdown of a US Navy EC-121 Incidents – 1968 and 1969[140], by Richard A. Mobley.

Richard A. Mobley is a former naval intelligence officer and the author of *Flash Point Korea: The Pueblo and EC-121 Crisis,* published by Naval Institute Press on October 9, 2003. [141]

(Note from the author: Information on Central Intelligence Agency (CIA) websites are in the public domain and may be reproduced, published, or otherwise used without the Central Intelligence Agency's permission. [142] [143]

---

140 *Historical Crises in North Korea* [PDF 1004.1KB**]. The articles are UNCLASSIFIED in their entirety.
Source: Central Intelligence Agency https://www.cis.gov/about-cia/site-policies#copy
Information presented on this website is considered public information and can be distributed
or copied freely unless identified as being subject to copyright protection.
141 https://www.amazon.com/Flash-Point-North-Korea-Pueblo/dp/1557504032
142 Source: Central Intelligence Agency https://www.cia.gov/about-cia/site-policies/#copy.
143 https://www.cia.gov/library/center-for-the-study-of-intelligence/csi-publications/csi-studies/studies/vol-59-no-1/pdfs/Studies-Extracts.pdf.

Association of the US Army, *The First Korean Conflict Echoes in Today's Challenges (1950s Korea Conflict)*
https://www.ausa.org/articles/korean-war-echoes-today%E2%80%99s-challenges.

Echoes of the Korean War, by no specific author, publisher Foreign Languages Publishing House (1996), Pyongyang, (north) Korea. No specific author and no ISBN – Printed in the Democratic People's Republic of Korea No. 604173.

This booklet is available through https//www.ebay.com, and a third-party provider, Shifoying Dongli 105, Building 5, Unit 10, Room 302, Beijing, Chaoyang District 0024, China.

The US Imperialists Started the Korean War, by Candidate Academician Ho Jong-ho, Doctors Kang Sok Hui and Pak Thae Ho, publisher Foreign Languages Press (1993), Pyongyang, (north) Korea, ASIN: B0000CP2AZ. Printed in the Democratic People's Republic of Korea
https://www.amazon.com/gp/offer-listing/B0000CP2AZ

This book is only available from third-party sellers.
1) Hippo_books   2) Discover-Books   3) Breaktimebooks

Red Wings over the Yalu, China, the Soviet Union, and the Air War in Korea, by Xiaoming Zhang, publisher Texas A & M University Press, College Station (2002). ISBN: 1-58544-201-1
(Cloth cover) and ISBN: 1-58544-340-9 (soft cover).
https://www.amazon.com/Red-Wings-over-Yalu-Williams-Ford/dp/1585443409

Air Combat over the Eastern Front & Korea, a Soviet Fighter Pilot Remembers, by Sergei Kramarenko, publisher Pen & Sword Books Ltd, 47 Church Street, Barnsley, South Yorkshire S70 2AS (2008). ISBN: 978-1-84415-735-8 (hard cover)
Translator: Vladimir Krupnik and John Armstrong
Editor: Sergei Anisimov

English text: Christopher Summerville

https://www.amazon.com/Combat-over-Eastern-Front-Korea/dp/1844157350

ABOUT THE AUTHOR

Sergeant First Class William R. Graser, US Army (Ret)

William R. Graser was a Sergeant First Class recruited by the US Army Security Agency in 1965, and upon completion of basic training completed specialty training at the US Army Security Agency Training Center and School, Fort Devens, MA. During the Cold War era, his assignments included South Korea, Vietnam, Thailand, West Germany, occupied West Berlin, and US Army Security Agency's headquarters at Arlington Hall Station in Virginia. Sergeant Graser was awarded the Legion of Merit Medal for his exceptionally meritorious conduct in the performance of outstanding services and achievements while serving with the US Army Field Station Berlin.

Graser, author and retired soldier, continued to serve his country as the senior volunteer/family readiness group leader (2007-2012) with the 1st Battalion, 304th Regiment, 4th Brigade, 98th Division (Training), US Army Reserve Center, 64 Harvey Road, Londonderry, New Hampshire. Twice he received the Patriotic Civilian Service Award for organizing mobilization events and unit recruitment efforts during this period. In December 2015, Graser published *Veterans' Reflections: History Preserved*, revised April 21, 2016. [144] [145] "His method, which waves the veterans' own stories into an historical overview of a specific conflict, is extremely effective. The soldiers' accounts go well beyond the war's scoreboard and reveal some of the actual fears and experiences of the participants. Anyone can tell the facts behind a story, but those who have lived it can share insights no secondhand history can match."

---

144   Publisher: iUniverse ISBN: 978-1-4917-7285-0 (Soft Cover), 978-1-4915-7286-7 (eBook), Audible (Amazon).
      Highly recommended by *Pacific Book Review* and *The US Review of Books Star*.
      Author's website: http//www.graser-vetsreflect.com
145   William R. Graser, known as Harry F. Fraser

Dedicated to the author's first cousin, Specialist 4 John William Graser (January 24, 1949-May 27, 1968, who served his country as an infantryman with the US Army's 1st Battalion, 7th Cavalry Regiment, 1st Cavalry Division (Airmobile). On May 27, 1968, he was killed in action in Thua Thien Province, Republic of Vietnam.

https//www.graser-vetsreflect.com

CPSIA information can be obtained
at www.ICGtesting.com
Printed in the USA
JSHW061559041222
34154JS00003B/13